SPAIN

The inside story of La Roja's historic treble

SPAIN

The inside story of La Roja's historic treble

GRAHAM HUNTER

BackPage Press

BackPage Press

Copyright © Graham Hunter, 2013

All rights reserved

The moral right of the author has been asserted

First published in the United Kingdom in 2013 by BackPage Press

ISBN 9781909430105

A catalogue record for this book is available from the British Library

Design and typeset by Freight Design

Printed and bound in Scotland by DS Smith

www.backpagepress.co.uk

Contents

Author's
Introduction

The genesis of this book can be traced back to mid-morning on June 13, 1982. My friend Graeme Runcie and I were over halfway through our 2000-mile pilgrimage from Aberdeen to Málaga to follow Scotland at the World Cup. The train had crossed the border at Irun: we were in the Basque Country. The sun was up, rehydration had taken place.

Out in the corridor, a drunken Englishman, who'd decided to don a kilt and follow the Tartan Army, wielded a bottle and attacked a passing Spaniard for absolutely no reason at all.

Instinct took over and I dived in on behalf of the terrified local, broke up the skirmish while others joined the peacemaking effort.

But by the next station the Guardia Civil stomped onto the train, wielding guns, and while they got the right man, they also heard tales that I might have been involved and decided on a 'take one, take 'em all' approach. A mere six years after the death of General Franco, Spain's dictatorial leader between 1939 and 1975, being on the wrong side of one of these guys was not a groovy situation.

There we were, the thug, the peacemaker and the rifle, on the platform in the blazing sun as the train, ponderously, began to inch away.

Just then, one of the locals who had intervened leaned out a window, rattled off a spray of Spanish to the armed cop who thought for a second, nudged me with the butt of his gun and indicated that if I could race along and catch the open door which was being held for me then I was now noted as a force for good, not a thug, and I was back in the game.

If Scotland had shown a turn of pace like I did then, perhaps that tournament wouldn't have ended the way it did for us.

Right at that moment I knew that Spain was for me.

I loved the pompous grandeur of the big old stadia, the searing heat, the way the game was discussed – yelled about – in bars, the fabulous, analytical coverage in the printed media, the 'oooooooooooyyyyyy!' when the ball fizzed past the goalframe. The one thing I didn't like about Spanish football was the football Spain played. Over-wrought, sluggish, precious, lacking an identity.

Then came changes: Pep Guardiola, Albert Ferrer, Miguel Ángel Nadal, Fernando Hierro – football with skill and guts; Gaizka Mendieta, Kiko, Fernando Morientes, Raúl and finally Xavi, Iker Casillas, Fernando Torres, and Andrés Iniesta; David Villa, Xabi Alonso and Cesc Fàbregas.

The country where I lived, where La Liga's teams completely fascinated me had, by 2007, a national team where the dominant values were technique, intelligence, team spirit, hard work, skill and a will to win like never before.

Having worked around the Spain camp for other reasons at World Cup 2006 in Germany, I covered them for UEFA.com at Euro 2008 and 2012 and worked as a FIFA TV producer at World Cup 2010. What united those jobs was the need to watch and listen to everything: every press conference, every training session, every post-match mixed zone or man-of-the-match interview. Sometimes my role involved sharing hotels while on the road with the Spain squad, sometimes to be invited into their dressing room, as after the 2010 and 2012 finals.

To achieve the core work of interviewing them, arranging features with them, recording short match promos, we needed trust, many off-the-record chats ... and the players needed to feel that when they worked with me, Adam Goldfinch (a masterly cameraman), Dani Huerta (a super Spanish journalist), Fede Ardiles (golden-voiced and versed in television techniques) and even Glenn 'The Shadow' Post, they were in professional hands. Regularly the players asked if they could stay and chat longer, to hide from the mayhem of the Spanish media – I think they enjoyed interacting with us.

Certainly, I enjoyed my work and thank those organisations who hired me. Going back and starting all over again, generating new information and interviews for this book, taught me that while it's fantastic being involved in the day-to-day news, it needs this exercise in order to achieve perspective and to join all the dots.

But thanks above all to Spain. They've been the dominant force since 2007 and their trophy treble is unique in football history.

Two things, in particular, lift their efforts above the black-and-white fact that no other country has had the talent, the nous, the hunger and the organisation to win the tournament hat-trick.

The first is that their brand of football is what we need boys and girls around the world to copy. If you eventually prefer a team playing more direct football, the long ball game, or whatever coaching philosophy you favour, then that's fine. Football is a big house. Just make sure that the skills, game intelligence and team spirit which Spain have gifted us for the last six or seven years are taught as the foundation stones of any football programme, amateur or professional.

Secondly, the players, staff and directors who have carved out these triumphs are as thoughtful, down-to-earth and friendly a bunch as you'll meet in top-level sport anywhere. I think these triumphs have been created not just by innate talent but by intelligence and strategy and carried out with style, wit and panache. If I've not brought that out in these pages then I've not done what I set out to.

Finally, although fans go to massive lengths to follow their team around a tournament, it's important to understand what a gargantuan effort it is for a squad to play elite club football all year and then yomp its way through the hurdles and pitfalls which these behemoth tournaments throw up. Climbing Everest it might not be, but a mountainous achievement it most certainly is.

I've been extremely proud to be given the friendship and access which helped me offer this record of what they have done.

Viva La Roja.

Graham Hunter
Barcelona, September 2013

Unloved

Around 300 Spanish fans bunch around the Spain team bus as it tries to reverse away from the scene of their humiliation, inch by careful inch, so as not to add injury to the insults being directed at the team, the manager and the federation president.

> *Piss off Luis!*
> *Get lost Grandad!*
> *Villar, resign!*

And that one catches.

> *¡Dimisión! ¡Dimisión! ¡Dimisión! (Resign! Resign! Resign!)*

The supporters are furious and tired, out of pocket and embarrassed at the 2-0 defeat by Sweden they have just witnessed. Their language and tone are in tune with those the Spanish media will invoke over the next few days.

> *TECHNICALLY BANKRUPT – Diario AS*
> *OUT!!! – El Mundo Deportivo*
> *LUIS - GO NOW! – Sport*
> *LUIS'S TEAM IS A DISASTER – La Razón*

Spain are 20 months from winning the European Championship.

— Murcia
— *October 9, 2006*

Spain open the doors to the training sessions in the days prior to a friendly against the Argentina of Leo Messi, Carlos Tévez, Kun Agüero and Javier Mascherano. The idea is for three days of goodwill, a truce. However, the players are now admitting to each other that they do not even want to go out and train because the atmosphere is so toxic.

A banner is held up: Luis, cabrón, que vuelva la ilusión [Give us back our hope, Luis, you bastard].

Xavi is furious. Most fans are supportive, but pockets of them hurl abuse at the team and at individuals. "They are getting away with just saying anything they like to us!" he rages.

The day before the game, Luis Aragonés writes on the federation website: "I will stay on regardless of the result against Argentina. There is no doubt that parts of the media have mounted an orchestrated campaign against me and have laid all the blame at my feet, entirely unfairly. No, I feel neither beaten nor humiliated. I am still confident that we can turn things around. Yes, I've had to listen to a few insults but I've always found that those who spend their time insulting other people end up being on the receiving end of the same thing. There is no cause for alarm."

Spain beat a strong Argentina team 2-1, but Aragonés' name is violently whistled and jeered when it is announced along with the line-up.

Xavi will later admit that, during these darkest days, he and some team-mates accept call-ups to Spain largely because of their admiration for Aragonés. Otherwise, they are sickened by the stark difference in enjoyment, appreciation and success they have at club level compared to their experiences with *La Roja*.

El Mundo Deportivo: Chaos Takes Root

Yesterday there was an inappropriate level of euphoria after the win over Argentina. What we are seeing of Aragonés implies that we are dealing with someone prone to huge mood swings. The image we have of him and the federation is one of histrionics and confusion.

Luis Aragonés: "No matter how much I'm attacked I'm not going to quit. In football whatever has to happen, will happen."

Fernando Torres [2013]: "At that moment, the criticism and the insults were aimed at the coach. They were just baying for his resignation. Our backs were up against the wall and there were so many calls for him to go that you were almost starting to believe that we would lose him."

— Spain vs Latvia
— Carlos Tartiere Stadium, Oviedo. September 13, 2007
Six wins, one draw and a defeat after losing to Sweden, Spain beat Latvia 2-0 to go second in Group F.

Despite this obvious upward trajectory, prior to the match the insults from fans and media have reached such a pitch that Aragonés cancels the PR-friendly open training session and tells his players that he will not speak to the media post-match, no matter the result.

Centre-back Juanito tells the rest of the squad the abuse is such that he feels as if they are training and playing in a foreign country. The fans heap insults on Aragonés, whistling and jeering him during the game. On the final whistle, they turn on the team. Aragonés, furious, rips up his plans and chooses to be driven the 500km from Oviedo to Madrid rather than re-join the federation charter flight as scheduled, because the media are on that plane. In solidarity, almost every player refuses to talk to the media post-match. José Manuel Ochotorena, the goalkeeping coach, recalls the rising tensions between the national coach and the nation's press.

José Manuel Ochotorena: "Luis began to issue the squad list on the internet. I remember the dreadful press conference in Oviedo. We had lost against Northern Ireland and the press had started speculating constantly about him resigning. Then there was the whole Raúl thing. Luis is not the kind to back away from a confrontation so there was a really heated discussion. People were insulting him personally. It was really dreadful."

El País: A Third Division Win
Totally discredited on the pitch, off it things are just as painful. A clueless coach and a bunch of characterless players unable to mount a rebellion and unwilling to raise their voices as crisis looms.

El Mundo Deportivo: Sack Them All — Quickly
This should break things once and for all. It won't be a surprise if Spain don't qualify for the Euro. This display was the perfect image of our grotesque football

federation over which Ángel María Villar presides. This job arrived too late in his career for Aragonés. The situation is explosive, unsustainable and pathetic. Can someone please sack them all for the good of Spanish football!

Spain are nine months away from winning the European Championship.

— Spanish federation training ground, Las Rozas, Madrid
— October, 2007

Since losing 3-2 to Northern Ireland in Belfast a year ago, Raúl, Spain's all-time record goalscorer, has been dropped. It is now two days before a make-or-break qualifier in Denmark. Lose there and it's highly likely that Spain won't be going to Euro 2008. Sweden would be favourites and both Northern Ireland and the Danes much better placed to finish second.

After evening training it is twilight and a clutch of fans are pressed against the gates of the training ground. Responding to pleas for an autograph, Aragonés wanders over. One fan demands, loudly and aggressively, when Raúl, the crown prince of Madrid, will be reinstated. What the hell is the coach playing at?

Aragonés tries to count to 10. He tries to walk away. But months of tension and abuse have been slowly eroding his self-restraint. He turns and explodes. Nose-to-nose with his abuser, kept apart only by the metal fence, he growls: "Do you know how many World Cups Raúl has been to?"

Silence.

"Three! And do you know how many European Championships Raúl has been to?"

Silence.

"Two! So, three and two, that's five. Tell me how many [of the five tournaments] he has won! Come on! Tell me! Tell me how many he's won!"

Silence.

Aragonés has one more attempt at walking away before turning back again.

"How many? Not one!"

This is all captured by a television camera and broadcast to the nation. The fury of a fighter, but also of a man prodded, abused, insulted, attacked and misrepresented until he can take no more.

Spain are eight months away from winning the European Championship.

— Denmark vs Spain
— *Aarhus Stadion, Aarhus, Denmark. October 13, 2007*

Sergio Ramos [2013]: "The criticism was still ferocious; it felt like everyone was gunning for us."

Joan Capdevila [2013]: "We felt completely isolated."

Spain lose Fernando Torres and David Villa to injury ahead of the Denmark match. Aragonés ignores the still more furious demands for Raúl Gonzalez Blanco and promotes Espanyol's Raúl Tamudo, who scores. Albert Riera gets one and Sergio Ramos puts the finish to a wonderful 28-pass possession which typifies the football Aragonés has been aiming at. Objectively, it is a complete triumph for Spain's coach. They win 3-1 away from home and, now, are very nearly through to the finals. In interviews for this book, every player marks this down as a turning point of immense significance.

The Spanish newspaper Marca acclaims the moment with: "Luis better not think that this is his victory. It is ours for insisting that he play Xavi, Cesc and Iniesta together in midfield."

— Spain vs Sweden
— *Estadio Santiago Bernabéu, Madrid. November 17, 2007*
— Spain vs Northern Ireland
— *Estadio de Gran Canaria, Las Palmas. November 21, 2007*
Having been as low as fifth in the seven-team group and nine points off top a year ago, Spain will now qualify for Euro 2008 if they beat Sweden in the Spanish capital. However, sections of the support and media now have a blood lust. So rabid is the pro-Raúl, anti-Aragonés – and even anti-national team – fury that despite the prize on offer, some players fear that the support will be drowned out, or at least undermined, by abuse of Aragonés. This, after all, is the Bernabéu, the domain of Crown Prince Raúl.

Iker Casillas: "I only ask that the supporters get behind the team and, by implication, get behind the coach, too. Just as we the players all are. The objective is to qualify and everything else needs to be set aside. We must be with the coach. Whether people do or do not like his way of working, his personality, he is the guy who can take us to Euro 2008. There will be

80,000 people there and, obviously, they will all have their own opinions and there will be discrepancies between those for and against. But this is not a Madridista stadium this time – it must be a Spanish one."

Spain defeat Sweden 4-0 and Northern Ireland 1-0 in Las Palmas four days later. Not only have they qualified, they go to Austria and Switzerland as Group F winners and their FIFA ranking has risen to its second-highest position – No.4 in the world.

Weeks earlier, Aragonés has referred to the unlikely prospect of him staying beyond Euro 2008 as Spain manager with the phrase: "All milk has a sell-by date, after which it goes off." When his players exact some revenge on a superbly organised Northern Ireland side in Las Palmas to secure the top spot in the group, they have a big night out which ends in the hotel disco. Aragonés, having initially left them to it, eventually joins in and is grabbed by every last man in the squad and thrown in the air several times, as if after winning a trophy, while they chant over and again: "This milk will never go off!"

The Spanish public and its media, and the footballers of the Spanish national team, are now completely at odds over their views of the manager and the brand of football which he is developing.

They are seven months away from winning the European Championship.

— Onda Cero Radio Station, Madrid
— *January 29, 2008*

On the football programme Al Primer Toque (One Touch), Aragonés tells the journalist Alfonso Azuara that, having explained once why Raúl is not being chosen for Spain, he will not answer any further questions on the Real Madrid captain. Azuara calls him "cowardly" live on air.

"You are the coward who is lying to his listeners," Aragonés repeats over and again, gesticulating angrily at Azuara. The temperature and tone are those just preceding a bar fight.

The radio station host demands that Azuara ceases and desists. It is all captured on the studio camera and made available for viewing.

Spain are six months away from winning the European Championship.

— María Zambrano train station, Málaga
— February 5, 2008

Aragonés has qualified Spain for Euro 2008. His squad are in Málaga to play the World Cup runners-up, France. They have gone 12 matches without defeat, but the Spain party is ambushed in the middle of Málaga's train station by a group of fans chanting: "Raúl selección! Raúl selección!" (Raúl must play for Spain!) while waving aloft white No.7 Real Madrid shirts and red No.7 Spain shirts. Live on television, of course. The country still appears firmly pro-Raúl, completely anti-Aragonés. Recently, the national manager's home has been daubed in pro-Raúl graffiti. It is a police matter.

Aragonés is convinced that Raúl's agent, Ginés Carvajal, has organised the protest. Two weeks later there is a summit, called by Carvajal, between the coach and the ostracised striker.

> **Luis Aragonés:** "Neither of us has to bend over here. Spain was split down the middle on this issue and it is time to end it. There is nothing personal between us."

> **Raúl:** "The national team is more important than whether or not I go to the European Championship. I support the coach and whichever group of players go, but I want to see an end to speculation that I or my people are organising fans to go to Spain games to sing in support of me returning to the team."

Spain are now only four months away from winning the European Championship.

— TVE Studios, Madrid
— April 15, 2008

Enough is enough: the hatred, the calumnies, the professional insults, the acid-drip corroding of squad morale, the outright lies. Aragonés does something remarkable. He agrees to trial by television. He appears on the programme, 'Tengo Una Pregunta Para Usted' (I've Got A Question For You), where he is grilled by an often hostile studio audience, defending robustly his position on Raúl in particular.

Spain are nine weeks away from winning the European Championship.

— Spain vs Peru, friendly
— *Estadio Nuevo Colombino, Huelva. May 31, 2008*
— Spain vs USA, friendly
— *El Sardinero, Santander. June 4, 2008*

Aragonés' team has not lost for approaching two years, during which time they have defeated Argentina, England, Italy, France, Denmark and Sweden. Nevertheless, two hard-fought 1-0 wins in the final warm-up matches before Euro 2008 are enough to spark an avalanche of doubts and criticism in the media. Enough for Aragonés' players to be whistled at throughout, booed off the pitch and sent to Austria with the very clear message that their fans neither trust nor respect them.

In added time during the Peru game, Joan Capdevila scores the winner with a volley, the goal of his life.

Joan Capdevila [2013]: "We played a friendly against Peru, in Huelva, which we won in the 91st minute and our own fans were whistling. Then we went to Santander for the last match before the Euros and they were still whistling. We were all saying to each other, 'We've won both games and they are still booing! What kind of result do they expect? 5-0?'

"The press were heaping the pressure on us. People believe what they read and if the papers are saying that Spain are no good then they come to the games expecting us to mess up and ready to boo."

Such is the incontinence of ire shown by some supporters that Spain feel forced to make the final training sessions in Madrid closed to the public. There are some countries where this would be the norm. Not Spain.

El País: June 3, 2008.
The coaching staff have decided to make the next two sessions behind closed doors with the aim of at least being allowed to work in peace. Aragonés, his staff and the players are finding it just tiresome that last week, even before the poor reception for the Peru game, some fans turned up simply to shout insults and others to yell their continued support for the absent Raúl.

Fernando Navarro [2013]: "It is a particularly sharp memory for me because the USA game was my debut. It was glaringly obvious to the team that people had no faith in us. They thought that history was about to repeat itself and we would immediately trip up in the tournament. We knew that we were fully capable of making our mark and there was a real sense that with the talent we had in the squad we could get the victories. Having said that, there is no doubt that some around the squad were a bit down because of the public's evident lack of faith in us. I wouldn't say that it undermined morale because we were pretty sure of our own capabilities. It was just a sad situation to feel that people lacked belief and turned that into insults."

Santi Cazorla [2013]: "Because I was a late call-up I had an easier time of it in terms of the fans, but most of the other guys were involved when we were in the doldrums and the fans had completely lost the faith. Those players had to suffer the abuse, the whistling, and the negative press coverage. It was a total nightmare and the person who had to bear the brunt of it was the manager. It was always there at the back of your mind during every team talk, but what I found was that it gave us an extra edge. We would go out with the captain's words of encouragement ringing in our ears, thinking about what everyone had endured and you would just think to yourself, 'This is it. Make or break. I am part of this and it is time to step up and stuff people's words right back down their throats'."

Six working days after being booed off the pitch in Santander, *La Roja* will kick off Euro 2008 Group G against Russia.

Spain are now just under four weeks away from winning the European Championship.

Across a little more than 26 magical, electric, explosive days, the quality of Spain's swashbuckling play will energise football fans across the world. They will score 12 times in six games, Xavi will be man of the tournament – although how the judges separate him from Marcos Senna would be fascinating to know. *La Roja* will not concede a goal after the group stage.

They are about to conquer Europe, but right now they feel unloved, abused, misunderstood and the catcalls of an unhappy support are still ringing in their ears.

— Italian airspace, just over Genoa, destination Madrid
— June 30, 2008
Less than a month after he and his team-mates were jeered out of El Sardinero

stadium Pepe Reina has a microphone in his hand. The captain may be flying the Milagros Diaz, but the exuberant Liverpool goalkeeper is in charge.

"¡Pensamientos Positivos!" he chants. [Positive thoughts].

"¡PENSAMIENTOS POSITIVOS!" the entire front half of the aircraft roars back at him. They know what is coming next.

Reina: *"¡Esta leche nunca caduca!"* [This milk will never go off].

"¡ESTA LECHE NUNCA CADUCA!"

Reina: *"¡Si Luis no sigue, no volvemos!"* [If Aragonés doesn't stay we're not coming back].

"¡SI LUIS NO SIGUE, NO VOLVEMOS!"

Most of those on board have had only a couple of hours of sleep and it is quite possible that none of them has ever drunk this much alcohol in their lives. In 24 hours, Carles Puyol will be so hungover he won't be able to speak to the Spanish Prime Minister.

Spain land at Barajas Airport in Madrid. Well over a million jubilant Spaniards are on the streets of the capital waiting for them, even though temperatures are tipping 90 degrees. Police have asked that no more citizens attempt to head for the centre of Madrid where, in Plaza Colón, a massive celebration is going to be held at the end of Spain's open-topped bus ride.

Nobody has come armed with insults. There will be no cat-calls, no mention of Raúl. Collectively, no memory of the last two years during which Spain's players and staff were tormented. They are all winners. It never happened.

The air stewardesses dance the Macarena; Puyol races up and down the aisles dishing out cans of beer. The chanting of Aragonés' favourite sayings begins again.

"¡El dueño del juego es el dueño del balón!" Whoever owns the ball, owns the game.

However, the players also want to make their feelings known to federation president Ángel María Villar one more time.

"¡Luis renovación! ¡Luis no se va! ¡Luis renovación! ¡Luis no se va!" Give Luis a new contract! Don't let Luis go!

Just short of 8pm that night, the Milagros Diaz opens its passenger door. Iker Casillas, Aragonés and the trophy advance in unison and another day of mayhem is unleashed.

There is another fridge full of cold beer and champagne on the bus which will take 90 minutes to ferry the European champions from Barajas to the city centre.

Once they are all on the temporary stage in Plaza Colón, Pepe Reina adopts, and adapts, the manager's motto: Whoever owns the microphone owns the night.

One by one he calls his squad mates to step forward and receive the adulation of the raw-voiced crowd. Exaltation, relief, pride, adulation, alcohol, lack of sleep, plus a showman who would put Barnum and Bailey to shame.

The Pepe Reina show is available on YouTube and words alone may not do it justice. This apparently off-the-cuff, boisterous and entertaining performance shows the union between *La Roja* and the people of Spain. Those who doubted them – abused them, even – are now unified in their adoration of their *selección*.

Pepe Reina: "No.1 – the real hands-free, the guy who made this dream possible by stopping two penalties ... Iker Casillas!

"No.2 – the Chorizo, the biggest sausage in the world ... Raúl Albiol!

"No.3 – the wild boar from Besòs ... Fernando Navarro!

"No.4 – the marshal of the penalty box, the boss of the defence ... Carlos Marchena!

"No.5 – Tarzan, the man who eats pineapples ... Carles Puyol!

"No.6 – the guy who was fighting with the Sun King, because he doesn't like the rays ... Andrés Iniesta!

"No.7 – Spain's No.7. Because he was the top scorer. Because he's got big balls. El Guaje! David Villa!

"No.8 – Humphrey Bogart, it's him, yes, Humphrey Bogart. The authentic and the genuine guy with that mop of dark hair. Xavi Hernández!

"No.9 – El Niño. Yes, my boy. Spain's favourite kid ... Fernando Torres!

"No.10 – the real McCoy, even though he is a bit dopey ... Francesc Fàbregas!

"No.11 – the authentic Garrincha. Yes, yes Garrincha! ... Capdevila!

"No.12 – the one for the fans. He is small, very small, still in the juniors ... Santi Cazorla!

"Right, the No.13. The guy who cleaned me out of €500 in the penalty competitions. Andrés Palop!

"No.14 – it's like he was the son of Johan Cruyff. The real and genuine ... Xabi Alonso!

"No.15 – he paid homage to our dear Antonio Puerta, may he rest in peace. The mythical ... Sergio Ramos!

"No.16 – the real Falete [Gypsy Flamenco singer], the real ... Sergio García!

"Who is the No.17? ... come on! The real gypsy, our main man, the Güiza ... hey! Where is Güiza ... the guitar! ... Dani Güiza!

"No.18 – the second dude who is the real McCoy, even though he's a bit dopey, too. Álvaro Arbeloa!

"No.19 – the samba, the Brazilian-Spanish samba. The real conga-drum ... Marcos Senna!

"No.20 – what quality. My God. Divine and exquisite ... Juanito!

"No.21 – he's really small. He's about a metre and a half tall but he's got quality to die for ... David Silva!

"No.22 – Diego Armando Maradona ... he is the authentic Galactico, the authentic Rubén de la Red!

"No.23 – a humble announcer, here with all of you ... Pepe Reina!"

To get his sign-off you'll have to know that the Spanish for mushrooms is *champiñónes*.

"Waiter! Waiter!" *(Camarero! Camarero!)* he bawls out to the now slightly puzzled throng. "A plate of mushrooms please!" *(Una de champiñónes!)*

And, of course, at the mention of *champiñónes* the whole of Spain gets the pun at once. *Campéones, campéones oé, oé, oé...*

And they are. Champions of Europe, about to conquer the world and then become the first team to win three consecutive tournaments.

Why Spain? Why now? This is the inside story of how they did it.

Aragonés
versus Raúl

The defenestration of Raúl Gonzalez Blanco by Luis Aragonés may not be the most obvious catalyst for three tournament wins and global acclaim, but this was the moment the atom was split and the power of this Spain team realised. At the time, the story shocked the nation, divided it too.

It was portrayed in the Spanish media as a heinous, unjustifiable act of vindictiveness rather than the bold act of renewal it has proved to be.

Raúl was a god. For *Madridistas*, he had become a legend by the age of 17 – the Atlético Madrid starlet who abandoned the *Colchoneros* and crossed the city because Jesús Gil, the club president, wouldn't pay for repairs to his dad's clapped-out old car; who then scored against his old team on his home debut, in that ferocious city *derbi* and who was champion of Spain in his first season at Real Madrid. He left *los Blancos* a three-time Champions League winner, all-time record goalscorer in that competition; six-time Spanish champion and winner of two Intercontinental titles. Like Iker Casillas now, Raúl was simultaneously captain of Madrid and Spain. He was iconic, revered and, if times were bad, a single spark of hope and defiance.

So when Aragonés, this lumbering, aggressive, foul-mouthed, Easter-Island faced, eccentric Atlético Madrid legend with a blue-collar attitude and a losing national-team record, kicked little Prince Raúl with the halo above his head out of the national team, in October 2006, the story was simple. Aragonés was treated as the devil incarnate and the demands for his immediate dismissal were deafening.

While his squad stayed loyal to him in person, they didn't help the Spain coach by losing two of the next three games – away to Sweden and at home to Romania.

Had it not been the case that the president of the Spanish federation, Ángel María Villar, was irrevocably behind Aragonés, then he would have been dismissed and probably excommunicated.

Moreover, Villar twice refused Aragonés' offer to resign.

History has always been written by the winners and it's clear that this gruff, visionary, brave pensioner got it right.

Seeds of Raúl's downfall were planted at the 2006 World Cup in Germany. He remained captain, but during the tournament he was used by Aragonés for only 144 of the possible 360 minutes. It was a clear indication that change was coming. In stark comparison, Cesc Fàbregas, aged just 17, drew glowing praise from Diego Maradona for his World Cup debut and was given 214 minutes. Sergio Ramos, aged just 20, was given the starting right-back role despite having played all season at centre-half. Marcos Senna, in his first tournament aged 29, was immediately a stalwart. These were the portents of what was going to happen over the next 24 months.

In truth, Aragonés' error was not going far enough, soon enough. For example, when Asier del Horno was injured and out of the tournament, Joan Capdevila was not called up. Andrés Iniesta and Carlos Marchena barely played; Joaquín and Luis García were still considered vital.

Three key moments shaped Aragonés' future thinking and drove his polemic actions.

Diego Torres of El País wrote at the time – and neither protagonist has been willing to confirm or deny it since – that a group of players, including Pepe Reina and David Villa, were a little late for the midnight curfew to get back to the team hotel in Kamen, near Dortmund. According to Torres, Raúl, as captain, went to the coach to point out that there should be the normal sanction for breaking curfew. Aragonés appreciated neither the intervention nor the advice. It may have been pure fluke that Villa, who was threatening to take Raúl's place and who would eventually also take his No.7 shirt, was involved.

The players had given advance notice to the Spanish FA administrators that they would be a little late; the coach was cool with it and, unfortunately for the captain, bristled at interference. He did not need his elbow nudged in terms of what to do and, still more importantly, he would rather have seen a captain fighting for his squad and defending his players: all for one and one for all.

Aragonés had listened to his captain's wish that the team stage its training camps in the five-star Calderona Hotel near Valencia rather than the new, custom-built but functional hotel at the Las Rozas Spanish federation training centre. He had also agreed to reduce the 23-man squad to 18, to ensure fewer players went without game time. Aragonés had shown some flexibility, but he had bent far enough.

Another moment which hardened perceptions came when Raúl equalised against Tunisia with 20 minutes of the second group game remaining. He wrenched clear of Mariano Pernia and Xabi Alonso and ran 20 metres to jump into the arms of his Real Madrid team-mate Michel Salgado, a substitute. Briefly the two men were joined by Carles Puyol and Sergio Ramos, then Joaquín and Fernando Torres, but as soon as Raúl had finished embracing Salgado he was out of there, sprinting past one substitute goalkeeper, Pepe Reina, to high five another, the former Real Madrid No.1, José Antonio Cañizares. Finally, he trotted back on to the pitch before giving one of those dark, meaningful looks back at the bench, towards Aragonés.

To us non-combatants, these things may initially seem insignificant, but there are many in the game who believe that how a team or individual celebrates is demonstrative of morale and that in these white-heat moments, mutual regard (or disregard) are seared into team-mates' souls. It's something about which, for example, Pep Guardiola feels strongly about.

Victor Muñoz won 60 Spain caps and nine trophies with Sampdoria and Barcelona, one of which was the Copa del Rey under Luis Aragonés' management. Muñoz told me: "There are things which are sometimes not accorded the importance they should be. Luis, within his own personality and his way of thinking, has his own very clear set of priorities on such matters."

Lastly. With only seven minutes to go in the first knockout round game against France, Spain were tied at 1-1. Yet they still managed to lose 3-1 and go out. Patrick Vieira's 2-1 goal stemmed from a moment when Thierry Henry and Carles Puyol competed and the Frenchman used all his savvy to earn a free-kick when there really wasn't a foul.

This is most definitely not a sin beyond redemption – Pablo Ibañéz had acted similarly to win Spain the penalty from which they scored. However, it is yet another example of La Roja failing to win in extremis. They are 1-0 up and can't win. They are drawing with only a handful of moments left, but once again it is the opponents who find something extra, not Spain. Late, winning goals are just not their thing. Not yet.

Just before Euro 2008, furious at a goal Peru scored against his team in a friendly, Aragonés delivered a tirade which applies perfectly to what happened in Hanover against France, and against Northern Ireland in that shocking 3-2 defeat during which they twice led.

"When you are winning you have to know how to compete! Nobody has become a champion with defensive errors like this. Just because you want to 'play' the ball doesn't mean that you have to concede a stupid goal! There are certain times, and zones, when you have to get rid of it. Defensive security must be more important than anything else. To defend better, the first element is security right across the team. My players know my wishes. When we are winning we must let the opponent in as little as possible, let them have the ball as little as possible. Sometimes we still get stretched, we let the lines of strikers, midfielders and defence part so that there is space between them. The recent tournament winners kept clean sheets. Spain has this great ability to flow up field and create chances, but I want us to operate more as a team, more in unison."

From that moment until victory in the final of Euro 2012, Spain played 42 competitive matches, conceded only 20 goals and lost twice. The changes Aragonés made in personnel, playing style and psychology were important and effective.

These were some key factors in how he analysed Raúl. At 29, he might have been in his prime, but in the three years since Florentino Pérez had made the ludicrous decision to dismiss Vicente del Bosque, Madrid, now captained by Raúl, had hired six managers. The team did not look as fit, the club had become a soap opera. It was debilitating. Steve McManaman, Raúl's Liga and Champions League winning team-mate, explained to me his sympathy for the side effects all this had on the Spain captain.

Steve McManaman: "In 2003, when we visited a thousand places around the Far East, didn't train well but smiled and waved at people, I knew in pre-season that this club wasn't where I wanted to be. Raúl took the captaincy of Madrid, which he'd just inherited from Fernando Hierro, really seriously.
"Spain was still an underachiever at that time so Real Madrid was probably bigger than the national team for a guy like him. He took what was happening to heart; the play was poor, the constant influx of coaches inhibited the team

and he lost three or four players around him: Hierro, Fernando Morientes and Claude Makélele for sure, who had made him a better footballer. Even Zidane's form dropped, too. I'd not be surprised at all if Raúl didn't enjoy those three or four years after 2003."

Throw in a tough knee injury and you can easily argue that Raúl's form at the time he was permanently dropped in autumn 2006 gave Aragonés a context for his decision.

In the two seasons before, and the one after the World Cup in Germany, Raúl registered three of the lowest five goals totals in his career.

However, Aragonés based his decision on bigger, more permanent criteria. The Spain coach wanted a change of philosophy; a quicker, more possession-based style, more patience, more use of established young players, like Xavi, Cesc and Iniesta, plus room for emerging talents like David Silva and Santi Cazorla. Aragonés wanted to make the system fit these players, not vice versa.

Raúl is hugely intelligent in football terms. I spoke to him only a couple of times on Spain duty but he always displayed both courtesy and a clear, articulate understanding of the game he had mastered. Even as an icon, the crown prince of *Madridismo*, he repeatedly admitted that his was a playing style majority-based on hard work, intelligence, fitness, speed and hunger – not pure technique. Many of his goals were 'percentage' goals – drawn from the fallibility of the opponent. An offside line which was sloppy; a keeper rebound; a mis-control by the centre-back. His reading and anticipation of play was peerless.

More, he was the kind of player around whom a team is shaped. For all the skill involved in the process, Raúl was at his best with a vertical style of play. The midfield wins the ball, the wingers are fed, and the ball is centred. Or, the ball is played up to, and laid off from, a traditional No.9, such as Morientes.

He wasn't the participative and speedy footballer Aragonés wanted. The coach was moving to a 4-3-3 system where Raúl would be, at best, third choice behind the emerging Fernando Torres and David Villa. If some of Raúl's brilliance was based on what you might call speculative football, Aragonés wanted to move to control and security. Raúl emanated from the old school of strikers accustomed to picking the best out of a volume of opportunities, rather than participating patiently in meticulous build-up, where the goal opportunities become of higher quality.

Now Aragonés wanted domination of the ball, rapid circulation of possession; he wanted Xavi, often, to be in charge when the ball was played vertically, rather than the striker to demand that the ball was played forward when he had made a run.

Aragonés could not predict he was about to oversee the implementation of a style which would bring two defeats in 42 competitive matches, but he knew how to reach out for it. That's why he dared to incur the wrath of most of the footballing nation in order to achieve it.

The great myth is that Aragonés kicked Raúl out in a fit of pique, that their personal dislike was such that a you-or-me ultimatum was inevitable. The fact that Aragonés was the Real Madrid youth product who ended up one of Atlético's all-time legends and that Raúl's career path took precisely the opposite trajectory framed the narrative perfectly for the many who wanted to understand it as nothing more than a bitter division of *Madridista* and *Colchonero*.

Raúl had 102 caps and 44 goals and was discarded by an embattled coach who had promised to resign if Spain didn't go past the World Cup quarter-finals, but who instead, having failed to reach even that stage in Germany, had led his team to defeats against Sweden and Northern Ireland. No wonder Aragonés had a bullseye on his back. The battle became bitter and immensely divisive. The country took sides and the media, largely, bet that Rául would be back and Aragonés sacked.

However, all of that poison was the by-product of, rather than the driving rationale for, the brutal curtailing of a great footballer's international career.

There is a curious little anecdote about the final impetus which steadied Aragonés' nerve.

Spain's basketball team won the world title in Japan, shortly before the football squad flew out to Belfast to face Northern Ireland. *Baloncesto* is massive in Spain and general delirium had followed the national team's victory. Some of their best players had been exported to North America – the Gasol brothers at the LA Lakers and Memphis Grizzlies for example. This, it was held, had brought a toughening of mentality, a winner's attitude to match the team's talents. If basketball, why not football?

The coach of the national football team took notice. Before leaving for Belfast, Aragonés said: "With each game, it is clearer that this is a special generation of technical footballers we have here in Spain, but the defeat in the World Cup affected us a great deal. We need to do a profound analysis to draw the right conclusions. We need to learn from those around us in Spain who are winning [the basketball world championship]."

Elsewhere, but within the same day, Raúl either hadn't understood what the team line was or didn't care: "We've all really enjoyed seeing the basketball lads win, but that's got nothing to do with football. Spain has never seemed to be competitive in the big tournaments and we've never found the answer as to why. You have to hope that one day we will."

Gradually this was becoming a battle of two, distinct, points of view and two extremely strong characters.

Gaizka Mendieta was a national team-mate of Raúl's for six years and played for Aragonés at Valencia. He told me: "I got to know Luis well when he was my coach. He's a born motivator but, for him, black is black and white is white, there are no grey areas. His point of view is: 'You are going to play like this and this ... if you don't want to play that way, you are not getting picked.'

"It's a basic principle in football that you follow through and do what you say and Luis is a man who will tell you things right to your face and then do what he says, for good or bad. At that stage Raúl no longer fitted his view of how he wanted Spain to be.

"Raúl being who he is, it nearly cost Aragonés his job, because of a couple of bad results, but he did what he needed to regardless of personal consequences and it worked well."

Four years after Aragonés guillotined Raúl's international career, he said: "We decided on two major aspects – to change the way we played so that we used the best footballers who would ensure we had constant possession of the ball. At that time we simply couldn't compete with a team like Germany because of their physical power, but now our rivals cannot live with the tempo of our one and two-touch circulation of the ball.

"The other key thing was to erase the egos. After the loss to Northern Ireland I met with my staff and decided that it was time to prize team-play ahead of ego. It wasn't only Raúl who stopped being chosen but Joaquín, Reyes, Salgado, Cañizares and eventually Albelda.

"We built a group where everyone knew their roles, there were no great egos and there was no difference in importance between those who played more regularly and those who came off the bench.

"I had two sports psychologists with the team in the 2006 World Cup, one of whom had worked in the great North American sports at the top level. I learned from them that you can't make a strong, winning group if there are strong individual egos there.

"I put together a squad of great players who were even better as people. When I arrived I had a squad, but by the time I left we had a team."

Euro 2008

There came a stage when the German team couldn't get a touch. They looked at each other as if to say, 'What the hell is this?' Even in that moment I was thinking: 'This isn't going to end here. This is just the beginning.'

Fernando Torres

Euro 2008

This turns out to be the musical tournament. Not because of the operatic triumph of hope over fear in an epic quarter-final, nor the soaring notes of seven goals scored in two games against Guus Hiddink's Russia. This is not a metaphor. It really is a tournament played out to music: opera by Verdi, pure flamenco, White Stripes, Jambao, *Y Viva España* – a little of everything. However, the very first notes, brassy, Tyrolean and earnest, played by an old-fashioned oompah band, sell us a dummy.

The music and costumes of the civic ceremony to greet the players in Neustift, 15 miles south of the Austrian city of Innsbruck, initially make it seem as if Spain have made a serious error, locating themselves in what appears to be a village stuck in the 19th century.

Everything revolves around the fact that Luis Aragonés has a secret weapon called Kurt Jara.

Back when old *Zapatones* (Big Boots, one of Aragonés' many nicknames) was playing for Atlético Madrid, Spanish football had a problem. Franco's dictatorship wouldn't allow foreign players to 'pollute' the cherished Primera División. That led to a legion of what are known as *Oriundos* arriving to play for the top clubs: players who either earned dual citizenship – principally South Americans – or who faked it, bought it or begged for it. This was still the era in which Alfredo di Stéfano played international football for Argentina, Colombia and then Spain; the rules were far more lenient then.

The significant trade in falsified papers and passports saw Franco's government relax the rule in 1973 and allow Primera teams to sign two non-Spanish, non-*Oriundo* players in the hope of ending the problem of falsification and corruption. Valencia immediately signed Salif Keita (the uncle of the former Barça midfielder Seydou Keita) and, from FC Wacker Innsbruck, Jara – a World Cup-calibre Austrian midfielder.

This was the hothouse moment in Spain when Madrid signed Gunter Netzer, Barça signed Johan Cruyff and the newcomers were treated like something between gods and extra-terrestrials. Jara probably earned more fame than he otherwise might have done at a time when a Di Stéfano-coached Valencia were a punch-bag to the heavyweights. He was greeted as a saviour.

The Austrian's second match for *los Che* was at Atlético Madrid – Aragonés scored in a 3-1 win for the home side. Jara went on to get goals at the Camp Nou and the Bernabéu, to defeat Barça at the Mestalla and to score in his last game against Atlético, by now coached by Aragonés. The big man liked Jara, the two spoke for a while, and that was that.

After he stopped playing, Jara coached his hometown club, FC Tirol Innsbruck. His reputation grew when his team eliminated a Fiorentina side featuring Francesco Toldo, Angelo Di Livio, Rui Costa, Enrico Chiesa, Predrag Mijatović and Moreno Torricelli from the UEFA Cup the following season.

However, by the time the Euro 2008 first-round draw ordained that Spain play their three Group D fixtures sequentially at Innsbruck-Innsbruck-Salzburg, Jara was outside the game, analysing matches for Austrian television, but still based in the region. Thirty-three years had passed since his conversation with Aragonés, but he had a reason to get back in touch – Jara believed the Stubaital valley could provide the perfect tournament base for Spain.

He reached the coach and pitched his spiel at a good time. The draw had derailed the Spanish Football Federation's (RFEF) plan to train in Solothurn in Switzerland, almost equidistant between Basel, Berne and Zurich. Travel from Solothurn to two Austrian cities would have been a ludicrous own-goal in terms of the distances involved.

Jara then needed to persuade the regional Tyrol authorities to make a major financial investment in developing facilities. A pact to bring *La Roja* to the place from which they would plan their assault on Europe began to take shape. But it was not simple.

Neustift, a tranquil countryside resort 16 miles from Innsbruck, was Jara's preferred venue. It features elegant, old-fashioned chalets, hill-walking, glacier-climbing – and very little else. There wasn't a single football pitch and Spain required a minimum of two, preferably three. Top quality, of course.

However, everything else about Jara's proposal convinced Aragonés. He liked the fact that there would be no other teams nearby – Spain would be the darlings of the local population. They could also get first dibs on lots of quiet, isolated accommodation where families, girlfriends and the national media could stay in this respectful, well-ordered little countryside community at the far point of a valley dwarfed by craggy, elegant hills and mountains.

On the other side of the deal, the Tyrol authorities had to stump up €1m – a huge financial risk.

"We had to bank on the idea that hosting Spain would promote the region as a potential summer training camp for other teams – Spanish, hopefully – in the future. That was the idea of how to amortise the investment," Jara explains.

Then, as would happen two years later in South Africa, Mother Nature intervened. Such a vast quantity of late snow fell in the spring of 2008 that by May 5 construction had yet to begin on the new facilities. There were still no football pitches in Neustift.

One month before kick-off, the faint-hearted within the RFEF must have feared that Spain had found a new way to screw up a tournament. No bad decisions by referees or linesmen; no missed penalties or goalkeeping errors – this time they were sabotaging their chances before a ball was kicked. A snappy new development.

However, within four weeks of blistering work, from that date to Spain's arrival in Neustift, everything was fixed thanks to the importation of German technology and a massive human effort which shredded all health-and-safety guidelines in terms of man-hours in a working week.

"I don't think there's a team at this tournament that have better training and living facilities than us," the Spain coach announces not long after arrival.

— Day One.
— June 5, 2008. Neustift
Spain's players touch down around the middle of the day at Innsbruck Airport with the previous night's booing at the Sardinero in Santander – following the uninspired friendly display against the USA – very much on their minds.

A little bit of fussing around to get everyone on the team bus (carrying the slogan: *Pase lo que pase, España siempre* – Whatever Happens, Spain Forever), then a 30-minute drive to Neustift and out into the grey, damp Tyrolean afternoon.

Spain are at the tournament; out trot the future European champions, stiff as boards and patently bemused by the kids in lederhosen, braces, and alpine hats with little feathers in the sides. As the teenagers stomp, and clap their hands against their heels, slapping hands in what looks like a cross between Morecambe and Wise's 'Bring Me Sunshine' and a Morris dancing convention, Santi Cazorla (23), Cesc Fàbregas (21) and Sergio Ramos (22) giggle, point and clearly don't know what the hell to make of it all.

The music is all oompah, brass and accordions. The Spanish, not the most widely travelled as a group, mostly have their ties askew and top buttons undone; they look uncomfortable and a tad embarrassed. These guys aren't allowed to ski, they take most of their holidays in Mallorca, Miami or Sardinia. Their draconian timetable, stripped of almost any leisure time, doesn't allow them to experiment with off-piste holiday tourism.

What they see is the strangest, most old-fashioned foolamajiggery which, as far as they are concerned, stands as much chance of being a practical joke as a traditional welcome from their alpine hosts. They look like a bunch of young guys who will find the Stubaital valley claustrophobic, cloying and risible.

Then Neustift plays its trump card. A little cluster of kindergarten-aged kids, dressed in the red and yellow of Spain's flag, begin to sing the children's song *Veo veo* (Spain's version of the game I-spy). It is charming, it hits a chord with the millionaire footballers and the atmosphere changes. In one quick, basic move Neustift has got under *La Roja's* skin.

Later, Carlos Marchena points out: "These cute little kids were singing in our language, not an easy thing to learn at their age, and it was really touching. I thought: 'They've put a lot of thought and effort into this.'"

Xavi: "It was a beautiful place, just a stunning valley, but the welcome from the people was the most impressive thing."

Kurt Jara is standing beside me and my colleague Dani Huerta and, on seeing Aragonés and his men so clearly touched and in good humour, noticeably relaxes. He elbows me, winks and grins: "We know how to look after them here."

The ubiquitous Manolo el del Bombo (Manolo with the Drum, Spain's most famous fan, whose adoration for the national team cost him his home life when he came back from an away trip to find his family gone and the house empty) begins wandering about and is mobbed – more in demand in Neustift than at a Spain game.

When the tubas and accordions segue into *Y viva España*, that's that. Neustift adores *Das Spanische Mannschaft* and *La Roja* love them right back.

"I understand from Aragonés that things have changed dramatically with Spain in recent years," Jara tells us. "I've watched them a lot. He tells me the players' attitude has changed greatly because of the influence the Premier League has had on those who went there and expanded their knowledge. I'd like Austria to win this tournament, of course, but I think Spain might do it."

Having arrived, the inventory is positive, if not problem free. Medical tests show that all the players are pretty burned out and most of them show serious iron deficiency. David Silva has an ear infection while David Villa has suffered a micro-tear in his thigh as a result of a collision with Carles Puyol against the USA. It is viewed as a run-of-the-mill battle scar and is almost entirely obscured by his excellent form at the start of Euro 2008. But it is an injury which will return, with the potential to add to the many twists which have historically derailed Spain's tournament challenges.

When the first training session is cancelled, I surmise it is to allow players to tend to these bumps and bruises. However, on interviewing for this book they correct that impression. In fact I'm struck by how much reverence still exists towards Aragonés from his players for the tiny surprise of allowing them the rest of the day off.

"Yeah, it might seem crazy still being impressed by that detail," Capdevila tells me five years later. "But we had just arrived in Austria, we'd eaten at 2pm and the boss says: 'Right lads, you are now free until 10am tomorrow.'

"The best we could normally have hoped for was to eat lunch, have a siesta and then not train till about 7 or 7.30pm, but no. Luis wanted to give us a pleasant surprise, he wanted us to relax and that's what we did. Everyone mixed; most of us spent a little time with the new guys; old friends who had changed clubs caught up with each other and those who had families nearby went to check they were installed safely. We all went out to dinner together – it was a terrific way to start."

— Day Two.
— *June 6, 2008. Neustift*
Russia are first up. Five days away.

Aragonés has used the cancellation of training in order to have another of his legendary pep-talks, from which players almost always emerge smiling and laughing thanks to his eccentric expressions, his mispronunciation of his players' names or simply because of his immense, bear-like energy for the coming fight.

However, now he is drumming home a message that he'll repeat all the way to the final: "We're not here to play games – we are here to win. We are the best squad at the tournament and if you guys give your utmost and we fail, it will simply show that I'm a crap coach."

The surprise is that, despite his squad having been assessed as fatigued, there begins a series of double-training sessions. Spain are out and warming up from about 10.45am, in full tilt by 11am and winding down around 12.15pm. Three players are pre-selected for media duties which they conduct sitting at a table in front of a marquee full of around 60 journalists from a confetti of countries. Other players not in the press conference attend to petitions from Spanish radio, television and a handful of the most respected press journalists.

From there, it is back to the Milderer Hof hotel just over a mile away: lunch, siesta, social time and back on the training pitch by 7pm.

The morning sessions focus on stretching, jogging and the famous passing drills called *rondos*, where one or two guys wear bibs and start in the middle of a circle of team-mates. The ball must be kept moving, usually via one-touch, at high speed around the circle, while the one or two in the middle press and try to either win the ball or touch it to disrupt the passing. Team-work, technique, touch, sharpness, pressing, fitness and team spirit all in the one exercise.

Before the end of the session there may be a mini-match or two, some crosses and shots for the goalkeeper; nothing too technical.

At night it is much more about exercises which translate directly into match situations: set-up play and shots or headers, free-kicks – both attacking and defending – then another mini game. The players are constantly busy, their work is short, intense, interesting and wholly aimed at stimulating sharpness.

— **Day Three.**
— *June 7, 2008. Neustift*
Not every day is based around double sessions but they are staged sufficiently often to be fascinating. It is also surprising and intriguing that every session is open to media and fans (bizarrely, the only one behind closed doors is before the final group game against Greece when qualification is assured, there is major team rotation and, it appears, less to hide).

Marcos Senna [2013]: "If you are happy with the sessions and if you like the coach's manner you could train three, four even five times a day – especially if you are in a competition as important as that one. We were delighted to go out there and truly enjoy the work. Even after a long season, if he'd told us that we were doing double sessions every single day in Austria then there wouldn't have been a single problem."

Santi Cazorla [2013]: "The atmosphere was amazing, everyone was up for it. We wanted to train, to follow instructions and work hard. No-one complained about the workload. We had double sessions, which was great. We were there for a month and everyone was determined to be on peak form."

Meanwhile...
The sight of 600 Swiss volunteers wearing coloured boxes on their heads will prove to be one of the more arresting line-ups witnessed at Euro 2008, but shortly after that performance at the opening ceremony the hosts are covering their eyes for other reasons: their favourites are defeated 1-0 by the Czech Republic and star striker Alexander Frei ends his tournament early with a knee injury.

— **Day Four.**
— *June 8, 2008. Neustift*
If this is summer in the Stubaital, they can keep it. It's cold, cloudy and wet. It rains so often and, with so many of *La Roja's* travelling fans arriving in this quaint and now overcrowded little valley to tramp around the training ground, you can come back from a morning's work with mud up to your shins.

And the flies. Flies on your hand, up your nostrils, buzzing next to the players' microphones and under your laptop – anyone here for the glamour will have a screaming fit and retreat within 48 hours.

Yet here is a slice of life: local families turn up; camera crews from around the world want a piece of the action; hard-looking armed cops with Alsatian dogs are at the corner of every pitch; there are former players, parents, wives, kids and girlfriends. They are all at Neustift, watching the future champions of Europe begin their quest.

> **Meanwhile...**
> *A Polish tabloid mocks up a picture of Leo Beenhakker, the national team's*
> *manager, clutching the severed heads of German counterpart Joachim*
> *Löw and Mannschaft captain Michael Ballack before the teams meet. The*
> *Germans respond by leaving Poland in pieces – Lukas Podolski scoring twice*
> *in a 2-0 win.*

— Day Five.
— June 9, 2008. Innsbruck

By the day before the first group game, against Russia, several things are clear. Firstly, Fernando Torres, off the back of a record-breaking first season at Liverpool, shows no signs of slowing down in Austria. *El Niño* is in the groove.

"A lot has changed in the four years I've been with Spain," he says. "I've drawn confidence from this season and I'm here at the end of it very hungry to add a trophy. The Champions League semi-final left a bitter taste – we came so near to winning such an important title [Liverpool were defeated by Chelsea in extra-time]. Now this is my last chance this season to lift a top-class trophy – something I've always dreamed of."

Secondly, it's clear that Marcos Senna, for all Xabi Alonso's legitimate claims, is Aragonés' go-to man. Senna is imperious, looking sharp as broken glass.

Marcos Senna [2013]: "Once La Liga had finished, Luis gathered us all together for a meeting and told us that we had so much quality that if we all believed we'd win it then Spain *would* be champions – we were just that good. He told us to go home and spend our few days off imagining being winners of Euro 2008. And he made me think. I'd had a good season, I was at my peak and I realised: 'We have such unbelievable players that we really are going to win.' By the time we reached Neustift I was totally in my zone."

Finally, there is the positive impact of the last two squad picks: Santi Cazorla and Sergio García.

While Raúl's absence is reported as a national calamity, almost asphyxiating all further debate about Aragonés' choices, there has still been a proper sprint for the tape. Joaquín, David Albelda, Luis García, Pablo Ibañez, Pernia, Albert Riera, Raúl Tamudo and Bojan, all serious candidates, have been pipped by the

Villarreal midfielder and the Zaragoza striker. When the group of 23 is named, Andrés Palop, Cazorla, García, Fernando Navarro, and Rubén de la Red don't have a cap between them.

At the time, the coach says: "I don't look at which team is first or third or wherever. I want players who fit my needs, who have had a good season personally and who are on form. Sergio García may well be used as a second striker [at Real Zaragoza, who were relegated along with Murcia and Levante that season] but he'll be useful to us on the right wing."

Speaking to me in 2013, he recalled: "I'd been watching Cazorla for two years and when my scouting team came back with good reports in the final two months I decided that he'd come, and that he might have an important role to play as a substitute when games were stretched and mature. I knew that we were talking about a player with a very big future."

Santi Cazorla [2013]: "I remember it so clearly. I had just finished training with Villarreal and as I got into my car the phone rang. It was Hernán [the Villarreal press officer] telling me I was on the list. Up until then I hadn't allowed myself to believe I'd make it. Sure, my name had been bandied about a bit because I'd had a good season, but you never really believe it until you get that call. It took me two hours to get home but it wasn't until several hours later that it really sank in. The phone had been ringing off the hook with people congratulating me, but once I had a moment to myself … what a feeling! It was incredible.

"Aragonés had been in charge of Oviedo when I was coming through there, but I was just a kid then and he didn't know me. However, I remember watching him at training sessions – we were doing pretty well at the time. In fact, he and I didn't have any contact until he called me up. That was why I was so taken aback to be selected for the Euros."

So surprising, so late are their inclusions that they are the only two not inoculated against a type of tic found in some rural areas of Austria each summer, whose bites cause encephalitis.

From the start, they embody the changes taking place within the camp, even if only for their manner and attitude. Cazorla, a likeable, infectiously funny guy by nature, constantly sports a face-splitting grin. García shows the mentality of a player brought up at FC Barcelona and taught the value of intensity in training. Both work their socks off, neither looks the least bit intimidated and throughout every training session perform as if their lives depend on it. They inject a squad with a lot of games in its legs, and which won't be without some issues to deal with in the days ahead, with energy, fun, hunger and youth. One up to Aragonés before a ball is kicked.

> **Meanwhile...**
> *The arrival of the Dutch in Berne turns half the stadium orange. It also leaves Italy looking a little off-colour. That's a symptom of their opening 3-0 defeat in Group C and their inability to quell a feverish performance from the Netherlands which spikes when Dirk Kuyt reacts to his saved shot by lifting a cross calmly for Giovanni van Bronckhorst to nod the third goal.*

— **Day Six.**
— *June 10, 2008. Innsbruck*
  Spain v Russia
Uno y dos y tres … ganar y ganar y ganar!

The first rival is Russia, but it had so nearly been England. The difference was made in the final night of qualifying, at a rain-soaked Wembley; the night Steve McClaren became 'The Wally with the Brolly' as he sheltered from the rain on the touchline while England's hopes of playing in the finals were washed away.

Croatia had already won Group E when they arrived in London while England needed a draw to make it. They recovered from 2-0 down thanks to goals from Frank Lampard and Peter Crouch. With 25 minutes to play, England had the point needed to send them to Euro 2008. Instead of shutting the game down, they pushed for a winner and the cost was the time and space needed for Mladen Petrić to fire a long-distance winner past Scott Carson.

Thanks to Russia beating Andorra 1-0, despite missing a penalty and having Andrei Arshavin sent off, England were out. Arshavin got a two-game ban, which was only the beginning of Spain's good fortune. Pavel Pogrebnyak, Russia's principal striker, who scored 10 goals in Zenit St Petersburg's victorious UEFA Cup campaign, abandoned training on June 7 and headed to Munich for a knee operation.

"Against Spain we'll be missing the only two players in my squad who can change games, decide games, in a single instant through their own skills," Hiddink declares. Naïvely, I reckon.

He goes on to reveal he's unhappy that Roman Pavlyuchenko has failed to keep himself in shape in the lead up to the tournament, admitting that the striker, on whom he'll now have to rely, has put on a couple of kilos and will be submitted to the equivalent of a pre-season training schedule in order to approach fighting-weight.

"He wasn't in great shape when he joined us, but he's made progress," is the Dutchman's downbeat, and unnecessarily open, assessment.

Russia's technical director, Victor Onepko, adds: "Pavlyuchenko is good, but lazy. He's strong, big, and shoots off either foot, but when he doesn't want to train, he doesn't train."

Way to back the team, lads.

In terms of omens, Hiddink was coach of South Korea when Spain were eliminated from the World Cup in 2002. Xavi, Puyol and Casillas were there during that shoot-out disaster. Aragonés, at least, knows Hiddink well. They were direct opponents as coaches as far back as 1991/92 for Atlético Madrid and Valencia; a year after the Dutchman left Valencia, in 1994, Aragonés took charge at the Mestalla. Meanwhile Russia, it is widely noted in the Spanish media, were Spain's victims (disguised as the USSR) when they won this tournament back in 1964.

Right now, Innsbruck is all of a quiver. Never mind the Scarlet Pimpernel, the man they are seeking here, there and everywhere is Roman Abramovich, famously a financial backer of the Russian Football Federation. Discos are suddenly charging €800 for bottles of vodka and champagne, farmers are making hay while the sun shines by renting out fields for helicopter pads and the ratio of Aston Martins, Ferraris and Lamborghinis to Volkswagens changes from 1:10,000 to 1:1. The Russian oligarchs have hit town.

The Tivoli-Neu Stadium, home to FC Wacker Innsbruck, is bursting with life, colour and great waves of noise. The true fans have taken over and the corporates are hard to spot. The local organising committee has added a temporary extension to the ground; instead of the normal 17,000 capacity there are 31,000 inside the stadium. To the right of the main stand are stunning mountains and the flight path for the local airport – it feels like a busy, important, lively place to start a tournament campaign. It feels like the right place to be.

Aragonés, as is predictable from training, selects: Casillas; Ramos, Puyol, Marchena, Capdevila; Iniesta, Xavi, Senna, Silva; Torres, Villa.

Some in the Spanish media call it a 4-1-4-1 formation (Senna holding), but it lines up like a 4-4-2 and in many attacking phases it will perform like a 4-2-4.

The squad has been told since day one that sometimes those on the bench will be even more important than those who play. It sounds like gibberish but it's a central part of the dismantling of the *ancien régime* of Raúl, Helguera and Guti. This is a band of brothers.

Down in the changing room Aragonés lets the players get ready, get a feel for the pitch. Then he calls them back in. He's dressed in waterproof training gear and football boots. He moves as if there is a primeval force bursting to escape his body.

The players gather around him, so do the staff. Back and forward he stomps, aluminium studs on his football boots clacking harshly on the tiled floor with a rhythm that accompanies his staccato delivery.

"Everybody goes out onto that pitch with a positive attitude." Clack, clack, clack, turn.

"Everybody convinced." Past the massage tables, back to where he started.

"We'll stick a leg into every tackle." Clack, clack, clack, turn.

"But we are smart out there. We're not going to suffer. We're going to do this together. Together. And if we get the chance to hammer them, we *hammer* them." A final turn, before he stomps back towards the far wall.

"And we run ourselves into the ground. Be smart, too."

Then he pauses; says nothing for six long seconds as he paces some more. He stops, faces the players standing stock-still by their lockers: Xavi, Villa, Torres, Puyol, Iniesta. There is total command in his voice.

"Listen to me. The moment has arrived. After two years when they've all battered and beaten us. But now we are going to show them. *Now* we are going to show them.

"We run ourselves into the ground and when we are exhausted, because you've done your job, you raise your arm and a team-mate will be there to take your place. Let's go!"

There's an explosion of roars of *"Vamos!"* (Let's go).

They surge into a huddle, every player, every staff member; Casillas in the middle, all hands extended into the centre, everyone touching.

Casillas shouts: '*Uno y dos y tres'* (One and two and three) then every voice roars back: '*Ganar y ganar y ganar!'* (Win and win and win!)

Every match will follow this ritual. It becomes Spain's mantra.

And now it's game on.

Russia play on the front foot, just like a Hiddink team. It's not a brutal game, but Russia's physique is superior and as they sweep forward, particularly via overlapping wing-backs, they have the upper hand. But, it turns out, they are also lackadaisical.

Nineteen minutes have gone by when Roman Shirokov, a 26-year-old Zenit defensive midfielder deployed at centre-back, screws up. Strolling out of defence, he panics as David Villa presses from his left side. His limp pass in the vague direction of Pavlyuchenko and Dimitri Sychev is simply a means of avoiding responsibility. What he doesn't know is that Joan Capdevila is about to unleash the pass of his life. Fifty metres away from Shirokov, Capdevila anticipates the Russian's folly. He edges between the two Russian strikers and uses his weaker foot, the right, to cushion-volley a simply unbelievable pass 60 metres down the channel, to where Fernando Torres is now isolated one-on-one with Denis Kolodin. The Liverpool striker jinks one way before going the other and hones in on the goalkeeper, Igor Akinfeev. Shirokov has compounded his original felony by allowing Villa to run off him and sprint to be unmarked at Torres' right hand. Having isolated the Russian keeper, *El Niño* dinks the ball into the path of Villa, who scores.

There's delirium, but before that begins we see a microcosm of what will make Spain special. Torres' generosity is rewarded by Villa running away in the celebration with his arm around the neck of his strike partner and pointing to Torres' chest. The gesture is unmistakeable: 'He gave me the goal on a plate.'

"Sometimes there's an ego in being a striker, you want the goal," Torres admits after the tournament. "But not this time; this time we just wanted to ensure that the team won."

Fernando Torres [2013]: "I love playing with David, because we're mates, because he's super-talented. Austria was one of our best experiences and we defied critics who said we couldn't function as a partnership. We've been playing together since the under-21s and it's always worked brilliantly. It's an instinctive mutual understanding forged through our playing time and our friendship off the pitch. Our wives are good friends, too.

"I could have gone for that first goal but … put it like this: the other day at Chelsea we were watching a video clip of a striker one-on-one with a keeper when there was a free striker to his right ready to take a pass and score. Now if I were the coach in that situation and the first striker didn't square it for the simple goal, then I would have taken him off immediately because he's not a team player. You have to put the team first, every time. That's the way I see it; the way I've always seen it. I love scoring goals, but if I see a team-mate who's in a better position, then I pass the ball to him. It was nothing to do with the fact that it was David or because I was thinking about giving him a confidence boost, but because he was perfectly positioned to put the ball in the net. That's always been my response and despite the fact that footballers have a reputation for being self-centred, I'm not going to change."

Russia hit the post within moments when Dmitri Sychev's cross from the right wrong-foots Carles Puyol, Marcos Senna and even Andrés Iniesta. But Konstantin Zyryanov's shot rebounds off the woodwork.

Then, just before the break, Spain produce something sensational. David Silva works back, regains possession and frees Capdevila, the left-back, just outside Spain's box. The Catalan is a converted winger and gallops away, first down the left, then cutting in to feed Iniesta. The Barcelona midfielder twists and turns Yuri Zhirkov until he looks like a dog chasing his own tail, then Iniesta sends a delicious pass outside Kolodin for Villa, who sprints between Hiddink's centre-backs and slides the ball past Akinfeev.

Box to box; wonderful skill and very direct. What's more it's part of the new Spanish DNA that they almost automatically produce a goal just before half-time or just before the end – mentally and physically quicker and fresher than opponents time and again.

Although Russia continue to threaten intermittently, Villa completes his hat-trick, and Shirokov is again made to look as if he is a *Russia's Got Talent* winner given a shot on the big stage based on a strong public vote rather than any real defensive co-ordination.

Twenty one minutes earlier Torres has been substituted off, for Fàbregas. It's obvious he doesn't like the decision. It's not a tantrum, but it will draw a reprimand from Aragonés the following day. When Villa scores his third, he runs to the bench, brushes past everyone else and embraces Torres, who's now wrapped up in his anorak against the heavy rain and looks just a little embarrassed to be centre of attention. Later he admits to having felt hugely honoured and fortified by this gesture. It's the most individualistic of Villa's Euro 2008 goals. That he chooses to share it with Torres, on the bench, underlines the strength of their relationship.

Significantly, it is a positively viewed version of the very thing Raúl was marked down for by Aragonés during World Cup 2006, when he ignored some of his team-mates to celebrate a goal with his 'inner sanctum' of Salgado and Cañizares on the touchline. Villa's celebration is looked on as a gesture to a friend who feels hurt; Raúl's as a gesture of defiance to the coach (and damaging to team spirit). The margins are fine. Not all coaches would have seen a major difference.

Spain concede when Shirokov's near-post header drops perfectly for Pavlyuchenko to ram home with his forehead.

However, *La Roja* are rampant; Fàbregas and Santi Cazorla nip about like imps, doing gleeful damage to Russia all over the pitch. It's no surprise when Villa's last contribution of the match, in added time, is to meander forward exhaustedly, lob the ball to Xavi, whose volley is saved but drops for Fàbregas to not only score his first headed goal as a professional but, importantly, his first goal in 27 international matches. That statistic has been the subject of tension and criticism. Fàbregas is already a hugely important figure at club level for Arsenal so the spotlight is harsh. The team converge on him, both joyful and relieved that this important, popular footballer has the monkey off his back.

Spain 4 Russia 1

Spain: Casillas, Sergio Ramos, Marchena, Puyol, Capdevila, Silva (Alonso 77), Senna, Xavi, Iniesta (Cazorla 63), Villa, Torres (Fàbregas 54)
Goals: Villa 20, 45, 75, Fàbregas 90

Russia: Akinfeev, Aniukov, Shirokov, Kolodin, Zhirkov, Sychev (Bystrov 46), Zyryanov, Semak, Semshov (Torbinsky 57), Bilyaletdinov, Pavlyuchenko, Bystrov (Adamov 70)
Goal: Pavlyuchenko 86

Meanwhile...
Zlatan has landed. Ibrahimovic scores Sweden's first goal of the finals by striding on to a lay-off from Henrik Larsson and rifling a volley into the top corner in his side's Group D opener with Greece. Peter Hansson almost seems apologetic after he adds an untidy second goal in a 2-0 win.

— Day Seven.

— June 11, 2008. Neustift

Inside the camp, it's already clear that this tournament has a different feel.

Aragonés has guillotined Raúl's international career principally for footballing reasons, but as a positive by-product the coach has removed a stultifying sense of hierarchy. Now something new is bubbling through: hunger, friendship, togetherness. The objective is to win, but this group has decided there will be nothing finer than doing it with friends, rather than colleagues.

Back in Neustift the Spanish federation has erected a canvas pavilion so that the media centre is right next to the training ground. This is to accommodate the travelling army from Spain's vociferous and often critical television, radio and newspapers, plus those from the rest of the world who were expecting the car-crash performance usually provided by the national team at tournaments. Someone, however, has omitted to provide translation services. With three players on press conference duty almost every day, this is a problem.

Paloma, the RFEF press officer, co-opts me to take notes and make sure that all the foreign media get a rough Q&A transcript at the end of every gig. In exchange, a little storeroom will be converted into our studio, somewhere to carry out the one-on-one interviews and to keep the specially-constructed lighting rig and cloth backdrops for filming. Even before the Russia win, as we set up our mini-studio, one of the longer serving federation men happens by and stops for a chat.

"I really believe something could happen this time," he says. "The atmosphere has changed so radically, and for the better, that I think this tournament could actually be when we punch our weight."

There is tremendous spirit on the pitch and the training sessions are full of high jinks between Reina and Casillas; Fàbregas and Xavi; Capdevila and Cazorla and the work is undertaken with real appetite. What we don't see is how much fun the squad are having off the pitch, too.

José Manuel Ochotorena won three Spanish titles and two UEFA Cups as goalkeeper for Real Madrid, was *Zamora* (the goalkeeper with the best record in La Liga) in season 1988/89 for Valencia and went to Italia 90 as a back-up to Andoni Zubizarreta. He became goalkeeping coach at first Valencia, then Liverpool and then the Spanish national team. He is at Euro 2008 to coach Iker Casillas, Pepe Reina and Andrés Palop.

'Ocho' recalls: "You'd go into one of their bedrooms and there'd be a group of players there, a mix of Barça and Madrid and there was always such a good atmosphere. We also had a list of favourite songs we'd sing along with and after every game we'd go back to the hotel and we'd all start dancing and singing – the hotel staff, too! I suppose the most important thing about the team was the level of respect they showed each other despite being cooped up together for so long. That's worth mentioning, I think."

One of the kit men, Félix Martín, a veteran of 13 tournaments with Spain, also makes it clear: "Players didn't head off to their rooms ever night alone like they'd done in previous competitions, so I told them this was the first time I'd seen such unity."

They meet over Cola-Cao (a chocolate drink), cards, football discussions, table tennis, Playstation – not every squad member, but about two-thirds of them on a good night.

"Fourteen guys all congregated in one team-mate's room to chat and have a laugh – I'd never seen that in all my time with Spain," agrees Casillas.

Often, one player's room would be chosen as the main hub. When they check in at the Milderer Hof hotel next to Neustift, Spain's players are enormously amused to find the five-star, Hollywood-style suite hasn't been assigned by the Austrian owners to Luis Aragonés, nor to Captain Casillas. Not even to one of the star strikers. That privilege falls to Joan Capdevila whose humility goes about a mile beyond self-deprecation. His king-size suite has a living room, three bedrooms, a bathroom, a shower room and a nice balcony. Heaven.

Capdevila doesn't mind at all when the rest of the squad come round to his territory every night. He isn't bothered by the relentless jokes about who he'd had to sleep with to get the best room in the whole of Austria. However, when it comes to sleeping alone in a cavernous, creaky, apartment, there *is* a problem.

Capdevila is petrified that either there are ghosts or someone is trying to break into his suite while he sleeps.

Santi Cazorla: "How Joan ended up with this enormous suite nobody knew, but there were three huge bedrooms and a living room all for him, so the rest of us would pile in every evening after training to play cards and talk. I was in there every night and he began to tell me that he was hearing noises in the middle of the night, as if someone was there. He's *such* a scaredy-cat. I thought it was hilarious."

In the end Cazorla takes one of the spare rooms and Capdevila, reunited with peace of mind, goes on to produce an epic tournament.

Fernando Torres and Marcos Senna, who have the rooms directly underneath and next door, respectively, often can't get to sleep for the noise booming out of Café Capdevila. A small price to pay for squad harmony.

Meanwhile...

The main build-up to Portugal's match against the Czechs is conducted in England, where Manchester United have been left fulminating over Real Madrid's covetous comments about Cristiano Ronaldo. It perhaps does not help that the Portuguese forward cuts a dashing figure in all-white; scoring one goal and setting up another during a 3-1 victory which puts his country into the quarter-finals.

— Day Eight.
— June 12, 2008. Neustift

Talking football with Fernando Torres is immense fun: he's sharp, clear-minded and articulate. During his career he's been a gigantic footballer. It is true, however, that his countenance can betray emotions a little too clearly.

On leaving the pitch against Russia nine minutes after the break it was easy to read that he was upset – despite him doing very little to aim his fury at Aragonés.

Immediately post-match the coach pointed out that "it was only my intention to look after him. He's vital to us and he's had a long, hard season with Liverpool". How astute Aragonés will prove to be on that point.

Some of the Spanish media poke and prod at the occasionally irascible 69-year-old in the following 48 hours and he snaps: "Whether I've had a word with him or not is an internal matter, but I can assure you that things didn't stay like they were in Innsbruck. You can't just let that pass. I fully comprehend that a player can get angry. I was a footballer and I got angry. I'm with Torres up to that point. But I don't want to suddenly see those who aren't picked or who are replaced getting pissed off. If you don't start, you make sure you are ready to come on and make an impact. If you are coming off, then the first person to be annoyed with is yourself."

Torres and Aragonés have already formed a successful partnership, taking the club both of them love, Atlético Madrid, out of the Segunda División and into the Primera back in 2002. However, to date, of the 41 games he's featured in for Spain under Aragonés, Torres has played 90 minutes only 11 times (scoring in 10 of these matches).

In season 2007/08 he has produced 33 goals in 44 Liverpool appearances – a contrast to the two in nearly two years for Spain since qualifying for Euro 2008 began in September 2006.

"I was a little angry when I was taken off, but I was mostly annoyed with myself," Torres explains about the Russia match.

This echoes the analysis provided by Aragonés. Torres is frustrated, he's simply shown too much of his angst. Will the media let it go?

Meanwhile...
Austria's Ivica Vastić gets the goal in a 1-1 draw with Poland to become the oldest player to score at a European Championship. At 38, Vastić is just a year younger than Croatia manager Slaven Bilić, who also refuses to act his age by celebrating with childlike enthusiasm as his side beat Germany 2-1.

— **Day Nine.**
— *June 13, 2008. Neustift*
In the pre-match press conference for the Sweden game, the Spain coach tells me: "I've had a chat with him [Torres] but there has never been a problem. Sometimes you build a paternal relationship with players and I've been with him a long time now. However, he's only in my teams on merit."

Fernando Torres: "I was angry because after a pre-tournament match against the United States in Santander, he [Aragonés] had told me that I had nothing to worry about and that I would be a starter in Austria. I'm not sure why he decided to tell me that – perhaps because he had taken me off at half-time in three successive pre-tournament matches against Italy, Peru and the USA. Whatever the reason, he took me off. I was angry at the time but Luis didn't say anything to me after the game against Russia and I thought that was the end of it. I never expected the media to make so much of it. Maybe that media attention was the reason Aragonés called me in and told me that as far as he was concerned it wasn't an issue. He even told me: 'Spain is Torres and 10 others.'"

The issue draws comment from Henrik Larsson, the former Sweden and Barcelona striker, who leaves no doubt around how important a player Torres has become. "Fernando, in my opinion, is the new world superstar. I've watched all his big matches, the European games for Liverpool in particular, and we are talking about one fantastic striker."

On the Wednesday between the games, *La Roja* train in the morning and then get complete liberty to enjoy a day off and report back on Thursday at 10am. I bump into Pepe Reina's dad, looking after the keeper's young daughter, Grecia, at Thursday training. He played with Aragonés in the 1974 European Cup final. His presence here is an indication that, tucked around the valley where the Zückerhut (Sugerloaf) and Elfer (Eleven-shaped) mountains tower over the chalets, are the kids, wives, girlfriends, friends and parents of *La Roja's* 23 footballers. Many of the players go for pizza and a beer, one or two go into Innsbruck, a few just play with their kids – limbs are rested, minds cleared.

Then, on the Friday afternoon, just over 24 hours before kick-off against Sweden (again in the Stadion Tivoli Neu), one Swedish tabloid reckons it has a belter of a story.

I'm sitting next to the Sky match commentator Martin Tyler, talking about shared experiences at the 1982 World Cup, when a reporter begins wandering around the press conference crowd, showing off the article in his paper that morning featuring a lurid headline detailing how they have caught a Spain player out on the town drinking just two nights before this crucial group game.

Given the nightlife row which had hurt Sweden before their 2006 qualifier with Liechtenstein (Zlatan Ibrahimovic, Olof Mellberg and Christian Wilhelmsson were banned for breaking curfew), perhaps the reporter and his editor believe they have a massive scoop. Sure enough, there is Sergio Ramos with his arm around a fan who has asked for a picture. The snap is clearly taken in a pub or club and it is used as a huge splash on the page.

Taking the newspaper in one hand and the microphone in the other, the Swede wanders right up to Luis Aragonés.

"We caught your player out, drinking, in a local club right ahead of the game against our national team and here's our newspaper picture to prove it. Now, what do you think of *that*?"

Zapatones peers, stone-faced, over his glasses and, with those great big hams for hands, reaches out to take the tabloid so that he can examine it for himself. There's total hush.

Aragonés peruses the picture and article, considers it for just a beat or two and says: "What I think is you'll need to get a better photographer because Ramos has a night off again tomorrow and you never know, I might be out dancing with him. I like disco music, although I prefer flamenco.

"On his day off this is the sort of thing he's meant to be doing. I was worried you were going to show me something worse."

With that he disdainfully passes the paper back to the crestfallen journalist. The crowd roars with laughter.

Then Aragonés warns Sweden will play English Premier League football. They do.

He demands that his wide players prevent the ball into the box to stop Zlatan getting goal chances. They can't (but, in the end, it doesn't matter).

> **Meanwhile...**
> *Gianluigi Buffon saves a penalty, Italy's blushes and the aspirations of his country to reach the quarter-finals of the competition after a 1-1 draw with Romania. All without using his hands. The goalkeeper sticks out his right boot to prevent the Romanians taking a late lead which would have left his side floundering in Group C.*

— Day 10.
— *June 14, 2008. Innsbruck*
   Spain v Sweden
Uno y dos y tres … ganar y ganar y ganar!
   Torres pays his manager back by giving *La Roja* the lead.

Xavi's corner after quarter of an hour is a training ground move. The ball is pushed short along the byeline to Villa who looks like he's going to return it to Xavi, who's moving inwards from the corner flag. Instead Villa cuts it diagonally to his left, where Silva is unmarked on the edge of the box.

He controls with his left and then dinks the ball towards the penalty spot, right in front of Petter Hansson, who is comprehensively turned over by Torres. The striker extends his leg to poke the ball into the near-post gap which Andreas Isaksson has just vacated.

As Torres jogs off to celebrate Villa simply erupts out of thin air, Bruce Lee style, to envelop him in a flying embrace. The match tension is broken and so is Torres' drought. Butch couldn't be happier for Sundance.

Ten minutes before the break Spain's left side allow an easy cross, just as against Russia – this time from Freddie Stoor. Ramos is out of position, Ibrahimovic gathers the ball, Ramos is already falling, and Zlatan shields possession muscularly. His turn is now easy and he pretty much shoots through Casillas' dive.

And so, 1-1 it remains, well past the 90th minute.

But, wait, the man with the king-sized suite hasn't had his say yet. Nor has old Aragonés.

With time nearly up, The Wise Man of Hortaleza [another of his nicknames] is still on his toes. From the technical area he's bellowing at Villa not to drop back and defend, to stay up beyond the centre circle.

"*Villa, Villa, Villa*! Get yourself there … just stay there between them." Still focused, still attending to the details which will change their tournament.

Suddenly, under pressure, Joan Capdevila lumps it forward. They call it a *pelotazo* in Spain.

Torres has dropped deep off Villa to go hunting possession. When he and Stoor both jump for the ball, which is returning to ground with snow on it, the pair land in a heap on the ground.

One bounce and possession is 60/40 in Petter Hansson's favour ahead of Villa. But somehow the striker's quick feet squeeze the ball out beyond Hansson and despite Mellberg trying to close in and Sweden's huge keeper racing out to block, Villa twists slightly to his left, opens the face of his right boot and finesses the ball beyond Isaksson into the far panel of the net.

Villa sinks to his knees and the adrenaline bursts out of him in a primal roar. But that's not the centre of the action. Marchena has jumped into Casillas' arms while almost every other player, those stripped for action and all the subs, are now in a pile of jubilant bodies right in front of the dugout, to where Villa has sprinted to celebrate with everyone else.

Aragonés, more emotional than he will eventually be after the final in Vienna, tearfully joins in – hugging players, properly sucked in by the moment.

"That's not my style, but it really got to me to see all the squad celebrating together like that," he explains post-match.

It is two years since Raúl equalised against Tunisia in the World Cup and went off to celebrate with Salgado and Cañizares, to the exclusion of other, not particularly enthusiastic, squad mates.

Everything has changed. It is also a Spain record. Aragonés, the most vilified *La Roja* coach in history, has now equalled the all-time number of victories, held by Javier Clemente, but his 36 wins have come in 51 rather than the Basque's 62 internationals.

Sweden 1 Spain 2

Sweden: Isaksson, Stoor, Mellberg, Hansson, Nilsson, Elmander (Sebastian Larsson 79), Andersson, Svensson, Ljungberg, Henrik Larsson (Kallstrom 87), Ibrahimovic (Rosenberg 46)
Goal: Ibrahimovic 34

Spain: Casillas, Sergio Ramos, Marchena, Puyol (Albiol 24), Capdevila, Iniesta (Santi Cazorla 59), Senna, Xavi (Fàbregas 58), Silva, Villa, Torres
Goals: Torres 15, Villa 90

> *Meanwhile...*
> *The wheels come off the bus which Greece had insisted on parking in front of goal. The holders are excluded from the last eight by a vibrant Russia, who beat them 1-0 thanks to Konstatin Zyryanov's strike. European football has moved on in this tournament, even if Greece have not.*

— Day 11.
— June 15, 2008. Neustift
After two years of horrible abuse from press and fans alike, Aragonés has pulled it off. The spirit in the Spain camp has changed from 'We are not amused' in the Raúl era to 'All for one and one for all'.

"It's totally the manager's merit," offers Iker Casillas, squad captain but also club-mate of Raúl at Real Madrid. "He's achieved the ideal of building a team that always plays to win and which has a sensational atmosphere. Don't have any doubts – that union you see on the pitch is the fruit of the work we do off it."

Spain are Group D winners, they are in the quarter-finals and they will play in Vienna. Their superstitious fears about the 'curse of the quarters' rest on whoever emerges from Group C.

It won't be Holland, aggregate 7-1 winners over Italy and France in their first two games. Romania sit second after two matches while France, European champions in 2000, and Italy, reigning world champions, are joint bottom.

> **Meanwhile...**
> *Turkey's hopes of reaching the quarter-finals are pronounced dead 75 minutes into their final group match, with the Czechs 2-0 up. A mere 15 minutes later the Turks are playing with such vivacity that when Nihat Kahveci whips the third goal in off the underside of the crossbar to record an incredible 3-2 victory it seems a natural conclusion.*

— **Day 12.**
— *June 16, 2008. Neustift*

So, now it's back into the micro-cycle of play-recuperate-rest-train. In Neustift, Spain have a double session just ahead of the dead rubber against Greece – in Salzburg.

Every bus journey – and there are plenty of them – is owned by Sergio Ramos. He is the music man, his is the soundtrack of the tournament – dominated by *Aire* (José Mercé) a flamenco track about opening up the windows to the new morning, letting in fresh air, new air, happiness into the house. Good theme.

The other track repeated almost until it wears out is *Se Parece Más A Ti* by Jambao – a dirge so fatally gloppy and repetitive that any self-respecting music fan would ship in a couple of own goals just to get home early. Lucky for them that Gerard Piqué (Stone Roses, Elvis Costello, Oasis and James) hasn't yet broken through.

The best explanation comes from Aragonés' audio-visual assistant who prepares scouting videos but who also claims some credit for the nature of this musical tournament.

Javi Enriquez: I had prepared a CD by Julieta Venegas with songs on it like, *You Are The One For Me* and *Now Is All There Is* but it didn't make much of an impact on the lads. So I asked Ramos and Reina about the songs likely to go down well and used them instead. We won the first match, against Russia, and when the players came onto the bus at the end I had our driver – who was the spitting image of Obelix – slam on the third song. Everyone was tapping along to the music, really getting into it. I pretended to the federation delegate that the players wanted the volume turned up and there was this great sense of building euphoria. Their developing confidence and determination was almost tangible, all through one song – *Se Parece Más A Ti* – which became like an anthem for us throughout the tournament."

The Greeks were tournament winners four years earlier, playing with a style which Otto Rehhagel has honed to perfection: a tight-marking, speculative, grey approach which doesn't thrill.

On the way, they had helped eliminate Iñaki Sáez's Spain from Euro 2004 via a 1-1 group game. But even though only four short years have passed not a single player in red from that draw would take part in the rematch, and only four of those used by Sáez in Porto were even in the 2008 squad.

Things are grim for the holders, too. Having lost their opening matches against Sweden and Russia, Greece are already out.

Training has shown that neither Puyol nor Silva are fit to play a third group game, but also that Aragonés wants to shuffle the pack. It's clear that Xabi Alonso and Pepe Reina are going to play, while Fàbregas' performances in the last two matches and Sergio García's work rate in training also mean they've earned starts. As has Dani Güiza, the one guy on the trip who has been looking alternately fed up and anxious.

He was *pichichi* (top scorer) in La Liga that season with 27 goals for Mallorca (only beaten to the European Golden Boot by Cristiano Ronaldo). Güiza hasn't found it easy to hit the net in training, hasn't even come on as a substitute and, despite knowing that Aragonés will take him to Fenerbahçe, who he has agreed to manage after the tournament, the Andaluz striker has the countenance of a man who's lost a tenner and found ten pence. Now his chance has arrived.

> **Meanwhile…**
> *Both Joachim Löw, the Germany manager, and his Austrian counterpart Josef Hickersberger are sent to the stand. It is not clear if they were simply complaining about the standard of a game which seems like a polite kickabout until Michael Ballack skelps home a free-kick for a 1-0 win.*

— **Day 13.**
— *June 17, 2008. Salzburg*
Then, suddenly, it is Aragonés who has the dour, unhappy face.

On the evening before the Greece game, the Spaniards sit in front of the hotel television and watch Italy not only beating France but leapfrogging Romania, who lose to Holland.

Italy – *bloody Italy* – are *La Roja's* opponents in the quarter-finals.

"Not at all the rival which I most fancied playing in the last eight," Aragonés confesses. "Really, really complicated. They looked like they were dead and buried in this tournament and here they are, in the knockout round – again."

The fact that Spain haven't beaten Italy in a competitive match for eight decades becomes the most quoted fact in the tournament.

Meanwhile…
Andrea Pirlo and Daniele De Rossi score as Italy beat France to progress to the quarter-finals despite entering the final round of games with one goal and one point to their name. Holland take their total to nine of each after a 2-0 win over Romania.

— Day 14.

— June 18, 2008. Salzburg

   Spain v Greece

Uno y dos y tres … ganar y ganar y ganar!

Otto Rehhagel liberates his team, the five-man defence becomes a system with flying wing-backs and the match is fun as a result.

Spain go one down to a lovely Greek free-kick, ending in a thumping Angelos Charisteas header reminiscent of how Rehhagel's mob won Euro 2004.

Alonso, later given man of the match, nearly scores from his own half, almost breaks the post with another volley and generally peppers poor old Antonios Nikopolidis, who has announced he is about to retire, with shots all night.

The Spain equaliser is straight off the training ground – a move I've seen them work on over and again during the previous few days. Fàbregas surges forward from midfield, Güiza makes one of those NFL wide-receiver runs where he heads long, checks and then uses the little bit of space he's gained on his marker by dropping back one pace to wait for Fàbregas to deliver him the ball. It's a lovely chip forward, Güiza heads it very deliberately into the path of De la Red who's been tracking the play and his volley screams into the net off Nikopolidis's arm. Practice has made perfect.

The winner is a perfect illustration of the football Aragonés decided to adopt following the Northern Ireland defeat in 2006.

Spain keep the ball. Teams haven't yet learned not to chase them for possession.

Spain always finish the first half and the second half much fresher than their opponents, ready to exploit gaps and dips in concentration.

Spain score when the other team is still on the pitch in body, but already in the changing room mentally.

Against the Greeks, Güiza nods the winner in the 88th minute from Sergio García's cross from the right wing.

In the 17 matches since their last defeat, by Romania in November 2006, *La Roja* are not only unbeaten, they have scored 32 times while only conceding eight. But just check out how often they've caught the other team sneaking out of the match before it's over.

Against Greece in 2007, David Silva's winner comes in the 90th minute.

In the qualifier at home against Denmark, Villa scores in the 45th minute of a 2-1 win. He does the same thing away to Latvia in a 2-0 win. Then in September 2007, in a vital qualifier away to Iceland, Andrés Iniesta's equaliser comes in the 87th minute.

At home against Latvia, Fernando Torres gets the second in the 86th minute; away against Denmark, Sergio Ramos scores a beauty five minutes before the break and Albert Riera kills the match in the 89th.

In the spring of 2008, Italy and France are both beaten 1-0 – Villa and Capdevila each scoring in the 79th minute.

Capdevila adds the winner against Peru in the 90th minute then Xavi gets the only goal of the game in the 79th minute versus USA in the days before Euro 2008 kicks off.

Already at this tournament, Fàbregas has hit the fourth against Russia in the 90th minute while Villa robs Sweden of their draw with his 92nd-minute goal.

In due course, opponents will get savvy. They will put banks of seven, eight, even nine men behind the ball and not tire themselves out by chasing possession. For the meantime, *La Roja* has created a private scoring zone – just before half-time, just before the end.

Greece 1 Spain 2

Greece: Nikopolidis, Vyntra, Kyrgiakos (Antzas 63), Dellas, Spiropoulos, Basinas, Karagounis (Tziolis 74), Katsouranis, Salpingidis (Giannakopoulos 86), Charisteas, Amanatidis
Goal: Charisteas 42

Spain: Reina, Arbeloa, Albiol, Juanito, Fernando Navarro, Sergio García, De la Red, Alonso, Iniesta (Santi Cazorla 59), Fàbregas, Güiza
Goals: De la Red 61, Güiza 88

Meanwhile...
A little goes a long way for Russia. The diminutive figure of Andrei Arshavin is in the starting XI for the first time following suspension and steals the show in a 2-0 win over Sweden. A generally eye-catching performance is epitomised by his contribution to Russia's second goal but more impressive is the ease and intelligence with which he conducts the Russians from midfield – orchestrating progress from the group to meet the Dutch.

— Day 15.
— June 19, 2008. Neustift

From the moment Howard Webb (who Spain will meet again in this story) blows his whistle to end the Greece game, there are 94 hours until kick-off against Italy. Almost every last second of them is spent talking about omens, about the curse of the quarter-finals, about not beating the *Azzurri* competitively since the Olympic competition of 1920. And about Mauro Tassotti elbowing the nose off Luis Enrique's face in the last eight of USA 94 (an incident which was David Villa's first-ever memory of watching Spain play on television).

In the end it's pretty handy that a row springs up, just to get everyone's minds off Roberto Donadoni's team and how Spain might as well not bother turning up.

Throughout the tournament thus far Aragonés has been a little niggled by Sergio Ramos. Unhappy with his decisions about when to go and when to stay against Russia; unhappy with the way he was brushed off by Zlatan in the build-up to his goal; unhappy with one or two minor habits which have been developing around the team sessions at the Milderer Hof hotel.

The coach chooses to stage Ramos' ticking off on the training field – in public but out of earshot.

The day after the Greece win, Aragonés is happy to explain why he chided the defender. "Sergio's a great guy and a fine professional but there are certain codes of behaviour he needs to adhere to. It's not about his football, it's something to do with our life off the pitch. It's time for him to understand certain ideas that, because of my experience and veteran status, I am firm about."

The story is that Ramos has been a little too laid-back around camp, frequently the last down to breakfast and that he hasn't realised that his coach – a stickler for rules – is losing patience.

Part of the price to pay for Aragonés' unyielding loyalty to his players amidst a storm of criticism over the previous two years is total adherence to his rules. Meeting every single deadline assiduously is one. If breakfast is at 9am, then 9.01am won't do. Late is late, and late is disrespectful to those who are following rules. One minute is anarchy.

Moreover, Aragonés is a great student of body language. He'll read a great deal into what he sees while he's unnoticed.

Particularly first thing in the morning.

His audio-visual analyst confirms how keen Spain's coach was on making sure he was well placed to see every single player as he arrived down to the breakfast room in the morning.

Javi Enriquez: "Luis tended to have just four hours sleep a night and I'd stay with him till about 3am as we worked over video footage. Then we'd usually have breakfast together at 9.30, although Luis would be up and about and in the restaurant at 7.30am."

Aragonés' words about Ramos are said with affection and only a gentle reprimand. But they are given to a media which, even now, is thirsty for old-style bust-up stories. Once they are published and broadcast back in Spain, Ramos isn't happy.

Meanwhile...
A blond moment in the first quarter-final costs Portugal a place among the last four. Germany's Bastian Schweinsteiger, the peroxide-haired midfielder, celebrates his first start at the finals by scoring once and creating two more goals with free-kicks in their 3-2 win. His substitution late in the second half receives appreciative applause from both sets of supporters.

— Day 16.
— June 20, 2008. Neustift
The next morning, while Aragonés waits to brief his squad before beginning training, Ramos wants explanations. Although the media are 70 or 80 metres

away, the cameras have long lenses and only someone illiterate in body language could fail to spot that this has the potential to kick off.

Remarkably, nine minutes later Aragonés is back in control, things have been resolved (although this would only become clear later) and *Zapatones* has got away with criticising his player in public – in theory an error and a violation of his own code.

To both men's credit they are the types to speak bluntly, to heat up quickly but neither particularly bears grudges. Ramos felt no rancour that Aragonés had criticisms – only that they were evidenced in public. Moreover, the defender tuned in to what his coach had to say, irrespective of his irritation.

Sergio Ramos: "Neustift was one of those stages you go through as a footballer. I didn't enjoy it as I should have done. When you begin a tournament not playing as you'd like to it's hard to be a bundle of smiles. Things worked out well in the end and that's all that we were aiming for. I got a bit of stick from Luis, he was very demanding. But I feel this was wholly positive. Immediately I felt that if the manager was being this demanding with me it was because he felt I had extra to give. However he did 'give out' to me quite a bit. His main point was: the first job is to defend, so defend. Once I got up past the halfway line he was more liberal about me taking chances. I've got great affection for him and I'll always be grateful for everything he taught me."

While that storm was brewing in its teacup, Aragonés began work on a bigger, more important theme.

He now admits that, three full days before the Italy game, he had, "begun to note a few moments of pessimism". The antithesis of what he has been trying to convince these players for two years. *His* Spain aren't here to lose to anyone, least of all because of superstition, jinxes and a creeping fear that this result is pre-ordained.

Spain aren't only feeling jinxed because it is the quarter-finals (they had lost at this stage in 1986, 1994, 1996, 2000 and 2002), nor because they have failed to beat Italy competitively since the 1920 Olympic tournament, but because of the date. June 22 is pure voodoo.

On that date in 1986 *La Furia Roja* were beaten on penalties by Belgium in the World Cup quarter-finals; On the same date at Euro 96, Spain, despite having a perfectly good goal chalked off, lost on spot-kicks to England at Wembley –

again in the last eight. Finally, both Rubén Baraja and Fernando Morientes had goals incorrectly disallowed against Guus Hiddink's South Korea on the same date in 2002, before Spain lost the shoot-out 5-3 and exited the World Cup.

Amidst all the voices warning of impending doom, news of little morsels of good fortune falls on deaf ears.

Luca Toni is out of sorts, Gianluca Zambrotta sluggish, Fabio Cannavaro injured. Then, during Italy's last group game, the victory which eliminates France, both Andrea Pirlo and Rino Gattuso are booked and suspended for the Spain game.

Asked about the huge importance of both being absent, Aragonés seizes an opportunity to get a laugh and diffuse some of the tension. "Pirlo, okay, they'll miss his creativity. But let me tell you that if Rino Gattuso is some sort of vital reference point for the way Italy like to play then ... well, then I'm a priest!"

However, back in Spain Luis Enrique has recalled the last competitive fixture between these two nations, during USA 94, and how *La Furia Roja* were in line for the semi-final, 1-1 and dominating Italy in Boston, until Mauro Tassotti's brutal elbow in the face of the then Real Madrid midfielder.

Tassotti wasn't sent off (he was retrospectively banned for eight games), Roberto Baggio scored the winner with two minutes left and Spain were so unnerved by the incident (Luis Enrique's nose was shattered and there was blood all over his face) that their levels of concentration and intensity plummeted.

Enrique lets rip: "This is a vendetta, this needs to be revenge for USA 94."

He has the theme entirely wrong. Those were the days of the *Furia Roja* – Red Fury. If Aragonés has done anything in the two years since losing to a technically inferior but far more streetwise France side it is to ensure his team knows how to deal with pressure and how to win whether or not they are playing well.

He wants focus, ball possession, ice-cold blood in his men's veins. The last thing he needs is for this to become violent, personal or driven by revenge.

On the training ground he is in search of intensity. There is a double session on the Friday, two days before the match in Vienna. But it's not a positive experience.

In all the practice matches, and Group D games, goals have rained in. However, this one finishes 1-1 thanks to Sergio García for the reserves and David Silva for the first team. There's a lack of precision during the match. Sergio Ramos gifts the ball to García for his goal, passes go astray and only three or four of *Los Rojos* emerge from the practice with kudos.

At one stage Aragonés intervenes in exasperation, patently troubled by what he's witnessing. "Take the corner again and let's see if we can at least get a goal," he roars out midway through the 40-minute full-scale practice.

There's a well-known Chinese journalist, based in Beijing but often on the Spanish scene for his newspaper, going round exclaiming that the fact there were paragliders descending from the towering Tyrolean hills with Spanish flags fluttering in the wind behind them was, in Chinese wisdom, "a bad sign".

"If the flag comes down it's negative and a portent of doom," he tells anyone who will listen.

Not if he has been sent by Italy coach Roberto Donadoni himself could he better feed the paranoia of the twitchy Spanish media.

However, that isn't the only aerial threat on Aragonés' mind. He imposes seven corners on the practice match, even when the ball doesn't go out of play, and invents four or five free-kicks in addition to those legitimately awarded. Defending against the high ball to Luca Toni (who has had a brilliant season with Bayern Munich, 39 goals and 12 assists in 46 matches, but who Paolo Rossi has described as having had "twenty chances without scoring one" in the tournament thus far) is evidently on his mind.

"We are going to play a national team which, if you take a look at all the trophies they have won and the power of their current squad, could make things very complicated for us," argues Aragonés during the countdown to kick-off. "So what I want from my players, from now until the end of the match, is utter and complete conviction that we are going to win. Any side which thinks it wants to defeat Italy requires total self-confidence. Given all my years in football I know one thing for sure – the guy who goes out totally convinced that he's going to win is far more likely to play positively. If one guy has negative vibes then the whole group can suffer from that, too.

"A national coach's job is technical and tactical but on occasions it's psychological, too. I've had a brief chat with the group after the Greece victory and I've told them there are things to fix – but I look at the lads and I'm sure there is no psychological thing about Italy weighing down on their shoulders."

He is lying.

> **Meanwhile...**
>
> *A goal from Ivan Klasnić in the final throes of extra-time causes Croatia manager Slaven Bilic to race down the touchline in celebration. By the time he has returned to the dugout, Turkey have equalised. The Turks have become synonymous with big finishes in these finals and carry it on to win 3-1 on penalties. Bilic wanders slowly out of sight.*

— **Day 17.**

— *June 21, 2008. Vienna*

Arrigo Sacchi, verging on a holy figure in Spain given the playing style and triumphs of his AC Milan side, and Italy coach last time the *Azzurri* eliminated *La Roja* from a quarter-final, sums the whole thing up beautifully.

"It's very evenly-matched but that's just an advantage for Italy. When a contest is this tight, Italy has become accustomed to winning it nine times out of 10. It's a question of culture, of footballing tradition. For any Italian, football, fundamentally, is only about winning. Nothing else. In comparison the Spanish live for the spectacle, for the beauty of the game. That means they have concentrated more on technique than being practical about victory. Just look at this tournament. We've been capable of taking the most ferocious criticism after losing the first game 3-0 to Holland, using the attacks to improve by some kind of osmosis, such that now the fans and players and media are wholly united behind the objective that the *Azzurri* win and go into the semi-final. Italy is the team which was dead, but now not only is it able to walk, it's running!"

Exquisitely constructed, brilliantly argued. But wrong.

Damiano Tomassi, the former Italy, Roma and Levante midfielder says: "Italy will go through because of our mentality, our spirit and our ability to cope with pressure. That's what we are made of. Spain has developed a more efficient playing style, but they are still overcome by taboos. They are terrified by the quarter-final jinx. They never get through; it's as if they are even petrified of the words 'quarter' and 'finals'."

Casillas admits that when Italy versus Spain in the quarter-final was confirmed he thought: 'Italy, the team which does a lot with very little.'

Torres recalls his feelings: "The quarter-final – our brick wall, where all our old ghosts suddenly appear." This is a golden generation, but one which is still wrestling with fear.

Poor old Tomassi. At almost any time over the previous 88 years he'd have been on the money.

> **Meanwhile...**
> *There are 55 shots traded between Holland and Russia in their semi-final. When the dust settles it is Guus Hiddink's troops left standing. Dutch aspirations of reaching the next round are mortally wounded in extra-time; Arshavin is the triggerman, crossing for Dmitri Torbinski to score then adding the final goal in a 3-1 win over 120 thrilling minutes.*

— Day 18.
— June 22, 2008. Vienna
Spain v Italy – quarter-final
Uno y dos y tres ... ganar y ganar y ganar!

As they go out to the pitch Aragonés is still talking, still priming his men psychologically. "Let's do this, let's make them run themselves ragged chasing after the ball!"

Casillas picks up the baton: "Two years we've been waiting for this – two years preparing for this. Let's not forget that. Let's make the people who came here to watch us enjoy themselves."

The match is as the two Italians had suggested it would be. Though Spain dominate possession and create good chances, Italy are a wolf in sheep's clothing: nerveless, sure that a good meal is coming along soon and, in the meantime, happy to feed off the pressure.

An hour has passed. Luca Toni is causing havoc in the penalty box. Casillas comes out to block and then, somehow, gets back on his line as Mauro Camoranesi fires the loose ball at goal through a crowd of legs. Casillas saves with his left boot, even though he's moving to his own right. Both remarkable and crucial.

Senna fires in a long-distance drive which Gigi Buffon spills; hope stirs for a minute, but the ball doesn't trickle over the line, nudging gently off the post and back into the arms of the Juve legend.

Cazorla, set up by fellow substitute Dani Güiza, has Spain's best chance but his shot zooms across goal and squeezes beyond Buffon's left-hand post. The image of Senna and Villa sinking to their knees in frustration, while Casillas puts his gloved hands to his head, betrays frustration, perhaps even the familiar self-doubt.

Marcos Senna: "I'm a Brazilian, I love playing for Spain and when I was young if my country weren't playing I always supported Spain. But I've never suffered from any quarter-final phobia, nor are Italy any kind of *bête noire*. So when the game was drawing towards penalties and Iker made a small error with a kick-out, I was sure I'd seen some legs begin to tremble and some minds turn to the fact it was Italy, the quarter-final, and penalties were looming. I just started shouting at everyone, rousing them up and bawling at Iker to concentrate. He just gave me this look as if to say, 'What's up with this guy?' But at that moment I felt like Aragonés' man on the pitch and it was my duty to re-emphasise his message that we were better than Italy and there was no reason we were going to lose."

Iker Casillas: "We all felt that Italy had got through by the skin of their teeth. We had come out of the group with nine points, eight goals and only three conceded. They had only four points, just one win and had also conceded three. And yet here we were again, facing them in a penalty shoot-out."

Before a shot is fired in anger Casillas seeks out Buffon. They pass two or three words, there's a smile, an embrace – what's about to happen is vital to each man, but not sufficient to spark gamesmanship, enmity or a lack of grace. Different heights, but two big men.

Luis Aragonés: "I told the players: 'I don't want anyone refusing a penalty because that would be a very bad sign.' I picked the three best takers from training to go up first – Villa, Cazorla and Senna.
"There's often a psychological disadvantage in going first, but if I could have chosen that night, it's what I would have opted for. Italy won the toss, they chose to let us start and it just gave us the chance to edge ahead. A small mental edge."

If Aragonés has chosen well. *If* the first man scores.

The Austrian cops have told us that there are 30,000 Italian fans, passionate and noisy, but only around 12,000 Spaniards in the Ernst-Happel Stadion. That kind of split on a hot, humid night in Vienna should ensure the *Azzurri* dwarf the Spanish roar – but they don't. Not only is the travelling red army suddenly filled with conviction, the shoot-out is also going to take place at *their* end of the pitch. Details, tiny details.

In Neustift, Aragonés has made everyone practise spot-kicks. The only ones needing no encouragement are the three keepers – Casillas, Reina and Palop. From the first training day they have been involved in a little competition amongst themselves, right at the end of the session. It is fascinating. Usually, but not always, it's 10 penalties each and while they admit to the winner being bought a beer or a tapa by the losers, there is also hard cash involved. It is competitive, it is fun and only a few of us in the media stay behind to watch. From that day until this it's become a familiar tradition of Spain's tournaments. With the arrival of Víctor Valdés, who doesn't take part, it's now an eye-to-eye, toe-to-toe slugfest between Casillas and Reina.

The best I've ever seen – and it was just epic – was in Gniewino, en route to winning Euro 2012. But more of that later.

I asked Spain's keeper coach about this fascinating 11-metre gunslinger-battle.

José Manuel Ochotorena: "They've had this private competition since they first came together in the national side. They'll bet on who saves the most penalties in training and the stakes will be things like a cup of coffee, a beer, €50. But I can promise you, they take it very seriously and will play to the death. On more than one occasion, we've had to stand about waiting for them because they've drawn and want to play on and on until they get a winner. Some evenings we're literally dragging them away as the lights are being switched off. It's some spectacle, I can tell you, and they'll sometimes get a handful of fans who stay back to watch and support one or the other. It's just another example of the strong relationships within this group. It's indicative of what makes the team so special and so successful."

Casillas is a phenomenal goalkeeper and a born competitor. But I can't help believing that facing penalties from Reina, over and over, has honed his reflexes, his philosophy, his nerves. Having taken so many himself, I think it helps him get inside the mind of the taker, too. Suffice to say, during the three tournament wins Casillas has saved four penalties.

José Manuel Ochotorena: "Before any shoot-out we'll have done our homework. We'll know which players are likely to take penalties, their body positions as they take it, whether or not there are specialists who are used to taking penalties. Players always have a favourite area of the goal but you can't rely on that. It's a personal, internal thing and there's no way to know what's going on in the striker's or the keeper's head. Iker has a strong character and he's taken to his role as leader in the group like a duck to water. If you watch him in moments of high tension during a match you'll see that he can change in an instant from being completely normal to becoming cold and calculating. He manages tense situations with ease and much better than many others in football. In the run up to a match we'll pass him all the info we have. But often, and in this case it happened, he'll tell me that he wants to follow his own instincts. As we prepared in Vienna that's what he said, that he was in the right frame of mind, that he had all the information that he needed and that he was going to let his sixth sense take over. At the end of the day you have to respect the player. It's him out there on his own after all. It seemed to work pretty well."

Before there has even been a huddle, before most players can take a sip of water, Aragonés goes straight to Villa. He'll take the first one. The potential for a small edge is in his hands.

Santi Cazorla has his back to the coach but as he turns round Aragonés barks out: "Cazorla second."

Santi Cazorla: "From the moment I became a professional until then, I hadn't taken a penalty. You're asked: 'Do you want it or not?' and you say 'yes, yes!' which is contradictory because you're only thinking about not failing, because if you do miss and Spain are eliminated, then that's forever. But you just accept the risk, and the responsibility."

Joan Capdevila: "If I'd known Santi had never taken a penalty I'd have fainted on the spot."

Senna intuits that he's next – the boss loves him, he strikes the ball well and he's without nerves in this situation.

Everyone is still milling around, no huddle, when Güiza, a protegé of Aragonés and a second-half substitute on the night, is crouching down and suddenly finds his man-mountain coach towering over him. The instant that Aragonés tells the Mallorca striker that he's No.4, the boss knows that he's chosen the wrong worker. Body language, the expression on Güiza's face, his lack of an enthusiastic reply while he ties and then re-ties his boot laces all tell Aragonés this is the man of straw.

"I could see I'd made a mistake, but it was too late to change my mind," Aragonés confesses later.

Then, with the players finally all grouped together around the 69-year-old, Aragonés calls Cesc Fàbregas as the fifth and, hopefully, final taker.

Given that Casillas has dissuaded 'Ocho' from giving him any advice or information, Reina is at a loose end. Casillas doesn't want any input. Reina knows that if he was on the pitch he would be the sixth taker (and I'd have bet my house, my premium bonds and all my Paul Weller CDs on him scoring). Instead, he's gone looking for team-mates to help.

Before he walks up and kisses the ball, places it on the spot and begins the shoot-out, Villa, the regular Spain and Valencia penalty taker, indicates to Reina that he'll accept some quiet counsel.

> **David Villa:** "Pepe advised me that I should aim my strike low and to the keeper's right and that's just what I did. Getting that first penalty in the net took a lot of pressure off all of us. History owed us one and had done so for a long time."

Spain 1-0 Italy

Fabio Grosso, scorer of the winning penalty in the World Cup final against France in Berlin two years earlier, ambles up, full of graceful athleticism, and shows how pressure evaporates if you've already conquered the world from the spot. He barely breaks stride, opens the instep of his left boot and sprays a wonderful shot into the right-hand panel of Casillas' goal frame.

In the main stand, Casillas's mum, Doña María del Carmen, faints. She's out cold for five minutes. Once treated by the Red Cross she's fine, but she's missed her son confirming his conversion from Iker to *San Iker* (Saint Iker). "I've done this before," she says. "Whenever I watch him playing and the commentator announces that there's a dangerous free-kick coming up I just shut my eyes. I can't bear the tension."

Spain 1-1 Italy

> **Santi Cazorla:** "Pepe [Reina], who's been a great friend since our days at Villarreal, came up to me and said, 'Wee man, how are you feeling? Just stay calm and take your time. They don't know you and my advice would be to

send it straight down the middle'.

"Then we were all lined up and I looked at Buffon and thought to myself, 'If I send it down the middle and he stays put, I'm going to look like the biggest idiot in the world'. I was standing there and all these thoughts were going round and round in my head. 'What do I do? Ignore my own instincts and follow his advice? Or go my own way and take the consequences?'

"So I just went my own way and scored. Pepe came up to me afterwards and said 'Congratulations – you've got a big pair of balls on you. You just ignore my advice and still manage to score!'

"In truth, I really appreciated it. That was a tough moment and I was grateful for the gesture of support."

Cazorla's penalty mimics Villa's. Buffon goes to his left, the ball nestles in the opposite corner.

Fernando Torres: "The Italian sense of assuredness was remarkable. You looked at them during the shoot-out and they were all in little groups of one and two, laughing, smiling, joking, relaxed. We, on the other hand, were all encouraging each other, arms linked around one another, tense but supportive. You just got this impression of one team which was used to it, one team which wanted it."

Spain 2-1 Italy

Iker Casillas: "I'd faced [Daniele] De Rossi in the Champions League and he'd put the penalty straight and high above me and I just figured to myself that rather than repeat that he'd put it to the natural side for a right-footed player – into his left, my right. That's just what I thought in the moment and I went for it. I stood still and tall for as long as possible then just flung myself."

Casillas saves, fabulously.

Spain 2-1 Italy

Marcos Senna: "When I first signed for Villarreal back in 2002 I chose the number 19 for the back of my shirt. One of the club directors came to me and told me: 'That's an unlucky number around here, perhaps you'd better think again.' But I liked the number and I told him I wasn't superstitious like that. Then in the January of my first season I did really bad ligament damage to my knee against Betis, was out for several months, and the director came to me again. I ignored him, got back to playing and immediately was injured in the knee again. Out for most of the season. This time he insisted that I was suffering the jinx of the number and although I stopped and thought about it, I made a point of not giving in to some sort of made-up hoodoo. So when I scored against Buffon in Vienna there's this lovely shot of one of the best keepers ever diving the wrong way, my penalty hitting the net and you can see the number 19 clear as day on the back of my Spain shirt. At the end of the tournament I went back to the same guy at Villarreal and said: 'Aren't you pleased I didn't listen to you now?'"

Spain 3-1 Italy

Mauro Camoranesi, South American-born just like Senna, isn't remotely stressed by the situation he and his team are in. His face betrays no more tension than if he was choosing between a nice Pinot Grigio or a complicated, dark bottle of Barolo. He barely seems to move his right leg but the ball screams into the top-right corner of Casillas' goal. The best penalty yet.

Spain 3-2 Italy

Dani Güiza: "I wasn't used to this kind of thing. This was my debut at a big tournament and I could feel the pressure. I saw the boss naming the guys one by one and could feel he was coming for me. When I didn't score it was the worst moment of my career, I was in tears – quite sure that I'd messed it up for everyone. The world caved in on me."

Buffon again dives to his left, his favoured side, and easily blocks the striker's faltering effort.

Spain 3-2 Italy

But even before he steps back between the posts, Casillas begins to rescue Spain.

He sees Güiza is destroyed, in tears almost before Buffon has stood up in triumph.

"Don't worry Dani, don't worry – I'll save the next one for you!" roars Casillas as the distraught striker heads back to the group.

Later, he recalls: "You spend a month, cooped up in a team hotel with a guy and you see him in pain, the first thing that comes to mind is to help him, to make a human gesture."

His words have an immediate psychological effect on the group.

Aragonés will later say: "Iker didn't even think about it, he just reacted to support a team-mate. But I could see the instant impact his words had on the group. They weren't thinking: 'He's missed, here we go again,' they were thinking: 'We've still got Iker!'"

The Italian fans, now certain that this is once again their moment, are reprising their *Seven Nation Army* chant from World Cup 2006. Di Natale runs up looking confident, but puts his effort in exactly the same place as Güiza and Casillas emulates Buffon, saving low and to his right.

Spain 3-2 Italy

As Casillas saves from Di Natale, the line of red shirts bursts forward from the centre circle. One man is left behind. In that second Cesc Fàbregas knows it's all on him. The 20-year-old Catalan hasn't taken a penalty since he was 15 and in the *cadete* (under-16) team at the Camp Nou with Piqué and Messi. Now he has the chance to eliminate the world champions.

Momentarily he's lost in the significance of it all. Then he's on the move. Pacing forward. Ready.

> **Cesc Fàbregas:** "When the boss called out my name as the fifth taker, it was a surprise. I hadn't even taken a competitive penalty since I was 15 years old and he hadn't been picking me as a starter. But I immediately felt an immense confidence because he chose me in fifth position – that's usually where you put the guy who you're most sure will score. Walking up for the penalty, you feel that life is presenting you the challenge, that your country needs you and I wanted to answer. After so much talk about me being on the bench, my attitude, my form and so on all I wanted to do was score for my country and give them some joy. I normally put my penalties to the side that Buffon dived. This time, I don't know why, I just hesitated that split-second

longer before committing myself and I could see where he was going. So I changed my mind at the last instant or else I might have missed."

Spain 4-2 Italy

Initially the players run to the winning goalscorer. Then the group abandon Fàbregas and swamp their captain, upon whom realisation has gradually dawned that Spain are in the semi-final, the curse of the Italians, the curse of the quarter-finals and the curse of June 22 are all now over. His smile becomes a roar and then he disappears under Villa, Cazorla, Puyol, Fàbregas and company.

Eventually, Casillas goes to the fans and uses his arms to signal: 'This was for all of you.'

Then, in the dressing room, a royal visit. King Juan Carlos has always followed football passionately – Spain and Real Madrid in particular. This time he's visiting an old chum in Aragonés. Once, a considerable time ago, Juan Carlos, Aragonés and Alfredo di Stefano dined together on an occasion when the King was to award the Wise Man of Hortaleza Spain's gold medal for sport.

"Very nice, but, your majesty, wouldn't it just be more convenient to give me and him [Di Stefano] some sort of monthly financial stipend as well?" Aragonés teased at the time.

"I've practically known the man since he was only a prince and now every time we meet I ask him how the financial idea is going. He always tells me to keep at it, to keep plugging away."

Aragonés is in high spirits. Five years later he admits he was economical with the truth on the night before the Italy game, when he claimed there were no nerves, no talk of the jinx. "In the build-up to the Italy quarter-final I was struck by all the media and the fans thinking we were automatically going to lose again and I saw nerves in some of the players. I took the captains [Casillas and Xavi] aside and asked them to help me re-double my efforts to make their psychology more robust. My message, over and again, was that we were the better side and we'd go through. No doubt."

Cesc Fàbregas: "The dressing-room scenes were delirious, everyone was just so full of joy and the King was there telling us how well we'd done. But this is just a match, just one small win. I didn't come here to end the curse of the quarter-finals but to win this tournament – we all did. If the boss decides to drop me for the next game then no big deal. I'm here for the team whether it's for 90 minutes or one, just for extra-time and penalties or really whatever he wants. I don't want the glory, I want Spain to have the glory. This country deserves to end all the misery it has suffered in tournaments for so long."

Five years later, at Chelsea's Cobham training ground, a few days before scoring in the UEFA Europa League final over Benfica, Fernando Torres tells me: "We'd been pretty confident, but then you draw Italy, a team that had kicked our butts in so many tournaments. You start getting flashbacks of the worst moments. But Aragonés made it a challenge for us to beat everyone, not just Italy. Press, fans, Italy and whoever came next, all the way to winning it. You walk out thinking that you will change history, you win on penalties and *that* is the moment. All the anxiety, all the fear just melts away and it's as if you've won the whole tournament. When we beat Italy we were all totally sure we'd be champions."

Spain 0 Italy 0 (Spain win 4-2 on penalties)

Spain: Casillas, Sergio Ramos, Marchena, Puyol, Capdevila, Iniesta (Cazorla 59), Senna, Xavi (Fàbregas 59), Silva, Villa, Torres (Güiza 85)

Italy: Buffon, Zambrotta, Panucci, Chiellini, Grosso, Aquilani (Del Piero 108), De Rossi, Ambrosini, Perrotta (Camoranesi 58), Toni, Cassano (Di Natale 75)

— Day 19.
— June 23, 2008. Neustift
Fate has a little slap in the face waiting for Aragonés.

UEFA announces that Russia, who have torn an otherwise impressive Holland side to shreds in the last eight, are the home side for the semi-final. It means that with a clash of strip colour (red) Spain will have play in yellow – a colour Aragonés both fears and hates. He's been known to send players home from a training camp if they turn up dressed in yellow.

My *Revista de La Liga* colleague, Gaizka Mendieta, who played for Aragonés at Valencia, confirms: "Luis is certainly a little idiosyncratic. I remember once going to a local council event at the Valencia town hall and the Mayor's secretary happened to be wearing a yellow dress. Luis couldn't even look at her. He said to us: 'Just keep her away from me, I don't even want to be near her.'"

Of course, we tease Aragonés about playing Russia in yellow. "It's *mustard*, not that other colour ... *mustard!* Golden if you like, but so long as I don't have to put one of those jerseys on, then fine."

Wisely, I think, we leave it at that.

— Day 20.

— *June 24, 2008. Neustift*

Part of what makes the re-match so appetising is that Russia have begun to play spectacularly now that Arshavin is free of suspension. His trick in the 23rd minute against Sweden, to send Konstantin Zyryanov free down the right wing in the creation of Roman Pavlyuchenko's opening goal, has been the technical moment of the tournament. He added the second goal, hit the post, was named man of the match and then produced a goal and an assist in extra-time to eliminate Holland.

Back in Neustift, Xavi is enraptured. Before the semi-final I chat about the Russian with the Barcelona midfielder.

"Another little guy who can rule the world," he points out, returning to a theme we've previously talked about in Barcelona. "Do you know I'd never even heard of Arshavin before this tournament and he's absolutely superb? He's just one more example of how football is for the smart guys, not the big guys who can run all day."

Aragonés really only has one concern – that the 4-1 victory over Russia in the group stage may have fostered complacency.

The red Spanish caravan pulls out of its tiny Tyrolean hideaway – destination Vienna once more. A thousand kids with their parents turn up and Aragonés gives the local cops permission to let all of them stream forward in search of autographs.

One of the cops' Alsatian dogs gets over-excited and bites our cameraman, Jürgen. Bad dog.

And we are told an interesting little detail – the bulk of players' luggage has been left behind in the Milderer Hof hotel and either after the 3rd/4th play-off on Saturday, or the final on Sunday, *La Roja* will flit back to Neustift to collect their gear, before setting sail for Madrid. It's a small psychological touch. Aragonés hopes that it feels like they'll expect to be coming back because they've won, not deflated after a play-off. Tiny details.

— Day 21.
— June 25, 2008. Vienna
The Arshavin buzz plays right into Aragonés' hands.

Santi Cazorla: "Before the Russia game we were all a bit worried about Andre [Arshavin]. We were in the team meeting room waiting for the boss to start the briefing and we all began talking about how well this guy was playing, the damage he was capable of, and so on.

"Luis arrived, stopped just inside the door and demanded to know what all the chatter was about. One of us said 'We've been talking about Arshavin, *Mister,* because he looks like the kind of player we'll need to be wary of'.

"'Nonsense,' Luis said. He instantly told us he'd heard that Arshavin downed an entire bottle of vodka on his own to celebrate beating Holland. 'He'll be no threat at all, in fact I'm not sure he'll make it onto the pitch'. It wasn't true and Luis didn't mean any harm, but it sure as hell took the pressure off. We laughed, deep down some were reassured and the boss told us: 'Pavlyuchenko is the danger man.'

"In fact, every team talk was like that. We used to look forward to them knowing that, somehow, the boss would find a way to make us laugh and relieve the pressure. I don't know what it is, but he's just got a talent for bringing humour to the most stressful of moments."

Sergio García: "He had us all in stitches of laughter that day. He made preparing for the game so much more enjoyable. I'd never had a coach who liked to muck about a bit before a match."

Carles Puyol, a few months after the tournament, says: "It was the best team talk of my career."

Meanwhile…
Stick a fork in them, they're done. Turkey bow out in a semi-final against Germany but do not go down easily. In trademark style, they make it 2-2 with only nine minutes left through Semih Şentürk. Five minutes later, they are outdone by Philipp Lahm, who scores to put Germany in the final.

— Day 22.

— June 26, 2008. Vienna

    Russia v Spain – semi-final

Uno y dos y tres … ganar y ganar y ganar!

Aragonés was only spinning a yarn, but in the event Arshavin doesn't do himself justice on a steamy, rainy night. Just as the coach predicted, however, Pavlyuchenko does indeed threaten. Fitter, slimmer than when he arrived in Austria and with goals not flab under his belt, he's easily Russia's best.

"Come on, we'll take this opportunity!" is Casillas' rallying call in the tunnel before kick-off. Spain play as if they have taken Russia a little too seriously. Alternatively, perhaps the first half evidences the effect of 120 minutes and penalties against Italy only four nights previously.

After half an hour David Villa tries a shot at goal and immediately pulls up with a recurrence of the thigh problem incurred by colliding with Puyol against the USA. It will prove the end of his tournament, but he has already scored sufficiently to win the Golden Boot. What's more, he has hit the net in each of his four games and that's enough to ask of any striker. Anyway, Spain are unshackled and there's no stopping them now.

Unfortunately for him, with his morale in his boots because of the immediate diagnosis that there's a tear in his muscle, Villa is in the showers when Spain make the breakthrough.

Just after the break Iniesta, enjoying his best game of the tournament, essays a diagonal shot at goal. Xavi, whose quick pass has begun his team-mate's forward drive, anticipates what might happen, bursts forward and diverts past Akinfeev.

"A moment of complete happiness, perhaps the most magical I'd had in football until then," he will say later that year.

That is that. Spain tear at Russia. It is a footballing spectacle. Over the years since Euro 2008, almost every opponent has attempted to shut Spain down. To suffocate them. Very few go toe to toe, but it *is* an approach that can be rewarded, as Portugal and Argentina discover. Twice at this tournament Russia try to slug it out and the aggregate score is 7-1. Italy, four years later, will follow suit – but we'll come to that.

Fàbregas creates the next two goals – for Güiza and Silva. The first assist pass, a sublime volleyed-chip, is a work of art.

Spain are breathtaking, bold and sumptuous to watch. There's also a visual reminder of what, apart from talent, makes this group so special.

The unhappiest Spaniard in the Ernst Happel stadium, Villa, runs the furthest along the touchline and celebrates the most unashamedly when Güiza scores the second, certain that *La Roja* are in the final. For now, the fact that he won't take part is irrelevant.

When Fàbregas presages how the final of Euro 2012 will open up, with a goal assist for Silva, Villa erupts again and joyously launches his water bottle high into the Austrian sky.

Pase lo que pase, España siempre – Whatever happens, Spain forever – a phrase made reality in Villa's unselfish reactions.

More music at the final whistle – the mustard-shirted players gather in a circle and dance around roaring out the trumpet chorus of the Triumphal March from Verdi's Opera 'Aida'. You *do* know it, you've heard it sung by the fans at a hundred Champions League matches.

Russia 0 Spain 3

Russia: Akinfeev, Aniukov, Vasili Berezutsky, Ignashevich, Zhirkov, Semak, Zyryanov, Semshov (Bilyaletdinov 56), Saenko (Sychev 57), Pavlyuchenko, Arshavin

Spain: Casillas, Sergio Ramos, Marchena, Puyol, Capdevila, Iniesta, Xavi (Alonso 69), Senna, Silva, Villa (Fàbregas 34), Torres (Güiza 69)
Goals: Xavi 50, Güiza 73, Silva 82

— Day 23.
— June 27, 2008. Vienna
Russia had previously won the battle of the hotels – nipping in to book the place on the edge of the Danube which *La Roja* wanted. As the morning of Friday June 27 dawns, however, I'm certain that there are few complaints. Spain have instead installed themselves in the Vienna Hilton which sits, gloriously, on the edge of the extensive, verdant Stadtpark and the Danube canal – a 15-minute drive down Lassallestrasse and then onto Handelskai to reach the Ernst Happel stadium.

Neustift has been brilliant: an oasis of calm, far from the madding crowd and unaffected by the brutal storms which cause the television signal for the Germany-Turkey semi-final to be lost for 20 minutes and the International Broadcast Centre to very nearly blow away. Kurt Jara has come up with a location where the integration of families with the players can happen very nearly unnoticed (the Spanish media know but leave well alone).

Joan Capdevila [2013]: "Everything's rosy now that we are winning, now that we are the best in the world – it's fine that the players are allowed to spend the night with their wife or girlfriend during the tournament. It's fine that we were sent out on the town to drink as we wished after winning the last-16 match against Portugal in the World Cup. And in Euro 2008 we used to have a few beers in one of the rooms, usually mine, after a match. But I guarantee the day that we start losing … well, I remember when I was in Coruña in the era of *Super-Depor*. We were winning all the time and we'd go out on a Tuesday night and the people would be lining up to buy us drinks. Then we started to lose the odd game and you'd go out on a Sunday after a match and the same people would be abusing us and calling us drunks. Mark my words, if we [Spain] start losing, they'll all be lining up to scream insults at us once again."

The tension leading up to this tournament has been immense. Constant criticism in the press, the idea that the team is without a spark, that the defence is leaky, that Aragonés still is not the right man. The entire, endless Raúl farrago. Had Spain been based in or near a metropolitan area and players been out for a beer, or been spotted emerging from the hotel or apartment of a girlfriend or wife, the unofficial embargo on private lives would have been strained, probably broken by news media or paparazzi.

It has worked. It has, in fact, been vital. A little bit of magic at the end of a picturesque Tyrolean valley. The Jara-Aragonés partnership has become a hidden, but immensely important, impetus towards a winning atmosphere.

Nevertheless, Vienna is glorious. Neustift was grey and grizzly. Private, but damp. The elegant Austrian capital sports temperatures soaring through the 80s under a violently azure sky. This is the precise moment for a city of empire, history, power and beauty. Spain is ready to emerge as the belle of the ball.

Training is at the Franz Horr Stadium and, unlike Neustift, it's a bit of a hassle. The little stadium, where Austria Vienna play, is a bit run down. Crowds assemble outside, it's tough for the team bus to get through and the world's media have crowded in to the concrete tribune alongside the pitch.

Everyone apart from Villa takes part. His absence is Spain's first setback. Had the third group game been critical, it's probable that Puyol, Xavi and Silva would have been in doubt but, as it turns out, no other player has missed a competitive minute through injury or suspension.

After training everyone has the rest of the day off until 9pm.

Although it's been difficult, stuck away in the Tyrol, from the start of the tournament, Puyol, Iniesta and all three physios have tried to find themselves the treat of a sushi restaurant every time the coach gives them a free afternoon or, better still, a free day.

Carles Puyol: "Raúl, Fernando and Juan, our physios, plus Andrés – we're all great friends and we've sought out good Japanese restaurants together. Little by little we've been joined by new disciples – Fàbregas, Alonso, and Xavi – but we are the nucleus. We are the Sushi Crew. There's a good feeling. It's just another of the small keys to our current success."

— Day 24.
— June 28, 2008. Vienna

To the Ernst Happel, a happy hunting ground so far, and more training. But first a little chat.

Aragonés starts off by telling his playing group: "You don't play finals, you *win* them. Nobody remembers the beaten finalists. They remember Spain for *fiestas* – bah. We'll show them a *fiesta* when we win. Nobody, *nobody* remembers the runners-up."

Time and again he emphasises these same points: they are here to lift the trophy. *'Pensamientos positivos!'* he'll roar endlessly during the next 24 hours. Positive thoughts.

Later, in the hotel's conference room, there's more detail, but the tone is still jocular and idiosyncratic. Throughout the tournament Aragonés has shown his propensity for mixing up names. Fàbregas has always been 'Fabrikas'. Briefings about opponents are often confusing, because it's not always clear who's being talked about.

So, picture this scene. It's the night before arguably the biggest match in Spanish football history. Aragonés is in full flow and, it transpires, one of those present will become our fly on the wall.

Joan Capdevila: "It's the middle of the team talk and the boss is beginning to tell us that he's not sure if Wallace will even be playing. His point is that if Wallace is playing then ... and then he notices Xavi with his hand half up. "'Yes, Xavi?'
"'*Mister*, I'm pretty sure his name's Ballack.'
"'Ballack? Wallace? I prefer Wallace. I'm calling him Wallace from now on.'"

It's summer 2013 when the left-back shares that story and it still leaves him laughing out loud.

After the final, some of the players gleefully remind Aragonés that Wallace *did* play.

"Doesn't matter – he didn't win, did he?"

Joan Capdevila: "Other coaches can be great motivators but Luis had that something extra. Not only did he always help us bond as a group, he somehow managed to strip all the tension away. That was completely new for us."

During the team talk it's not all positive.

"The Blond Fella," Aragonés continues. "The one with that weird name [Schweinsteiger] – he's been sent off more than once and if we're smart you never know whether that might happen again. I don't want us to lose our discipline, but if I were smart I'd pass a little comment, I'd maybe make a face at him, see what he thinks."

He notices Casillas having a wry laugh, right in front of him.

"What you think skipper? Yes? No? Very well, maybe we can say the odd thing because he's a hot-head, he's lost his rag before and these are games you don't play – you win."

Another golden moment from Aragonés that evening goes like this: "And don't be chatting to the referee or the linesmen and calling them ref or lino! Even in my playing days I used to make sure I knew their first names – each of them. Now that you are all a lot better known, famous, make sure that when you see them, going out to the pitch or inside the stadium, wherever, give them a high five, put an arm around their shoulder and make sure it's 'Hi, Joseph', or whatever. They like that. Show some balls, learn their names. You'll see, the guy will go away thinking 'Bloody hell, he knows my name!'"

They take him to heart. Four years later I'll see one of these players putting exactly this idea into practice in the Ukraine during Euro 2012.

It's time for rest, the last night before Spain's first final in a quarter of a century. Golden time. But, this being Spain ...

Marcos Senna: "The fans had been great all tournament, noisy, supportive, totally different from the couple of years previously. However, the night before the final they were in the hotel. To be more specific they were in the bar. You couldn't move because they were everywhere. And they started singing. All the songs you want to hear in the stadium were echoing up from the team hotel bar the night before we played Germany. I just couldn't sleep. No way. So I took a sleeping pill and drifted off to the sound of them singing about victory, singing *¡Y Viva España!*

"When I woke up, I'd slept okay – but the songs were still in my mind. I could hear them from the night before, echoing around my head. I knew we had to win. I knew we couldn't let them down."

— Day 25.
— *June 29, 2008. Vienna*
  Spain v Germany
  – The final of the UEFA European Championship 2008
Uno y dos y tres … ganar y ganar y ganar!

It has all been for this. "If we are not in the final then I'm a crap coach and I've organised a crap team," Aragonés told them, well over a month before.

Spain's royalty, football's royalty – they are all here. At home the streets are silent, yes even in the Basque country, even in Catalonia.

Before leaving the Hilton, Aragonés seeks out Torres.

El Sabio and *El Niño*. The wise man and the kid. They've worked together at club level, now they are about to conquer Europe.

Torres has been in two UEFA European Championship finals before (UEFA Under-16 in 2001, UEFA Under-19 in 2002) winning each 1-0 and scoring each time.

Aragonés trusts him. They won Spain's Segunda División in 2002.

Aragonés needs him. David Villa is injured and Fàbregas, with one goal in 31 internationals, will play second striker.

So the coach takes matters into his own hands. He goes to Torres, looks him sternly in the face, announces to him that Spain will win the final 2-0 and that he, Torres, will score both goals. At which point he grabs the striker with those two big bear paws and kisses him on the forehead.

"It's something I did at Atlético," he reveals later. "And it worked."

"I came up a goal short," says Torres through that perpetual, shy grin.

Now we are in the dressing room. There's nothing new.

'Pensamientos positivos!'

'Uno y dos y tres … ganar y ganar y ganar!'

Aragonés is up to his high jinks before the kick-off.

José Manuel Ochotorena: "I remember that if players weren't doing well he used to tell them that they had a stammer in their legs. And the team talk I'll always remember is the one before the Euro 2008 final. He made us laugh by describing some of the Germans as having a stammer in their legs, too. He took all the tension out of the situation and somehow managed to transmit this sense of calm. The players went out onto the pitch looking forward to the game, determined to enjoy it. As they were lining up in the tunnel he went up to the German players and tapped one on the chest [Podolski] as if to say: 'Aren't you in good shape?' He then gave [Joachim] Löw a big hug as if he'd known him for years and said, 'Don't worry, it'll all be over soon'. Then he went up to say hi to the referees. It was brilliant."

Fernando Torres: "When we were waiting in the tunnel, ready to go out, and the tension was rising, he went up to the Germany captain [Michael Ballack] and said: "Good luck, Wallace." He looked at us, smiled, and winked. What a way to take the pressure off! What a character!"

Germany start well. Spain don't.

Thomas Hitzlsperger shoots on target. Casillas saves. Ramos misplaces a pass while being pressed by The Blond Fella and Miroslav Klose races into the box, but can't finish.

It takes about 15 minutes but, from then on, it's a technical knockout.

Ramos crosses and Torres hits the post with a header. *El Niño* begins to torment Per Mertesacker. Jens Lehmann saves astonishingly well as Christoph Metzelder involuntarily slices the ball toward the top corner of his own net.

The goal is smooth as silk, but also a little strange. Germany don't see fit to mark Senna, who passes to Xavi, also unmarked. Löw's team seems to be begging the man of the tournament to slice them open. Xavi. Unmarked? The flow of the ball has been precise and quick. Xavi takes, turns and releases a pass between Metzelder and Philipp Lahm, all in one velvet movement.

Torres is there. The striker's first touch, off the instep, is a mis-control, but it looks great. The ball goes on the inside of Lahm, Torres erupts around the outside. It's a race but Lahm looks sluggish and the Spaniard just manages to clamber past the defender, reach out a foot and dink the ball over Jens Lehmann.

The German keeper has been just slightly slow because, like Metzelder, he's assumed that Lahm, a flying machine, won't lose any race. Metzelder has stopped running and can't get back to the line.

Torres' right boot has clipped the ball such that it's spinning like a top, right to left revolutions. Another couple of inches and it'll go past the post but, instead, it nestles inside the panel of the net and that's that.

Fernando Torres: "I don't remember much about these moments so many years after but I know that when I saw Xavi getting the ball in space between the lines I knew that was very unusual. If he was unmarked then the pass was coming, so I set off. It came to me and bounced off my boot a little further than I wanted. Lahm was a tad slow because he thought the keeper would come and Lehmann evidently believed Lahm would turn and get a tackle in, so he delayed. I got a little touch on it and watched it spinning and spinning as it went near the goal and I know that if the pitch hadn't been watered properly, if the ground had been dry, the ball would have bitten instead of sliding and the spin on the ball would have taken it past the post."

Spain celebrate this less exuberantly than the majority of their 11 goals in the tournament so far – it's like they've always known that they'll take care of business.

Then comes a moment which Aragonés has nearly foretold. The player who laughs most when *El Sabio* goes over to pat Podolski on the chest is Silva.

Off the ball, just after an hour, the two players noise each other up and go forehead to forehead. Both men seem to make a slight forward movement then both Ballack (Wallace) and Schweinsteiger (The Blond Fella) rush to the referee with arms spread wide, heads nodding forward like toy dogs – claiming that Silva has head-butted *Poldi*.

Roberto Rosetti, the Italian referee, isn't having any of it. The Blond Fella rushes to the linesman to complain and, significantly, every last man on the Spain bench charges out to shout him down: coach, assistants, kit men, physios, subs – even Silvia Dorschnerova, who has been with the Spanish FA since 1982 and who is a much-loved match delegate, but who was born in Möenchengladbach.

Santi Cazorla: "They were all over us in the first 15 minutes and on the bench we were all saying that we'd have to turn things around, and quickly. Then Fernando scored and everything changed. Suddenly they were struggling to get the ball off us, we had complete control up front. Having said that, it was no walk in the park and we had a few hairy moments. We didn't manage to score a second goal and Iker had to make a couple of saves. I was completely fired up by the time the boss told me to start warming up and went out and ran my legs off, determined to do my bit for the team. It was a great feeling and then when the whistle went – what a moment! Indescribable! The best feeling ever."

Before the end, Ramos nearly scores with a header, Frings knees the ball off the line from Iniesta and a Senna-Cazorla-Güiza move so nearly ends up with Senna toeing the ball home from about half a metre out, but he just can't connect in time. Spain keep the ball like a personal secret.

Fernando Torres: "I think we showed our personality. The way we defended that lead I'd never, ever seen in such a big game. There's an entire history of teams who lead and then shut up shop, or a team which is 1-0 down and the ball just won't go in for them. But we kept playing, kept attacking and above all we kept the ball. There came a stage when the German team couldn't get a touch and they just looked at each other as if to say 'What the hell is this?' Even in that moment I was thinking: 'This isn't going to end here, this is the beginning. All these players love the ball, all of them have at least one more tournament win in them.' And so it has proved."

The whistle goes and this project has achieved its objective. Spain are champions of Europe.

I asked Thomas Hitzlsperger to describe the experience of playing them. This is what it was like.

Thomas Hitzlsperger: "Last time I had played Spain it was at under-21 level, against the Torres-Iniesta team and we lost, so I didn't have good memories. But we felt *in* the final. We went in with positive minds, relying on our well-known mentality and hoping that they would take a very wary look at us. They had the skill advantage; we had the advantage of being Germany. This was big. We knew they were better than us, but we really believed in our history and the fact that we still had some quality. We hoped it would be like playing England. You respect them but, generally, in crucial games we come out on top. We honestly thought 'We are better at this than them', we thought they might choke. But they didn't.

"We played 10 or 15 good minutes and if we had scored then you never know, but that was when their quality just took over. Look at the score and it only says 1-0, but we were well beaten. We had some problems coming into the game because there was animosity amongst our players. The Spanish team, I think, totally knew each other, played for each other and you could see that, finally, they had complete belief in themselves. They also knew each other's games so well. All this we could feel.

"Xavi and Iniesta always want the ball. It doesn't matter the occasion, the state of the game, the pitch – they protect the ball, they try to attack. Some midfielders, if they lose the ball they try to win it again, but they protect it next time by dropping deeper, making an easy pass. These two don't do that. They have absolute confidence and they always use the passes to create space or move forwards.

"Losing, even to a top side, was so disappointing. Devastating. But it isn't just that Spain put themselves across as humble – it's true. They are the best in the world at football, but they are great human beings. On the pitch they are there for each other, off the pitch they treat you with respect. They never come across as having big egos. They were celebrating their win but Mario Gomez told me that when he asked them to swap a couple of shirts after the game they were only too happy to stop celebrating, help him, have a little chat and wish him well. They could have said, 'Leave us alone, we are celebrating now,' but they didn't. They took time. Good team, great people."

And when he says celebrating, he really means it.

There's something called a 'flash' interview area in the reception area between the two dressing rooms, just at the point where the tunnel to the pitch begins. The world's television stations who have paid millions for the rights to broadcast this tournament live wait there in demarcated stalls – a moveable screen on either side of them and the front end open. A stall. It is to here that they will try to entice the winning players (of this or any other modern tournament) to speak live as soon as possible after the final whistle, so that the programme back home (be that Spain, Germany, UK, USA, Saudi Arabia, France, Brazil or wherever) is still on air.

It is often frazzled, but not this time. The players simply take over. Casillas, Villa, Sergio García, Güiza, Pepe Reina, Puyol and Ramos dance about, a few of them only in their swimming trunks, singing the *Seven Nation Army* chant while spraying champagne over every camera, every microphone, every presenter, Reina with the giant trophy balanced on his head. It's an uncontrolled orgy of happiness.

Villa and the Canal Cuatro reporter Juanma Castaño are good friends and, having utterly soaked him, Villa comes back with a towel to pretend to dry his hair (all the while this is going out live) and he takes the microphone to do the reporter's work for him: "Welcome to Vienna – you are live with the f***ing champions of Europe!"

Then, a little further down the line of their champagne supernova, Spain, led by Iker Casillas but with Rubén de la Red, Santi Cazorla and then about half the 23-man squad behind them, dance their conga line through the mixed zone where the German television stations who aren't live are interviewing Bastian Schweinsteiger. The Blond Fella's interview with ZDF TV is drowned out and he has to briefly pause but, initially, *Schweini* takes it in good spirit. Less so when the conga line doubles back a few seconds later and snakes past him in the other direction, singing ¡*Y viva España!*

Knowing Casillas, I'm pretty sure that, retrospectively, he wishes they'd chosen another way to celebrate.

Clothed, but not completely sober, the red army finally leaves the Ernst Happel, hits the airport and takes the Milagros Diaz plane back to Innsbruck. There, they jump on the *Pase lo que pase – siempre España* bus all the way down to Neustift, their little hidey-hole in the Tyrolean valley.

After a quick stop at the Milderer Hof hotel at 4am, it is a quick pizza in Café Anny before everyone moves to drink, sing and dance in the Dorf-Pub. It is wild, sweaty and totally deserved.

"It was like a sauna, but we drank enough liquid," Aragonés reminisces fondly. Herbert Hofer, owner of the Milderer Hof, has organised that the basement of the pizza place and the pub are basically off limits to the public, but open until breakfast for the European champions.

Beer is the order of the day, there are embraces, choruses, photos and no trouble. No paparazzi. Aragonés is the first to go, at 6am and, one by one, his troops follow him as they have done from the low point of Windsor Park, Belfast, to the summit of Europe.

Marcos Senna is one of the earlier players to leave, having been so drunk in the stadium that he reckons he could see four reporters when he was only talking to two.

Carlos Marchena: "One thing I'll never forget is myself and Raúl Albiol being brought back from the party in Neustift in the back of a police car, dressed up as cops because they lent us their jackets and hats. We just said to each other, 'Today of all days anything goes!'"

Marchena, the *Andaluz* from a little town of 16,000 inhabitants in Sevilla province with the record of never having played in a losing Spain side (which will last beyond World Cup 2010); Albiol the *Valenciano* from 700km to the north-east of Andalucia. Different accent, different upbringing, different allegiances. Brothers now.

The last to leave are Torres and Villa. Very different guys, very close friends. The *pichichi* of the tournament and the scorer of the tournament-winning goal. Little Austrian kids are en route to school when the saturnine son of a miner from Asturias in the north of the country and the tall, blond, shy *Madrileño* from the heart of the nation's capital make their way. *El Niño y El Guaje* – The Kid in Spanish and The Kid in Asturiano.

Once their differences might well have divided them. Under the Wise Man of Hortaleza Spain have done the wise thing: united, bonded, had fun and won.

Uno y dos y tres ... ganar y ganar y ganar!

Germany 0 Spain 1

Germany: Lehmann, Friedrich, Metzelder, Mertesacker, Lahm (Jansen 46), Hitzlsperger (Kuranyi 58), Frings, Podolski, Ballack, Schweinsteiger, Klose (Gomez 79)

Spain: Casillas, Sergio Ramos, Puyol, Marchena, Capdevila, Senna, Iniesta, Fàbregas (Alonso 63), Xavi, Silva (Santi Cazorla 66), Torres (Güiza 78)
Goal: Torres 33

The Wise Man
of Hortaleza

The word 'football' in the dictionary should always appear beside a picture of Luis Aragonés. His great mark on Spanish football history will be having dared to put the small but technically gifted players together in one team.

Xavi Hernández

The Wise Man
of Hortaleza

— **TVE Studios, Madrid.**
— *April 15, 2008*
The big, barrel-chested man has a countenance which suggests he was a New York beat cop in the 1950s and knows how to deploy a billy-club. He lumbers with the rolling gait of a former pugilist, down the long corridor towards an open door, through which shines the glare of television lights.

The long walk to the studio feels like that of the condemned man. This execution is being staged at the Estudios Buñuel in Madrid, where Sophia Loren, James Mason and Alec Guinness filmed the 1960s sword and sandals epic 'The Fall Of the Roman Empire' and there is acres and acres of space.

As the first camera zooms into his face, announcing his imminent arrival to the expectant crowd, he glances to one side, scratches at his upper lip, as if wondering: 'Could I still make a run for it?'

The theme music blares, 60 pairs of eyes glare back at him from the constructed amphitheatre where jury and executioners sit. Suddenly his nondescript, grey suit and watery blue-and-grey striped tie seem like a weak choice. One more step and he is in the harsh light. Beside him, the presenter is slick, slim and mock-sincere. In front of him, not only 60 critics but 60 minutes of broadcasting to millions around Spain – no holds barred, free interrogation, no subjects off limits.

The man facing trial is Luis Aragonés. He is Spain coach and there are just under two months until Euro 2008. He recently refused to speak to the media after a qualifying match, he abandoned the team plane and returned to Madrid by car and also threatened to announce all further squads by internet only. Yet he has accepted TVE's invitation to trial by television.

It is an astonishing development, one which even Eva Aranda, the producer of the programme 'I've Got A Question For You' (Tengo Una Pregunta Para Usted) could not believe when, via the Spanish FA, she got a 'Yes' to her request.

Previously – and since – guests on this show have included only heads of government, senior politicians and union leaders. Jerry Springer it ain't, but the event holds the potential for total disaster. This is live, the territory of the most skilled broadcasters, and, even then, hair-trigger dangerous – particularly given the addition of a combustible guest like the Spain coach.

Aragonés is volcanic – it is only a few months since he rounded on a critical fan outside the national training facility. That is not the image he is here to promote, but it is latent, and it may erupt. He might even storm off set. If that happens, if this is a catastrophe, then despite the fact there's very little time left before the European Championship, his tenure will be questioned still more stridently, his reputation will be further damaged.

Before the hour is out he will be asked whether he is too old to be national team coach, whether he is bitter and biased against Real Madrid, whether it is the power of Raúl's personality which is keeping him out of the national team and whether Rafa Benitez and Vicente del Bosque might be able to do a better job as Spain coach.

His questioners get the microphone, the host is next to invisible and while a research company has been employed to sift through proper demographics (there are men and women of all ages and the breakdown of the 60 begins with 18 Real Madrid fans, 15 Barcelona fans, eight Atlético fans and so on) it is clear that this audience is pro-Raúl. The subject which has dogged Aragonés for the last two years, sometimes driving him to distraction, is going to gnaw at him again. Live on television.

Before the trial starts, Aragonés wants to make something quite clear. "Neither my name nor my personality are meant for high media profiles. Nor do I desire them to be. I am here solely because of my job as national team coach. Two powerful reasons made me say yes to this. Firstly to defend football, a sport I am passionate about. There seems to be no respect for anybody in my sport. People undermine us and even get to the point where they insult us. The second, because people have managed to create an unbelievable deterioration in my reputation. People who neither know me, nor know what I am like or how I think. For these reasons alone I am here. Now, let's go."

In the end, it is a score draw or better for Aragonés. No swearing, no shouting, no storming off set. The questions give evidence of a lack of faith, of barely veiled frustration at Raúl's exclusion from the team; some of the questions themselves are insults packaged up as enquiries, but Aragonés copes well.

For an elite few who knew him intimately, perhaps this super high-risk strategy wasn't a massive surprise. This is a man who has confronted demons throughout his life.

In an era when talking about mental health was like hanging a 'don't give me a job' sign around your neck, Aragonés twice walked out – at Real Betis in 1981 and Atlético Madrid in 1987 – because of what to all intents and purposes were breakdowns. He took the Betis job in summer 1981 but quit in early September after one league match. He returned to the great love of his life, Atlético, and racked up over 100 games, winning the Copa del Rey and the Supercopa, and by 1986 was reportedly being paid about £200,000 per year. Aragonés drove Atlético to the final of the European Cup Winners' Cup in May 1986, where they were resoundingly defeated by Valeriy Lobanovskiy's Dinamo Kiev

In the pre-season training camp of July that year, he was confined to bed with flu-like symptoms, but was then overcome by depressive feelings. He told his players that he would no longer be able to coach them and then, despite feeling significantly better, took the advice of the club doctor, Enrique Ibáñez, to walk away from the job in an attempt to overcome the problem.

Enrique Ibáñez [1987]: "Due to the depression he was suffering at that time, he wasn't in quite the right condition to take a decision like he did and just announce it to his players. I am quite sure Luis will recover from this crisis, as he has from others previously, and it is then that he will be able to make a well thought-out choice."

While he was back by mid-season, he quit again – for football reasons this time – and was appointed as Terry Venables' successor at Barcelona in September 1987.

However, in January he was struck down again. Too depressed to leave his house, he missed training for several days and, once more, teetered on the brink of quitting. But this time things developed differently.

Notwithstanding that Barcelona were marooned in mid-table and it might have appeared handy that Aragonés could be quietly removed from post, Joan Gaspart, the vice president, helped introduce a doctor, José Pozuelo, who was a specialist in depression, anxiety attacks and bi-polar disorders. Aragonés rallied.

Then, in what became an unusually frank press conference held in the Quirón Hospital Clinic in Barcelona, Aragonés and Pozuelo confronted the entire subject.

> **Luis Aragonés**: "I am delighted to have had help from Dr Pozuelo because, if not, I might have had to quit this job like I have others at Betis and Atlético. Given the state I was in when we met I couldn't have continued coaching Barça."

There had been a scurrilous report of what had caused this depressive episode, and both men roundly denied that. Pozuelo also took a firm swipe at previous doctors, including Ibáñez at Atlético, for some of the terminology they had used in public about the coach and his suffering.

> **José Pozuelo**: "Luis neither suffers from cyclothymia, nor manic depression and some of the things said about him in public, misdiagnoses and lies, have not helped."

Pozuelo diagnosed a phobic disorder as the underlying cause of Aragonés' brief period of deep depression. Although it had hit brutally hard, the condition was treatable and shouldn't interfere with Aragonés continuing to work and achieve, he insisted.

> **José Pozuelo**: "He is suffering from a phobic-anxiety disorder which has a tendency to hit the highly intelligent and the highest achievers."

> **Luis Aragonés:** "I think the best therapy, now, will be to win the cup."

He duly did, two months later, when Alexanco's goal from a rebound off Gary Lineker's shot beat Real Sociedad 1-0 at the Santiago Bernabéu.

Then in 1991, once again coach of Atlético Madrid, Aragonés suffered the last of the major episodes which threatened his employment.

During late July and early August 1991, he could not work due to the anxiety he was experiencing. Pozuelo was called to intervene and Aragonés began to feel confident about how to deal with these severe attacks. Within a few days he gave an honest, in-depth interview about a subject that was still off limits in professional sport as in wider society.

Luis Aragonés: "At times I thought about giving it all up. When it happens the first time you clearly think it's something pretty grave. So when you are unwell you abandon your work and, in fact, three-and-a-half years ago when this happened for the third time, I took two years away from the game. I turned down offers because I was worried about what this was and whether it would occur with more frequency. Now I see no reason why it should come back and why I should stop. In Spain this kind of illness is compared to depression, or worse. The truth is that about 10 per cent of the world's population suffer from phobias of all kinds. I know people who are suffering from depression, and depressions which are lifelong. What I've got is not at all that serious. It's an illness that, with something like several days' rest, you can cure. As a sufferer you just feel what happens, and it appears without rhyme nor reason, depending on what kind of situation you are in. But to explain it to a non-sufferer is difficult. Obviously this might happen again, but experience teaches you what to expect and how to cope."

Life has been full of challenges for Aragonés. For those following his story, the challenge is to keep up with his nicknames. Born in the Madrid suburb of Hortaleza, he once explained that his brother was known as 'The Wise Man of Hortaleza' (*El Sabio de Hortaleza*). How it happened that the listener misunderstood the anecdote, or deliberately played with it, is lost in the mists of time. But in Spain, not just in the football community, if you refer to *El Sabio*, and especially if you use the Hortaleza bit, it will be understood that you are talking about ... *Zapatones*.

Zapatones, literally, means big shoes and so it is on record that Aragonés acquired this moniker for having big feet and for the trademarks of his playing career: a fierce shot and deadly free-kicks. However, the truth is this nickname was bestowed by a journalist because Aragonés walks like John Wayne, with a rolling, side-to-side gait. The Duke made millions of dollars and became a Hollywood legend. *El Sabio* got another nickname. Go figure.

When Aragonés was scouted by Real Madrid, he had the misfortune to be a tall man in a land of giants – talented, but not to the degree that when he arrived at the Bernabéu in the era of his idol Alfredo di Stefano, plus Gento, Férenc

A precocious Spain team triumphed over adversity in Nigeria to win the Under-20 World Cup in 1999. 'It's the strength and courage of that group that stands out. It became a template for future generations,' recalled their coach, Iñaki Sáez. Within 11 years, three of that team – Xavi, Iker Casillas and Carlos Marchena – would be European and world champions. *Photo: David Guttenfelder/AP*

Luis Aragonés' decision to exile Raúl from the national team decimated his support among fans and media. The pair agreed to a joint press conference in an attempt to diffuse the situation, but it would haunt the coach all the way to Euro 2008. *Photo: Paul White/AP*

Defeat by Northern Ireland in a qualifier for Euro 2008 saw criticism of Luis Aragonés and his players hit new levels. It was the moment when Aragonés decided to make major personnel changes within his squad, with Raúl and Michel Salgado the most high-profile casualties.
Photo: Offside/Marca

Aragonés returns from the Roi Baudouin Stadium in Brussels without the 1974 European Cup, but the career of the former Atlético Madrid player was not short of silverware.
Photo: Offside/Marca

Aragonés' success as a manager was punctuated by struggles with anxiety attacks brought on by phobias. The coach received help from Dr José Pozuelo while at Barcelona. 'Given the state I was in when we met I couldn't have continued coaching Barça.'
Photo: Offside/Marca

Vicente del Bosque sits dejected following his red card for a run-in with Kevin Keegan as Real Madrid lose a European Cup semi-final in Hamburg in 1980.

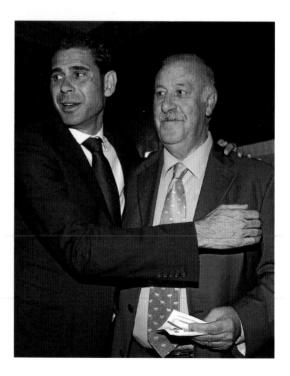

Fernando Hierro was Del Bosque's captain at Real Madrid until both were ousted. As director of football with the Spanish federation, Hierro appointed Del Bosque as national coach.
Photo: Offside/Marca

Spanish federation president Ángel María Villar appointed and then had the bravery and vision to stand by Luis Aragonés under intense pressure. Villar is the principal architect of Spanish football's golden era.
Photo: Offside/Marca

Ginés Meléndez was in charge of Spain's *categorías inferiores* during the three tournament victories and is confident of sustained success in the national side.
Photo: Offside/Marca

Toni Grande met Del Bosque when they were team-mates at Real Madrid and was later his assistant there, as well as at Beşiktaş and the Spanish national team.
Photo: Offside/Marca

Luis Aragonés arrives in Neustift, the quaint alpine village pitched to him as a training base by his former La Liga opponent, Kurt Jara. It would set the standard for Spain's low-profile, high-performance tournament digs.
Photo: Offside/Marca

The Spain squad were a little unsure of their surroundings on arriving at their training base. Their mood softened when a group of children broke into a rendition of *Veo veo*, Spain's version of I-spy. 'These cute little kids were singing in our language and it was really touching,' recalled Carlos Marchena, the Spanish defender.
Photo: Bernat Armangue/AP

Iker Casillas saved four penalties on the way to lifting three successive trophies with Spain, including this one, from Daniele De Rossi in the quarter-final shoot-out against Italy in 2008. It teed up Cesc Fàbregas to score the winner with the first penalty he had taken since he was 15.
Photos: Carmelo Rubio / RFEF, Martin Meissner/AP

Fernando Torres' shot decided the final in Euro 2008, but the striker watched the spinning ball unsure if the moment was his. 'If the ground had been dry, the ball would have bitten instead of sliding and the spin would have taken it past the post.'
Photo: *Offside/Marca*

Puskás and Raymond Kopa, he could thrive. He left, making pitstops at Oviedo, Recré, Hercules and Real Madrid's B team, then called Plus Ultra, before finally finding success at Betis and then glory at Atlético.

Between playing for and coaching *Los Colchoneros* he won five Copas del Rey, four Spanish league titles, the Intercontinental Cup, the Spanish Supercopa and the Segunda División title.

Atlético also reached the 1974 European Cup final, albeit via a thuggish semi-final at Celtic Park in which three Atlético players were sent off. Aragonés scored a brilliant free-kick with seven minutes left in the Heysel final against Bayern, up and over the wall and round the dive of Sepp Maier. However, disastrously, with about 20 seconds left, a speculative Hans-Georg Schwarzenbeck drive went right under the dive of Miguel Reina, father of Pepe.

The replay, two days later, ended in a brutal defeat for Atlético which would inspire Aragonés, later in his career (again against German opposition) to tell his players that "finals aren't for playing, they're for winning".

Aragonés was a fine player, an extremely successful manager, a survivor of depression attacks brought on by anxiety, nerves and phobias but, also, a deeply controversial man. In Spain, such episodes are famous.

Furious at the insults and intransigence of new Atlético president, Jesús Gil, Aragonés took him by the scruff of the neck and very nearly punched him during a heated dispute which, ultimately, led to the coach quitting, although the two had a fatal attraction for each other in ensuing years.

When Romario began to behave like a lothario under Aragonés at Valencia, late for training, up all night partying, more concerned about girls than *goles,* his coach fell out with him at great volume. Receiving yet another row from Aragonés on the Paterna training ground, Romario was biding time until it was over when Aragonés went nose-to-nose and bawled at him: "Look me in the eyes ... *look me in the eyes right now!*" Caught on film, the incident became infamous.

"A player who does not look right at you when he answers will lie to you," *El Sabio* subsequently explained.

When the Barcelona players he coached staged what became known as 'The Mutiny of the Hesperia' (named after the hotel in which they held their press conference), it was a brutally difficult situation for the coach. The revolt happened in April 1988. A couple of months earlier Barça had stuck by Aragonés when one of his phobic episodes left him temporarily too depressed to work. However, he is a players' man and it was the squad, not the directors, who had gone on to win the Copa that spring.

So when every player, bar three, agreed a statement demanding that the Barcelona president, Josep Luis Nuñez, resign, Aragonés saw his path as being clear – and sat in solidarity with his team at the press conference table. It cost him his job at the end of the season.

Samuel Eto'o, who still adores this tempestuous man he calls *abuelo* (grandad), was another to receive both barrels. On December 3, 2000, Mallorca equalised at home to Zaragoza. Aragonés signalled for the Cameroon striker to be replaced by Jovan Stanković. Eto'o gesticulated and growled at his coach before he was even off the pitch and sat down on the bench, disgusted with his manager's call.

Zapatones lost it. He stormed down the row of seats in the dugout, seized his striker by the front of his shirt and shook him while yelling in his face. Spain was transfixed.

Aragonés is irascible by nature and has a fiery temper when pushed, but if his manner can be like a bludgeon, his management can have rapier finesse. He has long placed a heavy emphasis on psychology in sport, especially when faced with the task of changing a losing dynamic. He explained it best, and most openly, back in 1998.

Luis Aragonés: "The coach is not the lead figure in a team, but it is a difficult job because it is so multi-faceted. For me, the most important of those, even though it is hardly spoken about, is the group psychology. Leading a group of young people who earn massive salaries and who all have their individual way of thinking – that is very complicated. Lately people only want to speak about tactics which, for me, is one of the least important things. What sells now about football is its tactics and its spectacle, but the coach is not, ever, the one who provides the spectacle – that is always the players."

Carlos Marchena: "One of the keys to our success in Euro 2008 was that we had gelled as a team. Until then it felt like we were a group of players from different teams. Aragonés deserves a lot of recognition for that. He did not talk about us as individual players, but always as 'the Spanish team'. He never referred to what we did or didn't do in our club sides. We had become a team and each of us was committed to a common objective, a single idea. We believed in the coach and it didn't matter whether or not we privately agreed with any of the criticisms leveled at Luis, we were single-minded in our determination to get behind him. It was abundantly clear to us all that these attacks could hurt him and hurt us as a team, so we chose as a group to shut the world out and set about the job of creating a truly great team. In effect, it served to make us stronger and everything that you see today is the direct result of that – of him."

José Manuel Ochoterena: "Luis' unfailing belief that this was the winning generation was a crucial part of their success. He drummed this message into them at every training session, every team talk. They were going to achieve great things and he wouldn't stop until they did."

However, Aragonés' use of psychological motivation also led to the biggest mistake of his career.

As Spain coach, Aragonés interpreted the form of the notoriously complex José Antonio Reyes as having been affected by the winger feeling intimidated by his Arsenal team-mate, Thierry Henry. In October 2004, on Spain's Las Rozas training ground, he ordered Reyes: "Tell that *negro de mierda* [black shit] that you are much better than him. Don't hold back, tell him. Tell him from me. You have to believe in yourself. You are better than that *negro de mierda*."

It was indefensible behaviour. Neither the words, nor the concept, nor the execution were acceptable. The outcry around the world when the incident was re-broadcast could easily have ended with the federation president, Ángel María Villar, sacking the coach.

The best that can be said is that those black players who defended him strenuously, Marcos Senna and Henry's friend Eto'o among them, have found some vindication since in that Aragonés has never again committed such a heinous breach of what is acceptable. In the subsequent decade, he has not given any hint that this was more than one horrendously misjudged piece of cod-psychology which did immense damage, but which did not betray firmly held racist views.

Spain suffers, in society and in its sport, from both latent and explicit racism. The country is not alone in that but there is far too little acknowledgement of it, still less education about how and why to eradicate it. To this day, you can witness morons at football grounds across Spain who think that it is acceptable to make monkey noises at black players. It is a bleak fact that Spain, as a nation, became far more vexed about Aragonés' exclusion of Raúl from the national team than his appalling choice of language in the Reyes-Henry incident.

During that torrid case of the People of Spain versus Aragonés it was often an accusation that, as one of the all-time Atlético Madrid icons, he was anti-Madrid.

Ironically, Aragonés' trajectory has similar themes to that of Raúl. The younger striker developed at Atlético until Jesús Gil refused to buy the player's father a new car to replace the clapped-out one which was not fit to drive the kid to training any more. That incident poisoned negotiations between Gil and Raúl's family and a future Real Madrid icon was gifted to them by their city enemies.

In comparison, not only did Aragonés, an all-time Atlético hero, begin in the Real Madrid youth system, he was very nearly recruited by Madrid to be their manager on four different occasions. Two Bernabéu presidents, Ramón Mendoza and Lorenzo Sanz, attempted to lure him.

In 1990, with Aragonés hugely inspired by what he had seen Arrigo Sacchi achieve at Milan, and instituting a high-tempo pressing style at Espanyol, Mendoza approached the Espanyol president, Julio Pardo, and asked for negotiations to begin.

At the time, Aragonés said: "It is between the two clubs. If they reach agreement then I would have no problem in taking over at Madrid."

Six years later, at 6.30 on the morning of March 12, 1996, the Madrid president Lorenzo Sanz woke Aragonés with a phone call offering him all the riches in the world if he would take over at Madrid. It infuriated *El Sabio*'s employer, Valencia president Francisco Roig. "I know Sanz woke him up this morning, I know that Sanz wants to rip him away from us at any cost, but Luis is a man of his word and he has big balls, so I am certain he will say no."

Over the years, such siren-song phonecalls from the Bernabéu repeated, but finally led to nothing. For a while it also seemed like that would be the case with Spain, too.

Aragonés, successful, forward thinking and now apparently fully in control of the career-threatening anxiety and phobic attacks, was an obvious candidate to take charge of the national team. Again there were four offers before Ángel María Villar got his man, the most notable in 1998 when he was the favoured candidate and asked for 24 hours to think over his decision. Ultimately he said no, went back to coach Betis and, at 60, seemed to many people to have lost his last chance.

Luis Aragonés [1998]: "The federation made me an offer but it was a restrictive one. It even named who I could have as my assistants, so I said no. Later they came back to me and opened up the conditions a bit but I said no again. The job of national coach is so different to that of daily work at a club – the responsibility you carry, the lack of time you get with the players, the obstacles the clubs put in your way. Moreover, the federation didn't handle it well enough."

He would get there, of course, but the strange thing is that Aragonés was one of those in Spanish football who needed the greatest epiphany in order to become evangelical about the new, technique-based, possession-obsessed and quick-passing playing style which gave a premium to Xavi, Andrés Iniesta, Cesc Fàbregas and David Silva.

Having been a player, indeed a man, to whom *furia* (intensity, passion, ferocity) meant everything, just six years before he became national team coach he made public his belief that all this tippy-tappy stuff would get Spain nowhere. In 1998 he evoked the *furia* spirit, arguing that playing to type was the only way to finally achieve something.

Luis Aragonés [1998]: "The best thing we can do is respect our own idiosyncrasies. Every country has its own way of living football and that is the way to act. Italy has won three World Cups with *catenaccio* and it is a world power. The Argentinians and Brazilians never waver from their personal football idiosyncrasies. Spain has ours too. Spanish football has never been exquisite and we should not obstinately try to go against DNA. *La Furia* was not just a nickname, it was not used to sell tickets, it was a philosophy which the national team needs to recuperate. We have dedicated ourselves to the idea that we all have to be brilliant on the ball. But no, we are not that kind of football. Right now we have a crop of 10, perhaps 12, players who have a terrific touch on the ball but they can't all play together. In this country a good player comes along and within a year and a half he is put forward as the best in Europe. It is a commercial problem, the need for the media to sell football as a product. People do not love football for the spectacle – they go to support the colours. They love football and they go to the matches because they love their team."

From Saul the tax collector on the road to Damascus, who became the most fervent disciple, Paul, the human condition has been full of conversions. However, having been opposed to almost every concept he went on to utilise in order to win Euro 2008, it's remarkable that it was Aragonés who transformed the national team. The coach accepted the responsibility of making Spain great while still totally dedicated to an old-fashioned *furia* philosophy. However, having taken the job, and assimilated the experience of seeing negative influences in one set of key players – the Raúl-Salgado-Guti-Cañizares clique – and positives in another – the Xavi-Silva-Villa-Iniesta-Fàbregas group – he almost instantly adapted as soon as the evidence told him his plans were out-dated.

Luis Aragonés: "I believed in this team from the day I began to work with them. When I took over in 2004 we decided to go for a particular type of football. Things didn't work out in Germany [at the 2006 World Cup] and normally the coach would have gone, but I was convinced that I had an extraordinary group of players on my hands, a one-off generation. Everything was against me at times, except the fact that I had such a wonderful team."

On the theme of Damascene conversions, the key man in Aragonés' reign, Xavi, did not enjoy the best of starts with the new man. The Barcelona midfielder was not called up for the new coach's first three games. Recalled in October 2004 for the matches against Lithuania and Belgium, the first thing Aragonés said to him was, "I bet you've been thinking 'That old bastard still hasn't called me up yet!'"

"Not at all boss!" replied Xavi.

"Come on, admit it. I know that's what you've been thinking. I'll be watching you closely."

Xavi remembers going back to his room in the squad hotel startled – but already resolved to impress this curious old ogre.

Even above Iniesta and Casillas, the Aragonés-Xavi axis is the point from which all good things have flowed from 2006 until today. From the instant that the Catalan began to understand the apparent eccentricities of his new leader, each had a massive impact on the other.

Xavi: "I just didn't quite make it to the Germany World Cup in good enough shape after my knee injury. Luis came to Barcelona to see me and then kept in touch regularly – he was preoccupied about me and my recovery. His support for me gave me so much confidence. I had never experienced anything like it with anyone else. He used to say to me, 'You understand how things are'.

"The word 'football' in the dictionary should always appear beside a picture of Luis. He's very, very smart. He'd look at you during a training session and say: 'You're acting a bit cocky. You've come here to train hard and I'm not seeing it! I don't like cockiness.' And with that he'd be off.

"Luis always gives things to you absolutely straight – never behind your back. I really think that his great mark on Spanish football history will be having dared to put the small but technically gifted players together in one team for Euro 2008."

In retrospect, the entire business makes the federation president who sought him out, appointed him and stuck by him through vicious times look shrewd.

Ángel María Villar: "We had thought about Aragonés a number of times and offered him the job before José Antonio Camacho took it, but he turned us down. Then, when Iñaki Sáez left, we decided we had to make him our manager. I had followed Luis for many years and he was the coach I admired the most. He had this great wisdom, years and years of experience and an in-depth knowledge of the game. He was a man who understood footballers inside out. We had a difficult period when we lost to Northern Ireland and then Sweden and Romania, but we started winning after that. Luis, who is an amazing person, was always ambitious and determined. He told me during qualification that we would be champions of Europe in 2008. And he was right."

Joan Gaspart was vice president at Barça when Aragonés sided with his players as they mutinied against their president. Yet not only does he maintain a fond friendship with *El Sabio*, as a Spanish federation director he was central in recruiting him for the Spain job in 2004.

Joan Gaspart: "I don't claim to be a clairvoyant so when Villar told me to meet Luis up some mountain peak in the Pyrenees where his family were holidaying, I didn't say: 'Voila! The very man for the job!' I knew he was a talented coach but the Spain job is a very different proposition. The matches can be months apart, it's not your own players you are working with, you are not in charge of their on-going training regime – it's a very different job psychologically. Nonetheless, I was very keen to meet with him and we had dinner. We had different ideas about the contract – the financial terms and other details – but agreed on a compromise position. Shortly afterwards, Villar agreed the deal and we signed the contract.

"That was the second deal he and I had concluded. Way back when we secured him to succeed Terry Venables in 1987 the contract was signed in the Avenida Palace Hotel in Barcelona and it was his friend, Fernando Díaz Plaja, who represented him. Fernando, who was trained as lawyer, was much better known as a writer and it is typical of Luis that he would choose a friend to do this for him rather than go for a specialist agent who perhaps would have got him a better deal. He will always put his faith in his friends first and foremost."

Twice when things were at their worst Aragonés offered his resignation, but neither Villar nor the federation directors would accept. In modern terms, it was an extremely rare show of perspicacity, faith and determination.

In my working relationship with Aragonés, I found him interesting, likeable and dynamic. What those who have been closest to him will tell you, almost without exception, is that this is a warm, funny, smart man who exaggerates his 'bear with a sore paw' act, particularly for the media. His goalkeeping coach from Euro 2008, for example, paints a clear picture.

José Manuel Ochotorena: "Luis is a lovely man, a very special guy who loves to chat. Sit down with him with some tobacco and a coke and you will be there forever. He is someone who really leaves his mark on you and there were several very emotional players after the Euros who recognised just how much he had meant to them.

"People get the wrong idea about Luis because their only experience of him is in press conferences where he is always prepared to actively defend his point of view, but he has a great sense of humour and those who actually know him will tell you how witty he is."

Aragonés has always believed in working harder than the next guy in order to succeed. Just as his faith in psychology is firm, and has paid dividends, his belief in scouting and video analysis is religious. He hired a youngster, Javi Enriquez, to film his players in action for their clubs, to film Spain training and playing, their opponents playing and training, and to put together both motivational videos and the musical score to which the players sang along while winning Euro 2008.

Enriquez, not short of some *cojones* himself, often used to sneak into opponents' training sessions masquerading as a Spanish television technician.

Javi Enriquez: "We were playing one international and they told us that the twin brothers on the other team wouldn't be fit to face us. I slipped into their training session with the guys delivering the technological equipment and found out that they would be playing after all. Later, Luis bet me a Coca-Cola that I was wrong and then I presented him with a piece of paper on which were written the brothers' autographs. It was great when I managed to put one over on him like that because it didn't happen often.

"Luis used humour to amazing effect and knew that a good laugh is a great stress-buster. He would pick up on the tension in a room full of players who were about to fight tooth and nail for their survival and he would make some ridiculous joke. Only once he saw that the lads had relaxed a bit, that their heads were clear, would he talk tactics. That was his great gift. He managed to clear his players' minds of all their worries. That, I'd say, is the ideal mental state for a footballer – when he is not thinking."

Raúl Albiol has been ever-present in Spain's three trophy triumphs, but has not enjoyed much game time. He made his debut in the make-or-break Euro 2008 qualifier in Aarhus, Denmark, which Spain won 3-1 despite a raft of injuries. It was a pivotal time in this story.

Raúl Albiol: "I'm sitting listening to the team-talk, half shaking with nerves over it all and then, suddenly, a mobile phone goes off. It's a cardinal sin and just for a moment everyone freezes, but it turns out to be the boss's phone. He picks it up and throws it right across the room shouting: 'Who the *hell* is calling me now?' The feeling of being worried sick that we are all about to play for our lives just evaporates at that moment. I'll never forget it."

When Aragonés made the decision to go on live television and face questions from a hostile public, he did so in tandem with his beloved wife, Pepa. Together they have five children and 11 grandchildren and all of them were in Vienna for the Euro 2008 final. Pepa has seen the real *Zapatones* all these long years – so different from the man portrayed, wilfully or not, in the media.

During the tournament Enriquez made a film of many of the private moments which led *La Roja* to ultimate victory. It was a revelation to Aragonés' wife when she watched it.

Javi Enriquez: "When Pepa saw the video she was in tears because she had never seen him at work before."

During one of the enforced sabbaticals he took from the sport following a phobic attack, Aragonés took a holiday in the United States.

Luis Aragonés: "I visited Warner Brothers in Los Angeles and saw Marlon Brando. His body double was working with him in a scene which involved the character having to jump over some steps and Brando was not doing the stunt. I said to myself: 'Hell, it's *all* a lie!'"

The sympathetic, kind, humorous and engaging man his friends and family knew followed Brando's lead. He donned the mask of the *El Sabio* personality, invested life in the *Zapatones* alter-ego, got grumpy, volatile and intimidating. And Spain, in due course, got the winning habit from him.

All the way from Marlon Brando in LA to Vienna, June 2008. An offer *La Roja* couldn't refuse.

The Kids
Are Alright

— **Barcelona**
— *December 19, 1992*

It is nearly 6.45pm on a cold, grey evening at Espanyol's Sarría stadium. In 2013, it is a petrol station but during the 1982 World Cup it hosted that all-time classic match: Italy 3 Brazil 2.

Los Pericos are hosting third-bottom Albacete and are winning 1-0, despite having missed a bundle of chances.

By coincidence – and we may just have to return to this little chap – eight-year-old Andrés Iniesta, a passionate Albacete supporter, is glued to his radio back home in Fuentealbilla, praying for an equaliser. This is his team's second season in La Primera and he fears relegation. They are fighting tooth and nail when it all clicks for Espanyol and they produce 40 seconds of world-class football.

Playing out from the back, they weave together four successive one-twos and Goyo Fonseca finishes with elegance. In that instant a small, dapper, bespectacled man leaps off the bench to acknowledge the exceptional football he's just witnessed.

Remarkably, it is Ginés Meléndez, Albacete's coach that day, celebrating the goal conceded by his team. Albacete are now 2-0 down with two minutes left and the result will leave them in the bottom three over Christmas, but this is a guy who lives for excellence, not expediency.

After the match, he says: "We were producing a really good second half and just when we were most dominant, Espanyol put us away with a move which was the best I've seen from any team this season. I got up to applaud them because if you are a good sportsman, if you love football, then you simply have to recognise the quality."

Ironically enough, on the last day of that season Albacete will beat Celta Vigo 1-0 to stay up and Espanyol will lose at Athletic Bilbao to be relegated. Both Iniesta and Meléndez will welcome us establishing the fact.

Flash forward 18 years and everyone is desperately looking for Meléndez.

When Iniesta scores the goal that wins the 2010 World Cup in Soccer City stadium, every media outlet in Spain wants to know: is this the apogee, or will we be able to sustain success? There was only one man to ask.

Iniesta had progressed through the youth set-up designed by Meléndez at Albacete before transferring to FC Barcelona's La Masía academy. By the time of that historic goal in South Africa, Meléndez had been in charge of youth development (*categorías inferiores*) at the Spanish Football Federation for 10 years. So in early July 2010, a path was trampled to his door by radio, television and newspaper journalists who suddenly took a much deeper interest in *categorías inferiores*.

When we meet at Las Rozas, the national training complex, Meléndez recalls: "They all rushed to me asking, 'How on earth can we keep performing at this level?' and I simply said, 'Don't worry, we have all the reinforcements ready and waiting in the wings'."

Spain had just finished runners-up to England in the UEFA Under-17 European Championship and in the three years since Meléndez's brave projection, Spain have won two UEFA Under-19 Championships, two UEFA Under-21 Championships and the 2012 UEFA European Championship in Poland/Ukraine. He wasn't joking.

When Spain lined up to face Italy in the final of Euro 2012 they looked like this: Casillas; Arbeloa, Piqué, Ramos, Alba; Xavi, Busquets, Alonso; Silva, Fàbregas, Iniesta. Those 11 players had amassed a remarkable 332 youth appearances for Spain. David Silva, the first scorer against Italy, led the group with 54 caps; Cesc Fàbregas, who provided the assist, 38. The lowest totals were Busquets (3), Arbeloa (7) and Alonso (10).

Whatever else is explained in this book, the single most important reason

Spain have won these three tournaments is supreme talent. However, each of these players has been carefully developed, both at club and national level. Moreover, Spain's record in youth tournaments provides irrefutable proof that the system is in place long before the players get to the senior squad.

Since 2001 Spain has won the UEFA Under-19 trophy six times (runners-up once); they have been UEFA Under-17 champions three times (and runners-up three times); they have won the UEFA Under-21 European Championship twice consecutively; they have finished runners-up in the FIFA Under-20 World Cup; have twice been runners-up in the FIFA Under-17 World Cup and, of course, won the Euro 2008, World Cup 2010 and Euro 2012 tournaments. There has never, in the history of organised football, been such an era of complete dominance.

There are clear, digestible reasons for this unique explosion of attractive, winning football.

For Spanish football development the magic number is 55. Every summer, culminating in July, Meléndez, his staff and the 19 regional scouts who work for him on a voluntary basis will meet and agree a list of the best 55 fourteen- and fifteen-year-olds in the country – five for each position in the under-15 team.

This process is duplicated for the under-16s, under-17s and under-18s, and while the under-19s and under-21s will gather an initial squad of only between 33 and 40 players, the process of selecting Spain's senior squad each season will start with Vicente del Bosque and his staff also picking what they consider to be the best 55 national team players.

Gradually those numbers will be whittled down, but it's what happens to the 14- and 15-year-olds which I find fascinating and explains one of the unique elements of Spain's development and domination over the last decade.

In December 2012, I was invited to the Spanish Football Federation's (RFEF) Christmas celebrations. Lunch with all the presidents of the Primera División clubs and then dinner, also at Las Rozas, with most of the federation staff, the principal Spanish journalists and one or two *extranjeros* such as Sid Lowe of *The Guardian* and Pippo Ricci from *Gazzetta dello Sport*.

The RFEF did me the honour of putting me at a table with Meléndez plus Spain's chief scout and analyst Antolín Gonzalo Martín, Antonio Limones, the executive who handles Spain's travel and accommodation, Javier Miñano, their judo black belt fitness coach, and Del Bosque's assistant Toni Grande.

During the speeches from the president, Ángel María Villar, and Del Bosque, Iniesta's name cropped up.

"He's one of my lads," Meléndez told me in a theatrical aside.

This fascinated me. Iniesta hit the FC Barcelona training system aged only 12 – surely the credit for his development was tripartite – his own, his parents and his club? Equally, over the previous few years I'd heard about the idea that the Spanish federation had instigated a system which inculcated personal, training and playing values, and attempted to turn out homogenised international footballers in a manner which was similar to the acclaimed system at FC Barcelona. Given that the national teams, at all age groups, gathered together a few times each year, training for a couple of days and playing a match or a tournament, I couldn't understand how such a concept was even feasible, let alone successfully implemented. The amount of contact time was minimal.

I went back to Meléndez to follow up our chat. He makes no claim to be either the sole or principal architect of this golden age, crediting the work of Iñaki Sáez and Teodoro Nieto before him, and giving due praise to a president whose initial vision all this was. However, he provided unique insight.

Ginés Meléndez: "In Spain we are almost further ahead than the clubs when it comes to spotting the cream of youth talent. There are tournaments where the best teams in the 19 regions compete at under-12, under-16, under-18 and so on. The 2013 under-12 national tournament took place a couple of weeks ago in Logroño and we have already selected 24 youngsters from that. Those same boys will be in the Spain Under-15 side in three years.

"The key research work is done by 57 scouts, nationwide, who work for us voluntarily. They are elected by their regional federations [Andalucía, Catalonia, Asturias, Basque Country and so on] and are paid nothing; they do it for the love of the game. We all meet up, once a year, in December and I explain to them precisely what I'm looking for. Then they call me, weekly, with information which is input to a database which I set up when I arrived in 2001."

An example: Teodoro Nieto spotted Xavi and decided to put him in the magic 55 during a regional competition where he was representing Catalonia in Tenerife, not when he was playing for Barça.

When Meléndez and his people have compiled their list of the 55 best 14- and 15-year-olds, they call them in for the beginning of an induction process which will mould them and, in some cases, make them world champions.

In July, the long list of 55 is finalised and the clubs are informed that their star pupils will be requisitioned as of September and – miracle of miracles – the clubs are obliged to hand them over. The big group is split into two and each group leaves their club for three consecutive days, once a month, between September and January, to live and practise at Las Rozas, just outside Madrid. There they will train, take school lessons and have a code of conduct drummed into them.

Ginés Meléndez: "I compiled a list of 10 rules which are presented to the lads in book form. They focus on things like punctuality, respect, friendship. The dressing room has to be left in perfect condition. Hotel rooms should be treated with respect. The boys have to show respect to the kit man, the masseur, their opponents, and the referee.

"The rules are important and we always enforce them. I remember one player who had a heated argument with the referee and we wouldn't allow him back until he made a personal apology to me. On one occasion I sent two lads home just for chatting in the corridor when they should have been resting in their rooms. It meant that they didn't make it to Europe with us and lost out on a medal. Later they came to me and said, 'That decision meant that we missed winning our medals, but it made us better people'. They all learn here, sometimes the hard way, but they all learn."

By January the group will be culled from 55 to 33, three players per position, and they will keep attending, three days (almost always Monday-Wednesday) until the summer when, competitive or friendly, there will almost always be a tournament.

This, as the national co-ordinator explained to me, is how it functions. "From the minute the boys arrive, aged 15, right up until they're 21, we work with them in exactly the same way, using the same training exercises, so that by the time they have worked their way up through the ranks the players have a perfect grasp of the Spanish game.

"We drill certain moves into them until they become automatic. The boys arrive with plenty of talent, but we have to give them order. Those are the two things that define our football – order and talent. Technical ability takes time to perfect and it's fundamental to what we do. You can't play the way we do without the technical side being perfect.

"We do endless *rondos* which teach them how to maintain possession and position. They need to know instinctively where to move within the team. Where do I go when the team-mate to my right has the ball? When do I press? What if that team-mate loses the ball? What then?

"It's like a training pyramid – it starts at age 15 and goes on from there. All the players who won Euro 2008, apart from Marcos Senna, had come through that system – they already had World Cup and European medals in the *categorías inferiores*. All the Spanish players at the World Cup had come through the same system and almost every single one of them had won trophies with Spain at youth level."

Xavi, one of the principal architects of this golden era, concurs.

Xavi: "My first experience of the national side was at a training camp when I was 16. I had to go down to Madrid and work with the other boys including Fernando Llorente, Iker Casillas, Fernando Soriano, Daniel Aranzubia, Fernando Varela, Pablo Orbaiz, Francisco Yeste. We all felt that those three days would set the course for the rest of our lives. I kept saying to myself, 'It's now or never. I'm either going to leave here a footballer or I'm not'. And as it turned out, I did.

"I played well and they picked me for the Meridian Cup in Portugal. Nigeria won it. I remember Barça signed Samuel Okunowo at that tournament, Simão was named top player and I was second. That same year, 1997, I went to the under-17 World Cup in Egypt with Casillas, David Sousa, Juanjo Camacho, Zuhaitz Gurrutxaga. We were third and Brazil, with Ronaldinho, won.

"I remember how fired up we were. We were desperate to win and there was great team spirit in the camp. There tends to be much more socialising, more talking at youth level. You're happier to open up about your worries because really you're all worrying about the same things. I reckon that it's fear that makes you so willing to share at that age. I made some great friends and I remember a lot of card games. I also remember Iker always producing the winning hand. From under the table, obviously."

In summary: for the last 11 years, at least, every Spain team, starting from the age of 14, has trained in a basic 4-2-3-1 formation and then been taught how to transform that into a 4-3-3.

The two systems have slightly different demands for the majority (although not all) of the 11 positions and so repeated practice, seven years of it in some cases, makes perfect. Spain's players will be drilled over and over again what to do in possession of the ball and when they lose it; how and when to press; how much distance is allowable between the lines of defence, midfield and attack. Heavy emphasis is placed on when to move the ball quickly; where each player must be in relation to the two around him; who will form their triangles, via which they aim to get numerical superiority in match situations. Taking talent and imposing order.

It also means that several players will reach the under-21 team having played, lived and won together for five, six, even seven years. When Thiago Alcántara, Isco, Álvaro Morata and David de Gea lifted the Under-21 European Championship trophy in the summer of 2013, Spain's Under-21 side hadn't been beaten since November 2009 – a run of 26 games without defeat, only three of which were draws.

Another factor is that the federation and club training systems in Spain are currently so effective that, reversing the situation which once afflicted the country's football, youth gets its chance early.

For example, the Spain team which won the Under-21 European championship in 2011 lined up for its first game, against England: De Gea; Montoya, Domínguez, Botía, Vilà; Javi Martínez, Ander; Jeffren, Thiago, Mata; Adrián. Between them they already had 944 first-team appearances for their clubs. The English players had clocked a similar total of game time, but those with most appearances had collected them loaned out by Premier League clubs to teams in the lower leagues. The Spain players were starters for Valencia, Atlético, Barcelona and Athletic, domestically and in Europe – astonishing experience and a factor in winning the tournament.

The Spain team which retained the title two years later against Russia began: De Gea; Montoya, I Martínez, Bartra, Moreno; Illarramendi, Thiago; Tello, Isco, Muniain; Rodrigo. Irrespective of the age-eligibility rules which demand squad regeneration, that team, with only three survivors, had still racked up 745 first-team appearances in Spain, England and Portugal.

The system works and within it, durable friendships blossom which break down both club and geographical barriers.

When they are aged 15 or 16 these kids are far from the first team and the hostility, media coverage and aggression which can emanate between rivals. Early integration bonds these players before club hostilities can divide them and this is a central factor not only in how Del Bosque combated the *Clásico*-wars of 2011/12 but in the squad spirit which has fuelled Spain's three tournament victories.

Ideas such as friendship, mutual support and respect, and debt to one's parents and community are easily mocked by those who see football as something like the movie Pulp Fiction: full of remarkable tough guys and winners and losers, where greed is good, values are for sissies and might is right. By comparison, the Spanish model is more like Mary Poppins, but it works. These are the motors of the *La Roja* machine.

Ginés Meléndez: "From day one we teach them values. We teach them what a winning mentality is and we also teach them about friendship, solidarity and team work: how to live and work successfully with other people.

"I can give you a great example. The national team was in Austria, preparing for the 2010 World Cup, and my under-17 side had made it to the final of the European Championship against England. It was a three-hour round trip to and from Liechtenstein to support the youngsters, but the senior players asked Del Bosque if they could go. He agreed and sure enough they all made the trek by bus. We lost the game – the first time England had beaten us in 10 years – and my lads were gutted, but as they headed out to pick up their medals, most of them in tears, there were Del Bosque, Ramos, Casillas, Xavi and company, waiting to applaud them and give them a sympathetic hug.

"When they are with the federation as kids they have two hours of lessons in the afternoons on Mondays and Tuesdays, but along with academic courses we teach them about friendship and team work. They learn all this stuff when they are still very young. You find the goalkeepers hang out together, the wingers together – the groups aren't necessarily defined by which clubs the guys come from."

Meléndez is a handy guide around this subject, a serial trophy winner with Spain's *categorías inferiores* and now the head of the youth programme, but there have been other architects and ultimately the system is no more than an effective hatching process for the latent natural talent. Talent is always the paramount factor and if the federation were receiving dull pupils, or training them poorly then the national teams would not be dominating.

Iñaki Sáez previously held a similar role to that of Meléndez, and coached the under-20 world champions in 1999, a squad which included Xavi, Casillas and Marchena. He spoke to me about this hothousing process and why talent alone is never enough.

Iñaki Sáez: "When they come for the first time, we don't exactly read them the riot act, but we are very clear about what we expect. Our main advantage is that they come to us knowing that they are the best. Then they come face-to-face with the best players from the clubs they play against week in, week out. They are now expected to befriend their rivals, start playing for their club-level opponents. Attitudes need to change and anyone who can't do that isn't asked back. We only want the good guys playing on the national team: guys who are clear about their role, their duty and who know how to work as a team. That's the essence of the current Spain side and it's all the more admirable because most of the players are drawn from those two great rivals Barça and Madrid. People, including some coaches, are continually taken aback by the friendship between Casillas and Xavi. It's as if they should be at each other's throats all the time because their club sides are rivals. Crazy! On the pitch you do what you have to do, but once the boots are off, it's real life, and friendship should be cherished."

Fernando Torres scored the only goal in the finals of both the UEFA Under-16 Championship in 2001 and the UEFA Under-19 Championship in 2002. His evaluation of his *categorías inferiores* experiences substantiates the claims of Meléndez and Sáez.

Fernando Torres: "When I was playing in Spain's youth teams it all felt a bit like being in a movie. You'd be called up and have to meet the rest of the squad in a hotel in Madrid. In the early days I didn't know a soul, but I'd seen a few of the other guys on television and I'd think to myself: 'What the hell am I doing here?' Then gradually I made friends. We'd exchange phone numbers and chat on the phone a couple of times before meeting up at the next Spain camp. That's how the friendships developed. In those days winning was actually less important than the experience of travelling abroad for competitions with coaches who would constantly reinforce to us that we were all born winners. That kind of self-belief is crucial for any football team and it's probably the key to the current team as well. That message – we are winners – was drummed into us as young lads so that it was what we were all thinking and saying to each other. I can't speak for the famous German mentality, but from the start that's precisely what Aragonés hammered into us prior to 2008: that we could and would win; that failure was not an option. I suppose it was pressurised, but coaches had been demanding exactly the same from us since the age of 15 and you don't feel pressure when you're that age. You're having fun, seeing a bit of the world and making friends."

Torres scored during the semi-final of the 2001 championship and revealed to the television cameras a t-shirt dedication to his friend Andrés Iniesta, who had returned home as a result of thuggish tackling by Germany earlier in the tournament.

Iniesta replicated the gesture as he celebrated the winning goal in the World Cup final, nine years later. At that defining moment, the first thing on his mind was commemorating the life and death of his friend (and Espanyol captain) Dani Jarque.

In 2013, Thiago Alcántara went up as captain of the victorious Spain team at the UEFA Under-21 Championship, having scored a hat-trick in the final, wearing the shirt of Sergio Canales back-to-front so that his injured team-mate's name was unmissable.

This kind of spirit is not exclusive to Spain, but it's a cutting-edge part of their success and, certainly in Britain, it is not the norm.

Fernando Torres: "I played with Dani Jarque and Andrés since the age of 15. That group of players are all 29 now and we've developed a strong bond despite the fact that most years we only see each other two or three times. We always want the best for each other and seeing Iniesta going out in the middle of that tournament because of an injury was heartbreaking – not just because the team lost a great player and would struggle without him, but because he's a friend. When stuff like that happens, a few of us will get together the night before the next match and write a tribute on one of our vests – it doesn't matter who wears it. It's a natural, spontaneous tribute to a friend. That day we did it for Andrés and Gorka [Larrea], who was also injured."

Gerard Piqué won the UEFA Under-19 Championship in Poland four years before he won the World Cup and is definitely more Pulp Fiction than Mary Poppins. Nevertheless, he told me that this glorious era has its roots in the values instilled in these players from an early age.

Gerard Piqué: "Much, perhaps all, of the current Spain success is down to our football upbringing. We were always taught: *'Win!'* but also that it wasn't simply about winning, more about how you won. The way you went about it on and off the pitch.

"Our dressing room is spectacular; we have a great winning atmosphere but not only on the days of games. If we are away together for a long time there are cards, beers, games, we share a great deal in situations like that.

"Compared to other nations? I'm not sure whether it's a [Spanish] cultural thing or it's something special to this big generation of talent we have right now, but I know the effect that winning together, repeatedly, has had on us. I won with Cesc and Mata, Iker with Xavi and Marchena, Fernando with Iniesta. Eventually, when you unite all that talent and all that winning experience you magnify what you've got and the whole is even greater than the sum of the parts.

"The emphasis I would put on our football upbringing, both at club and national level is like this. I've met so many guys with talent during my youth career – guys in the *categorías inferiores* for Barça who were made to triumph and looked like young candidates to win the Ballon d'Or. But they aren't dedicated, they don't follow the rules we are taught.

"The talent is a basic thing at this level, but with simply that talent, no matter how big, you are going nowhere. If you have effort and not a lot of talent you'll win things, but if you have that elite talent, and the football upbringing, and the massive work ethic plus a good feeling amongst your squad mates then you are brothers. Then you can achieve anything."

The poison which seeped into the *Clásico* between Madrid and Barcelona, courtesy of José Mourinho's scorched-earth tactics, was still being talked about at the 2013 Confederations Cup. Mourinho had left, for Chelsea, and some felt free to speak. Raúl Albiol revealed there was now tension between Álvaro Arbeloa and Iker Casillas, caused by the Portuguese.

Cesc Fàbregas left Arsenal for Barça and was immediately caught up in the conflict. Asked how things now stood between players of the two clubs, following Mourinho's departure, Fàbregas's reply illuminates the same principles behind *categorías inferiores*.

Cesc Fàbregas: "Things were a bit tense a while back, but everything's back to normal now and there's a great atmosphere in the Spain dressing room. Obviously you don't have the day-to-day contact that you get at club level so it's a bit different, but there's no way that that's going to affect my relationship with the likes of Sergio [Ramos]. I've known him since I was 17, we shared a room when we were in the under-21s together and when the rest of the squad piled into our room we all used to have pillow fights. I have loads of real friends in the national team."

That 2004 under-21 team also contained Roberto Soldado, Juanfran, Santi Cazorla and David Silva. Not bad for continuity.

However, what the Spanish federation achieves does not happen in a vacuum. They have the quite enormous benefit that their raw talent, even aged 14 or 15, will likely have grown up in an environment where technical skills are given the highest premium. *Fútbol sala* (soccer with small goals, small pitches and a smaller, heavy football) helps, as does the proliferation of *fútbol siete* (seven a-side astroturf football). The best young players are then given additional order, discipline, experience and responsibility by the federation system.

Furthermore, Spain's clubs have never banded together to seize power in the way those in England did in 1992, when they formed the Premier League. As a result, the top division in England is ahead of La Liga in organisation, rights sales and stadia. Its clubs control the relationship between their young players and the national teams at every age group.

Although the English system is different from Spain, the idea of that country's top clubs ceding their young diamonds to the English FA for training and education at St George's Park for three days each month so that they might become better friends and more effective for their country is a pipe dream.

The benefits of Spain having an FA president who not only was an international quality footballer – and a former team-mate of Aragonés – but who has been in post since 1988 give enviable advantages. Ángel María Villar is a football man through and through – not a former TV executive, chartered accountant or sharp-suited future conglomerate director. He has allowed countless youth and senior coaches liberty to work innovatively (and to be shielded from gargantuan pressure in the case of Aragonés) if *he* believes progress is being made.

Explaining the bedrock philosophy which he instituted and which has led to Spain's great footballing gold rush, he said: "I see the job of the RFEF as the promotion and development of football, as well as the provision of financial support. All of this is vital work, above all in terms of the lower categories. One of our priorities is to make sure that the youngsters starting out manage to get some international experience. We have created an infrastructure which includes staff who are not beholden to the senior coach. This has been important.

"In most federations, if things go wrong with the national team coach, the whole thing suffers. There has to be a flow of information and they [the coaching staff] need to be kept informed about what's happening at the training centre so that they can remain independent.

"We've managed to find very talented coaching staff in the lower categories and that's meant that our players are getting international experience. The players who have so recently won the European Championship and the World Cup are a product of this approach.

"There are three basic elements: the quality of the players who are very, very special, the coaching staff and this combination of day-to-day training at club level together with the international experience which has contributed so much to their development and to the bond they have formed as a group.

"This group has certain distinctive characteristics. They are talented players, but they have also developed a bond as a cohesive group. The dominant themes in the interviews they give are modesty, mutual understanding and respect for one's opponents. I can't think of a single exception to this, or a time when I've heard a player behaving arrogantly or boastfully. They play in a highly competitive league, but have somehow managed to prevent this from eroding the bond they have formed over the years. This particular group obviously has its own life-span, but I hope and pray that it will be as long as possible.

"It is the work of the players and the coaching staff which has brought us these trophies. No other team has ever achieved the like."

English Lessons

Fernando Hierro is sitting, beer in hand, underneath a black and white print of Alfredo di Stefano. It's Friday afternoon. Tomorrow is match day. Next to him is Ivan Campo, a fellow European Cup winner at Real Madrid. They are in a bar, but are untroubled by fans; there are no queues of Madrileños hoping to talk to them, touch them, demand autographs and pictures from them or phoning the club to report them for gross misconduct.

Beer. On a pre-match afternoon. The very idea.

Raúl Gonzalez Blanco, probably the most iconic Real Madrid and Spain player in modern history, is leaning on a drum. He is in full playing kit, standing on the wall behind the goal, a microphone in his hand as his adoring fans demand that their hero lead them in song.

Raúl roars: "*Vorwärts!*" Forwards! Which is a pretty complicated word for a foreigner. His team-mates and the Schalke fans roar back:

"*Vorwärts Schalke!*"

Then they all make the best job of helping the Spaniard chant:

"*Vorwärts Schalke!*

"*Kämpfen und siegen!* [Fight and win!]

"*Vorwärts Schalke auf gehts zum Sieg!*" [Forward Schalke to victory!]

It's a typical fans' song about struggling, overcoming obstacles and achieving victory. But it's not really Raúl territory.

These are astonishing moments for those who have known these regal, aloof men during previous eras in their careers. But things have changed.

Hierro is not in Madrid. The year is 2004 and he is in Harpers bar and restaurant in Manchester, a Bolton Wanderers player for a season, one in which they will claim a UEFA Cup place for the first time.

Raúl is not at the Bernabéu. It is December 2011 and he has just scored a hat-trick for Schalke 04 against Werder Bremen. The fans have roared his name until they are hoarse and he has trotted from the halfway line to stand up behind the goal and sing with his adoring public.

Both snapshots tell the story of Spain slowly waking up to the outside footballing world, learning from it, and changing fundamentally.

Raúl and Hierro were the crowned monarchs of royal Madrid, austere, ultra-Spanish. Most in their country would have bet their life savings that these two players were destined never to leave Los Blancos, let alone play in Bolton or Gelsenkirchen.

By spring 2011, less than a year after leaving Madrid, Raúl would admit to being stunned at how happy he was in Germany and of his regret that he had not taken this decision at a slightly younger age. He was fulfilled by the professionalism and atmosphere of the Bundesliga. On leaving, he made that crystal clear.

Raúl: "These two years have been extraordinary. I will never forget that and from what I have seen the people won't forget me soon, either. I have enjoyed every match and every journey. I have really felt euphoric, because I fitted in perfectly with my team-mates. Everything was just wonderful, especially the fans. Everybody had told me about them, but you when you see it for yourself, how they feel about their club – it's almost like a religion. It's just wonderful. I'm not just saying it – to play for Schalke has been one of the best experiences in my life. I have no words to express what the fans have given me. To pay back their love I should have scored more goals. I have felt at home here, equal to what I felt like at Madrid for over 17 years."

Raúl's former Real Madrid captain, Hierro, used to quite happily jump in Sam Allardyce's minibus for the drive from Bolton's Reebok Stadium to the Euxton training ground and then back, still covered in mud, to the showers at the

Reebok. For Florentino Pérez, Zinedine Zidane and the majority of the Madrid football media, this would have been an unbelievable spectacle.

> **Fernando Hierro:** "I was very lucky to experience what the Premier League is all about, the mentality, the football, the atmosphere and the spirit. We Spaniards were unused to leaving our country and playing abroad. It was normal for other players, foreign players to come to us and play in Spain. So the exodus of some of our players to the English league certainly brought lots of new inspiration and has enriched them.
>
> "They learn what football is about, how love of football is transmitted. You have to put all you have in it: spirit and lots of desire. It helps Spanish football as well; we can have up to 10 of our players employed in England at any given time, with a handful of them in the Spanish national squad."

Hierro and Raúl have helped show that even Spain's ancien régime endorse the changing times. However, the young musketeers have long since gone through the same induction to a new culture.

The young Gerard Piqué phoning the same firm of Manchester scallywags to fit a satellite dish on the roof of his Sale flat, naively unaware that it was these same men who had stolen the dish they had fitted on three previous occasions; Fernando Torres, confident that he had mastered English, but failing to understand a single word that Jamie Carragher was saying; Arsene Wenger taking 19-year-old Cesc Fàbregas aside on the Colney training ground and asking him: "I'd like your opinion on whether I should sell Patrick Vieira or not."

Talented young Spaniards getting used to the vagaries of the world outside their cosseted home life. Over the previous three decades while Brazil, Argentina, Germany, Italy, France, Holland, Denmark, Czechoslovakia, Paraguay, Chile, Peru, South Africa, Egypt, Zaire, Ghana, Morocco, Nigeria, South Africa, Zambia and even Greece won a tournament or two, *La Roja* turned failure into an art form.

The sharp irony is that today, with England now far behind them, Spain owe an enormous part of their tournament-toughness, the change in their competitive mentality and organisation to the English Premier League. Some of their finest young players have emigrated there and returned, cross-fertilising their new ideas and habits with those who have not, so far, played outside La Liga.

Because the last 50 years have seen a constant stream of La Liga clubs venturing out and winning international trophies and because their shores have been open to mass tourism since the early 1970s, it isn't easy to conceive of Spain as a closed and blinkered nation. However, for many of the country's leading football figures that description was not only true, it influenced first how they were taught and then how they acted from their initial childhood steps to the end of their careers.

Part of the blame lies with Francisco Franco, Spain's pernicious dictator from 1939 to 1975.

I am neither a sociologist, nor an academic. However, I have lived in Spain for 11 years and I know what I have seen, experienced and had related to me. During generations of dictatorial rule, a leader with a stunted, miserly, bitter and self-serving view of the world attempted to inculcate fear and loathing of outside societies among a general population who were told to believe that everything within heaven and earth could be found in Spain.

When things went wrong, it was because there were dark outside forces, conspiracies, demon foreigners who were against Spain.

Of course, Spain bred some liberal thinkers, audacious people, academics who knew the world was moving on and leaving their country behind. But the friends, families and communities around many generations of Spanish footballers taught them to have almost blind faith in the state, to always do things 'our way' and to regard the vast majority of foreign influences as negative or dangerous.

In his book, *A Time of Silence*, Michael Richards explains that Franco thought liberalism had:

…turned the [Spanish] state into a rotting corpse which would only be 'buried' by fascism and strict hierarchical authority.

His solution to "degeneration" was "treatment" through a physical and psychological quarantine. The sense of an attack on "our world" by "the forces of darkness", by something formless and chaotic was very powerful. Franco himself warned that "for the health of society, as for the health of bodies, a quarantine is needed for those who come from the plague infested territories".

Indeed Spain, in this period, could be visualised as a huge mental asylum or isolation ward. Once the true Spanish essence had been reconquered [Franco believed] it had to be kept pure from any contamination and so the country's doors had to remain firmly closed.

The boom associated with 1970s tourism to Spain and, following Franco's death, the return of thousands who had emigrated to other countries to escape dictatorship, began to allow foreign ideas to seep into society and culture. Nevertheless the effects of 40 years of brutal dictatorship needed time to dissipate.

For example, Carles Puyol was born just one year after Spain's first democratic elections since the 1930s. When Xavi Hernández, Iker Casillas and Carlos Marchena were babies, Spain suffered an attempted military coup.

In 1981, Antonio Tejero took 200 armed Guardia Civil and occupied part of the Madrid Parliament.

Jaime Milans del Bosch, who fought in the Blue Division which joined the Nazis on the Russian front, ordered tanks out on to the streets of Valencia in support, declaring a state of emergency. Valencia was completely sealed off from the rest of the country as Milans del Bosch and Tejero waited for military garrisons all over Spain to come out in support. In the end, only a televised appeal from King Juan Carlos peacefully quashed the siege. This was Spain, just one year before it hosted the World Cup: a country still gripped by uncertainty about how to think, act and teach in the absence of the strait-jacket of dictatorship.

The generations of apparently jinxed Spanish footballers at the major tournaments came from lineage which believed their values were the only values and that the outside world was probably corrupt and malevolent. It was not viable to argue that Spain's players caused all their own tournament misfortunes.

Franco's Spain imposed beliefs and norms which meant that their footballers did not possess all of the knowledge and skills needed in order to assimilate and overcome failure.

The generation of Xavi and Casillas were the vanguard about to be brought up in a society which could be falteringly self-confident rather than arrogant; ready to question, rather than be complacent; interested in the outside world, and not blinkered; deeply ambitious, not fearful of the unknown.

This generation needed a transfusion of international football and the rise and rise of the Champions League began to supply just that.

The European Cup, until 1992, allowed one club per country to enter and was knockout. It restricted to the elite clubs the process of players and coaches learning via experience, and that experience could be very brief. The Champions League eventually provided six European group matches for up to four teams. Now something like 60 Spanish players could earn experience of foreign travel, foreign food, strange pitches, odd referees, hostile crowds, different climates; gradually the differences between football cultures began to be eroded.

The next vitamin was televised football. For generations, 99% of what Spaniards viewed on television was their own product, with occasional sightings of UEFA football, or South American tournament finals. The way the game was refereed, what players could expect in terms of physical contact, the pace of a game, what was streetwise and what was cheating – all these concepts were embedded and unchallenged.

For this winning group, English football arrived on television schedules, once a week at first, but eventually almost without limit. Then came the exodus.

Gaizka Mendieta, an established Spain international and twice a Champions League finalist with Valencia CF, went to Lazio for €45m in 2001 and in 2003 helped Middlesbrough win their only knockout trophy, the League Cup. He still believes that leaving Spain in 2001, when José Antonio Camacho was still the coach, did not help his international career flourish. Nevertheless, he strongly endorses the idea that it was imperative for top Spanish footballers to experiment with, and take benefit from, other cultures while still at the peak of their careers.

Gaizka Mendieta: "Changing the mentality of the top Spanish footballers and adding toughness – that was something we definitely needed to improve. Spain was known as La Furia Roja [Red Fury] and certainly we saw ourselves as España de cojones! [Spain with balls]. Perhaps it transpires we exaggerated a little and it wasn't always reflected in our game – we were always a side who liked to play the ball.

"And I'd agree with people who say that our country was still developing in those days. Spain was a bit behind England and Germany in many ways. That was definitely reflected in our football.

"When the French team won the World Cup [in 1998], 12 of the 14 players they used to win the final were playing their club football abroad but, at that time, not one of our guys was. Having footballers with experience abroad definitely benefits the whole team. It won't automatically make you a better player, but it makes you more of a man, a more rounded footballer with a bit of world experience. It changed everyone's mentality – players, fans, media – when some of us went abroad. Suddenly, people were interested in other leagues and that opens your mind.

"There are a number of different factors in creating a successful team – the players, their innate talent, the manager, the directors, the federation, the group dynamic, timing and so on. But having the right mentality is crucially important. Spain was a nation which made it to the quarter-finals and no further. We were in a rut and needed to make that mental leap, to start believing that we could compete with Germany, France, with everyone."

The trickle of players who left Spain became an exodus, but their stories were not always the same. There were those who wanted better wages; those who felt badly treated by their club and had a canny agent with a contact in Poland or Slovakia; those who simply wanted a life adventure and invaded Scotland, Romania, Cyprus or Greece. Then there was the elite group of players who succeeded in England and returned better equipped to advance this golden age for the national team.

The remarkable thing, in retrospect, is that this armada of alpha-male players largely went to the Premier League because Spanish clubs did not trust them enough to give them the responsibility they sought in England. The goose laid golden eggs but wouldn't hatch them. The daddy of them all, Xavi Hernández, was very tempted to go to Manchester United well over a decade ago. By his own admission, only "pig-headed stubbornness" meant he decided to have one more try at establishing himself at the club he loved, Barcelona. Within a very short space of time after that decision, Fàbregas and Piqué chose a different path. They sought to better themselves at Arsenal and Manchester United respectively. When he was leaving Villarreal, Pepe Reina would have eaten his own football boots in order to sign for the club his father kept goal for in the 1974 European Cup final, Atlético Madrid. Instead, Liverpool put faith in him and put money on the table. Real Madrid were within an inch of buying Xabi Alonso from Real Sociedad in 2004 but, again, Liverpool were quicker and more brave.

Xabi Alonso: "It shows that Cesc went to England when he was 16, Torres at 22, I went at that age, Piqué spent a few years there, Reina too. Enjoying the chance to develop in one of Europe's big clubs, outside Spain, has obliged all of us to adapt and to become much better footballers. This obviously helps the national side."

Real Madrid did not have faith in their own youth product, Álvaro Arbeloa, until he knocked Barcelona out of the Champions League with Liverpool, played in the final of that competition and helped Spain win Euro 2008. Since Madrid bought him back again he has won five more trophies, including the World Cup.

Despite Spain's pre-eminence at developing young footballers, despite the avalanche of international trophies they won at youth level, it wasn't so long ago that there was a climate of suspicion about trusting them with first-team football at a young age and a willingness to, first, spend money on expensive foreign stars.

One of the most successful Spanish exports, and a touchstone player for *La Roja* in their last three winning finals, is Fernando Torres. He moved from the club he supports, Atlético Madrid to Liverpool in 2007.

Fernando Torres: "Traditionally, *La Roja's* biggest problems lay in the fact that Spanish players weren't given opportunities in La Liga's biggest clubs and nor did they tend to go abroad in those days. As a result they didn't get experience in the great European teams. Go to any Spain World Cup squad before 2006 and you'll see a mix of players from the big four clubs but also from five or six smaller clubs in Spain. We just weren't as competitive as we would have been if the squad list had been Chelsea, Arsenal, Madrid, Barcelona, Atlético, Milan, Inter. Spanish football was wearing blinkers – it didn't seem to even occur to anyone to play overseas and the country's hopes were therefore all pinned on the likes of Raúl, Pep, Mendieta. Look at Zidane's French team which won the 1998 World Cup. Look how it was composed.

"Our guys who were winning so much at Under-20 level with Spain were being told by their clubs that they weren't needed. They had better players. That is when you began to see this exodus of players with all the skills they had learned in Spanish youth football: Fàbregas going to Arsenal at 15; Piqué next; Xabi Alonso and Arbeloa joining them in England. People weren't scared to go abroad anymore. Suddenly those players were coming back from Liverpool and Arsenal to play for the national team. So, you then get a kid from Arsenal going to the World Cup aged 19 [Fàbregas]. If he had stayed at Barça in those days then he would probably have got his first cap aged 24, which is almost the age Iniesta had to wait until, even though he is a footballer with skills from another planet.

"The difference between the Under-21 side and the full national side is that at Under-21 level you are only playing against kids your age and size. If you triumph at that level but go back to your La Liga club and are told that you are going to get limited experience or you're playing in a side fighting relegation, then you don't get opportunities to improve, you don't gain experience. You can't then compete against the great international sides like France or Brazil, where the majority of their guys are at Milan, Juventus, Chelsea or Bayern.

"All those who went away to thrive in foreign leagues have helped so that, now, you have [David] Silva at City, Santi [Cazorla] at Arsenal and [Juan] Mata at Chelsea. Finally clubs like Barcelona and latterly Madrid are beginning to trust their home-grown players, but no good footballer from Spain is now afraid to go abroad to better his career and to become an improved player."

Torres himself was a key player for Atlético aged 17 and an international by 19. He is cynical, though. "If Atleti had been pushing for the title instead of in Division Two then perhaps I'd not have been trusted so early and if Spain were already world champions I'd have had a much longer wait to debut."

There is a myriad of things which change when a Spaniard goes, particularly, to England. Given how little the Anglo-Saxon majority in the Premier League care for trying to learn foreign languages, Spaniards are forced to learn English if they are to stick around. Spanish players in England talk repeatedly about the intensity and professionalism of football life there. Generally, although clearly not always, rules are tighter, timings are tighter, hierarchy is more clear-cut, and training is more intense. Generally, fans are more respectful in public situations and far more passionate and loyal in match situations. Players notice these things.

The play in England toughens them up. They return with a heightened awareness that their technique, their football intelligence and their tactical awareness set them apart, but they are no longer technically exquisite powder-puffs. The challenges which referees allow in England change the Spanish mentality about what is simply hard-nosed competition and what is an attempt to maim.

Even before the Euro 2008 final, when Spain defeated his national side, the great Rainer Bonhof, world champion in his playing days and still an astute talent developer, admitted that Germany could kiss goodbye to what was once a significant advantage. "Football has changed radically because now not only do the Germans play in Spain and the Brazilians play in Germany, the Spanish play in England, too. That mix of footballing cultures has totally erased the physical dominance we once had over the southern European teams."

The man who proved to be Arsenal's best player in his debut season of 2012/13 agrees.

Santi Cazorla: "Playing in England makes you much more competitive, different all round. Those of us who have had the good luck to work in the Premier League have brought something special back to the national team. That has been a very important factor in Spain's evolution."

What about those who stayed? What differences do they notice in their *La Roja* team-mates when they return from England, the football laboratory in which silk and steel have been inter-bred?

Joan Capdevila: "Guys go to England and are transformed by the experience. Look at Arbeloa, he changed enormously during his time at Liverpool and then he was able to come back and command a place at Real Madrid. I doubt he'd have made it if he hadn't had that time in Liverpool. Players come back so much stronger. Everything's different over there: the lifestyle, the daily routine. For example, here in Spain the evening meal is a big production. In England it's all over by 7pm. It must add a bit of order to people's lives and you see that reflected in the way the Spaniards play when they come back. They're much more focused and disciplined on the pitch. In fact, I'd be all for introducing a rule that says all Spanish clubs have to play a game in England once a month."

Given that Spain added English toughness and organisation to their existing high-functioning skill set and dominated the world for seven years, then what would happen if technical excellence could be added to English hunger and aggressiveness? Over to FA chairman Greg Dyke, or whichever former business executive is trying to reinvent the football wheel in London this month.

The Man Behind The Moustache

There should be statues of Vicente del Bosque in every Spanish city given what he has achieved for that country, but most of all in Madrid. The club should come out and declare its love for that man.

Steve McManaman

The Man
Behind The
Moustache

Around 60 minutes before the Euro 2012 final, Vicente del Bosque takes out his mobile phone and begins to tap out a text message in that old-fashioned style: phone held flat on the left hand, right index finger jabbing away. His fingers are those of a working man and the keys are small and fidgety at a time when tension is rife and history is beckoning. But he has something on his mind.

With music blaring out in the dressing room to dissipate nerves ("In my day the trainer asked for silence but now, you should hear the 'music' they play before a match. God wouldn't listen to it."), Del Bosque is overcome by thoughts of how it all began, and to whom he owes a debt. How a 17-year-old boy so tall and thin that he was nicknamed *palillo* (toothpick) was spotted in the beautiful UNESCO heritage city of Salamanca and propelled to fame and greatness; and Antonio Martín, or Toñete as he is normally known, the man he has to thank for it.

The last thing the coach of Spain does before his team become the first to win three successive continental and world titles, is to send a little gesture of thanks and friendship to the scout who set the whole odyssey in train 44 years earlier.

Toñete: "This will get me emotional just thinking about it. We exchanged text messages all the way through the World Cup, but I got this one just when I knew he should be in the dressing room and getting prepared for the Euro 2012 final against Italy. He wanted to thank me for everything. His message really only shared his gratitude for bringing him to Madrid and starting all this off. I thought to myself, 'how has this man got time to think of me when he is about to coach Spain to history against Italy?' And he did it again before the Confederations Cup final, too!

"He has a heart which is too big for his body. He is extraordinary. Being friends with Del Bosque, having taken him to start his career at Madrid, these things are far, far bigger than winning the lottery for me."

It was a typical gesture from a man whose nobility has always shone through, long before King Juan Carlos made him the first Marquis Del Bosque in February 2011. Friendship, respect, honour, dignity – these concepts matter much more to Del Bosque than victory, fame or wealth. He wants to win – from time to time he will make hard-nosed decisions and not flinch. However, if working in football were to rob him of some of those base values, he would quit in an instant.

What Del Bosque was taught by his parents, and the conditioning of life in Salamanca in Spain's impoverished 1950s, have been fundamental to what he has achieved and how he has done it. "I suppose everything I am today is a product of that childhood."

When Spain lost their opening match of World Cup 2010, unleashing a hurricane of criticism which would have enveloped lesser managers; when the *Clásico*-war in 2011/12 threatened to ruin all he had built with *La Roja*, Del Bosque's equanimity, class, compassion and calm led him through the tests.

He was badly wounded when Madrid brutally dumped him in 2003 after 35 years of excellent service as player and coach, but he has yet to hit back in the media, yet to vent any of his pain and anger. That's not his way. The most pungent thing he has ever said in public is: "Had they not removed me like that I am certain my team was equipped to carry on winning."

When his much-loved son, Álvaro, was beseeching him to re-instate Raúl and take his former Real Madrid striker to World Cup 2010, Del Bosque both appeased the lad and, elegantly, handled the growing public questions about a recall so that Raúl, scarred by his exclusion under Luis Aragonés, was done no further damage.

Football is fortunate that this gentle, interesting and humorous man exists at all. All it would have taken is one capricious moment from a fascist dictator or his secret police and Del Bosque would not have been born.

When he was still in primary school, young Vicente discovered his father

Fermín was a radical and committed fighter against the exploitation of working men and women. It transpired, to the great surprise of Del Bosque, that the stern and disciplined man who came to watch him striding through youth team games but who never commented on his boy's football development was also a genuine rebel. The Del Bosque home in Salamanca was a hiding place and distribution point for literature preaching democracy, workers' rights and the basic freedoms taken for granted around most of the rest of Europe. These were actions which could have resulted in the disappearance of Del Bosque's father under the oppressive dictatorship which ruled Spain.

Until his death in 1975, Francisco Franco's regime did not allow the vote, abhorred liberal or left-wing thinking, repressed cultural identity – particularly amongst Basques and Catalans – and tried to hermetically seal Spain off from the values and ideas of western Europe. Opponents betrayed by friends and neighbours, with or without justification, were often jailed and tortured.

Del Bosque learned that during the Spanish Civil War (1936-1939), just over a decade before he was born, Fermín del Bosque had been denounced by a neighbour, arrested without trial and held in a prison camp for three years.

During Franco's rise to dictatorship, partially backed by Nazi Germany, there was bloody slaughter throughout Spain. There was also poverty, starvation and disease. Hundreds of thousands died, some of those in concentration camps and prisons, due to torture and execution. Had Fermín been murdered, worked or starved to death, this was a time when there would have been few questions and certainly no call for justice.

Vicente del Bosque: "My dad was what we called a *progresista* and his imprisonment during the war was because of that. When I was about 11 or 12 I discovered that he was involved in receiving and storing propaganda leaflets. It was pretty explosive stuff. The atmosphere at home would be very tense at times like that. He listened to underground radio stations like *La Pirenaica* (a Russian Communist Party funded station which broadcast independent news and thought during Franco's reign, from Bashkortostan and then Bucharest) and Radio Paris. You have to remember the reality of the situation – we were living in poverty, unable to voice any kind of protest. Today I have plenty of right-wing friends because there is much more tolerance now. We have no problem in engaging in honest dialogue – that would have been impossible in those days. My father was overly responsible, fair and straightforward, to a degree that I'd say was noble. He was a man of good ideas, but too radical on many issues. His generation had to suffer a lot, to live through a war, and then endure the cruel after-war. It was in the kitchen that, gradually, he told us about his experiences – things which had marked him. He was a righteous man."

It was a childhood of sound formation but next to no money and certainly no frills. Typical of many great football stories, the young Vicente del Bosque traipsed around after his much-loved big brother, also named Fermín, kicking a ball throughout the streets, playing until dark and being told to go in goal because he was the smallest of the litter.

In the very early part of Del Bosque's life, Spain's football landscape, too, was radically different to that of today. Athletic Club, Atlético Madrid and Barcelona were the predominant forces. Madrid was a club whose important executives had been decimated by the war (either because of the vagaries of conflict or because they were anti-Franco) and which was re-building, slowly, under Don Santiago Bernabéu. Only once President Bernabéu began signing, or developing, superstars like Alfredo di Stéfano, Gento, Ferenc Puskás, Luis Molowny, José Santamaría, Raymond Kopa, Amancio and Ignacio Zoco did Spain, and Europe, fall under Madrid's thrall. The exponential factor in Madrid's favour is that this football explosion coincided with *televisiónes* appearing in some shop windows – little ragged-trousered urchins would gather in front of them and Del Bosque and his gang became captivated by the first *Galáctico* era.

The family was too poor for Vicente and Fermín to even attend the Salamanca matches which their father went to. The boys would sneak in when the gates were opened with 10 minutes left. A trip to watch Madrid, Barcelona or Athletic play was out of the question. Then grainy black-and-white images suddenly showed men in all-white kits dancing round tackles, conquering first Spain and then Europe. Di Stéfano, Gento and Kopa had Del Bosque hooked.

The majority of those who admire his work as a coach have not seen Del Bosque play. His 400-plus games in that famous white shirt were not as widely televised or recorded as those of the players he managed in Madrid: Raúl, Ronaldo, Guti and Zidane.

Del Bosque was a footballer of fine technical skills, good aerial ability and a knack of knowing when to hit the penalty box and either score or give an assist. Tall, elegant, not blessed with pace, his calm understanding of what to do made it seem like he was never hurried and the ball was his friend. He played like Trevor Brooking, the England international of the 1970s and early '80s; for a modern reference point, think of a cross between Sergio Busquets and Guti.

Toñete was trusted by Madrid and was to help discover a handful of players who would etch their names in the club's history. He worked to the rules of a manual put together by the head of *fútbol base* (youth development) at Madrid. The single most important criterion read: 'Remember to distinguish between a good player and one who is right for Real Madrid.'

It was an era when their six European Cup victories in 13 years made it feel that the next one was just around the corner – not, as it actually transpired, 30 agonising years away. In fact, Toñete was actually gifting Real Madrid the man who would coach them to two of their next three European Cup wins.

Toñete's recollection is that Fermín del Bosque, on finally handing his son over and heading back to Salamanca, had an expression on his face "as if his soul was broken". This man who had been imprisoned for his liberal beliefs, taken massive risks to advocate democracy and socialistic ideals, was handing his son to a club governed autocratically by a right-wing authority hate-figure who, even before the Spanish Civil War, had been a member of the *Juventud Acción Popular*, described by Dr Sid Lowe in his book *Catholicism, War and the Foundation of Francoism* as "uniformed, paramilitary" quasi-fascists. Madrid's all-powerful president, Santiago Bernabéu, also fought for Franco's forces during the war under the orders of General Augustín Muñoz Grandes, who would go on to head Hitler's infamous Blue Division in Russia during the Second World War. Young Del Bosque was going to work for a man who had opposed and taken up arms against everything that his father stood for.

In the radical summer of 1968, when the Prague Spring caused a Warsaw Pact invasion of Czechoslovakia, when liberals and anarchists on the streets of Paris nearly brought revolution to France, when civil rights protests in America and Belfast brought riots and retribution – in this most volatile, and febrile of moments in modern European history, a young man whose father had been put in a prison camp under Franco joined perhaps the most conservative football club on earth – Real Madrid.

It was a pivotal moment. For all his principles had cost him and the risks they still carried, Fermín del Bosque wanted his family to be tolerant and democratic and now he put those ideas into practice. Forty-four years later, the deft negotiations to bring peace to feuding Barcelona and Madrid players which helped Vicente del Bosque's side make history at Euro 2012 did not simply come from the pages of a management manual. The values he was raised to hold made him the man for those times.

Del Bosque also inherited his father's determination to fight for what is right. He was a founder member of the AFE, the Spanish footballer's union, while a young Madrid player. The AFE was born in 1978 and it was deeply controversial when, as membership grew, there were strikes and a Bosman-style battle against clubs who could retain a contracted player for his entire career. Joining a union at that stage was at very least a minor threat to your continued employment, most particularly at Real Madrid.

Ángel, a former Madrid team-mate, remembers the climate. "It wasn't easy to play for Real Madrid and be a member of a union, but we joined up. Not for ourselves, because we were comfortably off, but for the penniless guys who spent their nights in sleeping bags during or after their careers. We were demanding the introduction of a form of social security."

Between 1968 and 1984, when he retired, Del Bosque won La Liga five times and the Copa del Rey on four occasions. He played with some all-time legends of *Los Blancos* – José Antonio Camacho; Santillana; Juanito; Paul Breitner; Uli Stieleke; Gunter Netzer. Some may have endured longer, but in his prime none of them outranked him.

He played against Johan Cruyff, Diego Maradona, Luis Aragonés, Franz Beckenbauer, Jupp Heynckes, Uli Hoeness, Kevin Keegan, Graeme Souness, Gerd Muller, Johan Neeskens, Zico, Kenny Dalglish, Allan Simonsen, Hugo Sánchez, and Mario Kempes.

In his time he was coached by Miguel Muñoz, Luis Molowny, and Alfrédo di Stefano – five-star legends.

He had direct professional experience of the majority of the most important football figures across four decades.

His playing career, however, was scarred by one major flaw: Madrid simply could not win *La Séptima* (the seventh title). After six European Cup victories in the 1950s and 1960s, there was first an assumption that Madrid would continue to lift the trophy, then anxiety about when it would happen again, and finally a deep obsession. Across the four decades when Madrid sought *La Séptima* there were some epic, thunderous attempts. Del Bosque was part of many of them, as player and coach.

The first time I saw him play was in November 1975, when Derby County drew Real Madrid in the second round. Both legs ended 4-1 to the home team, but during extra-time in the return at the Santiago Bernabéu, Del Bosque flicked the ball to Santillana who lobbed it up over his marker and volleyed home in the style of Paul Gascoigne's famous goal for England against Scotland at Euro

'96. Two thundering ties to make you love football for the rest of your life: 6-5 to Del Bosque's side – but still not enough to drive them past Bayern Munich in the semi-final.

By season 1979/80, the European Cup was once again singing its siren song to Del Bosque and Madrid – the Santiago Bernabéu stadium was going to host the final.

Billy McNeill's Celtic threatened to end the dream in the quarter-finals, but the tie became a testimony to the fact that Del Bosque, now ageing, remained a wonderful footballer.

Celtic won the first leg 2-0 in front of one of those fevered Celtic Park audiences which make such nights gargantuan.

In the Spanish capital, it was bedlam and the second leg became another in a series of what are called *Los Remontadas Históricas de Madrid* – Real Madrid's historic fightbacks.

Black market ticket-touts were arrested the day before the game in possession of 700,000 pesetas from a mixture of stolen and fake tickets; more than 100,000 fans crammed into the historic stadium which then had fences and a small ash track around the pitch. Madrid's coffers benefited to the tune of 60m pesetas.

Pumped up, Del Bosque broke from the halfway line and started sprinting towards Peter Latchford's goal even before Károly Palotai had blown for kick-off as Real Madrid, in the very first seconds, tried for the long ball to the tall man for the knockdown.

Del Bosque's nice exchange of passes with Laurie Cunningham led to the crucial second Madrid goal, when Santillana headed down the Englishman's cross for Uli Stielike to score. Then, with four minutes left, Ángel crossed for Juanito to put the Scottish club out.

Celtic boss McNeill was incensed by refereeing decisions he blamed for the defeat. Despite that ire, his admiration for one player was undimmed.

Billy McNeill: "Once again Del Bosque stood out. I admired his performance against us just as in the first leg. He is one of the best players I have ever seen."

Davie Provan, a winger of the highest quality and today an eloquent and incisive football analyst on Sky Sports, recalled the performance of Madrid's No.6 over those two matches.

Davie Provan: "Back then there was very little European football on the television. It was our first experience of seeing many of the Real Madrid players, but Del Bosque had featured in big Billy's pre-match briefing.

"What often wrong-footed teams coming to play us then, and still does today, was the tempo – it was frenzied. That night we were so up for it, but I remember Del Bosque bringing the ball down and walking with it. Walking! That was his message to the rest of the Madrid team: *We* dictate the pace, not Celtic.

"His managerial career has been so good, so successful, that it has overshadowed what a fantastic player he was. His self-assurance then, and now as a manager, comes from class – real quality."

By the second leg of the semi-final in 1980, it seemed that Madrid were heading for the final and a chance to lift 'their' trophy in their stadium. Kevin Keegan's Hamburg, also featuring Felix Magath and Horst Hrubesch, had been beaten 2-0 in Madrid, but the night of April 23, 1980, at the Volksparkstadion in Hamburg, became perhaps the single most painful of Del Bosque's playing career.

Madrid were two down and thus equal on aggregate after just 17 minutes; Laurie Cunningham scored an away goal which meant Hamburg required two more to advance, but the Germans produced both within the space of five horrible minutes before half-time. Worse, Del Bosque was sent off with six minutes left, before Caspar Memering made it 5-1 to Hamburg. The red card came when, in an extraordinary moment for a man so placid and self-controlled, he took a swipe at Kevin Keegan with the intention of clipping him round the head. There is an emotive picture of him, a blanket over his shoulders, sitting on a kit box on the edge of the running track at the *Volksparkstadion* with the massive electronic scoreboard looming over the back of his head, showing 4-1 at the time. Elimination, humiliation, shame.

He had three more seasons to come, but this was the beginning of the winter years for Del Bosque, the footballer, at Madrid.

Due to injury and new signings, the next term he played only a moderate role as the Spanish champions advanced to the quarter-final, against Spartak Moscow. He got a testimonial five minutes in the Russian capital during a 0-0 draw and then the first half of what became a 2-0 home win. The nervous Bernabéu crowd were not generous with their former hero. He departed at half-time.

In El País the match reporter, Julian García Cancau, wrote: "The Bernabéu fans are going to push Del Bosque out long before his time. They have converted him into the scapegoat every single time the team around him is not functioning well."

Vicente del Bosque [1981]: "Fans need to realise that if I am on the ball so much it is because I have run sufficiently to get free of my marker. But I am tall, I am easy to spot and I appear slow. Moreover, I prefer to play football, not just to get the ball forward at the first opportunity. I try to wait for, or to create, the best opportunity for the right pass. I have been around for many years and I guess the fans tire of you, but that will change back. Passion for a player comes and goes with the Spanish public. Today they are on your back, tomorrow they glorify you again."

When Sergio Busquets, playing in a similar position to Del Bosque 30 years earlier, was hung out to dry following Spain's defeat by Switzerland in the World Cup, the coach's experience allowed him to empathise with his player and ignore the white noise which came after that upset. Busquets, like Del Bosque in his playing days, does work which is far easier to appreciate when you are the recipient of his support rather than the beholder.

In the cycle before the 2014 World Cup Xavi, still the brain of Del Bosque's Spain, is losing pace and athleticism with age. The fact that he has a coach with a personal understanding of the process should help manage a great player and a delicate situation.

The European Cup final of 1981 was Del Bosque's first and last as a player. Sadly it was a drab affair notable, unless you were a Scouser, mainly for its stats – Bob Paisley became the first man to win the trophy three times; it was the fifth consecutive victory by English clubs and Liverpool's hat-trick trophy. Alan Kennedy's goal with eight minutes remaining ensured Del Bosque left Paris without conquering Europe. For the meantime, at least.

One of Liverpool's key players that night told me what facing Del Bosque's Madrid had meant to them.

Graeme Souness: "I looked back at that final a couple of months ago because Jamie Redknapp rang me to tell me it was on television. I realised, watching it after such a long time, that for players like Del Bosque in midfield we must have been a nightmare to play against because we were already putting into practice many of the things which are in vogue now: pressing all over the pitch, full-backs pushed high up their touchline so that I stayed sitting in front of the two centre-backs, protecting them. I see much of that as central to the success of Barcelona and Spain nowadays.

"Those who criticise Spain for their manner of winning now know nothing about football. We were hugely successful at Liverpool and we were taught, from day one, to keep the ball. Don't try a pass through the eye of a needle; win the ball, circulate it, start again and again if you have to, but seek the right opportunity. Again, that's what Spain do excellently today. I'd put Del Bosque's Spain side up with Brazil of 1970, no question.

"Del Bosque has been a part of a change in the essence of Spanish football. In my day, and Del Bosque's, Spanish football was full of stuff you hated – dirty tricks, kicks and shirt pulling. Cynical and horrible. Now it's about quality, control, technique and winning and it's the most attractive stuff around. That's a remarkable change and they have a good man in charge."

Despite being plagued by injuries, Del Bosque had chances to augment his silverware in his penultimate season – and to add a European trophy. However, this was to become known as *La temporada de cinco copas perdidas* (the season of five lost cups) – both a nod in the direction of Barça's famous *temporada de cinco copas* (in 1951/52) and an acknowledgement that Real Madrid, in season 1982/83, lost five 'finals'.

La Liga – Madrid were expected to win the title ahead of the final day's fixtures, but were defeated 1-0 at the Mestalla by Valencia as Javier Clemente's powerful Athletic Bilboa won in Las Palmas to take the championship.

Del Bosque did not play in either the Copa del Rey final defeat by Diego Maradona's Barcelona or the Supercopa finals against Real Sociedad, which Madrid lost by an aggregate of 4-1.

The two-legged League Cup final was no better. Del Bosque scored in the 2-2 draw against Barcelona at the Santiago Bernabéu but at the Camp Nou, three days later, the Catalans won 2-1.

The coup de grâce came in Gothenburg, where Del Bosque was left out of the Real Madrid team which lost 2-1 to Alex Ferguson's Aberdeen in the European Cup Winners' Cup final.

Del Bosque's international career did not end with the number of caps his talent merited. A broken leg suffered before the 1978 World Cup denied him an opportunity to compete for a place in the Spain squad. He returned just before the tournament but Ladislao Kubala, the Spain coach, left him behind. In February 2013, a 3-1 win over Uruguay saw Del Bosque equal Kubala's record for the most matches as Spain coach: 68. He spoke kindly about the Hungarian, but the statistics tell a story. Del Bosque's 68-game record stands at 57 wins, five draws and only six defeats with 170 goals for and 45 against. The Spain team in Del Bosque's playing era, during Kubala's 68 matches in charge, had 31 wins and 21 draws.

The 18 games Del Bosque played for his country at least brought two notable benefits. First, he shared midfield with Ángel María Villar, the man who would re-shape Spanish football as its president from 1988 until the present – and who employed Del Bosque when replacing Luis Aragonés must have seemed an invidious task. Secondly, there was Del Bosque's only international goal, which came against Cyprus and in his hometown of Salamanca.

Del Bosque's last competitive match for Madrid was in the Copa in 1983, when Madrid drew Barça Athletic, now known as Barça B. The *Quinta del Buitre* (The Vulture Gang, a pun on the striker Emilio Butragueño's name) including Manolo Sanchis, Michel, Martín Vazquez and Miguel Pardeza were pushing through from Madrid's youth ranks and Del Bosque shrewdly went the other way. By 1984 he was preparing to coach in Castilla, Madrid's youth academy.

Del Bosque had always thought about precisely how to organise a game's tempo, how to prompt and push from midfield rather than just using the ball at the first opportunity. He soon found these were principles he could explain to others.

It is ironic that Del Bosque was both a lynchpin in the development of some truly great in-house talent but also the only Madrid coach to make Florentino Pérez's *Galáctico* philosophy properly successful. It was not his fault that the success of the latter deeply damaged the former.

The strategy was initially called *Zidanes y Pavones*: Madrid would buy the world's No.1 superstar every year, but theoretically promote excellent home-bred players from the *cantera,* too. Poor old Paco Pavón, an honest but not exceptional central defender, had the misfortune that his name was seconded to Pérez's scheme. The *Pavónes* were never given the time or encouragement to flourish.

This Bacchanalian behaviour inevitably made the club ill, but when the feast was high there was an orgy of terrific football, a sense that this was cutting-edge strategy and seemingly without horizon.

However, the young seeds from the youth system were almost immediately trampled upon. In those early, heady days there was no time for players such as Roberto Soldado, Juan Mata, Borja Valero, Álvaro Arbeloa, Álvaro Negredo, Juanfran and Javi García to find their feet and flourish. When the players in their way included Luís Figo, Zinedine Zidane, Ronaldo and David Beckham, that was comprehensible; by the time that became Michael Owen, Jonathan Woodgate, Carlos Diogo, Fernando Gago and Julio Baptista, far less so.

It became infamous that the *Galáctico* era, steered by Del Bosque, largely meant barren times for products of *La Fábrica* (Madrid's youth system). From the emergence of Iker Casillas from mid-1999 until Arbeloa was re-purchased from Liverpool 10 years later, no youth-team product hit the Real Madrid first team and stayed there. The last three to make it before the dawn of the *Galácticos* were Raúl, Guti and Casillas – each of whom had been significantly helped in his formative youth development by Del Bosque, while a *cantera* coach.

Presidents, first-team coaches and superstar players came and went, but Del Bosque endured in various roles, always inculcating the right values, teaching 'the Real Madrid way', making sure that footballers grew up with intelligence, technique, judgment, honesty, bravery and a will to win.

Midway through season 1999/2000, John Toshack's Madrid lay eighth. A long, simmering tension between the manager and his president, Lorenzo Sanz – not helped by losing the Madrid *derbi* to the Atlético of Claudio Ranieri and Jimmy Floyd Hasselbaink which would end the season relegated – culminated in the Welshman's sacking. It was a time for expediency and some pragmatism on the president's behalf. Presidential elections were just around the corner and a wealthy, politically active industrialist by the name of Florentino Pérez was beginning to make belligerent campaigning noises. Sanz imagined that it was more important to announce a star coach like Arsène Wenger or Fabio Capello in May or June, rather than try to persuade one to come midway through what appeared, to him, a doomed season. Instead, he promoted Del Bosque for the interim.

The quiet, moustachioed former midfielder very quickly confounded Sanz. So successful was he that, by May, a stellar coach was not required. From November 1999 to May 2000 lay the roots of the biggest treason committed against Del Bosque during 46 years in professional football. Despite a pair of four-goal thrashings from Bayern Munich in the group stages, Del Bosque and Toni Grande convinced his players that they could win the European Cup.

Vicente del Bosque [1999]: "I want to win the players over appealing to their competitive nature, without a lot of drama or false camaraderie. The football world seems, now, to be all about image and self-publicity, very little boot room. Let's see if we can win this squad over with a little bit of the boot-room work ethic instead of showboating."

In mid-November 1999, Del Bosque put together the majority of the technical team which would be in place when Spain won the 2010 World Cup. Paco Jiménez was returned to scouting opponents and potential transfer signings. Toni Grande came up from the *cantera* as assistant coach and Javier Miñano, previously with Madrid Castilla, became the first-team fitness coach. For several months under Toshack, the team had been operating without one.

> **Vicente del Bosque [1999]:** "This is my decision, which I think is vital, and that doesn't mean that I'm saying Toshack's methods are less viable than mine. I just believe that as we are about to turn the corner into a new decade and a new millennium it is the right time to appoint specialist and efficient collaborators and to know how to delegate."

Just before Christmas 2012, I asked Del Bosque to explain how he selected the location and training facilities for the tournaments his team won.

> **Vicente del Bosque:** "I set the parameters of exactly what I require and then the people around me in the technical team, discreet, excellent specialists, are in charge of their area. I have huge faith in them and their abilities. They handle the details of what we eat, where we live, how good the training pitch is – if I were to get involved with the doctors or the communications strategy or the training hotel then I would not be able to do my job properly. I let my specialists know what I want, they deliver and if the players are happy then they, too, will do the job I need them to do."

There are 13 years between these statements, yet they are almost identical in philosophy. Appoint excellence all around you – then delegate.

Back in 1999, Del Bosque's manner, his tactical changes, his history at the club, his use of Miñano, plus the lure of another European Cup were combustible influences, as one of his players recalls.

> **Steve McManaman:** "As a coach he was very honest and down to earth. He showed no airs or graces. We might not have been in crisis, but we were having a difficult time so he appeared a bit sour-faced and it wasn't a laugh a minute then. But most of the time you knew exactly how he was feeling. I recently watched the comments coming out of my old club Manchester City about Roberto Mancini and how much was said behind

people's backs. Well, there was none of that with Del Bosque. Everything – good or bad – was up front. He was the type of manager who didn't want to speak to his players constantly, only when he had something specific to say. Otherwise he kept with his staff. What was immediately apparent is that if we won and he was content with the form then, so long as you were fit, you would continue to play. That made people happy and motivated. It is also true that the immense sense of club history he brought with him, when he stepped up, added continuity and everyone around the club drew strength from that."

Aside from winning big trophies, showing a tremendous aptitude for gaining an edge in knockout football, even from knowing how to man-manage a group of superstars, there was another element which clearly emerged here and which correlates directly to Del Bosque's success in charge of Spain.

Under Toshack, Madrid were conceding nearly two goals per game. From when Del Bosque took over until they won the Champions League on May 24, 2000 that dropped to under a goal per game. Of the 38 games in La Liga and the Champions League, 14 were clean sheets. As national coach, his team played seven knockout matches without conceding on the way to their tournament wins in 2010 and 2012.

> **Vicente del Bosque:** "People highlight the attacking side of the game, which is fine, but if you rob the ball from the opponents 25 or 30 times in a match when they are trying to create scoring opportunities against you, that is equally valuable."

Iker Casillas, future Spain captain, was now promoted by Del Bosque to become the permanent Real Madrid No.1 in place of Albano Bizzarri. Four days after the goalkeeper's 19th birthday, he started against Valencia as Del Bosque won the first of two Champions League titles as coach.

To Del Bosque's enormous embarrassment, Sanz chose to interrupt the pre-Champions League final press conference to announce that the manager would be "renewed as coach" and "would stay at Real Madrid in one capacity or another for the rest of his life".

I was there in the ridiculously ornate Trianon Palace hotel in Versailles, a haunt for Generals Eisenhower and Patton, Marlene Dietrich and Queen Elizabeth II across the years, and witnessed Del Bosque's thinly contained anger that the press conference was hijacked by a grandstanding president. When Sanz wandered in, commandeered the stage and publicly confirmed Del Bosque's new contract, the manager feared that the focus on winning a Champions League final had been undermined.

> **Vicente del Bosque [2000]:** "It is a personal decision that I have decided to accept the club's offer and, as such, it is private. So I have got nothing to say. The club judges it appropriate to announce this now but, as far as I am concerned, it is a very minor subject compared to winning the final."

Real Madrid romped it, over-running and out-thinking Valencia in a 3-0 win, the goals coming from Fernando Morientes, Steve McManaman and Raúl. A festival of Spanish noise, colour and flair in the French capital, a fiesta for Real Madrid and an eighth European Cup.

> **Vicente del Bosque:** "This club, for its history and for its legend, always has the capacity to win the European Cup. *Our* cup. Football gives you second chances and this is a wonderful way to erase the memory of losing in Paris to Liverpool nearly 20 years ago."

Just as in the aftermath of the finals of the World Cup and Euro 2012, Del Bosque was quickly absent from the dressing room, foiling the plan of his players – later revealed by Fernando Redondo – to throw him into the Jacuzzi. This was the players' triumph and it was their moment to sing and drink and celebrate.

> **Steve McManaman:** "It was striking how he hid away. He really didn't want any glory, especially not to get in the way of the players in the limelight. He was remarkably humble."

And this is how Del Bosque sowed the seeds for the treachery done to him three years later. When Florentino Pérez won a substantial majority in the presidential elections within a couple of months, the new man in charge of the club was unexpectedly stuck with someone who was already a club legend, who had just won their eighth European Cup and who was safe in a new contract. The two men had only one thing in common: their feelings for Real Madrid. Politically, philosophically, strategically and in sporting and human terms, they were poles apart.

The uncomfortable truth for Pérez was that while the Salamancan kept winning trophies – two Spanish leagues, two Supercopas, the Intercontinental Cup and another Champions League – Del Bosque could not be sacked.

However, the division grew. There was brilliance to draw upon in the penultimate season – a 2-0 win at the Camp Nou in the *Clásico* Champions League semi-final of 2002 and then that awe-inspiring Zidane volley at Hampden to win Madrid their ninth European Cup – but it was also full of conflict. An El País magazine article detailing the republican, democratic and anti-Franco code by which Del Bosque's father had lived, plus the coach's own background as a union organiser were in opposition to the politics of Pérez; Fernando Hierro became a loud voice on behalf of the players, often in opposition to diktats from the president's office.

Steve McManaman: "There wasn't player-power like you find now in England. It was a powerful voice exercised always for the good of the team. In England there might be one or two idiots who want to argue with the coach and do so to see what benefit they can get individually. It wasn't like that under Del Bosque. Hierro was the No.1 man, then Sanchis, then probably Raúl, but Hierro was the player-leader on and off the pitch. He was the voice of the dressing room and I am sure Florentino heard too much from him. The last game of the 2002/03 season was the final straw. There were some disputes and when the club ordered us to go to the cathedral and the town hall because the city council demanded it, but then denied permission to follow tradition and hang a Madrid scarf on the Cibeles fountain, the dressing room decided that it was all off. The post-match celebrations on the pitch were muted, there wasn't as much of a lap of honour as expected and then chaos reigned. We had player meetings for hours on end until around 3am, when it was agreed that we wouldn't be the council's puppets just because the president ordered us to. Then, by 6am, it was all reinstated again and there were frantic text messages all around and search parties to make sure that all the players could be rounded up. It was a shambolic period and I think that might have partly dictated what happened next."

The five-minute lap of honour, Hierro's refusal to lead the players back out onto the pitch, Del Bosque's decision to allow his players freedom to make their own choices – these became reasons for the board to sack the best on-pitch leader and the most successful Madrid coach since the zenith of Puskás, Gento and Di Stefano.

The next evening his wife, Trini, drove Del Bosque to the Bernabéu, as she thought, for him to pick up some papers from his office and to meet with the president about renewing his contract which was to expire later that month. Halfway there, the mobile phone rang. It was Hierro. He had been kicked out of the club. No new contract, as had been promised.

"Look out boss."

"I suspect I'm going the same way as you in a few minutes."

The coach hid his suspicion from his wife and she was as shocked as the rest of the *Madridistas* when he returned to the car having been told he was out, despite seven trophies in three-and-a-half seasons.

Vicente del Bosque [2003]: "For about 20 days I had suspected this might be coming and I go proud of our work, our victories and in the sure knowledge that I have not committed any felony. What I and my assistants leave behind is something to feel satisfied with and now I find myself full of expectations for what lies ahead of me."

Jorge Valdano [Sporting Director, 2003]: "We simply told the squad: 'Vicente won't be continuing.' I know it is a decision which flies in the face of what the man in the street wants, what the dressing room wants, but those who govern a club have to govern it."

Florentino Pérez [2003]: "Real Madrid needs someone with a less out-of-date training manual."

Vicente del Bosque [2003]: "I have cried, of course I have cried – remembering the 35 years I have been with this club makes me full of emotion."

Without Del Bosque it took Real Madrid six managers and four seasons to win anything other than a single Spanish Supercopa. Real Madrid spent seven years unable to get beyond the last 16 of the Champions League.

Steve McManaman: "If that group of Del Bosque, his staff, Hierro plus [Claude] Makélélé and Morientes, who should never have been pushed out by Pérez, had stayed together they would have won more and more. No way on earth should Del Bosque have been treated like that. The deterioration started immediately and it went so far south that it was incredible. There should be statues of Del Bosque in every Spanish city given what he has achieved for that country, but most of all in Madrid. The club should come out and declare its love for that man, but too often it's the guys who love a club the most, who are the heart of the club, who get treated worst of all."

Ronaldo: "Del Bosque was a great coach and an incredible person. He knew that Real Madrid squad inside out and my year with him was one of my best. He was the ideal man to manage that dressing room and get the best out of our squad."

Del Bosque had an ill-fated spell with Besiktas in Turkey where, to put it lightly, he was appalled at the egos and lack of self-discipline – this from a man who had just managed *Los Galácticos*. It led to one of the few times in his career where he lost his temper.

Vicente del Bosque: "I had to watch my players strutting about like a bunch of little princes. They would be sitting in their rooms calling for cups of tea, pasta – I and my team had come from a world of top professionals who still managed to behave like normal guys. These fellows were used to being treated with absolute servility. There was no way I was going to tolerate it and I told them that in no uncertain terms. They were behaving like superstar players, which was a long way from reality, believe me."

A couple of quiet years later his regular lunches and cups of coffee with his former captain, Hierro, transformed into lunches and cups of coffee with the newly-appointed football director of the Spanish federation.

In the winter of 2007, Del Bosque received a phone call from Hierro, this time in the latter's professional capacity with the federation. Hierro was preparing for a future beyond Euro 2008 and beyond Luis Aragonés. Gradually it became clear that, win or lose, the federation and Aragonés were going to go their separate ways. Having been a prime candidate in 2004, before Aragonés was appointed, and enjoying Hierro's total trust and respect, Del Bosque profiled perfectly.

Between then and July 2008, when Del Bosque's succession was made formal, and shortly after mass celebrations across the country when Aragonés' squad won the European Championship, there was an arctic tension between the two men – one icon of *Madridismo*, one icon of Atlético Madrid. Aragonés often carped about lack of respect from the federation; his work was finishing with a replacement already agreed, whose identity was an open secret and who had been selected by one of his own former players, Hierro, who did not enjoy a particularly close relationship with Aragonés.

UEFA held a national team coaches forum in Vienna three months after Euro 2008. Del Bosque was there in his new capacity as Spain coach, Aragonés as the man who had just won UEFA's showpiece tournament. The great and the good from all over Europe were gathered for seminars, lunches, press conferences – the sharing of ideas and information. Aragonés and Del Bosque, chaperoned by Hierro, were like cat and dog, prowling warily around the five-star hotel. If one was in the bar, the other was in the conference room. If one was on the first floor, the other was down in reception. Hackles were raised.

There was a potential for conflict which was raised when, during the 2010 World Cup, Aragonés was repeatedly critical in his tone as an analyst as Spain needed some blue-collar effort to get through their group. After the tournament was won and Del Bosque came back with World Cup gold to match up against Aragonés' silverware, there was an opportunity for revenge.

Spain has a yearly award named after the Príncipe de Asturias, King Juan Carlos's son. It is somewhere between a Knighthood and a Nobel Prize. Across all other categories, previous winners include Václev Havel, Nelson Mandela, Woody Allen, Umberto Eco, Bob Dylan and Al Gore. In sport, Martina Navratilova, Seb Coe, Michael Schumacher and Carl Lewis are among the honoured. In 2010, the Spain football team won the Premio Príncipe De Asturias by a landslide margin. One Friday night in October they, plus a glittering gala of socialites, politicians, artists, scientists, writers and the royal family, gathered in Oviedo's elegant *Teatro Campoamor*. This is part of what the Spain coach said while addressing them.

Vicente del Bosque: "For over 100 years football has formed part of Spanish daily life and it is inexorably linked to the hopes and dreams of millions of Spaniards. We speak about it with such frequency and intensity that it is as if football were a member of each of our families. It is omnipresent, it leaves nobody indifferent. As such we [the squad] are the privileged beneficiaries of a status and responsibility which we cannot ignore. We are the standard bearers for a universal phenomenon which demands that you seek to better yourself every day. We are the few who defend the highest levels of a sport which the multitudes follow and practise. This squad which tonight receives the Príncipe de Asturias prize exhibits the values which soar over any particular trophy success and other material gains in professional football – these players are legitimate heirs to a tradition which honours us all.

"Their values, both timeless and decisive, are effort, talent, sacrifice, discipline, solidarity and modesty. These men who won the World Cup have been true to sportsmanship and honour. They reached the final defending those values – had it been any other way we could not have managed it. Spain winning the World Cup has been a reward for these values, but also the total conviction of all the players that our football proposition, our football philosophy, was the right one and that they were giving everything to it. Neither concept was doubted at any time. We all knew that this was the only way in which we could cope with the adversities and difficulties which will always arise if you try to achieve what we set out to do.

"This team feels deep satisfaction at having attained this unique success and at having made millions of Spaniards proud. The humility and modesty of this group of athletes became as powerful a strength in their favour as the sweeping football they are capable of playing."

All that having been said, in front of an adoring audience and flanked by his World Cup-winning players, Del Bosque strode towards Prince Felipe, accepted the award and then suddenly detoured into the audience. He knew where the man he wanted to find was seated. Calmly, with a big fraternal smile on his face, he reached out his hand and gracefully requested that Luis Aragonés, predecessor, critic, sometime rival, step out of the audience and stand, with the squad, to receive the thunderous applause of the opera house audience and the appreciation of watching millions on live television.

Evidently taken aback, and just as evidently thrilled and honoured, Aragonés accepted with grace. Arms raised in acknowledgement, Aragonés, Del Bosque, the remnants of the 2008 squad plus the new boys who had won the World Cup in South Africa stood at not only the zenith of their lives but of the history of Spanish sport.

Somewhere, looking down, Fermín del Bosque – republican, defender of democracy, preacher of equal rights, believer in the brotherhood of man and father of young Vicente, would have been very proud. Indeed.

The Rough
Guide to
South Africa

Although he had won all his matches since taking over, setting a record in doing so, Vicente del Bosque was still the new boy. The 2009 Confederations Cup in South Africa was his first tournament as national team coach and if that was significant for *La Roja's* fans and the voracious Spanish media, it was vastly more so for his players.

His contact with them had been sporadic, days here and there ahead of World Cup qualifiers. Those had been successful, but on this trip the coach would get a closer look at his players, and they could weigh up how much extra leeway they were going to get compared to the very firm hand of Luis Aragonés. Together, they would experience tournament football – the travel, the training camps – and knockout matches with no margin for error. Had Euro 2008 been a one-off, or had *La Roja* now acquired the winning habit?

From the outset, Spain got things wrong. For the sake of a few dollars more – well, several hundred thousand of them – the federation agreed to a friendly in Baku, Azerbaijan, five days before Spain kicked off the Confeds in Rustenburg against New Zealand. It meant nearly an extra 5000km on a plane, unnecessary time changes, and vast alterations in temperature for a group of players already exhausted at the end of a brutal season. No matter what was earned, it was a logistical error.

Sod's law kicked in. If you are nearly 5000km from home and you are trying to cram in a money-making smash-and-grab friendly (Spain won 6-0) in the full knowledge that it is probably not a great idea, something inevitably goes wrong. And it did.

One of the Spanish party – not a player – lost his passport and the team flight out of Baku was delayed until 3am. The passport was never found, players lost sleep and the staff member was left behind to sort things out. Bad start.

Fifteen hours later, via a set-down in Jo'burg and a 120km bus ride north to Rustenburg, the European champions were physically and mentally shredded. The temperature was 30 degrees lower than it had been in Baku. Del Bosque felt he had no alternative than to cancel the first training session, despite its high value in working out the kinks in various muscles and freshening tired minds.

Spain's group matches, all of which were won against New Zealand, Iraq and hosts South Africa, were in two different venues: Rustenburg and Bloemfontein. Those charged with planning this tournament on behalf of Del Bosque ignored the value of having one, well-planned, properly resourced base from which travel is easy, quick and safe.

After Spain played their first match in Rustenburg, a place they found hard to like, and with a training ground which was a 20-minute bus trip across the city from their chosen hotel, they then debunked to Bloemfontein. There, the training pitch and the Free State stadium playing surface were not well mowed, poorly watered, hard and uneven. In cold and wet conditions, the turf also began cutting up very badly.

In mid-winter, tournament organisers scheduled three games within six days on surfaces that had never been asked to meet the five-star demands of the world's best teams. It ensured that this was a pitch to impede Spain's style and inhibit the pace and finesse of their game. Match surfaces would be a bone of contention between Spain, FIFA and the local organising committee a year later.

Such obstacles are central to the challenge of winning the World Cup, making those that achieve it members of a most exclusive group. However, training pitches fall within the control of the federations who organise for their national teams to have optimum chances of winning these tournaments. During the process of review, assimilation and forward planning between the Confederations Cup and the World Cup, Spain decided that they would not move around South Africa dependent on their group stage matches, or the knockout round. Instead, they would attempt to mimic the success of their base at Neustift in 2008 by finding one relatively central venue which provided a first-class training centre, in a place notably more secluded than the Bloemfontein hotel they occupied during the middle sector of the Confederations Cup; somewhere from which they would have easy access to their own aeroplane.

They finally selected Potchefstroom, a base which helped them implement their particular brand of tournament management where players are allowed significant amounts of free time to explore their surroundings and relax with the friends and family who are installed nearby.

Equally, there were some positive influences from the Confederations Cup which steered preparations for the big one.

South Africa has a fascination for the Premier League which borders on outright lust. While Barcelona had just won the treble in velvet style, it was the Liverpool contingent, even ahead of Arsenal's Cesc Fàbregas, who were the big draws.

Fernando Torres was mobbed and the love for the English-based players moved Álvaro Arbeloa to reflect: "It seems to me a great idea to take these two competitions to South Africa. It is a great way to draw African football in to the rest of the world."

Although the squad medics were fearful about the impact of the cold when Del Bosque's players were allowed on an open-topped bus expedition at the Pilanesberg National Park Game Reserve – temperatures that morning were hovering around zero – the search to take pictures of lions, tigers, buffalo, elephants and rhinos was hugely popular.

These were minor notes, gentle advances, but helpful in giving all the players who attended the Confederations Cup a pleasant sense of the vast, interesting but conflicted nation they were returning to the following summer.

You can trace direct lines between summers 2009 and 2010 in other important matters. Just as the Confederations Cup began, David Villa, whose goals there put him second in Spain's all-time international scoring list behind Raúl, was the subject of a bid from Real Madrid. Barcelona also wanted him. They put in a counter move, but the price was too steep for the Camp Nou president Joan Laporta. Valencia confirmed they had an offer on the table, Villa admitted he had made his mind up about what he wanted to do, but that he was going to keep quiet about it and leave everything to his agents. In the meantime, it became common knowledge that Madrid were also signing Cristiano Ronaldo for a world record €94million. There was a frenzy about Florentino Pérez's rebuilding project, in the face of Barcelona's treble win, and Pérez added to it by commenting that Villa's move to Real Madrid was "just a matter of time".

In Bloemfontein, it was bedlam. Everyone wanted to pin down Villa. Was he going? What was holding everything up? Could a move from Barcelona dissuade him from joining *Los Blancos*? Speculation was incessant and began to suck other members of the squad into the media's sights. Would Villa's Valencia team-mates comment? Would the Barça and Real Madrid players offer opinions on the record, or titbits off the record? Raúl Albiol was also moving from the Mestalla to the Bernabéu; neither news story was positive for Spain and Del Bosque took note.

Twelve months later David Silva was caught up in a similarly lucrative, almost equally high-profile move from Valencia to Manchester City and the amount of time he spent on the pitch during the World Cup suffered as a result. The coach knows he cannot ask his players to put their lives on hold completely, but conduct a major transfer move during a tournament and under Del Bosque there is likely to be a heavy cost in terms of playing time. Villa told Barcelona that either they get their move for him signed, sealed and delivered ahead of the World Cup in May 2010, or he would not be joining them.

Another issue which crystallised for Del Bosque during the summer of 2009 was the need to ensure Andrés Iniesta made it to the World Cup by hook or by crook. The midfielder missed the Confederations Cup due to injury and while Del Bosque could not know that by May 2010 Iniesta's recuperation would still be in serious doubt, he did know that he did not want to try to win a tournament without him. During that first trip to South Africa, the coach admitted just how much Spain miss the little genius when he is not playing.

> **Vicente del Bosque:** "We took Pablo Hernández with us because we needed someone skilful and who gets beyond players wide on the right. We have Cazorla but he is just recovering from an injury. However, Iniesta is so important for us. His game has reached such a dimension that he permits you to do anything you want. You can ask him to play down the left, the right or down the middle and it makes no difference to him. He is the complete player. Amongst footballers in a squad, there has always been a hierarchy."

When they defeated South Africa, Spain claimed a world record of 15 straight wins, one more than Brazil, France and Australia had recorded for the previous best. They also equalled Brazil's world-record 35 match unbeaten run.

Perhaps this was not the tournament of their dreams, but between

Aragonés, Del Bosque and the players, a winning habit had been instilled.

> **Xabi Alonso:** "Let's not kid ourselves, this is not the World Cup, nor the European Championship. But it is a tournament for champions and that is important. We want to win. Planning for the World Cup next year, it is very positive to draw all this information about the host country in advance."

By the time the United States ended Spain's hopes of winning this trophy with a 2-0 win in the semi-final and brought their undefeated record to an end, both the manager and players had already begun to hint that such an eventuality was far from impossible.

> **Vicente del Bosque:** "It has taken us the maximum effort to beat Iraq and South Africa, so we cannot afford to get ourselves mixed up about what a challenge the US offer. Against supposedly minor rivals we have worked hard, with trademark humility. It would be fatal to assume that the US will not be even more complicated."

Many of *La Roja's* squad had previously suffered the ignominy of being jeered off the Santander pitch by their own fans back in June 2008, against the same opponents.

> **Xavi:** "We are favourites, we will be under more pressure than them. We have to accept that status. But this won't be easy, no way. In recent years the US team has evolved very positively, especially in the power of their attack."

La Roja had struggled to find top form against Iraq and South Africa, some absences were being noted (Marcos Senna, Iniesta) and the US had a team built to play quick, pressing, direct football.

Bob Bradley, the US coach, and his men won a victory which was theirs by merit for their simple, clear game plan and its excellent application. They squeezed and harassed Spain's midfield, Clint Dempsey and Landon Donovan showed the tremendous trait of using what little possession they did enjoy with the highest possible quality and intelligence. Subsequent years prove that Spain don't often lose this type of match. But there were clear presages of the manner in which Del Bosque's team would be defeated by Switzerland a year later in Durban and at Wembley to a Frank Lampard goal in 2011.

Spain shot at goal 29 times and won 17 corners, but they hit the target only eight times and they committed some horrible errors.

Bob Bradley: "Our game plan was to put pressure on Xavi and my players achieved that with great success."

The Barça player was robbed in the build-up to the second, decisive, goal but Joan Capdevila, Iker Casillas, Gerard Piqué and Sergio Ramos all committed rare errors for the goals which Jose Altidore and Dempsey scored. Spain simply did not play well.

In all my time covering this generation, a wide variety of the players have shared the same sentiments: 'If we are not sharp, if we do not press, if the pitch is poor, then we become a normal team and we are beatable.' This defeat, their first since 2006, was proof.

There were two, important, take-away conclusions from the experience. Del Bosque reflected on his tactical decisions: he left his strikers on and crowded the pitch with extra attacking midfielders; he encouraged the defence to play the ball directly and long and he allowed Piqué to go forward as an auxiliary centre-forward. Retrospectively the manager's analysis was that this had been an abandonment of basic principles, that it left Spain's football looking muddled and that he had learned a clear lesson: stick to the philosophy no matter the situation. This was one of the key influences on Del Bosque's decision-making when he resisted pressure to drop Busquets after defeat by Switzerland in the opening match of the World Cup.

Secondary to this was the immediate reaction to the defeat. Spain congratulated the US on their game plan and treated their media responsibilities in defeat just the same as in victory, but the end of their winning streak hurt the players. Faced with a trip back to Rustenburg and a thorny match to decide third or fourth place against the host nation, they could have dropped down into autopilot.

Instead, Del Bosque made four changes to his starting team and immediately applied the conclusions he had taken from the defeat by USA. When Fernando Torres and David Villa, who both started despite media criticism for not having buried chances against the States, again misfired, Dani Güiza and Fernando Llorente were brought on – strikers for strikers, team shape and tactics untouched.

Although South Africa were 1-0 up with 17 minutes left, Güiza scored twice within a minute just before the end to re-establish Spanish superiority. Katlego

Mphela added his own second in the 94th minute but, despite being taken to extra-time and suffering from tired limbs, it was Spain, thanks to Xabi Alonso, who got the winning goal and immediately reaffirmed their winning credentials.

The Spanish federation director of football summarised the post-tournament report articulately.

Fernando Hierro: "We don't have a magic wand here. Sport is about both winning and losing. We have recorded six wins in qualification for the World Cup next summer, the new coach has maintained our trajectory after Euro 2008. An experience like this one will strengthen the group and their desire to win. I am sad for the players, they so much wanted to reach the final and play Brazil. However, they have known how to accept defeat and how to react to it. This group had an average age of about 24, most of them have played many internationals but we have also promoted eight of our Under-21 players in recent seasons. Previously, Spain would head to a tournament with the tag of favourites without us ever having done anything to justify it. Now there is a reason. Now we don't have to shirk from the tag of favourites. We will be back here in one year and we will come to win."

World Cup 2010

This is not war. We compete, we fight to have the ball, but we are here to keep on playing the way that we know how, to be loyal to our style.

Vicente del Bosque

World Cup 2010

As Captain Guillermo Gómez-Paratcha gets Spain's Airbus 340/600 airborne, destination Johannesburg, Andrés Iniesta knows he is extremely fortunate to be on the flight to South Africa.

This has been the most soul-destroying year of his life. A thigh injury first sustained 13 months before the World Cup has since flared up on four further occasions. In the final third of Barça's league season, he has played approximately 30 minutes of football. With this track record, 99% of footballers simply wouldn't have been selected for the tournament.

This part of his story is already a matter of record – and, in Spain, of public debate. The hidden story, which only a select few staff and players on the plane currently know, is that spiritually and psychologically Iniesta has been in pieces. While all of Spain has been praying he'll be fit in time, a darker question has long been tormenting Iniesta's mind: might he be fit in body, but shattered in spirit and bereft of self-belief?

In his carry-on luggage, Iniesta has a DVD which will turn out to be a thing of magic. This plastic disc will ultimately be what success or failure for Spain in the World Cup turns on. It's just that nobody knows it yet.

The entire problem has its roots in Paris and the Champions League final of 2006. Central to the plot are two Dutchmen, Frank Rijkaard and Mark van

Bommel. Before the story is resolved, the latter will again inflict pain on Iniesta.

Rijkaard doesn't pick Iniesta for the Paris final against Arsenal, trusting the destructive Van Bommel ahead of the creative La Masia graduate. Barça win largely thanks to Iniesta's inspired performance, having come on at the break with the Cesc Fàbregas-inspired Gunners leading 1-0. Iniesta is champion of Europe, but describes the pain of not starting as "the worst moment of my life".

Ten days before his next Champions League final, against Manchester United in Rome, he suffers a 2cm tear in his thigh while drawing 3-3 against Villarreal. Three years on from the pain of Paris, Iniesta will not, under any circumstances, contemplate missing a chance to play 90 minutes and take destiny in his own hands.

Iniesta is 60 per cent fit and his thigh muscle so precariously held together by tiny fibres that club medics order him not to shoot at goal, in order to protect against more serious damage.

Iniesta is sublime that night, United are defeated 2-0 and the lingering soreness of Paris erased. But the agony of Rome is quite different and much more dangerous. Not only does he lose a huge part of season 2009/10 because of the same injury repeatedly returning, it corrodes his confidence.

Late in the summer of 2009, Iniesta is struck a devastating blow. His great friend Dani Jarque collapses and dies during Espanyol's pre-season training camp. The Barça genius and the Espanyol captain grew up together within the Spanish federation's *categorías inferiores* youth system and Jarque's sudden death precipitates a deep personal crisis. As he loses confidence in his body and ability as a footballer, now Iniesta is also examining questions of mortality and faith.

Andrés Iniesta: "I'd managed to create, let's say, an image of an Andrés Iniesta who played at quite a good level and the fact that I suddenly couldn't perform like that really overshadowed my life. I got to the stage where I no longer had confidence in myself. I'd lost certainty that I could still do the things I'd always done – it was very tough.

"I'm pretty sure people outside the club didn't realise how bad it got."

Twice between December 2009 and March 2010 he breaks down, but by mid-April he's training flat out. Then comes what feels like total disaster. On Tuesday, April 13, seven days before the first leg of the Champions League semi-final which Barcelona lose to Inter, and two months before Spain's World Cup kick-off, Iniesta is completing a shooting drill when his right thigh rips again. Even before momentum takes him off the pitch, he's already in tears. While the drill continues, he staggers over to the corner of Barça's Joan Gamper training ground and the physios, trotting over, see his diminutive frame wracked with sobs.

"That day was a killer, soul-destroying," he remembers.

Iniesta misses all but four minutes of the remainder of the league season, his fragile confidence once again in tatters. There's now a firm chance he won't make the World Cup.

Post World Cup, Vicente del Bosque underlines how great the dilemma was. "Muscular injuries can get right into your psyche. In theory you're healed, but in your mind you know whether you are right or not. If not, it can be confusing and damaging."

Spain's doctor, Óscar Celadas, goes further. "Before the full list for the World Cup was made public, Andrés was one of our guys who had had serious problems and there was a really big decision to be taken."

Naming Iniesta in the provisional squad becomes a gamble based on medical projections, not current fitness, but Del Bosque is certain that the midfielder's presence is going to be of transcendental importance.

So, in a double seat next to Víctor Valdés, his great friend and confessor from his very first days at the Camp Nou 14 years earlier, Iniesta is on the flight. The fact that he has once again aggravated his injury when Del Bosque dared to play him in the World Cup warm-up win over Poland is not the only problem he has carried on board. Physically he is healing, psychologically he is not. After dozing for the first half hour, he unzips his hand luggage, reaches for his personal computer and tries to draw strength and inspiration from the DVD which has been put together to save his World Cup.

All around him are the high spirits and activity of an expedition hitting the road. Sergio Ramos alongside Jesús Navas; Xavi next to Puyol; Fernando Torres seated with Xabi Alonso.

When Iniesta presses 'play' he sees the work of Emili Ricart. A physio at FC Barcelona, Ricart handles the recuperation and rehabilitation of that club's great stars post-injury. Fortunately his is a holistic approach. He knows that repairing the muscle, however long it takes, isn't always sufficient. If the injury has done damage to confidence and psyche, then physical rehabilitation will not come close to completing the healing. "Things had reached a stage where Andrés felt like this was a problem which was never going away – he was sinking," Ricart recalls.

The first images Iniesta sees are of Manel Estiarte, Pep Guardiola's right-hand man at Barcelona for the previous two years. The footage is from his former existence, as the Leo Messi of water polo, one of the greatest ever players in a sport hugely popular in Spain. The team he led failed to win gold at the Barcelona Olympics in 1992, conceding a winning advantage over Italy in the final with nine seconds left, then losing in extra-time. It was a crushing defeat for a Catalan superstar at his home town Olympics, provoking tears from a tough guy. The DVD jumps forward four years and Estiarte has fought back to win gold with Spain at the Atlanta Olympics.

Next, is footage of Fernando Alonso's 150 mph crash at Interlagos in 2003, his car disintegrating and the Spaniard being stretchered off the track. But that cuts to the Asturian driving to his first Formula 1 world title in 2005, becoming the youngest champion ever and celebrating madly on the podium in Brazil, the scene of his terrible crash two years previously.

Then there is Rafa Nadal beating Roger Federer to win a four-and-a-half hour, five-set epic final at the 2009 Australian Open. The Spaniard's first hard-court title leaves Federer in tears, unable to complete his loser's speech. The images flash forward to Federer fighting back to win the French Open later that year, becoming the sixth man to win grand slam titles on all three surfaces.

Finally there is Iniesta himself, down and out during that match against Villarreal in 2009, holding his thigh muscle, his face betraying the agony of the injury and the knowledge of its likely consequences.

The counterpoint? When he buries the ball into the top corner of the Chelsea net, stripping off his Barça top and running like crazy towards the corner flag.

Goal celebrations? Corner flags? Perhaps there is more of that to come.

— Day One.

— June 11, 2010. Potchefstroom

South Africa's N12 road is a thing of beauty, and of great danger.

It snakes from way down on the southern coast: George, where part of France's miserable World Cup is spent, through Gauteng Province, beyond Johannesburg to Witbank and, within a comfortable drive, onwards to Swaziland. The 130km stretch between Soweto and Potchefstroom, where Spain will live, train and plot victory, is remarkable. Once the township is left behind the land to either side of this dual carriageway is scrub. There are vast, flat acres of it and the cheapest way to keep that from becoming a huge, dense, jungle of grasses is to set fire to it. This is the Highveld, nearly 5000 feet above sea level; the altitude stings the inside of your nose and the back of your throat when you breathe in the thinned air. Combined with the smoke from the almost constantly burning bushland on that journey, it produces something joyful and evocative.

However, the smoke drifts, sometimes aimlessly, sometimes malevolently, across the freeway so that long minutes drag by when you struggle to see more than 10 feet in front of the windscreen. Orange flames lick upwards in the areas where the fires are most fierce, you can feel the heat even through closed windows. It's like nowhere I've been before.

Much more serious than the fires is the fact that delinquents occasionally stand on top of the infrequent pedestrian bridges to drop concrete breeze-blocks onto passing vehicles. My World Cup in Potchefstroom, this gentle, pretty, pocket-sized city, was extra enjoyable thanks to the hospitality of the Pukulani Lodge. However, late in the tournament our landlady, Juanita De Kock, revealed that only a few months previously her brother had been killed in just this manner on that route between Jo'burg and Potch, as the locals call the city.

These are the reasons why the Spanish federation's relentless travel and accommodation manager, Antonio Limones, has told Maphetle Maphetle, the ANC mayor of the city, that while they like the high performance sports centre of North Western University, they won't be doing Potch the huge favour of following the England and Australia one-day cricket teams who have stayed there unless there is an airstrip to land at. Spain's risk managers don't want to be repeatedly reliant on the N12 when getting to and from their travel hub, which will be Oliver Tambo Airport on the north-eastern side of Jo'burg.

The point will be emphasised at 2.30am following Spain's crucial 2-1 win over Chile in the final group game, when some thug standing at the side of the N12 launches a rock at the bus carrying the media home to Potch. The aim is to either injure the driver or make the bus crash – in either case stopping the bus so it can be looted and the passengers robbed. In this case the rock shatters the reinforced glass, penetrating the window and only failing to do worse damage because the strength of the glass prevents the missile hitting the driver. Imagine a bus carrying Casillas, Xavi, Del Bosque and Iniesta coming under that, or any other kind of assault, and it is simple to understand the federation's concern.

Maphetle Maphetle spends 26m South African rand, around £1.7m, on extending the semi-used military airfield so that a large passenger liner such as their Airbus 340/600 can touch down there and have enough runway to meet safety guidelines. Potch gets Spain.

As *La Roja* land on South African soil Captain Gómez-Paratcha bids his passengers farewell with the words: "Let South Africa quake, Spain have arrived."

Not long after, outside the student residences of NW University, where Linford Christie, Paula Radcliffe and Kelly Holmes have trained, Spain's weary squad sit in the low sunshine of the Guateng autumn squinting at the Zulu performers in traditional costumes, dancing, slapping their wellington boots and ululating. Some of *La Roja* wish they were back in the Tyrol: oompah bands, feathered hats, lederhosen and *Veo veo*.

Post-siesta, *La Roja* train. They *rondo* the kinks out of their muscles and begin some pressing exercises, but there are only 22 of them.

It is dark, cold, the trees rustle in the gentle wind and, then, across the Fanie du Toit rugby pitch, through the security perimeter and onto the football pitch trots Iniesta, the missing splash of red. By his side is Hugo Camarero, the federation physio charged with pacing the midfielder's rehab.

Recuperation from the latest version of his injury should be about a week, starting from the Poland match, but that takes him past June 16 and the Group H opener against Ottmar Hitzfeld's Switzerland.

However, when the federation doctor, Óscar Celada, tells us that "Iniesta is driven by such hunger to get back and play against Switzerland that we might have to try and put the brakes on him", it is not a code we need an Enigma machine to decipher.

> *Meanwhile...*
> *FIFA claims that South Africa will host a "Ferrari" of a World Cup. It certainly looks attractive as the hosts kick off with a draw against Mexico in Group A, although the competition might still require a tune-up. Or maybe it is just the vuvuzelas making that noise.*

— Day Two.
— June 12, 2010. Potchefstroom

This is one of those double-training days and already the Spaniards are in good humour. They can walk from their accommodation, past the heated outdoor pool, across a short green space, into the dressing rooms. From there, they move out through a tunnel and smack into the middle of the bleachers, which the scrum of media and the delirious locals will co-habit. Reporters hang over the railings calling out for the nod and wink which means an interview will happen; the locals holler, swoon and beg for autographs.

It being early winter, the mid-morning sun is strong, the sky is azure and the pitch cut so short and smooth it could be used to play billiards on. The Spanish federation director of football, Fernando Hierro, tells me: "It's thrilling to have facilities which are of this high quality. The playing surface here is stupendous." Xabi Alonso and Xavi emphasise how vital it is for Spain that the ball slides like a curling stone on ice when they pass, so that excellence of first-time control and quick distribution become even greater advantages.

What they don't know is that despite liaison with the NWU sports staff and the local organising committee during the winter about how to lay the pitch, how to maintain it, how to water it and how tightly to trim it, their pristine playing surface was very nearly washed away by forces no amount of planning could counter.

Spain's training pitch is newly constructed, just to the northern edge of the NWU Senwes cricket ground and surrounded by seven rugby fields. It also happens to be very near the banks of the Mooi Rivier, Beautiful River in Afrikaans.

The previous grass, kikuyu turf, which is *de rigueur* for rugger, had been replaced by a blend of rye-grass and some European seeds and it was all bedding down quite nicely when, just four weeks before Spain arrived, the rains came. Some of the heaviest and most persistent downpours in recent memory drenched the town and the river began to burst its banks. Spain's custom-made pitch was about to be completely swept away.

Professor Annette Kombrink, a formidable presence in this project and head of the local organising committee, intervened. All the navvies who were laying the runway extension at the military base were requisitioned, bussed down to the university and set about laying sandbags, digging trenches, and doing everything within their power to stem the tide. The rising water was first contained, then repelled and, gradually, it stopped raining.

As Del Bosque's boys sprint around the green turf, practising crossing and shooting, perfecting their *rondos,* playing a mini-match, they are blissfully unaware of the immense effort required to preserve their training pitch and avoid a last-minute disaster.

Meanwhile...
Diego Maradona, the Argentina manager and scorer of that 'Hand of God' goal, expresses a wish that the finals be played fairly, a comment which causes Robert Green to take his eye off the ball. The England goalkeeper spills Clint Dempsey's tame shot into his net, cancelling out Steven Gerrard's early opener and Fabio Capello's men must settle for a 1-1 draw.

— Day Three.
— June 13, 2010. Potchefstroom

The dozens of local black Africans who turn up to watch every Spain training session have had to negotiate several army checkpoints and the many without a vehicle have done so on foot, as part of a lengthy trek to catch a glimpse of the European champions. They stand in the bleachers, clustered tightly together and chant in what we are told is Tswana, a language predominant from the Highveld northwards. Joyful, indecipherable and harmonious background a cappella songs are punctuated by a change in tone and pace when a new name – Xavi, Iniesta or Torres – is introduced like a friendly face in a crowd of strangers. It is brilliant to be around.

Today is Sunday and a single session, with the players given the afternoon off. This accounts for their grumpiness when they are told to report, in full playing kit, to the meeting room in their student accommodation block.

This is the bunker from which Del Bosque will lead them to victory, where the opposition is meticulously picked apart, but today the players are to get the referee briefing which each squad must listen to before their campaign gets underway. The referee committee has sent them Horacio Elizondo, the official in charge of the Berlin World Cup final four years previously.

Group H is the last to kick off, meaning Spain are last to arrive, and they are a bit antsy. The World Cup has sputtered into life, intermittently entertaining but crackling with caution, conservative football and too few goals. The 14 games before Spain kick off average only 1.6 goals each. During Portugal vs Ivory Coast there are no goals and only three efforts on target, Italy vs Paraguay is a 1-1 draw with six on-target attempts, while New Zealand and Slovakia share two goals and hit the target only five times between them.

Elizondo tries to ensure that every player is clear about how strictly obstruction will be enforced; how much influence 'natural' and 'voluntary' body positions will be taken into account in judging whether a handball must be ruled as a penalty or not. After an hour-long refresher course, their Argentinian professor hits them with a Q&A. Casillas, Alonso and Reina are top of the class.

However, there is restlessness. Once Elizondo finishes and solicits any further questions, Xavi (given the nod from his captain, Casillas) is polite but extremely firm in asking the ref to take a missive back to FIFA.

"We've sat here for an hour listening about how the rules are going to be interpreted, but you go back and you tell Sepp Blatter that because FIFA aren't watering the pitches anything like sufficiently, and because they aren't cutting the surface short enough they are handing a premium to defensive football. If he wants good football and he wants entertainment, tell him to sort the pitches out."

There is no personal hostility, only passion, but it constitutes a natural punctuation point in the afternoon.

There is football currently on the television and it is a free afternoon – Del Bosque's boys are pawing the ground. They want out, but their route is barred.

FIFA have asked us to film each member of the squad individually in front of a green screen, so that the tournament will have a couple of poses for the television graphics and also for the massive screen at the stadium when the teams are announced.

I emphasise time and again that there must be no watches, no jewellery, that the keepers must wear gloves and to check that everything they have on is first-choice playing kit.

In record time, we are nearly ready to go, but Carles Puyol is jumpy. Instructions are for suckers, he is going first and he simply can't wait a second longer. I notice he still has his own personal brand of watch (CP5) wrapped around his wrist despite my briefing, but I say nothing and let him start. Elsewhere in the room there have already been boasts and bets about who will get it right first time because they are natural Hollywood material.

Puyi folds his arms, steps forward and gives a fierce look down the camera. He is ready to leave. Suddenly reminded that he wasn't supposed to be wearing his watch and that he is going to have to do it again there's a pause during which it is unclear whether or not the Barcelona captain is going to instigate a trade-union style walk-out, or deck me, but then the tension breaks into laughter and teasing. Puyol smiles ruefully at all the digs he's getting and off we go – everyone is into it now.

This is Víctor Valdés' debut tournament and when it is his turn I end up holding *his* watch while he's filmed. As he sets himself to leave the room he stops and checks back, having realised he's forgotten the expensive timepiece he usually wears around his wrist. He remembers I've got it and approaches with his hand out.

"Here it is, here it is," I say, "did you think I'd nick it?"

"Probably," he responds stone-faced.

A couple of days later, at the Durban stadium, pre-match, I am in FIFA matchday regulation uniform: hand-made Parisian-tailored suit, white shirt and tie – not exactly my normal choice of apparel.

"Nice suit," Valdés tells me after a fairly affectionate punch on the arm in greeting, "did you nick it?"

> **Meanwhile...**
> *Germany leave Australia reeling – after a 4-0 defeat – and also bereft of Tim Cahill, who is sent off for a tackle on Bastian Schweinsteiger. The Everton midfielder breaks down in tears afterwards, saying: "Dreams can be made and crushed in the space of hours."*

— Day Four.
— June 14, 2010. Potchefstroom
Training is sharp, particularly the night-time work, during which it's dark and winter-cold. It is as if the change of light and climate has transported the players back into mid-season mode.

Neither Villa nor Torres is 'in the zone' in front of goal – whether in mini-matches or the finishing drills. Juan Mata is, though, Joan Capdevila hits a couple of screamers and when Puyol loses a small-sided match he kicks the portable goal over in fury. There isn't a hint of over-confidence.

Álvaro Arbeloa says: "World Cups often start with drawn matches because of so many teams having a fear of losing instead of looking to score and win well, but we don't have responsibility to serve up good football. We are just here in search of victory."

Del Bosque appears preoccupied. During every training exercise, the coach has been pushing for speed of thought, elusiveness when being pressed and ruthlessness in front of goal.

It is not that he detects complacency, rather that he holds Ottmar Hitzfeld, the coach of Switzerland, to be an immense rival. As coaches of Bayern Munich and Real Madrid, these two men contested eight epic Champions League matches between 2000 and 2002. Del Bosque watched his Madrid side concede eight goals in two group-game defeats before prising Bayern out of the competition in a thrilling semi-final in 2000. The following year, Hitzfeld dealt retribution in the semi. In 2002, Del Bosque and Madrid claimed victory in a thunderous quarter-final.

While Switzerland don't possess players in the Bayern Munich category, they have conceded less than a goal per game in qualifying and just carved out two consecutive draws against Italy.

Del Bosque tells us: "I think the team is okay, confident in its possibilities but with the degree of self-awareness required for a competition like this. But in Spain it is on the tip of everyone's tongues that we are phenomenal, we are the tallest, the most handsome ... all that.

"We've seen at this World Cup already that there are very minor differences between all the sides and we may struggle to win this first game unless we do our jobs particularly well. However, there's such euphoria at home that it is impossible to turn that tide."

Meanwhile...
The Adidas Jabulani ball is getting a bit of a kicking by those teams who have conceded unfortunate goals. The Mexico goalkeeper Óscar Pérez is pictured in training fielding shots with an American football in a bid to read the unpredictable flight paths of the new FIFA choice.

— Day Five.
— *June 15, 2010. Durban*
The European champions head east and land at King Shaka Airport mid-evening on a grey and drizzly Monday, June 14.

The media straggle in around midnight, a handful of us in the team hotel, the rest dispersed around the grateful B&Bs which cluster the Moses Mabhida Stadium in Durban.

By morning, Spain awake to pleasant panoramic views of the Umgeni River and its wide mouth opening out onto the currently choppy Indian Ocean. Their hotel is pretty basic and the front desk staff have an air of the Three Stooges about them, but these are undemanding, easy-going guests: feed 'em, give 'em beds and get them to the match on time. *Pues, todo perfecto! [All's well]*

Tomorrow will be Spain's 50th match in World Cup finals. They have won only 22 and never progressed beyond the quarter-finals

La Roja's last match on South African soil, nearly a year earlier, was also Del Bosque's only competitive defeat since taking over in 2008. Rough and tumble on a dry pitch against a limited but clever, physical and quick USA side; precisely the type of challenge presented by Switzerland.

The Moses Mabhida Stadium is not only within sight of the hotel veranda, it is also cheek-by-jowl to Kings Park, home of the Natal Sharks and the venue for one of the semi-finals of the 1995 Rugby World Cup. Heaven forfend that the organisers could have saved a buck or two and converted it for football use.

Spain train in the afternoon and find the grass longer than their liking; irrespective of the threat of rain they would like the pitch watered heavily before the match and at half-time.

Del Bosque gets them stretching, sprinting, playing a mini-match, and then home to the Riverside Hotel. The technical staff settle down in the terrace bar outside the breakfast room to watch Brazil beat Korea 2-1. The tournament is not sparking and while Spain are here to win first and entertain second, there is a strong sense that the rest of the world is waiting for Del Bosque's elite, sometimes irresistible, European champions to start the party.

Meanwhile...
The North Korean coaching staff are upset by a question at a press conference, about how much influence the nation's leader Kim Jong-Il has in picking the team. An international incident is averted after Ji Yun-Nam restores some pride with a goal in a 2-1 defeat by Brazil.

— **Day Six.**
—*June 16, 2010. Durban*
Spain v Switzerland
Uno y dos y tres … ganar y ganar y ganar!

It is a sunny Wednesday morning by the Indian Ocean, a 10-minute drive from a brand new stadium, where Spain's World Cup will begin. By 6pm, the camp will be enveloped by dark clouds.

In the forecourt of the Riverside Hotel there gather army, police, media and private security, as players and staff board the team bus. Two routes are pencilled-in for *La Roja*, one is chosen at the very last moment. Team security is taken seriously. A helicopter chatters overhead, filming the journey for the international television feed.

After Iniesta reports no ill-effects from the final training session the day before, the line-up is confirmed: Casillas: Ramos, Piqué, Puyol, Capdevila; Busquets, Alonso; Silva, Xavi, Iniesta; Villa. 4-2-3-1. Del Bosque reads them the XI an hour before leaving.

Switzerland will be: Benaglio: Lichtsteiner, Senderos, Grichting, Ziegler; Barnetta, Inler, Huggel, Fernandes; Derdiyok; Nkufo. 4-4-1-1.

Just like the result is going to differ, wildly, from the opening game of Euro 2008, so does the team talk. Nothing bellicose. Compact. Low-key. Precisely 69 seconds long.

"Okay guys, what are our tasks today?

"Let's get our heads in this game. The thing I want you to watch out for is if they have a free-kick then those who are not in the wall need to watch for them being smart and trying to feed the ball to runners, so David Villa and Xavi – watch out. Don't let them surprise us.

"Pay attention to the fact that this is an important game – no red cards. If someone gets himself sent off then it's a problem for the team and a problem for him.

"Nobody gets suckered into making mistakes. For Andrés and David [Silva], make sure you are vigilant [in the wide positions], neither of you can lose concentration for a second.

"Think about winning and holding possession, think about using that possession to push the team forwards. Keep the ball moving. Sergio [Busquets], and Xavi, each of your positions needs to be dependent on the other – especially if one of you moves forward to initiate the play. If Piqué pushes on to start a move you have to compensate for that.

"But above all be conscious of looking out for your team-mates, be conscious of being a united team, please."

To shouts of *vamos!* they form their dressing-room huddle, every single player and staff member is in.

And then comes their signature tune.

One voice: *"Uno y dos y tres."*

All voices: *"Ganar y Ganar y Ganar!"*

My match position is 20 yards behind and to the right of Iker Casillas' goal in the first half, as is that of his girlfriend, the television reporter Sara Carbonero. Like us, the game is beauty and the beast.

Spain play with verve and width, they create one-on-one chances and Alonso hits the bar. Piqué's opportunity to score is easily the best, receiving a sweet pass from Iniesta, cutting inside the centre-back, Stephane Grichting, and shaping to put a right-footed shot to the left of the keeper. As he spreads his body, Diego Benaglio gets his left knee in place to deflect the shot wide.

The European champions have 24 attempts at goal, put eight on target, force 12 corners, commit 13 fewer fouls than the Swiss, don't see a yellow card (to Switzerland's four) but the beast is: they lose.

Six minutes after the break, Switzerland crash through the barrier of Spain's *doble pivote* in midfield, Xabi Alonso and Sergio Busquets, the latter of whom makes two key mistakes. First, he is out-jumped by Eren Derdiyok, who will later come close to making it 2-0 when he trickles an effort off the post. Second, and worse, the Catalan fails to track the run of the Swiss striker after their challenge.

Carles Puyol rushes forward to plug the gap, but Blaise Nkufo, having picked up possession, returns the ball to Derdiyok sufficiently quickly that the defender is taken out of the move and Piqué is isolated. Derdiyok sprints to a one-on-one position against Casillas, who attempts to dive in and tackle with his feet. The ball breaks off both men, hits Derdiyok in mid-air, deflects off Piqué, who is sprinting to cover the goal line, and as the Catalan defender falls, a victim of the chaos in front of him, the ball squirms out from underneath his body and lies there for Gelson Fernandes, who has been padding alongside as an interested spectator, to stab home. The Keystone Kops feel increases when the boots of both Derdiyok and Casillas catch Piqué in the face.

Of the 14 players used, six are World Cup debutants and there are hints that experience and cool heads are at a premium here. Minor chances arrive but Spain are having one of those days when the play is cogent but the finishing is fractured.

Torres, Navas and Pedro replace Busquets, Silva and another guy as the search for goals becomes desperate. The other guy, sadly, is Iniesta – easily Spain's most creative and threatening player on a brutally tough day.

With less than 15 minutes remaining, the player whose participation in this tournament had been so uncertain is challenged by Stephan Lichtsteiner and it is like watching an ocean liner plough through a rowing boat. Iniesta takes evasive action, leaping out of the way, but he feels an immediate problem at the back of his thigh. Post-match in the tunnel, it is a shock to witness up close the physical proportions of Benaglio (6ft 4ins) Benjamin Huggel (6ft 3ins), Grichting (6ft 2ins) and Derdiyok (6ft 3ins) while they shake hands or exchange shirts with Navas, Pedro and Iniesta. Of the 14 players Switzerland use, only one is under 6ft tall. Despite what I have been taught in Spain for the previous nine years, it suddenly feels as if the little guys could never beat these giants. Yet they have been doing that all their lives and Iniesta has been, by a considerable margin, the best player on the pitch.

There is a firm, sporting handshake between Hitzfeld and Del Bosque. In the dressing room, Arbeloa yells: "This isn't where it ends, this is where it begins."

To anyone who has played any kind of competitive football, the defender's words will immediately sound like dressing-room cliché. But when they look back over the tournament, most of the senior figures in this squad will point out that, for whatever reason, the full-back struck a nerve with all of them. Remarkably, they become the first rallying point.

Hearts and limbs are sore in Durban. Back home, knives are sharpening. Luis Aragonés says, in a television interview: "Opening games need to be played at 110%. It felt to me like these lads went out convinced they might win this fairly easily."

Spain 0 Switzerland 1

Spain: Casillas, Ramos, Puyol, Piqué, Capdevila; Alonso, Xavi, Busquets (Torres 61); Iniesta (Pedro 77), Villa, Silva (Navas 62)

Switzerland: Benaglio; Lichtsteiner, Senderos (Von Bergen 35), Grichting, Ziegler, Barnetta (Eggiman 92), Inler, Huggel, Fernandes, Derdiyok (Yakin 79), Nkufo
Goal: Fernandes 52

Meanwhile...
It's their party and South Africa want to cry after goalkeeper Itumeleng Khune is sent off against Uruguay in a match which they lose 3-0. Khune can perhaps console himself knowing he only conceded one of them but it is a result which shakes the hosts from dreams of the knockout stages.

— Day Seven.

— June 17, 2010. Potchefstroom

Some of the Spanish media, capable of balance in fair weather but hysterical at the sight of clouds, are demanding that Busquets be dropped. The defeat gave him his 14th cap but only his fourth competitive appearance. Suddenly, the argument is that the 4-2-3-1 formation is too negative and a *doble pivote* – two organising players together in the Spain midfield – is too much about protecting their own goal rather than creating chances.

Few outside the game, even after Barça's treble the previous season, are aware of precisely how highly his fellow pros rate Busquets' decision-making, positional sense, ability to rob the ball and his judgment of how to keep it circulating.

Back in Spain, the television channel La Sexta opens the debate with a poll: "Was playing a double pivot formation a liability for Spain? Ring us with your criticisms and suggestions – but time's running out for us to find a solution before the Honduras game on Monday!" Clowns.

Even the travelling media pack has had its confidence buffeted. The sports paper AS holds a referendum amongst radio correspondents (Onda, Cope, RNE, SER), newspapers (ABC, El Periodico, El Pais, El Mundo, La Razón) and television reporters (Punto Pelota, Canal+, Cuatro). Of the 12, only one radio (RNE) and one TV correspondent (Cuatro) think it is obvious that Del Bosque should continue with the same formation and personnel. Not a great show of faith in a team which qualified via 10 straight competitive wins.

Shrewdly, Spain produce an unscheduled briefing from Del Bosque. Media editors are looking for angles and they are clearly going to be negative unless there are positive new quotes to work with.

"I'm not here to debate with an authority like the previous Spain coach, but I do want to make it clear that there are not two Spains – that of Aragonés and that of Del Bosque. There is one Spain and we are all pulling in the same direction.

"Nobody in the tournament had as many efforts at goal as we did, normally we would have scored – it was just a bad day."

It is good, but there is better still. His players are given most of the day off to go to the Bona Bona Safari in search of Africa's fabled big five: elephants, lions, leopards, rhinos and buffalo. Right now victory is the endangered species.

Casillas stays to spend the day with his girlfriend, Sara Carbonero, one or two go out to lunch. The Sushi Crew from Euro 2008 hit the Cape Town Fish Market down at the Mooi Rivier mall. Busquets, hacked off at the result and the unfair critical landslide, opts for solitude.

Thinking strategically again, the Spanish federation open up the entire training base. The media are allowed to traipse round and film the accommodation block, the restaurant, the meeting and video analysis room and the leisure facilities, as well as up in the cricket club, where the video games, dartboards, table football, televisions and table tennis tables are all situated. This is very privileged access.

If you are a multi-millionaire footballer, used to five stars, it is a pretty spartan place to spend a month. Already a French government minister has used Spain's "student" accommodation to attack Raymond Domenech's squad for their overly luxurious quarters down on the Cape Town coast. Del Bosque's squad name their Potch residences 'The Convent'.

This flood of new information, new images and new quotes from Del Bosque buys a certain degree of respite from the 'Shock! Horror!' headlines back home. However, that neat little PR trick, authored by the reliable, likeable and forward-thinking Paloma Antoranz, who is in charge of media relations, is only the public precursor to the most fundamental moment of Del Bosque's Spain career, as important to his story as the dropping of Raúl was to that of Luis Aragonés.

Those who started the Switzerland defeat have the entire day off. Everyone else trains at 7pm local time but, and this will become a pattern, Casillas insists on taking part in the full goalkeeper workout, pushing himself at least as hard as Víctor Valdés and Pepe Reina.

There are *rondos*, shooting exercises, a mini-game and then dinner. After the meal, a meeting is called by Del Bosque and his director of football, Fernando Hierro. It is held in the cricket club: sufficiently far from the main accommodation that if there happens to be any harsh truths exchanged there will be no unnecessary witnesses.

This is a 'Chatham House Rule' get-together: even if some of the topic headings are going to be shared outside the room, there must be confidentiality around details and, above all, 'who said what'. It means a stripping away of hierarchy; every voice has equal weight for the hour or so that they meet, before authority is restored. No grudges will be held and no subject is off limits.

Although there have been a handful of versions of the roll-call, I am content that present are: Del Bosque, Toni Grande, Hierro, Casillas, Xavi, Reina, Marchena, Torres and Alonso. What is also now clear is that the players are unified in telling Del Bosque that they wholly support his ideas, his playing scheme and are tranquil about the fact that defeat by Switzerland was simply an accident.

The manager wants it made clear, and disseminated, that not only will he not be altering the formation, nor will he be looking for scapegoats and there is no way he will bow to media pressure about changes. Nobody will be dropped in punishment.

Hierro tells the current players he has never seen such harmony and conviction in a Spain camp and that he is still completely confident that the team can achieve something great.

Del Bosque's final message brings the meeting to an end: "We had to win six games to win the World Cup before that Switzerland result and we still only have to win six games."

Vicente del Bosque: "It was a moment of intense analysis. I wanted to know the players' opinions even though I had a firm view of how we should react. It was imperative not to single anyone out. In this world of football we all make mistakes, we all lose. If you look to blame as a remedy to that then we'll all lose all the time. Just because of one defeat we weren't going to start playing around with the team or the system which had brought us this far. The meeting helped to clear everyone's heads, get them focused on what my decisions were and to quietly spread that word. We also managed to analyse one or two things about the football we played against Switzerland with a view to assimilating what we'd learned. I think it was unexpected that there would be no drastic changes but I was clear about the way forward and about the fact that we could still win all six games to win the World Cup."

Meanwhile...
Manchester United confirm that Rio Ferdinand will not return to South Africa after tests show the England defender has suffered knee ligament damage in training. The France squad also seems resolved to return home following a 2-0 defeat by Mexico, some sooner than others after an ugly exchange between coach Raymond Domenech and striker Nicolas Anelka.

— Day Eight.
— June 18, 2010. Potchefstroom

It dawns one of those sparkling, crystal-clear winter days on the Highveld which would pass for the best of summer in Britain. A few players, Reina, Busquets, Alonso and Piqué amongst them, see the day a tad earlier than the rest of us.

They have permission to be up early and glued to satellite television at 3am South African time in order to catch the decisive Game Seven of the NBA Finals between the Boston Celtics and the Los Angeles Lakers.

The series is tied 3-3 and the Spaniards are yelling for the Lakers given that, behind Kobe Bryant, Spanish world champion Pau Gasol is the team's second most valuable player. The Lakers win and the decision to brave the freezing dawn is a good one. By mid-morning there is a spring in everyone's step as the starting XI are reintegrated into training.

There is stretching, endless stretching; *rondos*, endless *rondos*. A talk, a mini-game based on two touches and then one of those sessions which I have never understood. There are four tiny little goals forming the points of a compass and it is hard to tell which guy is playing with which team, but it seems to be all about walking the ball over the line between the two closely-spaced posts. I'm sure they do just it to confuse onlookers.

The daily press conferences are held in a lecture hall behind the gym. Today, we talk to Gerard Piqué and Xabi Alonso, but the tone has been set by the previous evening's meeting.

Gerard Piqué: "While I understand our fans' disappointment it was ridiculous that the Switzerland result brought criticism of our entire style of play. We played well but just didn't score. Believe me, my chance looked easier than it was, but if that had gone in we would have then hit another two or three – guaranteed.

"We've won the European Championship, we were unbeaten for 35 games, we won every qualifying match and arrived here as many people's favourites. You'd have to be pretty stupid to deduce that it's our playing style that needs changing.

"As for the nonsense about *doble pivote* and Sergio Busquets, I didn't hear anyone saying that when we beat Argentina and we played exactly the same way that day. Of course, then, everyone was praising *Busi* to the hilt. It's just a shame that people are always looking for someone to blame."

Xabi Alonso: "Anyone who starts having a go at the partnership between me and Busquets now, who didn't before, is just being opportunistic because of the result."

There is a night-time training session marked by three things. Firstly, it is so cold that the local fans who turn up do so in hats, ski jackets, scarves, gloves and often rugs or blankets. Secondly, although he is categorically ruled out of Monday's match against Honduras, Iniesta is at least trotting around and doing some stretching. Thirdly, Fernando Torres is beginning to muscle himself into scoring positions in training. He is converting some of them.

Things are looking up, but if the players do likewise then they will see their own breath in the cold, oxygen-thin, star-filled African sky.

Meanwhile...
England's goalless draw with Algeria is exacerbated after Wayne Rooney criticises supporters for jeering and a fan finds a way into the dressing room to make sure that the team hadn't misheard him. Germany suffer an unexpected defeat by Serbia and also lose Miroslav Klose to two bookings within the first 37 minutes.

— Day Nine.
— June 19, 2010. Potchefstroom
Honduras go under the microscope. The game is 48 hours away, so Saturday holds just one training session and it takes place in the evening, partly to get used to the routine for a late kick-off on Monday and partly to get used to the cold.

At 11am everyone is to gather in the meeting and video analysis room. Del Bosque wants all the available data at his fingertips but he will use a severe filter as to what he tells his players. He will be very specific, he will emphasise some key points, but he will strive to avoid overload. However, this is not an episode of Spooks and vast files of data do not just pop up on screen unaided. The information, carefully cut up into digestible video segments, needs to be sought, compiled and edited. It is as laborious as it is important. For this reason, poor old Antonio Fernández and Paco Jiménez, two long-time friends and colleagues of Del Bosque, were crammed inside a tiny plane the size of a phone-booth, last Wednesday. While Spain were being embarrassed by Switzerland, these two were in Nelsprit, watching Honduras lose by the only goal to Marcelo Bielsa's Chile.

Paco Jiménez: "It feels like I've been working with Vicente all my life. We started together as players at Castellon in the early 1970s and when Vicente began working at Real Madrid I joined him. Then, when Florentino wanted rid of us all, we both went to Besiktas. Eventually Vicente joined the national team when first Javi Miñano and Toni Grande were called to join him, and then me.

"Vicente and I won so much with Madrid – the Intercontinental Cup, two Champions Leagues. We won seven titles in just over three years.

"My job as a scout always involved trying to gather as much information as possible about our opponents. I'd then produce a written report and an audio-visual presentation for the players. The report covered everything: their playing style, their systems, a detailed account of how they moved line by line in defence, midfield and attack, their strategy and then an analysis of each player individually.

"In South Africa, I had to take several short trips by twin-propellor aeroplane to see a match maybe 1000km away. I made these journeys, of 90 minutes or even two hours, in tiny planes and one time I arrived and realised there were no stairs up to the plane. I asked how I was meant to get up there and I was told to jump on to the wing and crawl in through a window!"

This is how World Cups are won.

Meanwhile, the players are fed more than just information. If at Euro 2008 the doctor who controlled their diet, Jordi Candel, was colloquially known to his players as *Doctor Hambre* (Dr Hunger), things under Dr Celada have changed a trifle now. Well, not a trifle, perhaps a low-fat Greek yoghurt sprinkled with apricot shavings.

Javier Arbizú has been Spain's chef for over two decade and while the contents of the menus remain strictly controlled, there are now wider choices and some of the salad options are unlimited.

In Austria, Pepe Reina, Arbeloa, Rubén de la Red and Sergio Ramos used to sneak down to pinch stuff from the hotel kitchen. Nevertheless, every single Spain player loses a few kilos during a tournament like this, no matter how hard they try.

This is how they roll at mealtimes:

Training days

Breakfast (8:30-9:00): freshly-squeezed orange juice and coffee with skimmed milk, an egg white omelette with dried fruit/nuts, and a buffet made up of yogurt, toast, turkey cold-cuts, low-fat cheese, plus four choices of fresh fruit.

Lunch (13:30-14:00): various salads with asparagus and tuna, water, fruit, and a bottle of red wine split between every four players. The main course will be a choice of pasta, rice, lasagne, vegetable cream soup, fish, beef or chicken.

Snack (17:30): a fruit salad.

Dinner (21:30-22:00): water, fruit plus another bottle of wine divided between four. This time the choice is between a variety of salads, pasta, rice, lasagne, creamed vegetable soup, fish and chicken. No red meat is allowed at dinner.

Match days

Breakfast (8:30-9:00): as training days.

Lunch (11:30-12:00 on June 16, 13:30-14:00 on June 21 and June 25): various salads with asparagus and tuna, water, fruit, and a bottle of wine split between four players. Then there is a choice between spaghetti, creamed vegetable soup, potato puree or chicken breast.

Dinner (21:30-22:00 on June 16, 23:30-00:00 on June 21 and June 25): water, fruit and a bottle of wine between every four players. Then the choice between jamón serrano, pork chop, Spanish tortilla, sirloin steak and four types of pastas with sauce.

The seating plan frequently, but not always, puts at one table Alonso, Ramos, Reina, Casillas, Torres, Arbeloa, Albiol, Navas, Mata, Marchena and Silva. Another houses Xavi, Iniesta, Valdés, Javi Martínez, Capdevila, Fàbregas, Piqué, Puyol, Llorente, Villa, Pedro and Busquets. There is another for all the coaching and fitness staff, another for the doctors and the physios.

When red meat is served, it is in very small portions (no more than 100g), there is no sugar involved anywhere, no onions in the dishes on match day, always skimmed milk and players are always encouraged to opt for fish ahead of meat. Pepe Reina needs persuading.

Chef Arbizú began his visits to South African fish markets a year ahead of the tournament and has found it to be the most abundant, tasty fish assortment he has seen in his professional life.

> **Meanwhile...**
> *Nicolas Anelka is sent home in the wake of his outburst. Le Sulk presumably slams the door on his way out muttering about how he didn't want to play anyway and that it is a stupid World Cup. The Dutch have much less to moan about, reaching the last 16 with a narrow win over Japan.*

— Day 10.
— June 20, 2010. Potchefstroom

Andrés Iniesta is not the only one who has got here on a wing and a prayer. Fernando Torres, winning goalscorer in Spain's last final, has had to fight like a tiger to be in South Africa.

The problem erupted a handful of days after Iniesta's tearful breakdown on a Catalan playing field during Barça training, and it was to the *Ciudad Condal*, Barcelona, that Torres, a born and bred *Madrileño*, turned for solutions.

A meniscus problem in his right knee had not been properly sorted during a first operation so, on April 19, Dr Ramón Cugat, Spain's finest sports surgeon, attempted restorative arthroscopic surgery. On April 8, he had scored twice in Liverpool's Europa League 4-1 demolition of Benfica. The aggregate score was 5-3 because of two Óscar Cardozo penalties slammed past Pepe Reina in the first leg. Those penalties will play a part in this story.

Torres was in pain almost as soon as the match kicked off but remained on the pitch to seal the win which put Liverpool in a European semi-final.

On Monday, April 12, Torres attended Cugat's surgery for exploratory scans. Then on Friday 16, secondary scans in England finally showed the meniscus damage clearly; instant action was required if Torres was to stand any chance of making it to South Africa. Liverpool approved Cugat for the operation, but there was a stroppy Icelandic volcano, the air was full of ash and flights were suspended. A daring solution was improvised.

Torres was driven from Liverpool, down through England; he took the Eurostar to France and was then chauffeured the length of France and down into Catalonia to be present at Cugat's clinic first thing Monday morning.

Fernando Torres: "It was a really tough journey by road from Liverpool to Catalonia, but it was the only way.

"I guess the whole thing was a bit of an adventure and at least we had a pit stop for a sleep just outside Paris. But I was exhausted by the time we hit Barcelona on Sunday night.

"This knee problem resurfaced against Benfica in the second minute so I played the rest of the match with the injury. If I'd been thinking solely about Spain and the World Cup I'd have asked to come off. I wanted to get to the Europa League final with Liverpool, that was top priority."

I'm not awarding Torres a Purple Heart for valour, but I do think those who have attacked him over this issue should understand the choices he made, that he should have had his meniscus problem spotted and sorted months earlier, that he put his knee on the line for Liverpool, not Spain, and that it came at some significant cost to him.

The day is not without amusement as Raúl Albiol tells me that he would like to find, and deal with, whoever wrote a front-page article suggesting Iker Casillas let the goal in against Switzerland because his girlfriend, Carbonero, and her cameraman had a pitch-side position to the right of his goalmouth in the first half. The goal came after half-time. And it was The Times.

Raúl Albiol: "It is total crap that people are trying to drag Iker Casillas into some stupid row about his girlfriend being a TV reporter here at the World Cup. He is a great professional, our captain and one of the best keepers in the world. It's hard to put up with hearing the nonsense being spoken about him."

Fernando Torres: "Our bad day, our bad game has gone, but any rival can complicate things. We knew that from the USA defeat last year in the Confederations Cup. What's important is that we stay true to our philosophy and our style, not drive ourselves mad and start making weird choices in what we do.

"I don't know [if I'm ready to play] but I've worked hard with my team-mates, little by little forgetting the injury, training at the same level as the squad and it is up to the coach and whatever he decides will be perfect with me."

Torres will play, but far away from the microphones and the spotlights, something much more important is happening. The Spain physio Raúl Martínez has picked up the baton from Emili Ricart, the author of Iniesta's in-flight entertainment.

After his injury in the first game, Iniesta would admit he "felt all the ghosts of his dreadful year re-surfacing". Beyond physical recuperation, Martínez has been trying to work on the midfielder's psychology. The two have shared long conversations and Martínez has reinforced only positive sentiments. For whatever reason the cogs suddenly fit together and Iniesta tells the physio that despite having to sit the Honduras match out, his mind is at rest. Before the second Group H match he goes to sleep without fear that his body is going to let him down. Instead he is convinced that if his team-mates do their job and defeat Honduras, he is now through the worst and ready to influence matters.

By the middle of the day, the bus is on the road. They lay their heads down in five-star luxury in Sandton, but they will play in the Rainbow Nation's rugby stadium: Ellis Park.

Meanwhile...

The decision to send Nicolas Anelka home has the consequence of making Raymond Domenech look like the outcast – the France squad refuse to attend a training session, instead sending a statement articulating their opposition to the French federation. It is a message which their coach is then obliged to read out to the gathering media.

— **Day 11.**
— *June 21, 2010. Ellis Park Stadium, Johannesburg*
   Spain v Honduras
Uno y dos y tres ... ganar y ganar y ganar!

A year after this is all over, Iker Casillas will confess: "I had never in my life felt so nervous as against Honduras."

There are two changes to the team which started against Switzerland. Jesús Navas keeps his place at the cost of the man he replaced in Durban and his future team-mate at Manchester City, David Silva. The enforced absence of Iniesta allows Torres back in the starting XI, David Villa moves wide left and the Liverpool man is the single striker in the 4-2-3-1 formation. Crucially, as far as the players are concerned, Del Bosque has been true to his principles, true to his word and true to them. No scapegoats.

Before kick-off, Del Bosque's manner doesn't betray nerves. He doesn't reach for hyperbole, nor does he appear tense. As he talks to the players in the dressing room they don't even cluster around him; one or two are wandering about; in nervous tension, a ball is bounced. Del Bosque believes that the good work is done in the pre match-day team briefing. The dressing room, largely, is for getting changed in. Hence the 69-second team talk in Durban. Again, he'll underline key points but it will be brief, specific and clear.

"Come on ... what we need today is more mobility please. The guy who has the ball needs to have passing options not only beside him but behind him and ahead of him too. That's not just in midfield but defence and attack as well.

"Nobody needs to have the idea in his head that we are here to thrash this lot and put a huge number of goals past them. What we have to do is win. Nothing else. We must win.

"For that reason it's important to be aware of our defensive duties because we'll have to defend, too.

"I'm not asking more or less than you gave the other day. This time we'll finish our chances, but that's all I ask."

Xabi Alonso appeals for: *"Corazones y cabezas por favor!"* Hearts *and* minds, please!

They chant their chant.

It turns out to be a 6-0 game cleverly disguised as a 2-0 win. Before long, Honduras have been excused two penalties, one for handball, the other for a cynical shove in the back on Sergio Ramos at a corner, Villa has hit the bar and a crisp Torres performance has yielded two more goal-chances.

Villa's opening goal is a thing of beauty and a joy forever. Piqué's cross-field pass is chested down by *El Guaje* on the extreme left side of the pitch. He starts off with that hunched-back, scuttling run of his. When faced by Sergio Mendoza and Amado Guevara, Villa takes on the two big defenders like gates on a giant slalom, cutting across Mendoza then changing angles to move between the two men in a blur of red. Villa has made 20 yards, but he is still isolated at the keeper's right-hand edge of the penalty box. Osman Chávez makes a move towards the onrushing striker but then stops, allowing Villa to swerve to his right and then throw himself full length as the studs of his left boot give way underneath him. He levers his right leg into a sublime contact which curves the ball into the keeper's top right-hand corner, via a tiny deviation off the tip of one glove.

For the second goal, Villa's movement as the ball is sprayed out wide to

Navas on the right is exemplary. As everyone follows play towards the Honduras goal, Villa slams on the brakes. It is like a giant has lifted the entire pitch at the other end and tipped everyone towards the far goal, but Villa has gravity boots and he is anchored to the place he wants to be. Navas sees him, cuts the ball back diagonally and Villa's shot takes a flutter off Chávez's knee on its way in.

Emilio Izaguirre commits a penalty foul on Navas – Villa misses the spot-kick, an error his dad will phone to tease him about later.

There is also personal significance to the miss. Villa's two goals put him on five in World Cup finals, equal with Raúl, Hierro, Fernando Morientes and Emilio Butragueño as *La Roja's* all-time top scorer in the tournament and within five of equalling Raúl's all-time Spain record.

There's more drama before the end. Fàbregas is clean through and his effort is cleared off the line (bravo Chávez!), Ramos shoots narrowly past a post and the ultimate effect is that while Spain are out of jail and their fate is mostly in their own hands, they have by no means extracted all the goodness from the game.

Del Bosque's face, as his troops troop off, is thunderous. Puyol storms into the dressing room and hurls his shirt against the wall in fury. He thinks they have squandered a major chance to rule the group via goal difference if the results don't favour them after match three. Chile have beaten Switzerland 1-0 in Port Elizabeth to register six points and this, despite the relief, feels like an opportunity let slip.

Post-match, in the press conference, Del Bosque is pretty blunt: "I don't think that we've had a good game. Yes, we created a lot of goalscoring situations and we ought to have won by more goals, but I'm not totally happy – once again our finishing was off. What's more, I felt that we were too open and very vulnerable in the last half hour, and if we play like that against Chile we could be made to suffer."

Spain 2 Honduras 0

Spain: Casillas, Ramos (Arbeloa 77), Puyol, Piqué, Capdevila; Alonso, Busquets; Navas, Xavi (Fàbregas 66), Villa; Torres (Mata 70)
Goals: Villa 17, 51

Honduras: Valladares; Mendoza, Chávez, Figueroa, Izaguirre; W Palacios, Guevara; Turcios (Nunez 63), Martínez, Espinoza (Welcome 46); Suazo (J Palacios 84)

> **Meanwhile...**
> *An uneasy truce is agreed within the France squad as the players return to*
> *training. In Cape Town, Portugal put seven goals past North Korea, while*
> *South Africa-born Mark González scores on home turf for Chile in a win*
> *over Switzerland.*

— Day 12.
— June 22, 2010. Potchefstroom

Back at base Del Bosque still has things to say. Out of generosity, on what should be a quiet, contemplative morning for him, he speaks to all the Spanish media who have travelled to South Africa without having bought broadcast rights for the games or without a guarantee that they will get match accreditations to report from the stadia. It is typical of the Spain manager to be just as accommodating after a victory, which would have bought him private time, as after a defeat which required deflecting. Perhaps more stinging words from Luis Aragonés helped propel him forward. *El Sabio de Hortaleza* comments, post-match, for Al Jazeera: "Performing like this they won't get far. I didn't like it much. Xavi is being played out of position."

"We can't live on past achievements," is the nearest Del Bosque gets to a retort. In private, he is totally sanguine about what his predecessor is saying, as are his players.

Post-tournament, one or two senior players who are alumni of the class of Euro 2008 will reveal that they take time to think about what Aragonés is saying: not promoting his words over those of Del Bosque, choosing, instead, to not be stung by his criticisms but to examine them. Xavi and Torres believe that it is healthy to read between the lines rather than take Aragonés' criticism solely at face value. They reckon their old maestro is simply incentivising them from afar. Whether they are right or wrong, it is a positive way to treat the experience. *Pensamientos positivos*, as a certain grumpy old man used to growl.

Meanwhile, Busquets receives the most emphatic public support from his coach. Del Bosque tells his impromptu audience: "If I came back as a footballer once again I'd prefer to be [like] Sergio Busquets. He does everything, he's continually at the disposition of the rest of the team; he's a generous player, he just gives everything defensively and what's more he's usually the first to re-start our forward movements. When *Busi* is on form, the quality of our football is more fluid, quicker." It is a massive compliment given what a talented, intelligent and elegant midfielder Del Bosque was in his own day.

Once again, every player who has started against Honduras has the night off. Casillas, as before, is there of his own volition trying to out-work everyone else.

It is cold, dark, there is a healthy crowd in the bleachers and the session is good to watch. Again there is a heavy premium put on sharpness, quick reflexes, finishing chances, very fast, small-sided games in reduced areas. What stands out is that in the mini-match at the end of the session, Iniesta scores three times and gives four goal assists.

Something is happening.

> **Meanwhile...**
> *The hosts are knocked out but are not disgraced, winning 2-1 against France in their final fixture. It is a result which leaves Les Bleus bottom of Group A and will eventually cost Domenech his job. Argentina seem to have little time for such drama, taking maximum points from Group B with a win over Greece.*

— Day 13.
— *June 23, 2010. Potchefstroom*
Life and work around Potch is taking on a clear rhythm.

Players who have girlfriends or wives around are given a few hours off to go see them. A group of six players nip down the central plaza to an Italian restaurant (most of the Barça contingent plus Javi Martínez). Torres goes for a wander and causes one or two heart flutters when he gets back to the army check point to discover that he does not know where his accreditation is. Credit to the Bafana Bafana supporting soldier, he knows precisely who *El Niño* is but just won't budge an inch until someone from the federation comes out of the accommodation building and walks over to the security point to 'okay' Torres.

Meanwhile, Iniesta wanders downtown to the Mooi Rivier mall to idle around the CD library of the big audio-visual store. Unmolested, happy buying music, tranquil again.

If this is a slightly more relaxed day, it remains clear that excitement, or tension at least, is building back home. The Honduras game was the third-highest television audience for a football match in Spanish history (behind the semi-final and final of Euro 2008).

Ramos misses training because of rib damage; Torres works on, pain-free at least but not yet in the groove; Iniesta's tempo is increasing. He's going to make it.

And there is humour, albeit cruel and dark. During Monday's win, Piqué has accidentally been wounded again, this time by Izaguirre's flying boot. To the stitches over his right eye from the injury sustained as Switzerland scored, the defender adds three more, around his mouth and nose. I see him briefly before training and he mutters something about "feeling like Frankenstein".

On the pitch he is ripped to shreds by merciless team-mates. The back of his head is slapped, he is booted in the seat of his pants, his ear is pinged and he is mocked relentlessly. The team has won, the boys are in robust mood and Piqué's double wound on his pretty-boy face means they are going to have great fun tormenting the hell out of him this evening.

After training there is the half-hour evening meal and then, with no media around, the squad decides to celebrate San Juan.

Spain always has a big festival on June 23 for the summer solstice. Traditionally, there are fireworks and a bonfire. Exploding rockets over the Spain training camp in an area which is still tinder dry might not be *quite* the way forward, but a bonfire is built in the middle of the concrete courtyard, players and staff gather round it and when it has died down a little some of them, including Mata and Capdevila, take running jumps over the fire, as is traditional.

In fact, the whole idea has been Capdevila's. San Juan is San Joan in Catalonia, so this is his Saint's day. It is an important date to celebrate and one more excuse to get the squad together, to remind them of home, to pay respect to tradition – to bond. Perhaps it's emerging that I hold Capdevila in the highest affection. A sturdy footballer and ... a bit nuts. I have no higher praise. Back in Euro 2008 he awarded the same importance to San Juan but, in Neustift, it was raining. In his room he piled up some newspapers in a metal wastepaper basket, set it all on fire and jumped over it.

Later that night, there is another cricket club summit, called by Hierro this time and including Xavi, Casillas, Torres, Alonso and Marchena. Del Bosque, in attempting to lift the tension, has told the squad: "If we end up going home I'll take all the blame and all the pressure, don't worry about the reaction. Just go out and play with smiles on your faces."

It is well-meant but it jars with one or two of them. In this meeting, the players agree that it will be a complete disaster if they are knocked out. Not because of how much abuse they will get, but because this is the best squad

Spain has ever had. Player by player, they swear that they will not, under *any* circumstances, let this golden generation go to waste.

After defeat by Switzerland, the injury and form problems surrounding Iniesta and Torres and the criticism from Aragonés, momentum is beginning to swing.

Iniesta is noticeably happier and more sprightly. Torres' improvement is gradual, but it is there.

Now it emerges from FIFA that Villa is not to be banned for the Group H decider against Chile. Just before half-time at Ellis Park, Izaguirre had trod his studs onto Villa's toe in search of a reaction. The Asturian gave the defender an open-handed clip on the face. Some referees would certainly have sent him off. However, Yuichi Nishimura doesn't see it nor does he put it in his report. Case closed.

"It was an instinctive thing, I'm not proud – I'm going try to maintain better control if I'm provoked in future," Villa reflects.

From their first day with the federation, Spain's players are taught that it is a sin to be sent off. It is a betrayal of one's team-mates; it decreases the chances of success; it may well mean another colleague takes and keeps your place in the team. It is a commandment: Thou Shalt Not Be Sent Off. Villa has been lucky.

Meanwhile...
Otto Rehhagel resigns as coach of Greece following their elimination. It's the kind of decision which Capello is able to put off for another few days after his England side edge through following a narrow 1-0 win over Slovenia. The result sets up a last-16 fixture against Germany, whose win over Ghana doesn't prevent the Africans from finishing second in Group D.

— Day 14.
— June 24, 2010. Potchefstroom

Eleven o'clock, tick tock. Everyone is present and correct on the Potch pitch, which is strange because this is what tournament organisers now like to call MD-1 (Match Day minus one day). Thank the lord, too, because I'd been sure for years that the expression 'the day before the match' was causing malnutrition, illiteracy, religious intolerance and some cases of irritable bowel syndrome. Sorted now though.

La Roja work out locally because the Loftus Versfeld stadium in Pretoria has just hosted USA vs Algeria and the organising committee is concerned that if both teams train on the pitch tonight, it will not be in good condition for the Group H decider tomorrow.

The session starts with stretches, of course, *rondos*, sprints and ends with a full match, albeit only 15 minutes each way and on a three-quarters-sized pitch. Midway through, Del Bosque gathers his troops for a short briefing in the centre circle. He underlines some points made last night in the video analysis of Chile, concepts he wants to see in this mini-match and then repeated tomorrow at Loftus Versfeld.

For this short trip Spain will risk the bus on the N12. The real reason is that if things go against them then the next travel itinerary will be to Oliver Tambo Airport and onwards to Madrid. They won't need a flight back to Potch.

At Loftus there is another lucky break. While the pitch shows evidence of the shredding it took while the USA assured themselves of Group C victory, ahead of England, it is neither rock-hard nor is the grass long. These are two plus points for the Spaniards.

Del Bosque talks to what is a particularly large and internationally assorted media throng; the newbies who have arrived for this match have the feel of buzzards and vultures. Spain, the carrion.

Meanwhile, I grab Sergio Ramos and ask him what he was up to the other night against Honduras. His performance was not 100% disciplined and restrained and thus, perhaps, not quite what Del Bosque ordered, but it was thrilling to watch. He ran a trench into the right touchline, nearly scoring on three occasions.

"Yeah, I wanted to score and dedicate it to someone [female] whom I promised to get a goal for in this World Cup. I didn't score in Germany four years ago so I promised that over here I'd do a special celebration for her. Hopefully I can fulfil my promise."

Ramos lives with a swagger, a footballing Errol Flynn. He played with a pain-killing injection at Ellis Park, his ribs flaring with each swashbuckling run.

Sergio Ramos: "I'm delighted to be known as someone who hungers for the big games, the pressure games. Against Chile it will be a massive match, full of emotion. We know from experience that there are masses of people watching at home desperate for us to do well. I like to feel that they can identify with my pride in playing for Spain and my love for the national team jersey. I want it to show."

Meanwhile...
Italy's crown slips; the defending champions lose to Slovakia and finish bottom of Group F. Tata Martino's Paraguay lead it after a draw with New Zealand. Holland's coach Bert van Marwijk dismisses his side's performance in a win over Cameroon as "patchy". Paul Le Guen is even less happy and resigns as coach of the African side.

— **Day 15.**
— *June 25, 2010. Loftus Versfeld stadium, Pretoria*
 Chile v Spain
Uno y dos y tres ... ganar y ganar y ganar!

If this is an indication of what is to follow, it is going to be a bad night. There are about 90 minutes until kick-off, my phone is ringing off the hook and Manolo el del Bombo, Spain's celebrity superfan, is stuck outside the stadium with a combination of lackadaisical stewards and dopey local cops refusing to let him in because of his famous huge drum. He implores me: *"Amigo ... amigo ... help me amigo ... no me dejan entrar."*

Manolo the drummer is a lovely man-child, but he's no Keith Moon. His adult life has been dedicated to running his bar just outside Valencia's Mestalla stadium and travelling everywhere with Spain. Him and his big, black Basque-style Txapela hat. And his drum. Spain's one-man barmy army.

This is his seventh World Cup in a row. This tournament he has been dressed in a phenomenal red and yellow quartered suit and the federation have really looked after him, but now he is unchaperoned, stuck and swamped by fans. It is chaos.

Eventually, we get Manolo in and I don't think South African rugby or Ellis Park will really miss the Springbok training kit I liberate to bribe the guy who has been blocking Spain's vital drummer.

I bet the Spanish team were glad to see him there, to hear his infernal drum and to have him cajoling *La Roja's* fans into song, because in the hours before this match, every one of them confronted the fear that this might not be their night and their World Cup could be over. They all know that it will be regarded as a calamitous failure should the champions of Europe fail to get out of their group. They shirk away from the thought of the rabid nation that would await their early return. But their real fear is that of letting themselves down. They know

King Juan Carlos and Queen Sofia congratulate Aragonés after the final in 2008, although the Spain coach has a particular form of reward in mind. He had once joked with Juan Carlos about receiving a stipend from the royal family: 'Every time we meet I ask him how the financial idea is going. He always tells me to keep at it.'
Photo: Carmelo Rubio/AP

When asked if he would remain in post after the 2008 finals, Aragonés compared himself to milk with a sell-by date. The response of his players as they celebrated qualification at a hotel disco was to toss their coach into the air with the chant: 'This milk will never go off!' It was a ritual repeated after the final in Vienna.
Photo: Michael Probst/AP

Pepe Reina has acted as the master of ceremonies for each of Spain's tournament wins, whipping supporters into a frenzy as he introduces each member of the squad. He also took the lead as the squad carried the celebrations from the dressing room onto the flight out of Vienna in 2008.
Photos: Offside/Marca

The swimming pool at Spain's training base in South Africa. The jet-heeled Jesús Navas bet his team-mates he could run across the tarpaulin without getting wet. He won.
Photo: Offside/Marca

Spain convert space to suit their needs, adapting spartan surroundings to accommodate their equipment. In South Africa, that meant the bathroom became the boot room.
Photo: Offside/Marca

Spain play with intensity but training is something which can be enjoyed; Xavi and Iniesta play around to the amusement of their coach.
Photo: Offside/Marca

Carles Puyol had resigned himself to pulling out of the World Cup semi-final against Germany but intensive treatment in the 24 hours before kick-off left him fit enough to score the winning goal.
Photo: Offside/Marca

The World Cup final saw Holland betray their 'total football' heritage with a violently oppressive gameplan. Andrés Iniesta was pursued by his personal nemesis, Marc van Bommel, while Nigel de Jong's assault on Xabi Alonso became one of the tournament's most enduring images.
Photos: PA/Getty

The 2010 World Cup final brings Iker Casillas and Arjen Robben face to face; the Dutch forward one-on-one and certain to score, but for a quite unbelievable save by Casillas. 'An eternal moment,' the Spain goalkeeper told the author.
Photo: AP

Andrés Iniesta celebrates his World Cup-winning goal by paying tribute to Dani Jarque, his former team-mate who died in August 2009. At their most triumphant moments, many of the Spain players remember absent friends.

Photo: Martin Meissner/AP

David Villa missed the Euro 2008 final and all of Euro 2012 due to injuries, but started the final of the World Cup. He won the Golden Boot as top goalscorer at Euro 2008 and was joint top in South Africa.
Photo: Mike Egerton/EMPICS Sport

they are potential winners here. Fear crackles everywhere.

One senior player, whose identity I will preserve, turns to another en route to the match and tells his team-mate: "I'm crapping myself." His colleague is shocked. "The silence on the bus ride from the hotel to the stadium was terrible," Del Bosque will subsequently recall.

David Villa: "The hours before that game were the most nervous I can recall since I joined the national side."

Gerard Piqué: "There was so much silence, everyone was lost in their own world, thinking about what they could do to help the team get through."

While the guys are getting changed Del Bosque, fearful of transmitting his own tension, wanders about the special warm-up room which is needed when a dressing room is holding 15 sizeable rugby players rather than 11 footballers. Listlessly, he kicks a loose ball around.

Xavi: "You could see it on everyone's faces, this was an extraordinary tension." Either this is a sign that the players know they still are not firing on all cylinders and so are vulnerable, or that there is a deep, fearful determination that this will not, under any circumstances, be the day they follow the two finalists of the last World Cup, France and Italy, home in abject ignominy. Only when they have been out to warm up, sampled the boisterous atmosphere, let the cold, altitude-affected night air sting their nostrils, is the cloak of tension thrown off.

Del Bosque's team talk is shorter than a drunken Scotsman's temper.

"Okay, I say this every day but more than ever now, don't get suckered into making mistakes. And let's be united out there. If there's one guy with the ball there must be two around him. And just one detail. There are many, many lads back home for whom you are examples. Let's go out there and just do this for them."

Thirteen seconds. Everyone clusters and bows down into the huddle.

One voice: *"Uno y dos y tres."*
Every voice: *"Ganar y ganar y ganar!"*

Del Bosque's tactic is to surf on the slight buzz from the warm up, not to slow them down, to remind them that there is a world outside this bubble, and to go do their thing.

He heads out to the tunnel and for a split second Xavi and Casillas want their voices to be heard. They want the mood from the Potchefstroom cricket clubhouse 48 hours ago to be evoked. The captains want to crank it up, not protect any delicate nerves.

*"Never mind what we won two years ago, never mind going home with honour, never mind playing football with a smile on our face. This is life or death, this is the match of all our careers. We **must** win."*

Whatever else is said about Marcelo Bielsa's Chile, and I am neither a particular fan of his, nor impressed by what they do that night, they start the game like there are 14 of them on the pitch. There is double-marking on Sergio Ramos and Joan Capdevila if they attempt to burst up the wing. If a Spaniard turns in midfield there are two tackles to avoid before he can look up. More, they combine very quickly to counter and it is an asphyxiating match for the European champions.

Until, that is, a sublime intervention from David Villa, the man who escaped a ban to play in this game.

Chile playmaker Jorge Valdívia, talented but sloppy, is robbed by Xabi Alonso, deep in Spain's half and with hardly any effort. Worse for Chile, Gary Medel, a midfielder who is playing centre-back tonight, fed Valdívia and has continued his run in search of a return pass. Chile are exposed and Alonso sees it instantly. He clips a long pass to Fernando Torres and, seeing *El Niño* is going to win his race with Gonzalo Jara, goalkeeper Claudio Bravo decides to sprint out to rescue his defender. Well outside his area, Bravo slides into a powderpuff clearance, but Villa has anticipated what is unfolding. He is on the run down the left wing and as the ball drops to him 40 metres out he uses his left foot to crack a volley, while he's in full-flight. The ball arcs beautifully from left to right, bounces just once and curls into the far panel of the empty net.

It is one of the goals of his life and he scores it with his left boot, which carries the name of his kids, Zaida and Olaya, the number of his shirt (7), the Spanish flag plus a little logo to signify his marriage to Patricia.

Thirteen minutes later, Chile are trying to begin a move down their left, but the ball played to the full-back Jara is loose and Iniesta is on it. He intercepts, bursts forward, feeds a pass to Torres on his right and the Liverpool striker puts a perfect service back into the midfielder's path. As Iniesta glides on to it he sees Villa out to the left of the penalty area and fizzes the pass; Chile's defenders commit the cardinal sin of following the ball. Villa opens his body and returns the ball into Iniesta's now clear path and the midfielder uses his instep to cushion a volley into the far panel of Bravo's net. Unusually for Iniesta, he lets off steam, booting over the corner flag. Some of the pain of the last year is evaporating.

On the bus to the match, sitting next to his great pal Víctor Valdés (the first guy to look after him having arrived as a tearful, scared 12-year-old at FC Barcelona's academy), he had predicted: "I'm going to score tonight and I'm going to dedicate it to you."

While the players are celebrating, the Mexican referee is across the pitch sending off Chile's Marco Estrada. During the move, once Torres had fed Iniesta, the striker continued his run, looking for a back-post cross, but Estrada clipped his ankle and Torres went flying. It looked like an inadvertent error. Moreover, it was off the ball and during the move Spain scored. Nevertheless Señor Marco Rodríguez won't budge on his decision, the referee's second red card of the tournament stands.

Spain are 2-0 up and they are playing 10 men. When they concede a deflected goal within two minutes of the start of the second half, it simply makes things unnecessarily uncomfortable. Then, with about 15 minutes left, Marcelo Bielsa starts gesticulating to his team: *'This will do!'* Chile are told to defend at 2-1 down, and, although it is horrible to watch, that is what they do. For what feels an interminable time ("the most placid 15 minutes of our tournament" Del Bosque later calls it) Chile not only retreat behind the halfway line but a good 15 yards inside their own half. If Spain do not attempt to cross halfway, Chile simply let them have the ball for as long as they wish. They refuse to compete.

Previous Group H results mean that Switzerland, drawing 0-0 with Honduras at that moment, will not only have to win but to score two unanswered goals to qualify. However, if Switzerland score once, win 1-0 and Chile concede a third goal, then Chile are out. A far more threatening and more likely scenario.

Captain Casillas tells his defence that if Chile don't want to venture past the halfway line then Spain will remain group winners: there is an impromptu concord. Switzerland are effectively conspired against and it makes an unedifying, if understandable, spectacle.

So dedicated to winning a toe-to-toe contest for Group H leadership is Del Bosque that he has apparently never considered this scenario. When it dawns on him that Bielsa's team are no longer competing, he asks his assistant, Toni Grande: "What are they doing?"

Grande has done his arithmetic and tells his old friend: "They are through –

they don't want to risk conceding." Prior to that 15-minute *détente*, Del Bosque tells reporters: "Chile played with the conviction of kamikazes."

We are left with the facts that:

1) Spain have avoided Brazil: they'll face Portugal in Cape Town in the last 16.

2) Spain are the first side since 1986 not to have a player booked in the group matches.

3) David Villa now has Spain's all-time scoring record for World Cup finals.

4) Iniesta is man of the match and has scored his first goal for Spain in nearly two years.

5) Most importantly, Piqué tells everyone, it is his first game this tournament without needing stitches.

When they all get back to Potch in the early hours of the morning it is to find that a generator has broken down and there is no central heating. Several of the squad sleep in their quilted anoraks.

It's been emotional, but Spain are in the last 16.

Chile 1 Spain 2

Chile: Bravo, Isla, Medel, Ponce, Jara, Vidal, Estrada, M González (Millar 46), Valdívia (Parades 46), Sánchez (Orellana 65), Beausejour
Goal: Millar 47

Spain: Casillas, Ramos, Piqué, Puyol, Capdevila, Alonso (Martínez 73), Busquets, Iniesta, Xavi, Villa, Torres (Fàbregas 55)
Goals: Villa 24, Iniesta 37

> **Meanwhile…**
> *A goalless draw with Portugal is an affront to Brazil coach Dunga, who accuses the European team of adopting "negative tactics". Such criticism is the sum of seven yellow cards, a number of cynical tackles and a great deal of booing from supporters by full-time.*

— **Day 16.**
— *June 26, 2010. Potchefstroom*

The people of Potch have died and gone to heaven. Spain have qualified, the media pack are going to stay and spend money for at least a few more days, NW

University continues to receive a worldwide profile and the downtown mall is a footballing Hollywood.

There is a traffic jam of off-duty Spain stars in eateries. In one, Del Bosque is having dinner with his wife Trini and their children Vicente, Gemma and Álvaro, when they see Xabi Alonso, Fernando Torres, Raúl Albiol, Juan Mata and Sergio Ramos walking through the door. The Del Bosque kids insist on getting their pictures taken with the stars. Dad is just dad, but Xabi ... well, he's *Xabi*.

Again, only Casillas refuses to take the evening off.

The night holds particular significance for three peripheral men, two of whom will have a pivotal influence on *La Roja's* progress in the tournament.

Training is open and during the practice match there is a slight tangle of bodies. Fernando Llorente leans into Albiol in order to get his telescopic leg into a challenge. The defender falls in the least dramatic manner imaginable, but one of his studs has caught in the turf and Albiol is in trouble. He is stretchered from the pitch and taken to hospital. Llorente, the newbie, looks shell-shocked.

The match finishes and this time there is an improvised mixed zone round the back of the changing rooms. The players must pass the media on the way to their meal and the bedrooms, but at a distance of about 15 metres. The Spanish reporters are desperate to get Llorente's side of the story, but when he eventually emerges from the dressing room he has a bodyguard. Pepe Reina has one of his arms around Llorente's shoulder and is walking him along. Reporters petition the striker for an interview, but the response comes from the Liverpool goalkeeper: "Fernando has got his tea waiting lads and then I'm going to beat him at table tennis – can't stop, sorry."

It is another example of the tournament mentality central to this team's success.

On the positive side, word seeps out that the players have been promised a night out if they defeat Portugal. In Potch there has been time for families and girlfriends, CD shopping and the odd lunch down in the centre of the city.

If they get through, they're gonna hit the town.

Meanwhile...

FIFA announce an intention to post additional officials behind the goals to help with controversial incidents. The first games in the round of 16 do not provide working examples – Luis Suárez scores twice as Uruguay beat South Korea, while Asamoah Gyan is the extra-time hero as Ghana upset USA.

— Day 17.

— June 27, 2010. Potchefstroom

It turns out to be a very Carles Puyol day.

As at Euro 2008, the Barça captain is in charge of the sweepstake. Players and staff ante-up before the tournament starts. In play are the winners of each group, the identity of the top scorer ... which teams will be eliminated. Puyol is a good administrator and there's a tidy sum to be won. Every morning, players are presented with a photocopied sheet of the previous day's scores and scorers, and where that leaves everyone in the running for the total prize-pot.

There is much less free time between ties as the tournament enters the knockout phase, so the sweepstake ends after the group stage. Joint winners Mata and Piqué are going to share the loot.

More significantly, there's a strong rumour that Puyol has had a long chat with Fernando Hierro, once his implacable opponent for Real Madrid in La Liga's *Clasico* matches but now the Spanish federation's technical director. Puyol has told Hierro that he is going to retire from international football after the World Cup because his body is beginning to feel the strain of the extraordinary demands he has put on it during good times and bad for club and country. There is to be no announcement. Both Hierro and Del Bosque entreat him to think long and hard about it.

With just over 48 hours to go to the match in Cape Town, all the evidence at training indicates that Fernando Torres is winning his battle to convince Del Bosque he should start against Portugal. So far, everything about the World Cup has been going right for *El Niño*, other than the inconvenient fact that the tournament has come along two or three weeks too early for optimum recuperation.

Wherever he goes he is treated like a pop star.

South Africa lost Benni McCarthy, their talented and talismanic striker, just before the World Cup and the nation's football supporters seem to have adopted Torres as their favourite No.9. Girls want to touch him, police want his autograph, security staff want a photo with him and if he walks around the town of Potchefstroom crowds of schoolkids, on holiday for a month, flock after him like gulls following a trawler. It's a spectacle.

Of all the Spain players, Torres is the most elegant about giving his time. Morning or night he'll stop, either in the blazing sun or the evening, when the temperatures dip below freezing, to stand and sign dozens of autographs. All with that trademark shy smile of his.

"As far as the World Cup being in South Africa, I have to admit it feels like being in my own country," he says. "I actually feel in debt to the people here. Like the incredible fans in Asia when I tour with Liverpool, they live thousands and thousands of miles from where I play, yet they treat you like you were the striker for their country. It's remarkable. What's more, it's often the people here who have the least in life who can give you the most important lessons about being happy."

It seems crazy, but many modern young sportsmen, particularly in Spain, know little or nothing about the struggle against racism here – or even what apartheid was. Torres is different.

"When I play any tournament I study the country and I have done that with South Africa. I know a bit about the old history, apartheid, Mandela's ANC struggle, and that means we have to show support and respect for the country's push to move on from those crimes.

"The World Cup gives this part of Africa an unmissable opportunity to feel integrated into the world and no longer a scapegoat, so it is our duty to make the tournament a success and joyful.

"The Chile match was an intense game but beautiful, the kind I am totally accustomed to in England. I've had 90 minutes across three games in nearly three months and you can train to your heart's content but it doesn't bring you that finesse or match sharpness required to score. The World Cup is unforgiving and won't wait for me, but without game time I won't find my form."

This, bluntly, is Del Bosque's big dilemma.

Meanwhile…
Those extra officials might have spotted Frank Lampard's shot against Germany crossing the line, but England are robbed of the goal, sparking huge controversy. That is then deposed by a consummate performance from the Germans, Thomas Müller scoring twice in a 4-1 win.

— **Day 18.**
— *June 28, 2010. Cape Town*
Spain have come full circle. Six years ago, *La Roja* won their first match at Euro 2004 but were eliminated from the group stage by their neighbours and tournament hosts, Portugal. It was a humiliating moment. Far more significant than Iberian vendettas is the fact that the defeat in 2004 ushered in

Luis Aragonés and the beginning of a cycle of success. Knocking Portugal out of the World Cup would continue a steep upward trajectory.

Cristiano Ronaldo, club-mate to Casillas, Alonso and Ramos, is the main threat.

Gerard Piqué: "Ronaldo helped me immensely when I first moved to Manchester. He spoke more English and the two of us could also communicate in Spanish. He was fantastic and we actually supported one another a bit. Television has a role in him being misinterpreted – Cristiano is very sure of himself, he always wants to be the leader on the pitch, so people who only see him on television can misjudge him as arrogant when he is not. As a person and a friend he is fantastic."

Piqué had won his last three match-ups against Ronaldo, without conceding a goal – in the 2009 Champions League final against Manchester United and two Clásicos following Ronaldo's world-record transfer to Real Madrid. "What's important is never to give him space, or time to think, to make sure you don't commit a foul and that you don't let him get running at you with the ball. Then he's next to unstoppable."

Portugal and Spain are accommodated within five minutes of each other. Ronaldo and company are in a lovely, vine covered, boutique hotel which specialises in fine wines. Spain are in another rudimentary tower block. It appears that so long as they can sleep, wash in hot water, eat together and be fairly sure nothing will be stolen from them, all is well.

Both sides are within a short walk of Newlands Cricket Ground, an entrancing place whose main stand reminds me of San Mames in Bilbao.

The climate is fresh and sea-moist. Spain like the damp, razor-cut playing surface at Green Point Stadium.

Meanwhile...
Arjen Robben is afforded his first start and torments Slovakia in a 2-1 win. Robben scores a wondrous opening goal after 18 minutes – skipping in from the wing to whip a shot high into the net. The Dutch are joined in the next round by Brazil after they ease past Chile.

— Day 19.
— June 29, 2010. Green Point Stadium, Cape Town
  Spain v Portugal – World Cup last 16
Uno y dos y tres … ganar y ganar y ganar!

We've read the runes correctly. Two years to the day since his goal won the final of Euro 2008, Torres starts. Del Bosque repeats the starting XI for the first time since getting to South Africa. Portugal, in contrast, have been shuffling the pack all tournament and today will have three midfielders, including Pepe, as a barrier in front of the four-man defence.

Largely they'll attempt to suck Spain in, to catch them on the break, and to exploit width – Fabio Coentrão is having a particularly influential tournament – in order to cross for the battering-ram Hugo Almeida and team-leader Ronaldo.

The statistics tell us to expect a 1-0 result. Portugal are undefeated in 19, victory here will give them their all-time record and they haven't conceded in 20 of their last 24 matches. Spain have won 29 of their last 31.

Green Point Stadium doesn't have the traditional British-style tunnel, where the two teams line up side by side. Instead, before they enter the pitch, the players line up in two corridors facing into the central tunnel and are kept there interminably by the television director. This helps Spain employ a tactic they've discussed as an attempt to unsettle Ronaldo. His Madrid team-mates don't salute or hug him as they would normally when facing a colleague on international duty. They are deliberately cold and, because of the stadium design, they are at a distance, too. They want him on edge to increase any tension he may be feeling at only having scored once thus far.

"To arms! To arms! Whether on land or at sea.

"To arms! To arms! Fight for our country!"

The Portuguese players roar their national anthem. All bar Ronaldo.

Spain keep the ball for the first 59 seconds, stringing passes together before Torres nearly finds the top corner of the net and Eduardo makes a fabulous save, the first of three in the opening 10 minutes.

The riposte is fun. Tiago's long-range shot is palmed up into the air and Almeida, like a refugee from 1950s English football, bundles Casillas into the net as the keeper just manages to rectify his slip. Nat Lofthouse would have approved.

Then when Alonso gives away a free-kick 40 yards out, it is Ronaldo time.

With all the intensity of Jonny Wilkinson he paces out his run, fixes Casillas with that speculative stare of his and lets fly. The ball is like a paper plane: it seems to have a life of its own, it takes crazy changes of direction and if it hits you full-on, it is going to sting. Casillas does well to parry the ball up into the air with both hands from belly-button height and Piqué heads clear.

However, as the second half unravels, Portugal are being pinned back and Del Bosque decides to dare. Llorente is to be unleashed.

Portugal's centre-backs, Bruno Alves and Ricardo Carvalho, have been mugging Torres and moving forward with the ball. Del Bosque wants them subjugated. A technically talented Navarran, who also happens to be 6ft 4ins and 14 stone, is just the ticket. Llorente comes on and the sky seems lower.

Since Euro 2008 these players have been telling us: "Tournaments are won by the lads on the bench." Firstly, every player is responsible for maintaining a fun, professional and supportive atmosphere. Secondly, those who will not start and may not even come on must work flat out to ensure the coach has the maximum choices and to keep the starters on their toes. Finally, and most obviously, substitutions can change matches.

Of the four knockout ties, three are going to be tilted in Spain's favour by those who begin the game on the bench.

There are 55 minutes on the clock when Llorente, in full training kit and sitting on the bench, is told he is going on. By the 58th minute he is in play and by 59 minutes and 57 seconds, after a 15-pass move, Ramos curves a cross which drops between Alves and Carvalho. Llorente throws himself full length, heads on target and forces another fine save from Eduardo.

Spain smell blood.

Llorente ties up two, sometimes three players, head-flicking another cross just inches wide, holding the ball up, pushing Portugal further back and Spain further forward.

David Villa: "I'd never seen such overwhelming power in my life. He just gobbled up both their centre-backs for the last half hour of the game, drawing them to him and opening up space for those of us around him. That's no mean feat because both of them are big guys, very physical in the one-on-one clashes, particularly Alves."

When the breakthrough goal comes it is down to the disruption Llorente has caused Portugal's defensive structure. The move starts when Piqué sends a marvellous 40-yard pass for Villa, wide left. The ball is moved to Alonso, who pings an audacious pass to Iniesta, despite the midfielder being covered. Iniesta turns and tries to nudge the ball into Llorente's feet. Carvalho stretches a leg to intervene, but there are now *six* Portugal defenders within a metre and a half of Llorente. It's ludicrous. Carvalho's intervention comes straight back to Iniesta and the Barça man can see that because even the right-back, Ricardo Costa, has been dragged to Llorente, Villa is now completely free on the left of the box. Iniesta nudges another pass, but Xavi is in the way.

> **Xavi**: "I'd seen Andrés's eyes, I knew that there must be a player behind me and that was who he was aiming for, so I didn't take a touch, I just flicked it on."

This is the half-touch football Xavi and company have been taught since they were kids at Barcelona's La Masia academy. Charly Rexach, legendary winger and Johan Cruyff's assistant, often roared at his apprentices, "just use a half-touch!" when he wanted the ball to circulate still more rapidly than their fabled one-touch football.

> **David Villa**: "I was going to hit it with my right because that's how the ball looked like it would arrive, but Xavi's touch sent it longer and on to my left."

When Iniesta passes, Villa is onside. When Xavi flicks the ball it's tight as hell – television pictures have him offside by centimetres, but the flag remains down.

Eduardo, who has a heroic match, blocks with his knees, but they must be made of marshmallow because the ball flops back down in front of Villa and he stabs it in, off the crossbar, this time with his right boot.

Villa races to the corner flag to celebrate and the second player to join him, after Iniesta, is a substitute, Reina, *El Guaje*'s great friend, whose bald head gets a good-luck kiss from Villa before every game *à la* Laurent Blanc and Fabien Barthéz at France 98.

Just after the goal comes an incident which shows Portugal's defence is at breaking point. Carvalho has Llorente by the scruff of the neck. He is tugging down so hard to prevent him getting free that the striker's shirt is too badly ripped for him to continue in it. It's a penalty action, but it goes unpunished. Llorente has to go to the sidelines to get changed and briefly it is 11 versus 10 in Portugal's favour.

I say briefly, but it isn't a great pit-stop. So figure-hugging is the Spain top and so enormous is Llorente's physique that a top surgeon from Cape Town's Medi-Travel International Hospital needs to use a scalpel and anaesthetic to safely remove it. The replacement shirt isn't *quite* his size, but with a little butter and a crowbar Llorente is levered back into his work clothes and battle re-commences.

Eduardo produces the save of the match, from rampaging Ramos again, Costa is sent off in the last minute for elbowing Capdevila and the Argentinian referee, Hector Baldassi, trots alongside Xavi while the match is still in play, asking him for his match jersey later on.

Ronaldo has not had a sniff in the match. Capdevila, in particular, has blunted him.

> **Joan Capdevila**: "It was probably my best game for Spain. I thought they had a brilliant side. Everyone that day, right down to the assistant coach, actually told me it was the best game of my life."

Torres was patently disappointed to be taken off so early but at the end, beaming, he makes a point of seeking out Llorente for a big embrace.

Eduardo is sat on the turf howling inconsolably. Casillas has been his direct opponent and so it's less remarkable that he takes time to console him. However, that Reina also commiserates with Eduardo, who has the pain of defeat despite a magnificent performance, is unusually generous.

As the whistle goes I'm at the mouth of the tunnel, called to stand in for the on-pitch international television interview with Del Bosque and Casillas if reporter Sara Carbonero does not make it round from her match position in time.

As each of the Portuguese pass by, the pain of defeat is more obvious. Some are crying, one kicks the wall, another is swearing at the top of his voice.

Spain 1 Portugal 0

Spain: Casillas, Ramos, Piqué, Puyol, Capdevila, Alonso (Marchena 90+3), Busquets, Iniesta, Xavi, Villa (Pedro 88), Torres (Llorente 58)
Goal: Villa 63

Portugal: Eduardo, Costa, Carvalho, Alves, Coentrão, Tiago, Pepe (Mendes 72), Meireles, Simão (Liedson 72), Almeida (Danny 58), Ronaldo

> *Meanwhile…*
> *An uninspiring tie between Paraguay and Japan ends with our first penalty*
> *shoot-out. Yūichi Komano hits the crossbar with his spot-kick and Óscar*
> *Cardozo rolls the South Americans into the next stage with a calm penalty of*
> *his own. Are Spain – his next opponents – watching?*

— **Day 20.**

— *June 30, 2010. Potchefstroom*

The first thing of note is that the 11am flight from Cape Town to Potchefstroom airbase is not missing anyone. There are no walking wounded, no cops or paparazzi in pursuit, no black eyes, nobody in jail.

Once business was wrapped up at Green Point Stadium and everybody got back to the Southern Sun hotel, those reporters staying in the team base were advised about which pub to avoid that night (a Cuban place just around the corner). We complied.

Del Bosque's players are required to be on the bus to the airport at 9am. Apart from that they can, within the law, do what they like. Beers are taken, some go to the casino, some see girlfriends or girlfriends-to-be, some make it to bed around 2am, some can handle a fuller shift. The reporters are on a scheduled flight to Jo'burg at 8am, meaning a 5.30am departure from the hotel and there are one or two future world champions who have just made it in. We exchange friendly greetings, some of which are roared at us from across the otherwise empty breakfast room. They are in good humour and happy to see us up and slogging when they have only just finished celebrating victory.

Back at Potch, everyone is free until 7pm, training is recuperative and there are now only three guys, Víctor Valdés, Pepe Reina and the injured Raúl Albiol, who have not had game time. However, Reina's moment is just around the corner.

Adidas are team sponsors, extremely adept at keeping both federation and players happy with their work and they would like to borrow the studio we have set up in a lecture theatre on the Potchefstroom campus. It's how I meet Fernando Llorente for the first time.

The striker is contracted to Adidas and about to do a big interview for their site. While the crew set up the interview, he asks me where on earth my accent is from. He reckons I sound like the former Liverpool striker Michael Robinson, who starred for the team Llorente supports – Osasuna. We talk about Celts and the links between the north of Spain and Scotland, where I come from. Then it's time for his interview. It's not the last time we will hear of Llorente's family ties.

Un secreto a voces in Spanish literally means 'a secret being spoken about': an open secret. That is what David Silva's €33m move from Valencia (taking that club's sales to €73m since May) to Manchester City has become. It is confirmed today and there is nobody in Potch who thinks it hasn't affected Del Bosque's decision-making process in giving Silva no game time since the Swiss defeat.

— Day 21.

— *July 1, 2010. Potchefstroom*

It is a morning at the movies, but without the popcorn. Paraguay are the main attraction and Spain's video editor, Pablo Peña, has been splicing together the best cuts which go with the analysis Paco Jiménez and Antonio Fernández have brought back from scouting the South Americans' penalty shoot-out win over Japan.

Spain's players felt liberated against Portugal, much less tense in a knockout situation than throughout Group H. In their view it has been their best, most fluent and most attacking performance. FIFA's match report bears that out: 19 efforts at goal and 10 of them on target.

The video shows that Paraguay like to smother opposition and force their three lines tightly together; this looks like it will be something similar to the bruising experience against Chile, but without the 15 minutes played under a white flag.

When they have spare time in The Convent, the players play bingo, poker, *parchis* (the board game Parcheesi), swap DVDs, read, play table tennis and every computer game you can imagine. Sometimes there's cash at stake, others not. Xavi partakes, from time to time, but more than any other player in Potch he will watch the matches they have just played over and again. He is analytical, hooked on football but also eager to soak up details to help him and the team escape the suffocating blanket of defence consistently thrown over them.

What has emerged is that Spain do not stick firmly to the 4-2-3-1 formation. Alonso will liberate himself by 10 or 15 metres, Busquets will cover. Iniesta will come in off the right wing and often an offensive trio of Alonso, Xavi and Iniesta will be searching behind Torres and Villa in an urgent quest for space. The final frontier.

Is this any longer the *doble pivote* system over which the Spanish media has been in convulsions? It certainly is testimony to the training most of these players have had since they were 14 inside the *categorías inferiores*. A switch can be flicked between 4-2-3-1 and 4-3-3, like moving from third gear into fourth.

However, while Iniesta has been injured or recovering and while teams set out to frustrate and foul Spain, there has been huge responsibility on Xavi's shoulders. Whatever the formation, his position is not identical to the one he plays for FC Barcelona. Nor is he seeing so much of the ball. Often possession is coming to him either with his back to goal or when he is on the half-turn. He is being asked to play slightly more like Iniesta does, in the same spaces with the same lack of time, not always facing the play – looking for space rather than creating it by conducting the flow of the ball. He was rewarded with a man-of-the-match citation against Portugal, but still there is widespread preoccupation that perhaps he could perform better and that he looks troubled, unhappy even.

"Even the boss has checked with me that I'm okay," he admits. "People think I'm tense, but it's just that I'm intense."

Pedro, who has had a record-breaking year, becoming the only man to score in six different competitions (La Liga, Copa del Rey, Champions League, Spanish Supercopa, European Supercup and World Club Championship) is about to earn some game time. His training has been remorseless and while he and Navas share pace, Pedro adds much more goal threat. The Barcelona forward has yet to debut for Spain in a competitive match, but that wait appears to be nearing its end.

Pedro: "Our rivals know how Xavi and Iniesta play and how important they are to our style, so they are right on top of them in every game. Xavi, in particular, is being marked really tightly and aggressively. Teams are trying to snuff him out. But I thought both of them really sparked the team against Portugal, they were tremendous."

Xavi: "Paraguay need to be taken very seriously. They run like wolves, they press, they are complicated and even if they have less individual talent than Chile, the style is the same and they have come further. It's going to be a very tough night again."

— Day 22.
— July 2, 2010. Potchefstroom

Pre-match training will once again take place mid-morning in Potch. Last night's session was closed, but this morning sees Llorente lashing in the goals. That is not to overshadow Juan Mata, who won't get much game time this tournament but who scores in training more than anyone else.

While Spain were away in Cape Town defeating Portugal, the temperature in Potch sunk to minus eleven – and then it rained. Although there has been a cover on the training pitch overnight it has still frozen. Then melted. Then been rained on. The surface is cutting up, but that is nothing compared to the state of the Ellis Park pitch, where the quarter-final will take place. Since Spain beat Honduras there 12 days ago there have only been two further matches. The latest was Brazil's 3-0 win over Chile, five days previously. However, with the brutal dip in temperatures and then rain, the Ellis Park pitch is puffing and wheezing to catch up with FIFA standards.

Another whose lungs are not keeping pace is 61-year-old Manuel Cáceres Artesero, AKA Manolo el del Bombo. He has developed pneumonia and the Spain team doctors have advised him to go home, out of this freezing climate as soon as possible for treatment. This is not a man whose body is a temple – he is near pension age and he is quite seriously unwell. He is rushed home. The Paraguay game will be the first *La Roja* match Manolo has missed since his – and my – first World Cup, in 1982. It's a sad and limp way for this likeable eccentric's South African adventure to end.

Ellis Park is dilapidated in places. Inside the stadium, where I meet Del Bosque as he waits to go into the press conference, there is a part of the access tunnel where wires hang down, a bit of hardboard covers a gaping hole and the lights do not function fully. The *Mister* and I have finished our brief interview in a nicely lit and furnished television studio. He and I lean against the corridor wall and chat while we wait for what transpires to be a long Cesc Fàbregas and Gerard Piqué press conference to finish.

The coach tells me: "Cesc's pretty pissed off with me. And he's got every right to be, too." Del Bosque goes on to emphasise the importance of having a mix of young bucks and experience on the bench. Each of them, for slightly different reasons, stays ready for the chance to come on and play well enough to grab a start the next time.

Del Bosque surprises me a little by quizzing me about what the apartheid regime was like – growing up under Franco, Spain was not the place to be for freedom of debate and information, or liberal points of view. Slightly startled at having been put on the spot, I refer to what various South African friends have told me about their lives before and after apartheid.

In due course, while we mark time, I get my customary urge to bring all football chat back to 1983, the year my team, Aberdeen, beat Del Bosque's Real

Madrid to win the European Cup Winners' Cup in Gothenburg. I ask the Spain coach where he was on May 11 that year.

He does not know. He is highly amused to be told that I do. He'd just failed to make Alfredo di Stefano's squad for the final in which Aberdeen added to Madrid's miserable season, when they lost five trophies either in finals or on the last day of the season.

"How many of *my* team can you name?" he challenges me.

By the time I have rattled out seven names, the doors of the press conference hall are opening and Fàbregas and Piqué are emerging. "Here, you two," shouts Del Bosque. "Come and speak to someone who knows something about football." It's not the worst moment of my World Cup.

In the studio, Fàbregas gives a thoughtful, intelligent interview. Before we begin I suggest to Piqué that, for something fresh, he interviews his best friend.

"Done that, was crap at it, no thanks."

Foolishly, however, I let him stay in the studio while I interview Fàbregas for a piece which will be available to every television station in the world that has bought the rights to the World Cup. Fàbregas and I fall victim during the interview, forgetting that an unsupervised Piqué with time on his hands is a dangerous creature.

So heinous is his crime, mid-interview, that good taste forbids its reproduction.

Meanwhile...
Brazil are beaten for the first time since October 2009. The bruises will take time to heal since they lead the Netherlands until Wesley Sneijder pops up with two goals in the second half; the South Americans also give themselves a bloody nose when Felipe Melo is sent off for stamping on Arjen Robben.

— **Day 23.**
— *July 3, 2010. Ellis Park Stadium, Johannesburg*
 Paraguay v Spain – World Cup quarter-final
Uno y dos y tres … ganar y ganar y ganar!

The keepers are the captains. Justo Villar and Iker Casillas go head to head – and it's tails. Casillas concedes the kick-off so that he can change ends and play in the same direction as against Honduras, at this stadium, in the Group H game.

Paraguay play like Chile, but with bells on. Every Spain player seems to be surrounded by three men in red-and-white stripes. Not only are the European champions failing to fire up their game, Paraguay believe that a long ball or a set piece can yield a goal and just before the break that nearly happens. A long ball from the right is tucked away by Nelson Valdez, but the linesman has his flag up against Óscar Cardozo, who goes up for – and misses – the diagonal. If he does not make that action toward the ball, Valdez, who is onside, gets his goal. The break goes Spain's way.

Pepe Reina is a fanatic for detail. Encouraged by the equally detail-obsessed Rafa Benítez, for years his coach at Anfield, the keeper will study striker after striker on DVD, particularly their one-on-one finishes and their penalty taking.

Cardozo's Benfica have been knocked out of the Europa League quarter-final by Reina, Torres and Liverpool this season, but only after the Paraguayan striker scored two penalties in the first leg. Each of them was tucked away firmly to the goalkeeper's left. Having experienced that and seen the DVD compilation, Reina mentions to Casillas pre-match that if Paraguay get a penalty, or if the match goes to a shoot-out, then Cardozo's default action is to shoot to his right and the goalkeeper's left.

Paraguay get their first corner in in the 56th minute; Piqué dozes for a split second, Cardozo gets free and the Catalan hauls him down to the floor. Penalty.

Xavi thinks: 'If they score this, we are practically out.'

Villa thinks: 'Iker will save this. I'm going to be ready when he does.'

But Casillas is not working alone. Reina is up and jigging about, trying to get his colleague's attention. Reina roars at Casillas: "Remember!"

Then, just like in Vienna two years earlier, he leaves him be.

Casillas, a demon card player according to Xavi, runs through the percentages in his mind.

In their last match, Paraguay went through in a penalty shoot-out against Japan and Cardozo shot to his left, beating the keeper's right-handed dive. But his favoured style is to shoot to his own right and the keeper's left.

Cardozo will know I saw the Japan penalty, so he is thinking about changing sides. In all the tension, he may have forgotten that Reina saw two of his penalties up close this season.

I'm going left.

He does, he saves and when the ball is heading back up the field Reina is applauding his friend, and Casillas points over at him with both hands: *Your good call.*

Villa is ready. As play flows upfield, the striker gets in front of Alcaraz and wins Spain a penalty when the defender bundles him over. Xabi Alonso buries it, but Carlos Alberto Batres González does not even see the net bulge. The Guatemalan referee has been watching the edge of the penalty box. Three players appear to encroach but the Guatemalan believes that the furthest forward is a Spaniard, Cesc Fàbregas.

Before the match Paraguay's legendary keeper José Chilavert said of Batres: "He is the worst referee in the history of Guatemala and it's shameful that he has been given this quarter-final."

While Spanish bodies pile on top of the jubilant Alonso, Batres is blowing his whistle. Alonso must take it again.

This time the Spaniard knows he has not hit it properly and he's doing a jerky little hop and skip with his arms stretched out before Justo Villar has even dived to his left to palm the ball away, as if his whole body is screaming: 'Oh no!' However, this time Fàbregas has not encroached. He is first to the rebound. He gets a touch to take the ball past the dive of the goalkeeper and Villar takes him out. If you look in the Oxford English Dictionary for the definition of the word penalty, it will read: Cesc Fàbregas. Minute 63. Spain vs Paraguay. World Cup 2012. But Batres has something in his eye, possibly a symphony orchestra, two Mini Coopers, a packet of Penguin biscuits and a horse, because he doesn't see it.

Twenty minutes later, Andrés Iniesta hypnotises the Paraguay defence. He beats two defenders and draws another two toward him, the question marks visible above their befuddled heads as he cedes the ball to Pedro, one-on-one with the goalkeeper.

After all that has happened here, and all the history that has perennially prevented *La Roja* from progressing past the quarter-finals of any World Cup, all of Spain knows that even with the game tied at 0-0, Pedro *must* score or they will surely lose – to another penalty, an offside goal, a shoot-out or a dog running on to the pitch and dribbling the ball past Iker Casillas. That is how it goes with Spain and World Cups.

They think of Italy's Mauro Tassotti elbowing the face of Luis Enrique in 1994. They think of Garba Lawal of Nigeria trickling a shot past Andoni Zubizarreta in 1998. They think of the Egyptian referee, Gamal Al-Ghandour, disallowing Fernando Morientes' header in the 2002 defeat by South Korea on the false premise that Joaquín's cross had gone out of play.

Pedro *must* score.

But Pedro hits the post.

Hold on a minute, though. The ball rebounds right to the feet of the tournament's top scorer, the Golden Boot winner from Euro 2008, the most reliable striker Spain have ever had. David Villa.

Thirty million Spaniards breathe out in relief, cut short their curses and prayers, and they wait.

Villa opens up his body shape, strikes coolly with the inside of his right boot and the ball implacably seeks out the opposite post to the one Pedro just hit and rolls obstinately along the goal-line.

Twenty four hours earlier, in the middle of Potchefstroom's Fanie du Toit rugby ground, Villa sat in front of me, with that very ball in his hands. He looked at the printed insignia: *Jabulani, Kick-Off, Match 60, July 3, 2010 Paraguay v Spain. Ellis Park Stadium, Johannesburg*, and held it up to the camera.

Asked to dedicate a couple of words to the fans back in Spain he said: "I got the winner in the last match and, tomorrow, I hope to score with *this* football to put us in the World Cup semi-final."

And just as it reaches the post, which is still shuddering from Pedro's initial shot, the Jabulani clips it and rolls over the line – Spain's quarter-final jinx is dead, buried and gone for ever.

Adios Tassotti, *adios* Garba Lawal, *adios* Al-Ghandour.

Spain are going to the World Cup semi-finals for the first time in their history. Afterwards, in the pitchside television interview Casillas tells Sara: "You feel so many nerves, so much responsibility, but I'm happy for the work of the team, especially for those who are not on the pitch, who play fewer minutes. Above all Pepe Reina, who is a phenomenon. He told me where the penalty was going, so I did this for my team-mates."

Vicente del Bosque: "We weren't comfortable on the ball, they took away the thing which we are best at, which is all merit to Paraguay's tactics. Our attitude is completely beyond reproach and overall, without having played all that well, we still merited this. That is because Villa is on a scoring run at the moment, and we play this way because of a long process in Spain of preparing to do so."

Spain will stay overnight in Sandton, a classy neighbourhood in Jo'burg, and Del Bosque has sanctioned another night out.

Casillas and his girlfriend head off to find some peace away from the intrusive spotlight they've been under. For the rest, so long as everyone is ready to travel back to Potch at 10am the following morning, the night is their own.

This era has seen Spain tear up the rule book. They play little men against height and power. They ignore the idea that multi-millionaire footballers need five-star luxury during a tournament and house them in student accommodation. They are allowed recreational time with wives and girlfriends and there is no tabloid scandal. Every now and again they go out on the town to celebrate together. All because of a system in which, from an early age, they are taught discipline and respect; because egos are subjugated and because they know how to control and pass a ball.

Who knew?

Paraguay 0 Spain 1

Paraguay: J Villar, Verón, Da Silva, Alcaraz, Merel, Cáceres (Barrios 84), Santana, Barreto (Vera 64), Riveros, Valdez (Santa Cruz 72), Cardozo

Spain: Casillas, Ramos, Piqué, Puyol (Marchena 84), Capdevila, Busquets, Xavi, Alonso (Pedro 75), Iniesta, Torres (Fàbregas 56), Villa
Goal: Villa 83

> *Meanwhile...*
> *Argentina's defeat by Germany proves devastating to Diego Maradona. Pre-match in the tunnel he roars, 'We do our talking on the pitch!' over and again. But they are mute. Germany win 4-0 and Argentina seem tactically inept. By the end the coach and Leo Messi are in tears.*

— **Day 24.**
— *July 4, 2010. Potchefstroom*
    Three days until the World Cup semi-final
The morning after the night before, there is always a hangover. Puyol took the ball smack in his face making one block against Paraguay; it was so bad that he temporarily lost full vision. Fàbregas has shoulder damage and will need an X-ray; Ramos took a boot to the head and his eyebrow has been stitched. As for Torres, intuition tells him he is going to be dropped. In fact, he knows it.

Fernando Torres: "There are better and worse times during a tournament and I was never going to make being left out a problem."

205

However, away from all these trials, Andrésito Iniesta, a tormented soul just a few weeks ago, is currently the man of the tournament. He was the light in the darkness against Switzerland, creating his team's best chances. Against Chile he helped create and then score goals of velvet smoothness to win Group H. Iniesta's darting run and pass produced Villa's winner against Portugal. Then, when Paraguay resisted for 83 minutes, he danced past three tackles to give Pedro the chance to start the woodwork bonanza which ended with Villa scoring again.

David Villa: "Iniesta is a genius."

Xavi: "He's Spain's best player, no doubt. By a distance. He's been through so, so much suffering this season and it's done us all damage to see that. He's respectful, quiet, a great professional, he's earned his stripes – it's just a joy to play with him."

Back at base, it is back to basics. First teamers have the day off, but Casillas trains. The night session is mostly based around intense, small-sided matches aimed at keeping those who have the fewest competitive minutes sharp, thinking quickly, fleet of foot and with a feeling that their moment might be just about to arrive.

In Pedro's case, it is.

— **Day 25.**
— *July 5, 2010. Potchefstroom*
   Two Days until the World Cup semi-final
The further this bunch go, the more relaxed they are. Perhaps the mood is lightened because the next opponent is Germany. The Spain players admire this German generation because Jogi Löw's team play to win, they go out to dominate and beat opponents rather than to prey on another team's mistakes.

It should be intimidating, given that some highlights of the *Mannschaft's* tournament thus far have been the 12 goals scored in thrashing Australia, England and the Argentina of Leo Messi. By this stage, however, Spain would opt for a match against pretty much anyone if it means avoiding another set of space-denying, tactical-fouling giants.

Or perhaps the *joie de vivre* which settles on Spain's Potchefstroom retreat stems from an octopus named Paul. *Pulpo Paul* in Spanish.

England had woken up to the oracle powers of the *Octopus Vulgaris* much earlier in the tournament thanks to the fact that the star pupil of the Oberhausen

Aquarium, although a native of Weymouth, tipped Germany to beat England in the last 16.

The deal is that Paul's keeper places him in a tank which has two see-through plastic boxes with a piece of food in each. Each box is decorated with a flag of one of the two nations about to play. Television stations around the world love it.

So far at this tournament, *Pulpo Paul* (who made a damn good job of Euro 2008 in tipping four of Germany's six matches correctly) has got every single German result right, including a shock defeat by Serbia in the group stages. Ahead of the semi-final, *Pulpo Paul* plumps for *La Roja*. Fortunately he doesn't know about Carles Puyol's Sushi Crew.

One of its members, Raúl Martínez, has already played his part in treating the muscles and mind of Andrés Iniesta. Imminently he's going to have to go to work on his Sushi crewmate.

— Day 26.
— July 6, 2010. Durban

In October 2001 Kurt Jara, whose friendship with Aragonés would nine years later provide Spain with the base from which they win Euro 2008, quit FC Tirol Innsbruck, with whom he had won back-to-back Austrian championships, to become coach of Hamburg. He was replaced at FC Tirol by a slim, dark-haired German who bore a passing resemblance to Keith Richards circa 1962, before the Rolling Stones got big. His name was Joachim 'Jogi' Löw.

The revolution which Jara helped Aragonés begin, basing *La Roja's* training in the Tyrolean resort of Neustift, and which became unstoppable when Spain defeated Löw's Germany in Vienna that summer, now brings the European champions all the way back to Durban, where they so nearly derailed three weeks ago, for a rematch with Löw's fabulously attractive German national side.

Löw has been admirably daring. No-one, outside his technical staff, believed that taking Lukas Podolski and Miroslav Klose, who in the words of the legendary Gunter Netzer have both been "atrocious" in recent months for Cologne and Bayern respectively, would work. Yet it has.

When I talk to Casillas at the stadium prior to the last training session, he tells me that he fears "Germany are building a generation of international footballers to dominate for a decade".

Alonso, Villa, Xavi and Pedro all say the same thing to various Spanish media: they like the way Germany play; they respect them and think they are the best opponent left in the competition.

Jogi, smarter than your average coach, has taken a squad to South Africa which, if you discount 36-year-old Hans-Jörg Butt, has an average age of just over 24. Butt does not play and would not even have been here were it not for a genuine tragedy.

The previous November I took a call from my friend, Ronnie Reng, completely distraught at the fact that someone close to him, the Germany and Hannover goalkeeper Robert Enke, had committed suicide that day. If you have not read Ronnie's subsequent book about the depression and death of his friend, *A Life Too Short*, then I urge you to.

Enke had been scheduled to be Germany's World Cup goalkeeper. Rene Adler injured himself during the Bundesliga season and so Löw promoted Manuel Neuer. The 24-year-old Schalke goalkeeper is already one of the stars of the tournament and looks like a potential world No.1.

Perhaps Löw's other great masterstroke has been the selection and use of Thomas Müller. Long, lithe, electrically quick and imbued with a great joy in playing football flat-out, this kid also looks like a world-beater. However, the Uzbeki referee in Germany's demolition of Argentina hasn't helped the quality of this semi-final, cautioning Müller on a weak handball call, meaning he is suspended for the final four. Spain's little run of luck, so drastically different from their previous World Cup jinxes, is holding – in football terms, at least.

The Germans got the best hotel and we will be with them, back in the Riverside. Spain are in the significantly more downbeat Protea hotel which, besides being further away from the stadium, is less secure. Pedro and Busquets are robbed of about €2000 which has been left in their rooms while they and the rest of the squad are out for a walk along the beach.

Ask any Spanish journalist in Durban and they will tell you there is only one selection dilemma for the semi-final: to Torres or not to Torres. That is the question.

Everyone trains, including Fàbregas, who has been to hospital for a scan on his right leg after a bad impact in training last night, revealing heavy bruising and no bone damage.

Nobody in the media notices Carles Puyol finishing training and then wandering up to Raúl Martínez: "I'm in so much pain, I'm not going to make it for this game tomorrow. It's been getting sorer and sorer for days, particularly in training, and I think this is it. We're going to have to tell the *Mister*, I'm not fit to face Germany."

When he talks about it Puyol calls the problem his gluteus muscle, which is between the hip and the top of the thigh. But he is feeling a tight, pinching pain from there down the side of his thigh to just above the side of his right knee.

If *Puyi* tells you he is not going to be able to play it takes a very brave man to say, 'I can fix that', but that is what Martínez does: "Why tell the boss before you've let me have a look at this problem?"

Then he goes to work.

Before morning comes they pack in hours of agonising treatment. Puyol can suddenly move more freely and the Barcelona captain is nothing if not used to playing through pain. The Sushi Crew has rescued Spain.

Meanwhile...
A startling shot from Giovanni van Bronckhorst awakens the Dutch to the opportunity of winning the tournament — the full-back takes aim from 30 yards to start the scoring in a 3-2 win over Uruguay. Arjen Robben is also on the target and his influence on this tournament continues to grow.

— **Day 27.**
— *July 7, 2010. Moses Mabhida Stadium, Durban*
Germany v Spain — World Cup semi-final
Uno y dos y tres … ganar y ganar y ganar!

> *Uno de enero, dos de febrero,*
> *Tres de marzo, cuatro de abril,*
> *Cinco de mayo, seis de junio*
> *Siete de julio, ¡SAN FERMÍN!*

No, the dressing room anthem hasn't changed. Today is the Fiesta of San Fermín and this is the song every kid learns in Spain from when they are tiny.

> *First of January, second of February,*
> *Third of March, fourth of April,*
> *Fifth of May, Sixth of June,*
> *Seventh of July, SAN FERMÍN!*

This is when the world famous bull-running in Pamplona begins and around about 8 o'clock this morning the rocket will have fired, the runners will have poured forward down the cobbled street and the horns on hooves will have made chase.

Spain's chef, Arbizú, Javi Martínez and Fernando Llorente are all from this region and they have brought their red neckerchiefs to wear today. Del Bosque is not Navarran – he is from the beautiful university city of Salamanca – but his late brother and father are named Fermín, therefore this festival has always been special to him. During the day he finds his thoughts drifting to these two men and it is from them that he will draw some inspiration for what he says post-match.

The chaos of Pamplona is sadly mirrored at Durban's international airport today. Back in Spain, one travel agency has been advertising overnight flights into Durban on the day of the game, a hotel room during the day, a match ticket and return flights immediately after the match for €2000, or €3500 for business class. There are many takers.

One trouper, Manolo el del Bombo, has defied doctors' orders and, having spent approximately three full days at home fighting pneumonia, the 61-year-old has decided that Spain will not win the World Cup without him. He lands and gets a police escort to somehow make it to the stadium by the skin of his teeth, but he is one of the lucky few.

Scores of planes containing the super-rich, super-famous or super-important, including the Queen of Spain, Jacob Zuma, Leo Di Caprio and Paris Hilton, have arrived in private jets, landed in the slots needed for scheduled international and national flights and then refused to budge. You would almost get the impression that money has changed hands. Some flights from Cape Town and Jo'burg scheduled to get to Durban well in time for the semi-final do not even take off because there is such pandemonium at King Shaka Airport.

Themba Maseko, operations manager for the Airports Company South Africa (ACSA) which runs Durban airport, explains that these jets are meant to drop their passengers then move to the old Durban International Airport 60km away to park, but that many private aircraft pilots had refused.

"I am not blaming the VIPs. The people who caused the problem were the people flying the aircraft," he says morosely.

Just under 2000 people do not make it to the game, but Puyol does and so does Manolo.

Bastian Schweinsteiger, victim of the Vienna victory conga back in 2008, has confessed that "you are left with a certain feeling that you want revenge", but he isn't going to get it today.

The semi-final turns out to be a cracking game of football. Löw, like Del

Bosque, believes in the power of good scouting and preparation. The Spaniard, unlike Löw, has never composed a 100-page dossier on an opponent as the German manager did before beating Argentina 4-0 in the last round. Urs Siegenthaler is the German equivalent of Paco Jiménez and Antonio Férnandez and to help him in his scouting he has 56 students from the University of Cologne Sports School. They video opponents and break down the strengths and weaknesses, the mistakes and the habits, the pace and the power of every player the *Mannschaft* must face.

When Del Bosque makes one of the biggest calls of his career, to bench Torres, as predicted by the striker himself, it is the file on Pedro which Löw must open. The reasons for Del Bosque's decision are numerous: the Barcelona forward has had an utterly brilliant year; he is faster than inflation; he is a fighter; he has more goals in him than Navas, the most likely alternative, and he can be asked not only to block the attacks of Phillip Lahm, the raiding German left-back, but to pin him back by attacking that wing.

As it turns out, Pedro plays as if it were a kick-around in the school playground, showing no sign of pressure. He skips about, dragging two and three white shirts with him; he sets Villa up for a one-on-one chance with Neuer; he feeds Alonso and gets close to putting a shot on target. Del Bosque is not prone to hyperbole, but long after this tournament is won he will call Pedro's performance in the semi-final "stupendous".

For all their preparation, Germany find it hard to get any dangerous possession, but at the break it is 0-0 and history teaches that this national team is not beaten until the stadium lights are switched off and the janitors have gone home. That is emphasised when the referee fails to award a free-kick for a clear foul on Özil when Ramos clips his heel just outside the box in the seconds before half-time. So close to the line is the offence that some refs would give a penalty. Nevertheless, fate is now involved.

Before the pre-match team talks, and the studying of the tactical charts on the dressing-room wall, Pepe Reina questioned Puyol about a move via which, just over a year previously, he scored for Barcelona in a 6-2 win at Real Madrid. Using the magnetic pieces on the white board, Puyol shows Reina the concept and the practice.

By half-time in Durban the Catalan, who thought injury was going to ensure he watched this match from the stands, has noticed that Germany appear to be marking zonally and his path into the penalty box at set plays is almost unencumbered. Spain have so far played a couple of corners short, put one in looking for Capdevila, but nothing for Puyol. The Barça captain has, however, missed an easy scoring chance with a diving header which Iniesta puts on a plate for him.

Before they are even off the pitch at half-time, the centre-half has Xavi, who delivered the corner at the Santiago Bernabéu from which Puyol scored, by the arm and is instructing him.

"Let's use that move from the 6-2 win again. I'll speak to Ramos, Capdevila and Villa, you just put the ball on the penalty spot for me and we will see how they cope."

Neuer's goal is peppered, Pedro draws the best save from him, Toni Kroos does so equally from Casillas and the referee's mistake over Özil is annulled when he fails to give Ramos a penalty after Podolski brings him down.

Then, with 17 minutes left, Iniesta wins a corner on the Spanish left. I am at the mouth of the transport tunnel, right in line with the corner flag. As Xavi walks over to take the corner and settles the ball, I am aware of a little old lady, not in official uniform, who has materialised at my elbow without me noticing. She is diminutive, so I have to lean down a bit to hear her.

"How is the game going?"

"Well, it's pretty tense and pretty interesting," I reply. "We just need..."

I look up as I speak and Xavi appears to have used those four or five seconds to erect some sort of rigging so that he can dangle the football precisely where Puyol wants it.

Puyol, this battered, brilliant Catalan warrior filmed a television promotion with me back in Potch. He sits and stares stone-faced down the lens of the camera, holding up a rugby ball.

"They tell me this is rugby country. Well, I don't know anything about rugby."

He throws the oval ball out of shot to his right as a football is thrown to him from his left and he catches it.

"But I *do* know about football."

This is where he proves it.

Villa has been occupying Neuer on the line. For a split second, the keeper puts all his attention into shoving him violently with both hands and there is now no question of Neuer getting out to punch the corner.

There is a little triangle of players occupying German markers: Ramos to the left, tying up Klose, Piqué more or less static on the penalty spot and Capdevila to the right. The arc of the ball's movement is taking it towards Piqué, but as Sami Khedira bunches up every muscle to make the jump of his life, a dark shadow falls over the land. Puyol soars over them all, Michael Jordan-style, and crashes the best, most powerful header I have ever seen past Neuer.

Back by the tunnel I am finishing my conversation with the little old lady: "... we just need a goal." But my fairy godmother has vanished by the time Spain celebrate wildly and Puyol, carrying four of his team-mates on his shoulders, clenches a fist and wears an expression which says: Let's not make too much of a fuss of this ... back to work now.

FIFA give Xavi the man-of-the-match award. Since the first match of Group H, Iniesta has been Spain's best player against the Swiss; David Villa won man of the match against Honduras; Iniesta against Chile; Xavi against Portugal; Iniesta against Paraguay and now Xavi again. There is a pattern emerging.

Maybe Pedro would have won this award had it not been for what unfolds in the 81st minute. Capdevila starts a counter from his own box, Xavi rips out a searching ball into Pedro's right-wing run and the forward is racing through on goal. Arne Friedrich is tailing him, substitute Fernando Torres is available to the left. Pedro could shoot – he can see the whites of Neuer's eyes – or he could slide in Torres for a certain goal. Instead he tries to cut inside Friedrich, the German taps Pedro's ankle in the challenge, he loses his footing and the chance is gone.

"An error," Pedro recognises and, in future, alters his style to one where he almost always shoots low, hard and early. "I was so, so confident, I just didn't see Torres."

"Just as well we won because as much as I love Pedro, I was ready to kill him in that moment," Torres says retrospectively.

There is bedlam on the pitch after the final whistle and it continues into the dressing room, where Puyol immediately continues physio with Raúl Martínez on one of the massage tables. There remains quite an important game to be played.

Before we return to the dressing room, there are some epic phrases in the press conferences given by the two coaches.

Joachim Löw: "It is extraordinarily difficult to win the ball back if you lose it to Spain. Yes, they are definitely the best team in the world and they are going to win this tournament. In 2008 they won the European Championship in a spectacular way, totally convincing, but in the last couple of years they have evolved, introduced some changes and they now play as if they were on automatic. This team has a unique ability to dominate you and to control you. It is a marvellous team. These guys are the masters of football."

From a losing coach in a World Cup semi-final, this was breathtaking magnanimity. Just a little later he will go on, in private, to congratulate Xavi, to thank him for playing as he does and to tell the Spaniard that this is the best football team he has ever seen. The moment has not got the better of Spain's coach, either.

This is the son of the activist who sought democracy and workers' rights when such ideals could carry a lethal price. This was the footballer who formed a trade union. This was the manager who was sacked by Florentino Pérez for a more "modern" approach, for someone more "in-tune" with Real Madrid, for which read someone subservient, conservative, conformist.

> **Vicente del Bosque**: "Spain is a country which has changed greatly. Now we are integrated into the world, within the European community, and good things happen in our country. Sport is one of them. It is a privilege to have so many great sportsmen and women in Spain right now and for the football family, this is our moment. We have spent so long detached from this success that it was long overdue. I want to thank all the lesser-known guys who work in the youth development systems of our clubs. And all the former international players, plus the national team coaches who went before me. We have the obligation of representing our country as well as we are able and this is the moment to recognise all those who have done their utmost for the national team in the past. Some of their contributions have been anonymous but their work has helped us shine tonight. But this mustn't blind us. We are footballers, we have a trophy to win and this is a time to show restraint, not to think we are suddenly out of this world."

Del Bosque does not make it back to the dressing room in time to witness the great tenor, Placido Domingo, bursting in and adapting *Y Viva España!* to end not with *España por favor!* but *España campeón!*

However, Del Bosque is just in time for some of the comedy when Doña Sofía, the wife of King Juan Carlos, who is absent through illness, enters the dressing room. It's immediately evident that it's a while since she's played football for the royal household; a while since she's been in a dressing room.

Unchaperoned, she makes for the showers, is pointed down the corridor, and then propelled around the corner, where she comes face-to-face with her all-conquering football team and does a comic double-take.

Lacking a master of ceremonies, she starts clapping them ... and they all start clapping right back. Amidst the furore of applause, Joan Capdevila starts a manic little Riverdance of his own, in the corner. Sofía takes herself around the players, one by one, shaking hands as various players turn into royal couriers, desperately kicking or swiping boots, bottles, jockstraps out from under her before she trips over them and this becomes a diplomatic incident. This is a likelihood which increases when Carles Puyol, aware that he has been missing something, bursts into the room just as the Queen of Spain is about to make her speech. Sporting only a towel, he is a sitting duck for his team-mates, who roar: *Puyi! Puyi! Puyi!* Capdevila dances again.

After the Queen's speech ("nice job lads, tighten up on the finishing") Doña Sofía mistakes one of the federation officials, the former Real Sociedad president Luis Uranga, for Del Bosque, only for the coach to arrive in the nick of time, to bow and to invite her back on Sunday. Soccer City. The World Cup final.

Germany 0 Spain 1

Germany: Neuer, Lahm, Friedrich, Mertesacker, Boateng (Jansen 52), Khedira (Gomez 81), Schweinsteiger, Trochowski (Kroos 62), Özil, Podolski, Klose

Spain: Casillas; Ramos, Piqué, Puyol, Capdevila; Busquets, Alonso (Marchena 90+3); Iniesta, Xavi, Pedro (Silva 86); Villa (Torres 81)
Goal: Puyol 73

— Day 28.
— July 8, 2010. Potchefstroom
Three Days Until the World Cup final
They were both headhunted as kids under the FC Barcelona system run by a Dutchman, Johan Cruyff. Growing up, the greatest moment in either of their lives was created by a Dutchman, Ronald Koeman, whose goal gave their club the European Cup at Wembley in 1992. They were both given their Barcelona debuts by a Dutchman, Louis van Gaal. They were both kept out of that team by Dutchmen, Phillip Cocu, Frank and Ronald de Boer. They made their Spain debut together, 10 years ago, against Holland. They both won their first Champions League medal coached by a Dutchman, Frank Rijkaard.

With Holland already qualified for the final, who else was going to get Spain to Soccer City? Xavi's corner, Carles Puyol's intercontinental ballistic header. Now here they are in the gym hall at Potchefstroom's North Western University.

The press conference is packed, there are about 20 languages being spoken and Puyol, without the towel, is holding court.

No, he will not confirm whether he is going to retire after the competition.

Yes, it was his idea to come up with that rehearsed move at the corner.

He is not enjoying the focus being solely on him, at least until his semi-naked appearance in front of the Queen is mentioned. "It's the first time she's been in our dressing room and if I wasn't only wearing a towel, I'd have gone down on one knee."

He goes on to confess that although "what lies ahead is beautiful" he'll speak to Del Bosque and Hierro after the final about whether or not he will quit. For the moment: "I don't want the goal against Germany to be historic, I want a team-mate to go one better on Sunday."

Xavi is as confident with words as he is with the ball.

"I swear, I knew it was a goal from the moment my boot made connection with the ball from the corner. Somehow I just knew. I looked up, saw *Puyi* and thought, 'don't miss this one, this one's a goal'."

Better still is one of the men who snatched away Holland's first dream of lifting the World Cup, in 1974. Franz Beckenbauer. Doing some day-after publicity in Jo'burg Der Kaiser is comfortable admitting: "Spain were simply superior. We did well keeping the score down, Spain could have had more. I'm very confident that they'll win now."

Away from the press conference, Puyol relaxes in the company of his old friend Lu Martín, Spain's most charismatic, football-smart and occasionally eccentric journalist. "A fundamental change in my game is that analysis of matches has led me to use my brain more than my heart or my legs. I'm more preoccupied with controlling spaces in the match than following the ball. Before, basically, wherever the ball was, I went. I still take my share of knocks because I'm always convinced that I'll get to everything, but I've learned to think more on the pitch."

To enjoy himself, too.

"It's a great laugh having Piqué beside me for club and country, we joke a lot and I've learned a lot from him football-wise, too, but there has been a feeling of liberation for me since we won the European Championship in Vienna. I had just had a very bad year personally, and I began to understand that while we are professionals, we are here to win and to work within a structure, but we are also here to enjoy ourselves. To enjoy playing. I dumped a lot of anxiety. In sport you can lose, that's no problem, but what I don't believe we can do is betray our principles of how we play, what we believe in — that we want to win playing good football."

Night time is a hoot. Now, instead of 100 people there are 2000 at training. The locals, wrapped up in blankets, mufflers, gloves, ski jackets and balaclavas, are joined by media crews from Japan, China, USA, Australia, France, England, Mexico, Argentina, Germany and South Africa.

The training session is short, its purpose to give the substitutes a chance to sharpen up and run off some tension. Casillas is there, of course, and makes the night of one lucky fan when he gives her his training top as he comes off. Torres signs and signs and signs. Some of the players have a little game of crossbar challenge from the halfway line and Víctor Valdés wins out of sight, hitting four times.

The clatter of metal studs up the concrete corridor between the two bleachers signals that Spain are off to eat and our time in Potch is coming to an end.

— Day 29.
— July 9, 2010. Potchefstroom
Two days until the World Cup final

Morten Olsen, the Denmark coach, says something prophetic. Everyone else, Spain's players included, were talking about the debt both footballing nations, Holland and Spain, owe to Johan Cruyff and the football philosophy of Rinus Michels. Excitement is growing about an open final because Arjen Robben, Wesley Sneijder and Rafael Van der Vaart will not only want to beat *La Roja*, but to outplay them.

Olsen, who coached Ajax to the Dutch league and cup double, begs to differ: "If Brazil had beaten Holland, instead of the other way round, Holland would have been slaughtered at home. Not simply for going out but because of the disastrous way they are playing."

He is on to something.

The latest training sessions in Potch have been very interesting. One of the exercises has a goalkeeper and just one defender facing off against three attackers who start from the halfway line with the ball in their possession. The breakaway three must use their three-on-one advantage over the defender to score; it is about being smart, using angles, making good decisions. The defender must make brilliant choices about what space to occupy, how to jockey without committing himself at the wrong time and will be required to sprint over short distances. It is a test for the goalkeeper, too: how to communicate with his defender, how to close angles if the defender is beaten. There comes a stage when it is Pepe Reina and Joan Capdevila facing alternating sets of attackers. Capdevila's age, pace and athleticism have been under the microscope. At 33, he is a decent-sized unit and lightning speed has not been his calling card for a few seasons now. For a moment it looks like this might be a brutal test, but his football smarts, his positional skills and his communication with Reina are exceptional. His team-mates find it extremely hard to score against them despite the numerical advantage.

At a time when Capdevila's duel against the lightning-fast Arjen Robben is being pinpointed by the Dutch media as the way the final can be won, these are vital signs from the left-back.

At the conclusion of the final Potch training session, there is media mayhem. The press conference features Busquets, who nullified Mesut Özil's creative play while not giving away a single foul in the semi-final. His sidekick is Carlos Marchena, one of the original pillars of this golden era, dating back to the Youth World Championship win in 1999, who has now played in 53 straight internationals without losing, overtaking the record of Garrincha, the great Brazilian winger of the 1950s.

At these press conferences there is a lady from a Mexican television channel who is a real personality. Her questions are always bubbly, sometimes funny and this day she is going for the big one.

"Carlos, *Pulpo Paul* has had a brilliant World Cup, calling the winner of every match it has predicted. Now *Pulpo Paul* says Spain are going to win the final. What do you think?"

Marchena pauses, squints at the journalist and turns to one side. There is a gentle creaking as the multinational audience gently lean forward for what is clearly going to be a significant answer of depth and consideration.

Marchena leans into the microphone and says, deadpan: "Well, it's ... *an octopus!*" His audience corpses.

By this point, everyone who has secured an interview on the final open media day before press conferences at Soccer City on Saturday and the final itself on Sunday is keeping quiet about it. Everyone who does not have an interview is prepared to steal from friends and colleagues to get one, and worse besides. Gerard Piqué saves my bacon, agreeing on the quiet to nip into our studio, to talk Barcelona, Cruyff, Holland, Total Football, Spain and the World Cup final.

He finishes our interview with the words: *'Perfecto, Graham?'*

It is a sign. Everything is going to be *perfecto*.

— Day 30.

— July 10, 2010. Johannesburg
  One day until the World Cup final

It is 11.15am and Spain's luxury Hyundai coach, carrying the message *Ilusión es mi camino, victoria mi destino* (hope is my road, victory my destiny) on the side, is pulling out of the university gates for the last time: destination Jo'burg. For 30 days, access to this site has been precious and exclusive: training, press conferences, one-on-one interviews, filming, off-the-record briefings. Reporting *La Roja*.

As the bus turns the corner it is suddenly just a sports campus again. The restaurant, the bar, the cricket ground, these anointed locations where Spain's World Cup has been planned, where a minute ago there were armed soldiers, are now places anyone can wander in to. No army, no accreditation required, no Xavi, no Casillas, no Del Bosque. The magic has gone, but another carefully selected tournament base has given Spain an edge. A training pitch of exact quality, a tranquil local environment and one-star student accommodation. Which other international heavyweight does it like this?

As established, the N12 is a freeway of shocks, but the one which is about to arrive is completely unexpected. Halfway through our journey to Sandton's Da Vinci hotel, which we will share with the Spain camp, I take a call from the head of FIFA television. He's very happy with our work to date and he has a challenge. He has faxed the Spanish federation, officially asking whether we can film in the Spain dressing room after the final, should they win, and on the team bus to the airport.

"Could you please locate the federation president, Ángel María Villar, and persuade him. Thanks."

By 2pm I am in the bar of the Da Vinci hotel, writing up some notes, and chatting with two Spanish reporters, Lu Martín and the great Santi Segurola of *Marca*. Suddenly Villar appears, attracted by the fact that two of his favourites, Lu and Santi, are talking football. Santi is a huge fan of British football history and we have been talking about Alex Ferguson's Aberdeen era, Charlie Cooke, Kenny Dalglish and George Best.

Villar is in his element. A beer appears for him, and shortly we are talking about some of the greats of Scottish football – Billy Bremner, Dave Mackay, Jim Baxter – and the fact that Villar was in the first Spain team to win at Hampden, in 1975.

Needs must, however. "President, my bosses would like me to be able to take my cameraman into the dressing room if Spain win tomorrow and to be on that team bus with the trophy en route to the airport please."

Presidential pause. "We'll see."

Villar agrees to speak to Hierro, Del Bosque and to one or two of the players if necessary. He requests that we meet in the team's breakfast room on Sunday morning, by which time he will have a decision.

At Soccer City, I bump into Gio van Bronckhorst, who was a friendly and interesting player while at Barcelona.

"Fantastic goal," I say, in congratulation for his epic strike in Holland's semi-final win over Uruguay.

"I've got another one in my boots," he promises. This will be his last international. "Against close friends like Xavi and Puyol," he smiles.

Unbeknownst to me, sparks are flying while Spain are in the building. Shakira arrives for a sound test and run-through of her key role tomorrow in the closing ceremony. Her song *Waka-Waka* has been anthemic – everywhere during these weeks. Recording a video for it in Barcelona before the World Cup, she met Gerard Piqué. He has a big day tomorrow, too. Their eyes have caught. Within months they will be together and, in due course, parents of young Milan Piqué.

Meanwhile, David Villa is willing to stop and talk about the work ethic behind his goals.

"I was always taught, mostly by my dad, that talent isn't enough, you always have to work extremely hard. Now, I wouldn't like to have to play against myself. I know that whenever I'm up against friends in La Liga or in Europe they always tell me what a pain it is to try to mark me. Also, that they end up tired and flustered. I like hearing that."

Like most of the squad, his family are in town. His wife and his two girls will be at Soccer City tomorrow night. Does he worry what the price of failure might be for those who are there to watch and to support?

"If they are there, there's no way I'm going to put them through losing. I'll just have to make sure we win."

I tell him about being next to the distraught Portuguese players in the tunnel at the end of the match in Capetown.

"I've never cried on a football pitch. Not as a kid, not as a professional. If there has to be a first time then let it be tomorrow and let it be tears of joy."

Right now opinions, analysis and quotes are like confetti; what everyone wants is a hard news story. Will Torres be restored to the team? Is Wesley Sneijder fit?

The truth is, however, that this is a World Cup final of intricacy and depth – it does not need tabloid headlines in the build-up.

It is being called Cruyff's final. His emergence helped make the Holland team coached by Rinus Michels successful and seductive in the 1970s. His arrival and teachings at FC Barcelona changed the entire mentality of that club. The system he installed there produced Valdés, Xavi, Iniesta and Puyol then later Busquets, Pedro and Piqué.

Earlier in the tournament I talked to Xavi about winning the youth title in Nigeria all those years ago and the Cruyff DNA which is in any product of the Barça academy.

"I'm like Cruyff in that I'm a romantic. I think we are involved in a battle to defend the soul of football. That's the only way I know how to play."

Cruyff was one of the few predicting Spain would win the tournament immediately after the Switzerland defeat and before the final he says: "The last few World Cup winners have been sad to watch. They all have this attitude that if they keep the majority of players in their own half then they will feel more secure and the other side will make a mistake. I have had to watch games with Brazil, France, Italy and England recently where nothing happened. Against Germany, Spain just went out to enjoy themselves – in a World Cup semi-final.

"I'm going to watch this game with a few Spanish friends and take the view that no matter which team wins, I can't lose."

It is a bit startling to read Ronald de Boer, another Camp Nou alumnus and the brother of Holland's assistant coach, admitting: "Before the competition I thought Holland were spectacular. Now I don't enjoy watching them play at all. It's not exciting."

The Spanish media are fascinated by the fact that Arjen Robben and Sneijder have both been spat out of Florentino Pérez's Madrid, yet gone on to win a cascade of silverware this season at Bayern and Inter. Now here they both are in the World Cup final.

I am more interested in Van Bommel and Iniesta.

Only a few years have passed since Sandro Rosell argued in the Barça boardroom that the game favoured by the Brazil of Luiz Felipe Scolari and the Chelsea of José Mourinho, built around power and pace, should be adopted at Camp Nou. The coach, Frank Rijkaard, brilliant technically as a player but also a brute of an athlete, found it hard to put full faith in Iniesta and didn't pick the young midfielder to start the 2006 Champions League final, favouring Van Bommel. That moment began an epic story for Iniesta and now, face-to-face with his nemesis once more, it is nearing its end.

> **Meanwhile…**
> *The aggression and verve with which Germany have hunted success here is still evident in the third-place play-off, in which they beat Uruguay 3-2. Thomas Müller's goal wins him the Golden Boot on an assist tie-breaker over a group including Diego Forlan, who also hits his fifth in this game and wins the Golden Ball as the tournament's top player.*

— **Day 31.**
— *July 11, 2010. Soccer City, Johannesburg*
Holland v Spain. World Cup final
Uno y dos y tres … ganar y ganar y ganar!

Over cornflakes and coffee we strike a deal. Although Del Bosque and the players are fine about it, Hierro is not keen on cameras in the dressing room and is firmly against the triumphant bus ride to the airport being filmed. Villar, the president, is in favour, and so we reach a compromise. We can go into the dressing room all afternoon to film it being made ready for the players and, if Spain win, we will be welcome in their inner sanctum about five minutes after they all get in there.

No bus.

We set off from the Da Vinci hotel at 1pm, preceded by two van-loads of kit and with Toni Guerra as our guest. Toni is the head of a three-man team of *utilleros* (kit-men), with Damián García and Joaquín Retamosa, who take charge of a military exercise every time Spain's 3000kg of equipment moves anywhere.

Across Jo'burg to Soweto we drive, our cameraman Adam Goldfinch filming from the front of the car with his backside lodged in the windscreen to get a good shot of Toni while we discuss all the things he has to oversee before Spain can kick off the World Cup final.

Inside the stadium, the *utilleros* set to work. Each locker is decorated with a picture which has the player's shirt, number and name on it. The rule is that nobody gets to choose where they sit or who is next to them. It starts with No.1, Casillas, to the left of the tactical boards and ascends all the way to the last man, No.23, Pepe Reina. All the training kit, all the playing kit, boots, and flip-flops are laid out neatly.

The spare technical room in the dressing room (Del Bosque will find that he has his own small office in there, too) fills up with boots. Hundreds of boots, of all shapes, sizes and colours, some battered, some brand new, all now checked and polished, if need be.

Tactic boards are assembled, fruit bars laid out, the water boiler for tea and coffee is plugged in. Beer and champagne are, cautiously, secreted in the most low-key, discreet corner of this huge player area. Prepared, yes, but no jinxing.

Speaking of which, Spain are the designated away team. They will play in blue.

After about 90 minutes of watching and filming the *utilleros'* industrious routine there is a knock on the door. It is a blazered FIFA official.

"Do you have any special changes of kit planned for after the final whistle in case you win?"

Everything needs to be approved. No sponsor who has invested major money wants to see the winning team suddenly donning branded kit from a rival corporation. FIFA patrol this rigorously.

The question of a change of kit has provided both Adidas and the Spanish federation with a problem to solve. Shirts with a single star to represent a World Cup win are being prepared. Initially they are prepared in the blue Spain will play in, with the gold star above the crest. However, the players want to change into *La Roja* – the traditional, much-loved red. Adidas work all night, the strips are ready, but now the superstitious players do not want to see them or to check them. Adidas have also prepared a t-shirt celebrating the win which the players may put on after picking up the trophy.

Mr FIFA studies everything. Approves everything. Toni, Damián and Joaquín have done their job. Now it is over to the players.

Those 23 men are on the bus, heading towards the huge copper-coloured stadium which is shaped and textured like a huge car tyre laid on its side.

Inside the vehicle it is once again as quiet as a library. Many of the players are messaging each other on the journey via their Blackberry devices rather than talking or shouting. Dozens of texts are sent between them all during this period. No-one has agreed that this should be general policy – it just naturally evolves that way. Tension affects everyone in different ways. This time, fear is not the reason for the silence. Some are thinking about their nation and how they are making people feel back home.

Sergio Ramos: "I want to be a flag-bearer for the ordinary man back in Spain who is honest, hard-working and gets his job done with extra fire and passion on the day of a Spain game, so that he can get home to the sofa in his living room or join his community in the bar and watch us win."

The mood is reflective: 'What lies ahead? Am I ready? Can we win?' Reflection takes most of them to think of family, girlfriends and absent friends.

Jesús Navas and Ramos are preparing undershirts which will allow them to pay tribute to their former team-mate Antonio Puerta, who died after collapsing during a match in 2007. Ramos did the same for the Euro 2008 trophy presentation and the memory of his friend, with whom he played at Sevilla and in the *categorías inferiores*, has not dimmed one iota.

Llorente suggests to Iniesta that he will help him sketch out a tribute to Dani Jarque, the Espanyol defender and an international team-mate of Iniesta's at under-21 level, who died aged 26 in 2009, for the Barcelona man's undershirt. They get to it.

When the time comes, Del Bosque doesn't reach for stirring, patriotic, out-of-character rhetoric.

"Guys, you are not soldiers going into battle. This is football, not a war. We compete, we fight to have the ball, but we are here to keep on playing the way that we know how, to be loyal to our style. Humility, solidarity; be brave, start well, go after the game. That's important.

"Don't get tricked into doing anything daft. The only way to fail is to abandon what we believe in. Do it for yourselves, this is the biggest moment of your career, but if you need to think of anyone else, think of all the kids back home in Spain who are praying for you to win. Let's give them what they want."

The starting XI find this player tunnel huge, long and unsettling. They are held there, nervously waiting, for more time than they expect before going out to line up. Far away, on the pitch, they can see the golden trophy. It is hypnotising them.

Each player in the two teams has a mascot, a kid whose hand they have to hold. Piqué's has to haul him out of his reverie and starts to pull him along.

Earlier, on the television in the dressing room, they have seen shots of the captain of the outgoing holders, Italy's Fabio Cannavaro, holding up the trophy to the stadium crowd and then placing it on a pitch-side plinth.

"Nobody touch it!" shouts Casillas while they watch. "Nobody touches the trophy!"

Pre-match, on the BBC, Clarence Seedorf repeats a common analysis: "I think the key battle will be Robben against Capdevila."

Arjen Robben (pre-match): "I would much prefer to win a very ugly game than lose a beautiful one. The point is, we are in a World Cup final. From now on, how you actually play no longer matters. We will defend from the front; no-one here feels they are too special to get their hands dirty."

Maarten Stekelenburg, brilliant on the night, produces a fine save to prevent Ramos' header from going in early on. And then the thuggish nature of Holland's gameplan becomes evident. Even while the game rages on it brings them worldwide condemnation via broadcast and social media.

The referee, Howard Webb, tries to cope with Holland's attempts to kick Spain out of the contest, but he also makes mistakes. By half-time it is no exaggeration to say that Van Bommel, Nigel de Jong and Sneijder could all have been red carded. Van Bommel dives in and slices Iniesta to the ground from behind. Sneijder stamps his studs right into Busquets' knee with the Spaniard standing upright. De Jong infamously brings his right leg up to kung-fu height and puts his studs into Xabi Alonso's chest.

De Jong's assault on Alonso, and the determinedly destructive nature of the Dutch fouling, reminds me of my interview with Piqué on Friday afternoon in Potch. Piqué spoke about playing for Cruyff in the Catalan XI and we hit upon the word elegance. It was Cruyff's elegance in the early 1970s which first hooked me on international football.

Gerard Piqué: "Elegance is everywhere. It's how you dress, how you comport yourself, how you play. If you have elegance as one of your natural characteristics, then you need to expose it when you play football. The elegant players are not just better footballers, they are better because they are the ones the people want to see. That's better than being the tough guy who wants to hand out dirty tackles and fouls all the time."

By the end, Holland have committed 29 fouls, Spain 19. Nine bookings and a red card to five yellows. One of Spain's bookings is for Iniesta removing his shirt to commemorate Dani Jarque.

Spain's previous six games have produced a total of 19 yellows, only three of which have been for them. Holland finish the tournament as the team with the worst disciplinary record — twice as bad as anyone else.

Post match, the father of both schools of football will write a column which is scathing in the extreme of what he's witnessed.

Johan Cruyff: "A couple of days before the final I was asked: 'Can we [Holland] stop Spain playing in the way which allowed José Mourinho's Inter to eliminate Barça from the Champions League semi-final?'

"I said no, because I thought that my country's players would never dare do that and that they wouldn't totally renounce their style. I said that because even though Holland doesn't have such truly great players as before they do have a defined playing style. I was wrong.

"It's true they didn't line 11 men up on the goal line – but nearly. They didn't want the ball and, lamentably, they played really dirty, to the extent that they should have been down to nine men really early on thanks to two ugly challenges which nearly damaged me watching them!

"I'm not sore at having been wrong, just at seeing Holland choose such an ugly route to try to win this trophy. It was ugly, tough, vulgar, barely watchable, and with very little football involved. All of which did serve to unsettle Spain. If that's all you want to aim for then fine, but ... they lost, too."

Later in the game Johnny Heitinga is sent off for a second booking when he hauls Iniesta back in the middle of a one-two with Xavi. Puyol should have been sent off, too, for climbing on Robben as he broke through. Robben is a menace, but Capdevila plays him excellently, and he manages it half-lame.

Joan Capdevila: "Did you see the state of my ankle that night? Van Persie stamped right on it and the ref booked him, but it was so bad I was sure I wouldn't be able to carry on after half-time The ankle was already swollen up like a tennis ball. During the break I had to lie down because of the pain. I got some treatment, got it bandaged up tight and just forced myself to play on in the end. In a normal match you'd give up after an injury like that, but that day it was different."

At half-time, Seedorf gives a preview of the embarrassment which will be evident among many former Dutch internationals in the coming days, most notably Cruyff. "The Dutch tactic is just their aggression I think. They've been committing a lot of fouls and they are lucky not to have received a couple of red cards. Spain started well, after 15 minutes the Netherlands reshaped and since then all we've seen is fouls and tension."

Heitinga conjures up a miraculous block from David Villa close in, when the striker's volley seemed a certain goal.

Then, with 20 minutes left, a heart-stopping moment. Sneijder, although falling, spears a pass between Puyol and Piqué and Robben is free through the middle, just him and his former Real Madrid team-mate Casillas. The Spanish captain initially looks befuddled. He takes a couple of hops forward then a couple of steps back. Instead, he is undergoing the transformation described by his goalkeeping coach, José Manuel Ochotorena. Suddenly, there is ice in his veins.

Robben advances, he picks his spot and he correctly judges that Casillas, as a left-footed player, has a marginal preference for diving to his left in 50:50 situations. However, Casillas extends his right leg up in the air, stretched as far as he is able and Robben's net-bound shot clips the toe of Casillas' right boot. Unfeasibly, the ball deflects wide. The best save I have ever seen.

With seven minutes left, Robben again gobbles up a headed knock-on and powers through. Puyol grapples him, tries to bring him down and Robben insists on staying upright and trying to dribble round Casillas to score. However, his momentum is checked, Casillas dives at his feet and the second-best chance of the game is gone.

Ramos misses with a convertable header. Fàbregas is in prime scoring position but Stekelenburg produces a save with his outstretched boot which is almost the equal to that made by Casillas.

The climax of the story is near, but now the chief protagonist comes close to leaving the stage.

Andrés Iniesta thought he wasn't going to make it to this tournament. Once here, injury very nearly robbed him of a chance to play. Now, it very nearly all slips away from him at the last moment, due to the most uncharacteristic loss of one of the most even tempers in football.

Van Bommel has fouled consistently and now goes over the ball to plant his studs on Iniesta's ankle. No foul is given. As the play moves away, Iniesta get up and checks Van Bommel, knee to thigh.

Andrés Iniesta: "I was just being fouled for 80 minutes. Perhaps the referee, if he wanted to interpret it differently then maybe he could have sent me off. These things happen in football."

Howard Webb speaks to Iniesta, but that is all. The decision – which makes sense in the context of what has been allowed to pass that night – changes Iniesta's life, and football history.

Xavi: "They were feeling the pace more than us and we could have won it in extra-time."

Right in front of our pitch-side position, Fàbregas and Torres have been warming up. Fàbregas is bullish and ready to go. From the touchline he harasses the assistant referee, he harangues Webb. He sprints up and down. He gets on.

Torres is left there, feeling that his chance has gone and looking bereft. Then, suddenly, he is called upon. He always scores in finals.

Xavi: "The idea of going to penalties just terrified me. They were looking for it and getting to penalties with 10 men was already going to be a little triumph for them."

Gerard Piqué: "You begin to imagine taking a penalty because it's going to take a good psychological strength to take one in a World Cup final. Once you begin to think of the significance, your legs are going to shake. Once that starts happening, they are never going to stop trembling."

Instead, with just over four minutes left in extra-time, Navas, in a right wing-back position, sets off with a skip and a hop down the touchline. His inside pass to Iniesta, centre pitch, is shuttled on to Fàbregas, who supplies Torres out wide. He sees the run Iniesta has made forward – the little midfielder is at the far right-hand edge of the box. However, Torres slightly underhits the crossfield ball.

Van der Vaart is filling in for Heitinga at centre-back. As he attempts to clear, he slips and the ball is available on the edge of Holland's penalty area. Fàbregas has anticipated and takes a touch before cushioning a pass to Iniesta. Van der Vaart should be in midfield, marking Iniesta. Instead he is in defence, covering for Heitinga, sent off for a foul on ... Iniesta. There is one name cropping up here again and again and again.

Andrés Iniesta: "In that moment we were alone, the ball and I. I could hear nothing. As far as I was concerned, the whole stadium had fallen silent. I waited for the Isaac Newton effect, for gravity to make the ball drop and the second I had it at my foot, I knew it was going in, I just knew it. It had all come down to this moment. I knew exactly how to control it and where to put it: as hard as I could across Stekelenburg, so that he had no time to react."

Back in Fuentealbilla, where Iniesta was born, his dad José Antonio is watching at home, alone. His fear of flying is such that he took the train from Barcelona to Vienna for the Euro 2008 final and he often misses his son's biggest games. In such circumstances, he prefers to watch in peace and quiet. When his son scores, José Antonio turns off the television immediately. He cannot bear the tension of the next couple of minutes.

Iniesta's mother, María Francisca Luján, meantime, is equally stressed down at Bar Luján, in the centre of town, where Grandad Iniesta was the landlord for 35 years. On retirement, he converted every newspaper cutting he ever saved about his talented grandson into an archive which covers every millimetre of wall space. On the night of Iniesta's final it is packed, like most bars in Spain, and María Francisca is so uptight that she goes outside to seek fresh air and is still out there when her son scores his historic goal.

She misses him racing away to the left-hand corner flag, just as he had done at Stamford Bridge – the footage he saw on the DVD as the aeroplane took him from Spain to South Africa.

Now he is tearing off his Spain shirt so that the world can see his t-shirt: 'Dani Jarque, always with us.' Now he is submerged. Long after the tournament, he will admit that even in the heat of this moment, he quickly reckons on staying in that mad celebratory huddle for as long as Webb will permit, in order to use up time.

At the far end of the pitch, Iker Casillas sets off on a run, arms outstretched as if he is trying to build up enough speed to take flight. As emotion over-rides adrenaline, he collapses to his knees and tears overtake him.

Del Bosque is standing motionless, alone. He is in the perspex dugout, like a guy waiting for a bus to take him home to Salamanca after a long day at work. This night has been so mad that not until Webb blows the whistle will he relax. He begins to urge everyone else to stop celebrating, calm down and *pay attention!*

Four minutes later, that whistle sounds.

Fireworks light up the sky above Fuentealbilla. Only then does José Antonio Iniesta know for sure that his son has won the World Cup for Spain.

There is disbelief, there are tears, embraces, a search for friends and loved ones in the stands. Soon, they want their *La Roja* strips on, the new ones, red with the single gold star above the crest which will tell forever more that Spain won the World Cup.

Torres, carried off due to a groin strain, is helped to hobble up the stairs with the group, just as the trophy arrives in Iker Casillas' hands and is raised into a rain of ticker tape.

They gambol and sing and parade their trophy. Soccer City is theirs, forever.

Inside the dressing-room reception área, Juanma Castaño, on-the-spot reporter for Canal+, gets his traditional soaking in alcohol as David Villa and Xavi let him weigh the World Cup in his hands. The inner sanctum remains private as the players start to arrive in groups of three and four. Adam, my cameraman, and I get the wink, we are one of two crews allowed to witness the scene.

Rafa Nadal arrives and is more excited and more emotional than the players who have just won this exhausting match. His tennis triumphs are always marked by him pretending to bite the medal he wins, and he poses with several of *La Roja* who mimic his medal celebration, biting their winners' insignia.

Placido Domingo is here again. I invite him to try a few Clash numbers but there is no singing this time. It is a happy, if not quite orgiastic, scene. Perhaps the relatively sober atmosphere is to do with the fact that Doña Sofía has arrived, as promised, and this time with her son Felipe, the Prince of Asturias, and his journalist wife Letizia.

The *utilleros* pass me a beer and Pedro presumably mistakes me for Howard Webb as he smiles and says, "Thanks for everything", giving me a friendly embrace. It has been a strange month.

Sergio Ramos excuses himself. For the last couple of days he has been swapping texts with Arjen Robben, Wesley Sneijder and Rafael Van der Vaart. It has been a brutal night, Holland has renounced its footballing ethos and Ramos is going to commiserate with his friends. *Quid pro quo*, Phillip Cocu, a Barcelona legend, is on the Dutch coaching team and he eases in to seek out his former team-mates, Iniesta, Puyol, Xavi and Valdés, to tell them: "The better team won."

When these players look back on their photographs from this monumental night, they will not see many of Del Bosque in that dressing room with the World Cup. The coach takes Puyol aside: "You can't quit now, you have to reach 100 caps at least." It sways Puyol into changing his decision.

Over the coming days, Del Bosque will have some golden moments and much recognition for his achievement. Right now, he leaves the scene in search of his family; he is happy to leave his boys to it.

Not long afterwards, Gerard Piqué emerges. He is still in his boots, shorts and vest and he has the tiny nail scissors from the first-aid kit in his hand as he marches down the tunnel, toward the pitch. A couple of minutes later he is back, very distressed, demanding of a tournament official: "Where is the goal net? Where have the goal nets gone?"

When they show precious little interest in his enquiry or even basic politeness to him, he explains to me that he always cuts a souvenir piece of net but, this time, he has been too late. They are gone. I accept his idea that I join the quest and with the help of an apparently streetwise stadium volunteer kid, we trawl through the entire underbelly of Soccer City.

Everybody wants a piece of Piqué. The kid has made him promise that there'll be a reward of a Spain shirt in this for him, but when the extent of his inside knowledge turns out to be how to get to the vehicle tunnel to the pitch, Piqué very nearly eats him alive. Then we mistakenly burst in on a room where the take for the food, programmes and refreshments is being counted. Finally, we persuade the security into letting us into the stadium manager's office.

Yes, says one member of staff, the nets are here.

No, says one another, you can't have even a couple of centimetres from them. But, while we've got you here, can we have a picture? An autograph?

They are now dealing with an increasingly angry 6ft 3ins World Cup winner. As he poses for yet another photograph with staff who are not helping him in his quest for a memento, he turns to me and says, in Spanish: "I'll knock him down, we'll grab the nets and make a run for it." Part of my mind freezes, the other part *thinks* he's joking. Thankfully, the stadium manager finally arrives, as do some tournament staff. It ends in a net gain.

As the players prepare to leave Soccer City, we have a final chance to speak to them.

"Iker Casillas, world champion. How does that sound to you?"

Iker Casillas: "It sounds the best. It sounds like all the hard work, all the support from my parents has been rewarded. It sounds like it means millions of people, all round Spain, will be celebrating. That's good enough for me.

"Right now, an hour after the whistle, I still can't believe it. I don't think any of us have realised quite what we've achieved. We are all filled with such enormous happiness that there's no point in even trying to imagine what this will mean in a week or a month or a year. It's a dream, but one which doesn't feel real yet. All of us who are here are so because of incessant work since we were kids but also because of a radical change of style which was introduced to the Spain team four years ago. The decision was to rely on a generation of players who had been champion at under-16, under-19, under-20 and other levels and now that decision has borne fruit.

"During the match? That moment when it was just me and Arjen Robben … it was eternal. Absolutely eternal. So many things go through your head. Luckily the coin fell heads when I called heads, Robben wasn't definitive in his finish and we stayed alive. Now when you say 'Iker Casillas, world champion' it sounds incredible. I really still don't believe it. Back in Spain right now I can hardly imagine what it's like. The truth is that the youngsters of our country have the great good fortune of seeing their national team become world champions. I wish I'd had that opportunity as a kid. However, it's left me with the equal fortune of being the first Spanish captain to lift that World Cup trophy."

Gradually, the red tide is ebbing. Spain's media are down near the team bus. Iniesta takes Fàbregas' arm and hauls him away from an interview when the younger man has been praising Spain's goalscorer. "That's enough of that. Bus."

Quietly, Silvia Dorschnerova is slowly making her way to the bus, dressed in her elegant federation suit and carrying an impressive briefcase in her right hand. Silvia is the match delegate, organised, thorough, multi-lingual, smart. She keeps an eye on rules and administration, liaison with referees and tournament organisers. She has the World Cup in that briefcase, the trophy which will be passed from hand to hand, which will appear in a hundred photos as *La Roja* fly to what is a raucous welcome in Madrid the next day.

Millions take to the streets between the night of the match, the open-topped bus parade and the staged presentation, which turns into the Pepe Reina show as he takes the microphone to introduce every player and staff member on stage, in front of the adoring public. All in all it's not the worst day Spain has ever had.

Holland 0 Spain 1 (after extra-time)

Holland: Stekelenburg, Van der Wiel, Heitinga, Mathijsen, Van Bronckhorst (Braafheid 105), Van Bommel, De Jong (Van der Vaart 99), Robben, Sneijder, Kuyt (Elia 71), Van Persie

Spain: Casillas, Ramos, Piqué, Puyol, Capdevila, Busquets, Alonso

(Fàbregas 87), Iniesta, Xavi, Pedro (Navas 60), Villa (Torres 106)
Goal: Iniesta 116

At home, in Barcelona, Andrés Iniesta has a little treasure trove of golden memories from his career: medals, shirts, photos, boots, newspaper clippings. His most treasured memento will be the *La Roja* shirt in which he scored the World Cup-winning goal.

It is a while since he has sorted through his personal museum and as he archives this latest artifact, he chances upon another, from nine years ago.

Iniesta and Fernando Torres made their debut together in the *categorías inferiores* back in 2000, in a win over Belgium. The following summer they led the *Rojita* side sent to win the FIFA Under-17 World Cup in Trinidad and Tobago. Already Under-16 European champions, they journeyed to the Caribbean with high hopes, but failed to qualify from a group containing Oman and Burkina Faso. Parting at the end of a disastrous tournament, Iniesta and Torres swapped shirts, each signing one with a message for the other.

Now, returning as king of the world, having scored from a move which Torres initiates in Soccer City, Iniesta unfolds the No.9 shirt his friend signed for him all those years ago.

Torres' handwriting, even in magic marker, is clear to read: "Don't worry. Our World Cup is still to come."

It just has.

Everything You Always Wanted to Know About Winning Tournaments*

*But Were Afraid to Ask

— **Kaduna, Nigeria**
— *April 17, 1999*

Whatever was scuttling in the corner of Xavi's room was keeping him awake.

It wasn't one of the legion of cockroaches which ruled the joint. They were the size of roller skates, but their legs made a lighter sound on the pock-marked linoleum – he was so accustomed to it by now he had names for some of them.

It could be a rat. If so, this might develop into a life-or-death tussle.

But even if he decided to risk everything by shaking off the stale, flea-ridden sheets and confronting the demon in the dark corner, Xavi wasn't sure whether he could count on the support of Gabri, the team-mate who had been sharing his bed because the shabby hotel didn't even have sufficient rooms for the visiting Spanish squad. Xavi *thought* his pal had been ordered by the team doctor to move to another room so as not to contract this horrible virus with a quarter-final against Ghana looming. But his fever was so high, it was possible he had hallucinated that part.

Despite the Catalan's red-hot turmoil he knew that, today, a mutiny was coming. Things had gone too far.

Before Spain's under-20 team had set off for the FIFA Youth World Cup, the Spanish ambassador to Nigeria had stopped just short of telling them not to go. In a fraught meeting involving the Spanish federation, the squad – also including Iker Casillas, Carlos Marchena, Pablo Orbaíz, Pablo Couñago and Dani Aranzubía – plus extremely anxious parents, he listed the potential issues around the trip: gun-play; religious intolerance; corruption; malaria; poor sanitation and temperatures over 40 degrees.

Not without a major debate, they travelled.

As soon as they arrived at their first hotel, in Calabar, and before a match against a Brazil team featuring Ronaldinho, events made them consider abandoning the tournament and heading home.

Iker Casillas: "The first day we got there, already feeling down at the poor conditions and the small rooms with two to a bed, there was a big shoot-out on the street, right in front of the reception. Nobody even blinked an eye, apart from us! The people in the hotel told us that it was the norm and the only thing was to make sure we didn't leave the hotel."

A 2-0 victory over Brazil hit them like a shock of adrenalin so they continued, with wins over Honduras and the USA. Then, on to Kaduna.

Despite superb football and a clear line of progression which suggested Iñaki Sáez's team were now favourites to win Spain's first world title at any level, unhappiness continued to grow.

These were kids for whom routine and the familiar were foundation stones. They had travelled, but had never experienced what they considered to be third-world conditions, never been so cut off from home. Communication with Spain and their worried parents and friends was damn near impossible. Hotel phones you could forget; not one of the travelling party had a working mobile phone (federation included) and only the tiny handful of international media intermittently covering Spain had old-fashioned satellite phones of the kind previously employed only on the battlefield. One player, Gerard, was injured and had to be sent home, but they sent the request for a replacement into a telecommunications vacuum.

Iñaki Sáez: "I couldn't begin to describe all the problems we had. When we sent Gerard home we requested [David] Aganzo in his place. The problem was that we had no idea whether he was coming or not until he turned up on our doorstep. Contacting Spain was just so difficult."

There were lizards in their bedrooms; players often had to sleep head-to-toe in the same bed because the hotel simply did not have sufficient twin rooms; the sheets moved through their own propulsion thanks to the plethora of small insects which infected them; cooks in the hotel were seen turning fried eggs over with their bare hands on the skillet; when the players, as a last resort, asked for plain pasta, it arrived burnt. Word was circulated that one of the FIFA referees, Jan Wegereef of the Netherlands, had been hospitalised with malaria.

Everything came to a head in Kaduna.

Iñaki Sáez: "Xavi was a natural leader on the pitch, in terms of setting an example and in the way that he took command and urged his team-mates on. He was an obvious choice for captain [Orbaiz was the senior and on-pitch captain but Xavi was part of the three-man structure which is very common in Spain]. I'll never forget the day he and the other two captains asked to see me.

"We were staying in particularly shabby accommodation. The lads were having to sleep two to a bed, there were lizards everywhere you looked, a horrible dining room attached to a kitchen with a load of dented, dirty pots and pans hanging on the walls.

"Xavi got sick as a result of the appalling conditions and he ended up losing several kilos. Anyway, the captains sat me down and told me straight that the players couldn't take it anymore and they wanted to go home."

In these moments, things happened and decisions were taken which would subtly lay foundations for Spain's World Cup win in 2010.

Sáez listened to his players and then struck a deal. Firstly, he reminded them of the 15 or 20 kids they had left in Spain, most of whom were more than good enough to be in Nigeria, who would have cut off a finger to be there playing for their country.

'How can you let them down?'

Next, he emphasised that none of what they were experiencing was real. Sáez sold them the idea of the tournament as a bubble. The tournament would end, they would go home and they would discover – they did discover – that Spain had become hooked by their exploits. TV2 was televising the games in Spain – at least between power cuts suffered by the Nigerian host broadcasters – and the audience was around five million. This was a career-defining moment for many of them.

Finally, Sáez made the point that he, personally, had made a huge sacrifice that they knew very well had cost him a deal of mental agony.

Not long after defeating Brazil in the first game, the Spanish embassy informed Sáez that his mother had died. He considered that his greater duty was to remain in Africa and mentor this talented squad to whatever destiny held for them.

> **Iñaki Sáez**: "My mother had been very, very ill before I left, close to death in fact, and, spiritually at least, I had already made my final farewells. So I decided not to go back for the funeral when she passed away in the middle of the competition. The youngsters were aware of what had happened and I know that they really appreciated the sacrifice I had made to stay with them."

The pact was this: Xavi and Orbaiz would go back to the players, convince them to play Ghana and there would be a summit meeting the morning after the quarter-final. The captains understood Sáez's point of view and trusted him.

Moreover, he had appealed to their competitive instinct. Two years previously, Ghana had beaten Xavi and Iker Casillas in the FIFA Under-17 World Cup semi-final. Indeed, Spain had never beaten Ghana at youth level. "If you want to go home," he told them, "don't let it look like you are scared of Ghana."

The players were swayed. Casillas was picked for only his second game of the tournament because Sáez had seen the power and pace of the Ghanaian team lead to counter attacks and one-on-one situations in previous matches.

This time Spain dominated but after conceding a freakish, last-minute equaliser they faced a shoot-out; Casillas got a touch on George Blay's effort – the 18th penalty – and his save meant Spain were in the semi-final.

Carlos Lorenzana, a Spanish federation physio, arrived in time for the Ghana match and, afterwards, his input was vital. "Spain is enraptured with what you are doing," he told the players. "The worst is over, don't let the country down now." He also gave them the mother and father of all rows for daring to think of throwing in the towel – but it was the carrot, not the stick, which had the most effect.

Sáez negotiated a change of hotel and the federation employees bribed the new cook with pennants and key rings, leading to an improvement in the quality of the food. Spain beat Mali in the semi-final and then, on April 23, Sáez's birthday was celebrated in the Spanish embassy. Life was good again.

Spain thrashed Japan in the final to become world champions for the first time at any level. At the time of writing, only the senior team of 2010 have matched them.

In terms of the tournament mentality Spain have displayed in all three of their major wins, this was the tributary from which a great river was to flow. The federation learned that forward planning of accommodation and travel – particularly in Africa – was vital. They have since become exceptional at it and the triumphs of Neustift, Potchefstroom and Gniewino – the camps from which they won Euro 2008, World Cup 2010 and Euro 2012 – owe greatly to their experience in Nigeria.

From that 1999 squad, Xavi, Casillas and Marchena were on the pitch in Vienna when Spain were crowned European champions in 2008. All three were there at the end of the 2010 World Cup semi-final in Durban; three Nigeria alumni about to conquer the football world, in Africa, again.

The 1999 tournament forged strong bonds between them; Casillas and Xavi were the mainstays of Vicente del Bosque's captaincy team, and Marchena was one of the few included in the crisis meeting at the cricket ground at Potch after World Cup 2010 began with defeat by Switzerland.

Nigeria not only taught these three players the need for resilience, but also showed them the prize which can reward that quality and reinforced the humility which was a cornerstone of their federation training.

Iker Casillas: "Although it seemed illogical to us that FIFA brought that tournament to a country in the state Nigeria was in, it was only by being there that we could realise what real poverty and deprivation were. I saw people beating each other up for a scrap of food and now, whenever I eat I'm thankful for what I've got. I've seen for myself, not from some report, that people starve – I've never moaned about my lot since."

Iñaki Sáez: "When I look back now it's the strength and courage of that group of players that stands out; the way they coped and triumphed in a strange country and in enormously difficult circumstances. It became a template for future generations."

Spain didn't win in Vienna, Soccer City and Kiev specifically because of their experiences in Nigeria in 1999, but the tournament mentality learned there was seminal.

The following year, *La Roja* took silver at the Sydney Olympics. Sáez told me: "It was great having guys like Xavi who had been in Nigeria on the Olympic team. He kept saying how wonderful everything was because, 'you should have seen the dump of a hotel in Kaduna'. Those stories had taken on mythical proportions by the end of the Sydney Olympic final."

In Potchefstroom, in 2010, some of the world's greatest players, multimillionaires who might not only be sated by success but softened by it, lived in basic student accommodation: bare floors, a single bed, a tiny two-bar electric heater on the wall, unreliable central heating, a 16-inch television and a petite bathroom.

In Gniewino in 2012, the Hotel Mistral was of a different order, attractive and of a high standard, but it was isolated in a rural and extremely basic area around the training camp.

In both cases I wondered why boredom, restlessness, irritability and misbehaviour didn't encroach as I had seen within many other national squads in such circumstances.

Central explanations are that Spain enjoy their daily – sometimes twice daily – training, that they are steely in their professionalism (discomfort versus winning a major trophy is a no-contest) and that they largely enjoy being together.

I have witnessed how players' families are close at hand; I've seen players allowed to go out on the town during a tournament; beers in the team hotel; the occasionally spartan quarters these superstar athletes live in. It's a matter of record over the years that many international squads wouldn't have been able to cope with this. Drunkenness, paparazzi fights, cops, curfew breaches, ill-advised dalliances with kiss-and-tell females would have followed. But all these social policies which many of their rivals seem unable to handle are now a central part of the Spanish tournament-winning DNA.

Vicente del Bosque: "I think it's very beneficial for the group to go out and clear their heads, regardless of the result. Stress is a big thing and there's lots of pressure, especially in these types of tournaments. To have a chat over a beer, de-stress, I think is very advisable. You need to disconnect and take time out.

"It's important to have a lot of trust in them and I am quite lenient in that regard. If, on the odd occasion, one of them were to betray that trust or make a mistake, it wouldn't be the end of the world or necessarily mean that others would follow suit."

Four of Spain's 2010 world champions – Carles Puyol, Xavi, Marchena and Joan Capdevila – won silver medals at the Sydney Olympics in 2000 (Casillas opted not to participate in order to prioritise his Real Madrid career). At Espanyol's Sant Adrià training ground 13 years later, Capdevila recalled the experience.

Joan Capdevila: "Going to Sydney was the best experience of my life. I didn't have a clue about the country beyond what I'd seen on TV, but you know the best thing that happened there? We got to know each other and solid friendships were formed. It was great – all of us doing the sights together, going to see the kangaroos, moving about as one group. We hardly spoke about football at all.

"We were in Adelaide, then Melbourne and finally Sydney. We stayed in a hotel in the middle of Sydney, just us, and we could walk about freely there. Looking back I appreciate now just what an amazing experience it was. You have to grow up a bit when you go through an experience like that. The group bonded in Sydney."

Iñaki Sáez: "In Nigeria we were pretty much marooned in the hotel. There were police stationed outside and they wouldn't let us leave in case something happened.

"In Australia things were quite different and Toni Velamazan, the Valencia player who was a nice lad and one of our captains, came up to me shaking with nerves and stammering. He wanted me to allow the players a night out. "I told him that if they beat Italy [in the quarter-final] they could all go out and, what's more, he could decide on the curfew time. So, of course, they won and Toni told me they wanted to be out till 5am. In the event most of them turned up at the hotel at 2am or 3am and the stragglers were in by 3.30am, but the important thing was that they got to go out.

"Ten days training in Spain plus the 20 days in Australia was a long time away from home and usually tensions would develop. Some kind of argument would break out. It's one aspect of this job that's much more important than people think. You have to look after the players, negotiate with them. If you're willing to compromise a bit, they do appreciate it."

Spain win tournaments, principally, because they have the best players, but history is full of great teams who do not win. In this era, *La Roja's* truly great footballers have been guided, negotiated with and granted privileges by a series of man-managers, administrators and a federation president who know how to fine-tune them and the environment they work in; how to create what England, for example, find to be an almost mythical concept: the tournament mentality.

The nights out, the wives and girlfriends, the children who made the winning dressing room after the final of Euro 2012 feel like a crèche, the shopping trips, the sushi restaurants – as Capdevila emphasised to me, these are privileges which, when the team isn't winning, will be used to castigate the team.

Meanwhile, they have become weapons against boredom and stress within a group of more than 20 men who forge a winning spirit in situations which used to defeat them.

Fernando Torres was a part of failing squads at Euro 2004 and the 2006 World Cup before winning three tournaments with Spain and is perfectly placed to reflect on how and when the atmosphere changed, and what effect it had.

Fernando Torres: "Luis [Aragonés] always said that at all costs we had to avoid boredom setting in. According to him, boredom was more tiring than anything else and the federation has always done us proud in this respect by arranging base camps which allow us a bit of freedom. We tend to be out in the sticks, maybe a couple of hours away from any of our games, like we were in Poland, but it means that we can relax, pop in and out of each other's rooms, go out for a coffee, play a game of pool or a video game. If you're in a little village in the back of beyond, the locals tend not to be too interested in football and they'll leave you alone if you're out for a stroll.

"A bedroom is just to lay your head down at night and, generally, what it's like doesn't really matter. The important thing is spending the day with your team-mates. You'll see players having a coffee or a beer together after training and I don't see a problem in that. The important thing is that you're enjoying yourself and not worrying about however many days you have to spend there and how to get through them.

"Our families are put up in a nearby hotel and we get some time with them after training, a couple of hours to spend with our wives and kids. I don't think that that's a strange way to do things. It's the teams that don't do that that are a bit weird.

"As long as you trust the players in the squad and know that they won't take advantage, there's no problem. The management trust the players and, for our part, we know not to cross the line. If we're told to get back by 10pm, nobody's going to stroll in at 11. You don't want to be on the next plane home.

"Luis and Vicente both showed enormous trust in us, although Luis was a bit more vigilant. I guess it's always difficult to relax the rules at the beginning, but we've earned their trust and there's never been a single problem."

Santi Cazorla: "It's vital to keep talking to each other throughout the long tournaments. It's especially healthy if those with different points of view about something specific get to share their opinions, informally, at the same time. After every match we'd have coffee in someone's room and pick the game apart: 'The boss should have done this' or 'You shouldn't have made that move.' We'd argue back and forth about the tiniest detail, but that's what makes us so successful: talking; listening to the different opinions, listening to the captains. Even at half-time, the discussions would go on like that.

"*Puyi*, Iker and Xavi would point out where things weren't being done right. There's nothing to beat that spirit, that sharing of details at a tournament. You have to go to war, but how do you go to war? That's the key, and we seem to have it."

Fernando Torres: "The friendship within the team is reflected in the relationships our families have with each other. We'd have a day off at a tournament and I'll say to my wife: 'What do you want to do about lunch?' and she'll say: 'Let's give Santi's wife a buzz,' or whoever it may be.

"We all like to socialise together and we enjoy each other's company. That's been the secret of our success as a squad and as a team, that lack of egotism. Usually you are dealing with 15 egos in a football team, but in this national team, now, it's like there is just one.

"We all understand our position in European and world football and no-one's going to walk all over a team-mate just to get ahead. We are here to help each other."

Spain's record shows that, beyond talent, they have a system of tournament management which is exemplary.

Across 43 UEFA youth tournaments, from Under-16 to Under-21 level and between 1997 and 2013, Spain have won 14 and been runners-up six times. A huge record.

In the same time frame, at FIFA Under-17 and Under-20 level they have one win, three second places and one third place in 16 tournaments.

During the 45 matches in the knockout stages of those tournaments plus the three senior tournaments *La Roja* has won, they have participated in 19 penalty shoot-outs and won 14.

A pretty resounding testimony to the fact that, for the last 20 years, the Spanish federation has been educating players who can live together, pull together, go out together, conquer boredom, accept hardships, take their families along, subjugate club and geographical rivalries, outplay their rivals and win penalty shoot-outs.

If that's not a superior tournament mentality, I'd love to know what is.

Euro 2012

We expected to win it. In fact, winning was the only thing we could do.

Fernando Torres

Euro 2012

It transpires that in order to win Euro 2012, Spain not only have to overcome Italy, Ireland, Croatia, France and Portugal, but José Mourinho, too.

A foundation stone of all Spain's triumphant football since late in 2006, a period that has included two defeats in 45 competitive matches, has been an unbreakable spirit between players, whether starters or substitutes. In qualifying matches away from home on disastrous, cow-patch pitches, everyone pulls together. Living cheek by jowl for six weeks in order to win a tournament, everyone pulls together. Suddenly this unity is threatened by a new force in Spanish football.

From the day Mourinho takes over at Madrid until Euro 2012 there are 11 *Clásicos*. These matches produce 82 bookings and nine red cards, plus an additional expulsion for the Madrid manager. Barça players are booked 31 times and receive two straight reds. Real Madrid players are booked 51 times, receive five straight reds and two more of their players are dismissed for second bookings.

The *Clásico* has never been a flower-picking expedition for those of gentle disposition and refined manner, but the nastiness which erupts while Mourinho is in charge of Madrid, filling day after day of national debate, is like a corrosive acid to the Spain spirit.

Mourinho institutes a discourse that referees are prejudiced against Madrid when they play Barça; he consistently claims that Barcelona are theatrical – a theme he first introduced whilst Chelsea manager about the moment when Asier del Horno implanted one of his boots halfway up Leo Messi's thigh.

Under Mourinho, Madrid often play superbly. Their 2011 Copa del Rey final performance is first class; their victorious La Liga campaign of 2011/12 full of quality, hunger and excellence. Along the way, however, he both espouses and encourages 'win at any cost' tactics to fracture what he sees as unacceptably cosy friendships between key Spain players on either side of the *Clásico* divide. He expects his troops to follow orders. Tension mounts and players from both clubs begin to do and say things which threaten to do immense damage to the unity within the national squad.

Along the way, the signals given by Vicente del Bosque's shift from affable confidence that this harmony is indestructible, to concern that conflict between the clubs could infect his dressing room, then to the hardline: Anyone who takes this kind of behaviour into my squad will be excluded.

When Barça beat Madrid 5-0 in Mourinho's first *Clásico*, Sergio Ramos follows his red card for a bad foul on Messi by putting his hand on Carles Puyol's face and pushing him to the ground. Ramos and Gerard Piqué are held apart but patently indicate to one another that the argument will continue inside and, as Ramos departs the field, Xavi approaches the Madrid defender to remonstrate but is also shoved away, hand on chin. None of these are capital crimes, but they don't square with what these players feel about one another when sharing red shirts. Four months have passed since they won the World Cup and bathed in the adoration of the Spanish public.

By the Copa del Rey final of April 2011, tension is higher still. Álvaro Arbeloa and David Villa collide, no foul is given but, as he stands up, Arbeloa treads on Villa without acknowledgment or apology. Instead, Arbeloa and Ramos haul Villa upwards, one on each arm, as if to indicate he has been faking.

Xavi and Casillas face off and exchange complaints. The match develops via a knee-high challenge by Sergio Busquets on Xabi Alonso.

Within days, each of the UEFA Champions League semi-finals contains aggression and controversy. Pepe's red-card challenge on Dani Alves sparks Mourinho's infamous *'por qué?'* rant, in which he claims Barça's support of UNICEF may be helping them to win decisions. The second leg stokes legitimate fury from Madrid when a poor refereeing decision robs them of Gonzalo Higuaín's goal.

Before Spain's summer tour to North and Central America, Casillas admits:

"Xavi and I will have a little chat when we see each other again and, even if we both swear at each other a little, that will be that. I'm convinced that we don't need to have some sort of clear-the-air meeting. I made a mistake during one of the games against Barça, in the heat of the moment, when I tapped my face with the back of my hand to signify what I thought of them [It means: 'What a bloody cheek you've got!']. But I recognised and accepted my mistake."

Then come the moments which change everything. The Spanish Supercopa of August 2011 is balanced at 2-2 from the first leg in Madrid. At the Camp Nou, both teams play wonderfully. Messi wins it 3-2 with a remarkable late goal and then Marcelo earns a red card for a two-footed, off-the-ground lunge at Cesc Fàbregas. Both teams converge around the two participants, the benches empty. David Villa and Mesut Özil are red-carded. Mourinho sneaks around the back of the crowd and pokes a cowardly finger into Tito Vilanova's eye. Before it all dies down, Xavi and Casillas, again, end up recriminating with each other, face-to-face.

The Madrid and Spain captain gives an on-pitch television interview at the final whistle. He was half the length of the field away from Marcelo's red-card offence, but adopts the Mourinho doctrine in reacting to an incident which he hasn't seen properly.

"There will have been a tackle, they will have thrown themselves down as usual." He is talking about Fàbregas, who produced the assist for Andrés Iniesta's World Cup-winning goal allowing Casillas to lift the most famous trophy in football, one year previously.

Inside the Camp Nou, Mourinho justifies poking Vilanova in the eye by remarking that "football is a man's game".

Gerard Piqué says: "I don't believe this is down to the Madrid players. We've defeated them 6-2 at their stadium but none of this kind of thing happened. I have lived with them at competitions and they have been terrific people from the first minute. I don't think they are to blame, it's just that they are under the orders of a guy who is trying to damage Spanish football. Now they accuse the Catalans of being culpable for this, but the culpable guy is in charge at Madrid.

"When we all get together for the national side we will be open to making sure that the team is as strong as ever and that the atmosphere is as good as ever."

Iker Casillas's brother Unai, a diehard Barcelona fan, watching at home on television and beneficiary of close-ups and replays, doesn't agree with his sibling's assessment of the red-card incident. He assures his brother that he has got it wrong.

Casillas watches the television images of Marcelo's two-footed lunge at Fàbregas for himself and then contacts Puyol and Xavi and admits he said the wrong thing, and would they pass that on to Fàbregas please. He says: "Things can't go on like this. We have to sort it out." The gesture and his words are more than enough to heal the wounds from a poisonous series of derbies.

Those who drew a link between Casillas acting like a decent, mature, team-mate and the decline in his relationship with Mourinho, culminating in him being dropped from the Madrid first team, found support from Vicente del Bosque when the Spain coach reflected on his captain's club situation in September 2013. "Iker tried to restore harmony in the situation between Barça and Madrid and it cost him. When there were difficult moments in the national team Iker helped to protect the good atmosphere and the ability of Barça and Madrid players to pull together for Spain so that we could win the European Championship in 2012. This wasn't well received and restoring the peace has been detrimental to Iker. Everyone should take the stance that the Spain team is above, or at least equal to, the interests of any of our clubs."

When he finally left Madrid in 2013, Mourinho announced his regret at not having bought Diego López at the beginning of season 2011/12 to replace Casillas. Yet Madrid won the title that season, and came within a penalty shoot-out of reaching the Champions League final. Casillas conceded only 32 times in 38 league matches and a mere eight times in 12 Champions League matches. The stats make a mockery of Mourinho's statement.

Crossing the line drawn by Mourinho between the Spain players on either side of the *Clásico* – choosing to act with dignity – would prove a fundamental step toward victory at Euro 2012. However, Casillas would suffer immense pain and frustration the following season.

If there are comparisons between the way Mourinho handles Casillas and Luis Aragonés' decision to remove Raúl from the national team in order to better direct the group as a whole in the direction he believed was right, then neither the motive nor the end result show the Portuguese in a positive light.

Days after the 2011 *Supercopa* one of the most placid and easy-going of *La Roja's* players, Santi Cazorla, commented that, for Spain, the situation was "reaching its limit".

"As much as you want to avoid it, these situations do start to influence people's relationships. All the rest of us can do is hope that it's all sorted out as soon as possible, that some sort of agreement is reached. It is what everyone wants."

However, it took only until September 2011 for indications that Spain's summer in Poland and Ukraine might be sunny.

A fortnight after the fury of the *Supercopa* final, Spain are 2-0 down to Chile in a friendly in St Gallen, Switzerland, but fight back to lead 3-2. Very late in the game there is a tangle between Arturo Vidal and Iniesta. Unusually, Iniesta goes toe-to-toe.

In the blink of an eye, as Iniesta is surrounded by threatening opponents, Arbeloa is there dispensing protection and the *Clásico* divide closes a little. Busquets gets there to help his club mate, but Casillas, too, is off the bench and running over. Sergio Ramos arrives like a steam train to knock Felipe Seymour to the ground.

Vicente del Bosque: "Arbeloa is one of the lads who's given least appreciation for his football. But he gives everything all the time, he's a great competitor. People take into consideration everything which happened in the Madrid-Barcelona *Clásicos* but he's like that every time he goes to work – even in training. He'll not know whether it's Xavi or Xabi in front of him – they'll take a boot whoever it is. He's a top guy who, just like anyone else, it's possible to misunderstand. What he does for the national team stands on its own. Everything else, well you can like or not like but he's always given the national team what it needs."

Barcelona and Madrid, fighting shoulder-to-shoulder. Ready for what lies ahead.

— Day One.

— *June 5, 2012. Gniewino, Poland*

Those responsible for getting the world champions onto their flight to Gdańsk could be forgiven for that feeling every traveller has at one time or another: 'I'm *sure* something's been left behind.' As the Airbus A321 mid-afternoon flight takes off, it is indeed missing two essential items: Carles Puyol and David Villa. The defender and the striker have a combined total of 181 caps and each is a world and European champion at club and international level. Between them, they scored six of Spain's eight goals at the World Cup. It is a bad way to begin a title defence.

Puyol is first to drop, injuring a knee in the penultimate match of the season, the city derby against Espanyol, and immediately announcing that he needs surgery for the second consecutive summer. Iker Casillas and Vicente del Bosque receive direct phone calls to confirm the news and the captain admits: "*Puyi* is a big playing loss but at least as much as a person. He's laid-back with the whole squad, he's a force for unity and he's a great guy for helping the younger players. It's a delicate situation to lose him."

When Villa announces that he is not going to make it, the absence of *La Roja's* all-time leading scorer is enough to make many think Spain's goose is cooked. Villa is the leading scorer in qualification, and passed Raúl's *La Roja* scoring record against Scotland in Alicante. A fractured tibia suffered in the semi-final of the World Club Championship not only keeps him off the plane, it ultimately ruins the final 18 months of his Barcelona career.

Initially, Villa had been expected to make the squad for Euro 2012, but the Camp Nou medical staff sounded increasingly uncertain as the tournament approached.

Villa did get back in training sufficiently early, but he began to realise that he was neither sharp nor strong enough. Rather than exploiting Del Bosque's desire to wait until the very last moment – and perhaps even to use the group stage to get the striker ready – Villa takes the coach aside on May 21, six days before the final squad is named, and admits defeat.

On the federation plane there are now 140 passengers. Employees, directors, media and Manolo el del Bombo fill the other spaces, but the 23 important ones are taken by the players seeking to make history with a third consecutive tournament win.

After seven changes between the 2008 and 2010 squads, only four members of the World Cup group are not here for the third leg: Puyol, Villa, Carlos Marchena and Joan Capdevila are replaced by Juanfran, Jordi Alba, Santi Cazorla, who returns from the 2008 squad, and Álvaro Negredo.

It's destination Gdańsk, up on the Baltic coast of Poland and home to the Solidarność (Solidarity) trade union. It's partly due to the courage and obstinacy of Solidarność co-founder Lech Wałęsa that this country found its path away from martial law toward democracy.

All of that took place as the generation of Xavi, Casillas, Villa, Puyol and Marchena were being born and Spain itself was the subject of a brief military coup.

At Euro 2012 this group of players, defined by their unity as well as their talent, will play not in Donetsk, Lviv, Poznan, Warsaw, Kiev or Wroclaw, but instead will seek their destiny in a city where international renown, inspiration and democratic triumph are initiated by the motto: *Solidarity will not be divided or destroyed.*

On the tarmac at Wałęsa airport, Spain look relaxed. Slim, grey Brooksfield suits, white shirts, dark blue ties, one single gold star above the breast pocket which bears the Spanish Plus Ultra crest. Casillas breaks from the group when he spots a youngster in a wheelchair, amongst the dignitaries. Language is a barrier but after a pat on the shoulder and a ruffle of the hair, the kid has just met the captain of the world champions.

Gniewino, the base for Spain, is over an hour away, north-west and towards the coast. When they arrive it is the middle of the evening; the squad would welcome some food and respite but, of course, there is a ceremony.

This feels like an odd place for the federation to select. It's underdeveloped, rural, some grocery shops looking like little more than shacks – and it is damn cold. The locals are friendly, ruddy, shell-suited, a little perplexed by what is happening to their tranquil hideaway, but they want to make Spain welcome. Boys and girls in traditional costume dance and sing and then one of them seeks out a Spaniard to whom she will give a 'good luck' symbol. Llorente, sky-scraper tall, blond, blue-eyed and genial looking, is mistaken for the team leader and selected. In his outstretched hands he now has a massive loaf of bread and some salt. This summer, however, they want to eat cake.

For those wondering if the *Clásico* wounds within the squad have healed – and such questions still abound – the timing of an hour-long interview given by Xavi to Canal+ fuels speculation. The recorded piece is due to be broadcast after Spain are ensconced in Poland, but as soon as they fly out of Madrid's Barajas airport this excerpt is released by the television station to all media outlets:

Xavi: "We [Barça] congratulated them [Madrid] when they won, this is only sport after all. We have been respectful to them at all times: when they won the title, when they won the Copa final at the Mestalla. Despite that, I have not felt that they have been like that to us when we have won. This is a very personal feeling, simply my own view."

No sooner have Spain arrived than the *Clásico* divide is threatening again.

— Day Two.
— *June 6, 2012. Gniewino, Poland*
Spain's players averaged just over 4000 playing minutes this season between club and country but some have been on the pitch for well over 5000 minutes. Casillas is closer to 6000.

Puyol's absence means it's virtually certain that Gerard Piqué and Sergio Ramos will be the centre-half pairing. However, the latter has played 5375 minutes, while Piqué, disrupted by minor injuries and a tendency for Pep Guardiola to drop him more than in previous years, amassed only 3239 minutes of game time – a difference equivalent to 23 games.

They need to be together at peak level on the pitch. They *should* be training with identical intensity. But is that either advisable or feasible given the huge disparity in the demands already placed on their bodies?

Some players – including Álvaro Negredo, Jordi Alba, Raúl Albiol, Pepe Reina, Jesús Navas and the Real Madrid contingent – played their last competitive match weeks ago; the players from Chelsea, Athletic Bilbao, Atlético Madrid and Barcelona finished the season with either domestic or UEFA finals, or both.

The strategy around how to maintain each member of the squad at optimum condition is down to Javier Miñano, Spain's fitness coach, who in recent years has been round every pertinent club, including Chelsea, Liverpool, Manchester City, Arsenal and Manchester United, to collect precise details of how Spain's players train throughout the season and what individual plans, if any, they require to maintain.

Three fundamentals of the fitness work undertaken while Spain are winning tournaments are:

1) For all players, 99% of training will be with the ball.

2) There will be minimum disruption between what keeps a particular player fit and on form during the year and what he is asked to do with Spain.

3) All sessions must serve a secondary role in the fight against boredom and rust – they must be effective, but also fun.

Javier Miñano: "What I still find incredible is that these guys can compete right to the end of their club season, fighting for a trophy or European competition. They arrive at May physically and mentally exhausted, then they are willing to immediately change their 'chip' mentally and attempt to give everything they have to Spain. In the end, despite all the talent, this group's strongest suit is its unity, its ability to live and work together with maximum friendship and intensity."

While Gniewino does not possess the sunshine and native colour of Potch, nor the stunning beauty and rural charm of Neustift, in one way it is the epitome of what Spain seek when selecting their tournament base. The training pitch is not only superb, it is a 90-second walk from the terrace of their Mistral hotel. Down a set of concrete steps, across the athletics track and they are at work.

All around the training camp, which has a secondary pitch, a changing room, a gym and a spa up in the hotel, there are custom-designed fencing covers which are emblazoned with motivational statements.

La historia no te hace campeón, la humildad sí. History does not make you a champion, humility does.
La historia no gane partidos, el esfuerzo sí. History does not win games, effort does.
La historia no marca goles, el talento sí. History does not score goals, talent does.

Spain train twice. The morning session is all about clearing cobwebs: lots of *rondos*, lots of one-touch passing exercises across the pitch, stretching and then a mini game where goals are scored by walking the ball over the line of munchkin-sized goal-frames because Iker Casillas, Víctor Valdés and Pepe Reina are off training elsewhere with José Manuel Ochotorena. However, it is Javi Martínez, Valdés and Arbeloa [Barça and Madrid] who are first up with the media. From day one, Spain ignore the *Clásico* divide in daily work.

Álvaro Arbeloa: "I don't think pressure is our problem. We have come here to try to win. What is more difficult is that when other teams play us, they do so with 200% motivation because we are European and world champions. They have studied us perfectly and they know exactly what to do. Other teams constantly playing at their absolute maximum against us – that is more difficult than dealing with pressure. On the contrary, we have already won the Euros and the World Cup. Maybe, in fact, we are the ones with the pressure off us."

Arbeloa also shrugs off questions about Xavi's potentially explosive declarations in the television interview. "Fortunately we know how to separate club and country and if there are any differences then we are here to iron them out."
The evening training session is laid on for two main reasons: to keep the players happy in the amount of contact with the ball they are getting and to have a bit of fun.

They lark about with non-keepers in goal [Llorente, Torres, Martínez]; there are oodles of free-kicks taken; there is teasing, ear-pinging, plus we can see that satisfied smile which signifies that Del Bosque is happy in his work.

— Day Three.

— June 7, 2012. Gniewino, Poland

Far from Spain, on the cold, grey Baltic coast of Poland, we awake to the overnight news that Manolo Preciado has died, aged only 54. A funny, honest, vibrant football character whose life had been jammed full of tragedy, Preciado was in the process of taking over as manager of Villarreal. Spanish football has been overly burdened with these black, grief-filled days recently. Antonio Puerta, Dani Jarque, now Preciado – and the tournament has not finished with us yet.

There is no morning training session because this is the day when the refereeing briefing will take place. Pierluigi Collina, who refereed the 2002 World Cup final, is to visit on behalf of UEFA. Like Elizondo during the World Cup, Collina is to provide a short seminar for players to ensure they are up to date with the current interpretation of the laws most frequently applied. By the end of the tournament, UEFA will legitimately look on this process as a success as there are 231 fewer fouls in 2012 than there were at Euro 2008 – a drop of 20 per cent. The yellow card average is just under four per game. Once the opening match is over, there is one red card in the remainder of the tournament. The briefing is a small factor, but a significant one.

Still athletic and slim, the Italian arrives in a sports jacket, white on white shirt, jeans and white runners. Collina's briefing is three days before Spain play Italy. Slide by slide, every point is crystal clear. However, as one of those present explains to me with great amusement afterwards, the slide Collina has chosen to illustrate a straight-red challenge is an interesting one.

Collina shows the Spain players an image of Pepe's outstretched leg and boot impacting on Dani Alves in the Champions League semi-final at the Bernabéu: "Is this, or is this not, a direct red card?"

Xavi says: "Of course it is!" Casillas counter-argues. Other voices are raised in debate. The volume increases. Del Bosque, sitting in the far corner, simply smiles benignly, sure he is witnessing natural competitiveness – not a return to the animosity which endangered the harmony of his squad when the Mourinho *Clásicos* were a rolling soap opera. However, the Italian could have chosen any example to debate dangerous tackling. Given his audience and the situation, it's an intriguing choice of image.

The situation develops. "Okay gentlemen, you've got a month here together to argue all this out again," Collina jokes, trying to move onwards. He tells them that the challenge *does* merit a straight red and will do in the tournament. Now he shows a slide which is the aftermath of Pepe's red-card tackle, in which Barcelona's players surround the referee in search of punishment for the Madrid man. Collina tells them that this behaviour will receive a booking. He adds, as the embers of debate continue, that "this sort of haranguing of a referee simply does not work".

Spain's players instantly drop their arguments over the Pepe incident and unite in catcalls: "Don't be ridiculous – of course officials are influenced by players!"

"Well perhaps in amateur games," splutters the Italian to further jeering.

This is the generation of players told by Luis Aragonés that football is for the street-smart, ordered to know the first name of not only the referee but also his assistants. Like every team playing for the biggest prizes in football, Spain believe that if officials are put under moderate but repeated pressure then, sooner or later, you may get a break on a 50/50 decision.

The *Clásico* issue is dropped like a stone as soon as an issue which might affect *La Roja* is raised by an outsider. These 23 are now not Madrid, Barcelona, Athletic, Chelsea or Sevilla. They are Spain.

At night they train behind closed doors. Before they begin, they stand, lined up across the centre circle. Most of them played against teams coached by Preciado, one or two played for him. Del Bosque often played against him. They pay him silent respect.

— Day Four.
— *June 8, 2012. Gniewino, Poland*

Despite their pivotal shoot-out victory over Italy in the quarter-finals of Euro 2008, Spain still feel about *gli Azzurri* the way vampires feel about garlic. The teams met for a friendly in August 2011 and Italy won 2-1. There is tension in Spain about Sunday's opening game.

Del Bosque is now using a host of exercises in training to put pressure on his players to think, move, pass and press at their absolute optimum. Italy will be masters at defending space, but Cesare Prandelli has also made them a dangerous, attacking team and Del Bosque wants Spain's pressing to be intense.

What is strange, and what separates the two nations' football cultures, is that Italy has been embroiled in a far bigger crisis than the *Clásico* catfight. Concurrent football and criminal investigations into match-fixing began to emerge in June 2011; in May 2012, 33 matches were investigated and 19 people arrested, in addition to many more during the course of the scandal. Domenico

Criscito has been dropped from the Italian squad after being questioned by cops at the training camp.

Prandelli has told the Italian Prime Minister, Martio Monti: "If you told us that for the good of football we shouldn't participate then it wouldn't be a problem for me. There are things which I believe are more important."

For any other nation, this would be the death-knell of a title challenge, but this is Italy. Serious though these events are, they pale into insignificance compared to the *Calciopoli* scandal of 2006, the fall-out from which included Juventus being stripped of two Serie A titles, relegated to Serie B and, along with Lazio and Fiorentina, suspended from UEFA competition. Nevertheless, just over a month later, Italy won the World Cup in Berlin.

> **Gerard Piqué**: "It's just when it appears that Italy are in trouble that they are actually at their most dangerous. Not only am I sure that they will be a very tough first rival, I think they will be fighting to win this tournament right to the end. Nevertheless, I like our status as favourites. It shows that people respect us, it shows we have a very good team and I like that kind of pressure. Until 2008, when Spain reached knockout games they played not to lose. Since beating Italy four years ago, we always play to win. In fact, if we play as well as we can do then we will win this tournament."

Asked about his relationship with his likely partner at centre-back, Piqué adds: "Things are exaggerated from outside, I get on excellently with Sergio Ramos, I am proud to be part of this Spain team and to play with him."

Training has shown Pedro deployed at wing-back, Alba under Xavi's protective wing, Iniesta increasingly elegant and Negredo not yet scoring.

Even at this stage, most observers could get close to the team Del Bosque has in mind: in front of Casillas will be a back four of Arbeloa, Ramos, Piqué and Alba; Xavi, Busquets and Alonso will form the midfield trio; the only question is around the two players who will join Iniesta in attack. Silva, Llorente, Negredo, Pedro, Torres – names are swapped like trading cards in the school playground. Hardly anyone mentions Cesc Fàbregas.

> **Meanwhile…**
> *Andrei Arshavin has spent the domestic season on loan from Arsenal at*
> *Zenit St Petersburg. His return into the western consciousness is abrupt; the*
> *Russian emerges in Wroclaw to help dismember a Czech Republic side that*
> *are given very little say in their 4-1 defeat.*

— Day Five.
— June 9, 2012. Gniewino, Poland

Because the draw has been kind to the world champions and all three of their Group C games [Italy, Ireland, Croatia] are in the same stadium, *La Roja* are going to get to know the Hotel Gdańsk Yachting, at the city's marina, pretty well.

The first task on Friday is the bus trip from Gniewino to Gdańsk. Antonio Limones, as always, fields the enquiries of players keen to know who their neighbour will be.

He does not consult the squad when drawing his plan, but it has become the norm in all their hotels as they travel around the world that Ramos will be next door to Navas; Iniesta next door to Valdés; Torres, Mata and Alonso in a row; Xavi next to Busquets.

By this evening, a formal complaint will be registered with UEFA over the state of the playing surface at the Gdańsk Arena. Spain want the grass cut, watered, and then watered again. However, this warpath is preceded by more smoking of the peace pipe.

The press conference at the stadium features David Silva plus the World Cup winning goalscorer, Iniesta, and the World Cup winning captain, Casillas. The international media cannot believe their luck.

Iker Casillas: "If this tournament had been back in 2011, the state of things between Barcelona and Madrid would have been a problem. Not because we don't get along, but because the interests of the two teams kept clashing. Now, in hindsight, we are able to smile at it all. Back then there was real tension on both sides, but I believe that when someone makes a mistake you have to focus on their positive side. Now everything is magnificent, we have turned the page and we are focused on the national team succeeding."

However, this fear that the *Clásico* conflict might corrode Spain's chances of retaining their title was far from the national coach's sole worry. During his address to the Spanish Olympic Committee, prior to leaving for the tournament, a different concern was laid bare.

Vicente del Bosque: "The hardest thing is to keep on winning after you have tasted victory. You inevitably run the risk that the group of players becomes too laid-back. It is vital to have a healthy atmosphere in the dressing room and on the training pitch. The discipline you maintain in a team needs to be based on rules and respect. I'm not a great believer in orders or being overly controlling. We are famous for being 'good boys' but I can tell you that is not always the full picture. However, if anyone thinks that Spain has a permissive regime, then they are simply wrong. They say: Don't be too weak or you will get swallowed up, but don't be too bitter or they will spit you out. My way of leading the group is that tactics can both be taught and learned, but style is innate."

Meanwhile…
World Cup finalists Holland lose meekly to Denmark in their opening fixture. Germany start strongly, with a win over Portugal decided by that rare thing: a tournament goal by Mario Gómez, the striker whose errant finishing at Euro 2008 and then the World Cup became a source of ridicule.

— Day Six.
— June 10, 2012. Gdańsk, Poland
*   Spain v Italy — UEFA European Championship Group C*
Uno y dos y tres … ganar y ganar y ganar!

Gdańsk is an elegant city served by a plethora of low-cost airlines. It is summer and the Euros are on. *Azzurri* and *Rojas* deluge the city, congregating down by the river in the old quarter, which is just a few hundred metres from the Spain hotel.

Arbeloa has a gang of superheroes who try to follow him to as many big matches as possible: Superman, Batman, Captain America, one of the Incredibles and The Hulk. Manolo el del Bombo will have a supporting cast today. Italy have gladiators and centurions by the score. For nearly 90 years it was a case of *veni, vidi, vici* — we came, we saw, we conquered — when they met Spain in competition. Spain needed penalties to break that cycle and still have a point to prove over 90 minutes.

Del Bosque springs a surprise when he names his team, leaving out Negredo and Torres and fielding Fàbregas in the central striker role.

The coach has been shrewd. Back in August, when Spain lost in Bari, the Italy defenders loved their old-fashioned battle against Fernando Torres and Fernando Llorente.

Today Andrea Barzagli is not going to be fit to play and that will almost certainly mean Daniele De Rossi dropping from centre midfield to centre-back in a three-man defence. Del Bosque figures Italy would like nothing more than to try to dominate Torres or Negredo in a physical contest. Further, he reckons that, magnificent player though De Rossi is, he may be less comfortable working out how to play a Messi-style false No.9 who will drop away from the frontline, forcing the defender into a dilemma: follow the man or drop back and wait for the run?

Spain take the field: Casillas; Arbeloa, Piqué, Ramos, Alba; Xavi, Busquets, Alonso; Silva, Fàbregas, Iniesta.

Italy will be 3-5-2, attempting to flood the midfield and press Spain's wide men via the wing-backs. Buffon; Bonucci, De Rossi, Chiellini; Maggio, Marchisio, Pirlo, Motta, Giaccherini; Cassano, Balotelli.

It is a gem of a match. There are 28 efforts at goal and 15 on target.

Italy are significantly better for the first 50 minutes. Prandelli's side look fluent, and confident. Spain are a little creaky and Xavi keeps asking Arbeloa to step up and help cover Emanuele Giaccherini's work down the touchline; the Barcelona man is already part of a 3 v 3 in central midfield.

Andrea Pirlo, Antonio Cassano and Claudio Marchisio pepper the Spain goal. Cassano has been recovering from heart surgery and returned to full form only in late April, yet he sparkles here. Twice Italy blow the chance to lead. With referee Viktor Kassai about to call half-time, the former Barça favourite, Thiago Motta, flings himself at a diving header which Casillas barely manages to palm away.

Just after the break, Giorgio Chiellini hoists a long ball for Mario Balotelli to chase. He closes down Ramos who, instead of thumping it out of play, attempts an uncomfortable pass back to Casillas. Balotelli gets a foot in to block it, Ramos slips and falls off the side of the pitch and the Italian can close in on goal unopposed. Piqué is trying to press Balotelli while covering the pass to Cassano, who is waiting for a simple finish. Just as Balotelli is about to shoot, Ramos reappears, diving in to clear for a corner. It is a monumental recuperation. Prandelli, exasperated, puts Antonio Di Natale on for the Manchester City man. Presto.

De Rossi, strolling forward, feeds Christian Maggio. Cassano is occupying Arbeloa on the right touchline further up the pitch, so it has to be Xavi who trots over to close Maggio down. This leaves Pirlo in a little bubble of space 20 metres inside his own half and he is given the ball. Busquets is too deep to get close and when Spain's pivot attempts to make up the ground, Pirlo just drifts past him. Di Natale starts to sprint and Pirlo bends a beautiful left-footed pass around Piqué for the Udinese man to run on to. Di Natale opens his body position sufficiently to bend the ball around Casillas' left hand and into the small portion of open net he can see. It is a wonderful goal scored by the man thwarted by a blinding save from Casillas during extra-time in the Euro 2008 quarter-final and again in the shoot-out. After a four-year wait, this is catharsis for Di Natale.

Three minutes later it is level. Until now, bar some tidy link-up work, only his most loyal supporters would say that the Fàbregas idea has dazzled. He was goalless for Barcelona since January; following the defeat by Chelsea in the Champions League semi-final seven weeks earlier, he has had 25 minutes of competitive action because of a thigh problem. And now it is all on him.

In defiance of all of this, the goal is as if drawn by Del Bosque. His plan works to perfection. Silva has drifted into the false No.9 position momentarily. Fàbregas has dropped several paces deep and to the right.

Xavi feeds Iniesta, who has Leonardo Bonucci and Marchisio around him but nevertheless takes a perfect first touch and draws the Italians still closer. Silva is available, six feet away. He takes Iniesta's pass on his left instep and, as Chiellini is drawn out, swivels so that he can play a pass off the outside of that same left boot with his next touch.

It is a chain reaction, one of those long domino trails where you tip the first one over and, gradually, it knocks everything else in turn. Once Italy make a single slip, their defensive blocks topple one by one. De Rossi and Bonucci have gone towards Iniesta, so Chiellini must go towards Silva. Giaccherini has been just a touch slow in realising that Fàbregas has changed positions with Silva, and is running back to cover the Catalan, but he is late. Silva releases as Fàbregas sprints forward and, from parallel with the penalty spot, glides a left-footed volley past Buffon.

As the game opens up in the last 25 minutes Spain, as is usually the case, have not spent so much physical energy because they have had 60 per cent possession.

Navas, one of the substitutes, sends another, Torres, through for a one-on-one with Buffon, but the behemoth Italian out-psyches the striker; Xavi's through pass to Torres gifts another chance but when he cuts around Chiellini and lobs Buffon, the ball slides off the top of the net.

After the match there is an outpouring of anger. Spain's players, full of appreciation and admiration for their rivals, are enraged by the playing surface.

Cesc Fàbregas: "The state of that pitch was a pain. This should not happen in 2012. The grass was super-dry and desperately needed watering."

Xavi: "That pitch was prejudicial to our style of play. It was atrocious."

Andrés Iniesta [UEFA man of the match]: "It's a bittersweet feeling to get this award because we have not managed to start this tournament with a win. It is not an excuse for not winning, but that playing surface was disastrous for us. It was so dry that it impaired our ability to move the ball quickly."

Andrea Pirlo: "I was pointing out to Xavi before the game that the grass was not cut short enough, was also very dry indeed and became a real obstacle to quick passing. Given that Spain's game is much more technical than ours, it definitely prejudiced against them more than us."

Cesare Prandelli: "Yesterday I didn't know what we would be coming up against in this game, but I was smiling because this is a fantastic sport which I think we sometimes need to approach with less tension.
"What disappointed me was allowing them to equalise so quickly. We were playing the world champions but we should have made it more difficult for them after we scored."

Spain stomp off in high dudgeon, muttering about basic gardening skills and wondering whether playing all three Group C games in Gdańsk is such an advantage after all.

Spain 1 Italy 1

Spain: Casillas, Arbeloa, Piqué, Sergio Ramos, Jordi Alba, Xavi, Busquets, Alonso, Silva (Navas 65), Fàbregas (Torres 74), Iniesta
Goal: Fàbregas 64

Italy: Buffon, Bonucci, De Rossi, Chiellini, Maggio, Giaccherni, Marchisio, Pirlo, Thiago Motta (Nocerino 89), Cassano (Giovinco 65), Balotelli (Di Natale 56)
Goal: Di Natale 60

> *Meanwhile...*
> *The Republic of Ireland have come to the finals in good voice – supporters providing a boisterous atmosphere in an opening fixture with Croatia – only for their side to develop a stutter. The Irish fall behind after just three minutes and Sean St Ledger's equaliser is forgotten amid two further Croatian goals after the break. It is an Ireland performance out of tune with that in the stands.*

— Day Seven.
— June 11, 2012. Gniewino, Poland
Spain are given the night and the next morning off to see friends, family, girlfriends, wives – and fortune tellers, investment bankers and life-coaches if they want, too.

The Hotel Gdańsk Yachting may be a luxurious spot, light years from the farmland, cows and goosebump wind of Gniewino, but it is also Touristville. With Shakira and Iker Casillas' partner Sara Carbonero on site, there is an army of paparazzi, television news crews and rubberneckers.

Shakira, Piqué's partner, has flown in from Los Angeles. She will do some recording in studios in Gdańsk during the first stage of the tournament and has hired a villa on the coast of the Hel Peninsula, from where a launch or a helicopter gets her to Gdańsk in double-quick time.

There are requests for photos and autographs from fans; news stations begging for 'just a quick word'. This is their morning off, a reward for hard work and what Del Bosque regards as crucial disconnect time. But they are patient. They stand, they smile, they sign, they make their excuses and they leave.

Others, such as Fàbregas, keep their heads down today. Immediately after the match, he was out for dinner with his grandparents, Àlex and Isabel. As for many members of this squad, the opportunity to spend time with family is precious when football comes first for so much of the year.

By the evening, *La Roja* are back in their work clothes at the Hotel Mistral in Gniewino. All those who started are given the night off. Casillas trains again and Del Bosque again runs plenty of small-sided matches played with intensity, so that those who have not had game time are in competitive mode.

However, Del Bosque and his fitness coach Javier Miñano agree that this is as tired and overworked as they have seen this bunch of players at this stage of a season. At all costs, they must not overwork them.

> **Meanwhile...**
> *Two years after the squad splintered in South Africa, France are united in registering a first point in Group D. Unfortunately for them, England are also found to be cohesive. Both sides sit behind joint-hosts Ukraine after Andriy Shevchenko fends off age and a Swedish defence to score twice in a 2-1 win.*

— Day Eight.
— June 12, 2012. Gniewino, Poland

The fatigue affecting his players is not the only thing occupying Del Bosque's mind.

This is one of a handful of occasions when work takes us to the team hotel and I catch the coach in the mood for a brief coffee. It's the first time Del Bosque explains to me how delicate it is to drop guys in his squad who, at club level, "don't even know where the subs' bench is".

I had also been in the coach's company when news of Preciado's death came through. Del Bosque was sombre and reflective and made me consider the stresses and strains which he suffers in his job. Preciado, an opponent of Del Bosque's when Real Madrid played Racing Santander in the late '70s and early '80s, was six years younger than the Spain coach. Del Bosque explains that it all feels like a tremendous responsibility, that he had seen what victory had meant to Spain over the last four years, and that the country's thirst not only for another trophy, but for victory with style, was weighing on him a little.

Del Bosque is a remarkably balanced, calm man – not rare in football, but rare in serial winners. He also consumes the views of the written press every morning, when most in his position either do not read football journalism or at least claim that they do not. The Spain coach counts one or two in the media as good friends and reads six or seven news and football papers every day; he will talk to radio or television reporters in moments when 99% of managers would simply refuse.

Today, what he will read is going to underline the level of the expectation fuelled by victory in the previous two tournaments.

Carles Puyol gives his view of the Italy game via Twitter: 'It's the best match of the competition so far. If they would water the pitch the football would be even better. I'm very confident about *La Roja*! Iniesta is stellar!'

> **Laurent Blanc:** "To create that many chances against an Italy side which played really well and which is so good at defending means that Spain remain my bet to win the championship."

But what do Puyol or Blanc know? In the wake of the Italy game, Spanish newspaper columnists and reporters demand that there must be no more false No.9, that the *doble pivote* must be abandoned, that Ramos must be returned to right-back and that Spain must play much, *much* better. There is no acknowledgement of how well Italy performed [Mourinho as an analyst on Al Jazeera states that Italy, on this form, can make it to the final], or the fact that Spain end the match on top, or that Ramos and Piqué function pretty well at centre-back.

In the press conference, Sergio Busquets fights back.

> **Sergio Busquets:** "There is a lack of patience when Spanish international football is analysed. That was not just anyone we drew against, it was a very strong Italy side. But if we do not win these days, there always seems to be a 'but' from somebody or other. It is precisely what happened during the World Cup. As for the pitch, it is not just an excuse. It is so slow and spongy that you need two touches to control the ball, not just one. That slows down technical teams, fans get a worse spectacle and it gives an advantage to defensive football."

> **Meanwhile...**
> *The battle for the Golden Boot will end in a dead heat between six of
> the world's best strikers. Russia's Alan Dzagoev scores his third of the
> tournament in a 1-1 draw with Poland to get his nose in front.*

— Day Nine.
— June 13, 2012. Gniewino, Poland

Spain are beginning to suffer from the ailments which have befallen the previous great teams who have tried and failed to win three consecutive world and continental titles.

The intense media scrutiny is now a greater burden than ever; the loss of Puyol and David Villa is typical of injuries to key or ageing players; the tiredness observed by the coaching staff comes with endless working summers; Spain's players are aware of the huge effort from every rival out to dethrone the champions; all of it can lead to a decadent, *fin de siècle* attitude from superstar players who end up asking themselves: do I *really* need all this?

Consider first the leading brand in international football: Brazil. They were thrilling and peerless World Cup winners in 1958 and 1962, but lost the 1959 Copa America due to a 4-0 defeat by their most bitter rivals Argentina and a 3-0 loss to eventual winners Uruguay. Victory in 1959 would have given the South American equivalent of the hat-trick Spain are seeking in Poland and Ukraine.

Brazil won the Copa America in 1997 and 1999, but lost the final of the 1998 World Cup against France and thus kissed goodbye to another treble.

After Brazil won World Cup 2002, they added the Copa America title in 2004 and travelled to Germany for the World Cup but, with an overweight Ronaldo up front, were ousted by an ageing French team in the quarter-finals. France won the 1998 World Cup on home turf and conquered Europe thrillingly in 2000. However, when they reached Japan and Korea in 2002 they were decimated by injuries, tiredness, complacency and bad managerial decisions. The world and European champions finished bottom of Group A without scoring a single goal.

What of Germany? After Helmut Schön's great West Germany side won the European Championship in 1972 and added the World Cup on home soil in 1974, they reached the final of Euro 76 in Yugoslavia, where they faced Czechoslovakia. The treble was on. In a penalty shoot-out, with the score at 4-3 in their favour, the Czechs had one kick to win it and deny West Germany the treble. With all that in the balance, Antonín Panenka feinted to strike his spot-kick hard, but instead sand-wedged a little dink over the great Sepp Maier. In the process, Panenka gave his name to that most audacious of penalty-kicks, and it will be invoked twice during this tournament.

Great teams from three great football nations failed to finish the treble. However, further analysis reveals Spain's task is greater still. West Germany won Euro 72 and reached the final of Euro 76 in fewer total matches than it will take Del Bosque's squad to win Euro 2012. Schön's team won *two* whole matches at the finals in Belgium to become European champions in 1972. Four years later, the final tournament, in Yugoslavia, again began at the semi-final stage.

Euro 2008 was won over six fierce games after a long season far more demanding than was the case in the 1950s, '60s or '70s. Spain will play another six games in the defence of their title.

Brazil played six times to become continental champions in '97 and '99. However, the Copa America of 1959 was only four matches and the two World Cup wins either side comprised six games each (not the modern seven). Brazil also had it easier in their treble chances, but they blew it.

In winning the World Cup in 1974, West Germany played just one knockout match – the final. Everything else was determined by two group stages, a format far easier to manage and far less likely to produce shocks. Thus, if Germany had beaten the Czechs on penalties in 1976 they would have been first to win this trophy treble and it would have taken them a total of 11 matches, seven of which were on home soil. Yet still they failed.

Brazil came close to the trophy treble between 1958 and 1962, finishing third in the Copa America in 1959, but still only played 16 times and lost by an aggregate score of 7-1 to their biggest rivals.

By comparison, completing the treble in 2012 will take Spain 19 matches, in four different countries; they will be the first European team to win the World Cup outside their own continent and they will have coped with the constant pressure of a vastly more powerful and numerous media, and completed their task in the absence of their all-time leading scorer at Euro 2012.

France's path to the treble would have stretched to a marathon 20 matches as it featured two World Cups instead of two Euros, but they almost literally fell apart 16 matches into the chase.

Despite all that, large swathes of Spain's own media seem unimpressed with how business is being dealt with. There is a constant lack of faith in Del Bosque's basic game plan and a glutinous demand for three-goal wins in every match.

Today, the coach receives a couple of helping hands: one comes from Del Bosque's predecessor, by way of Cesc Fàbregas; the other from Giovanni Trapattoni, who won't countenance Ireland refusing to water the pitch in Gdańsk simply to reduce the quality gap between Spain and Ireland tomorrow.

Cesc Fàbregas: "Aragonés always told me that I was so busy giving assists it meant I would miss the chance to score myself. He saw I had the ability to get goals, to run beyond the defence and he told me that scoring goals is what really matters. He underlined that nobody remembers who was involved in the build-up to a goal, but everyone remembers who scores. And he was right. I used to be happier making goals, but once you discover what it's like scoring then you want a goal in every match. There is nothing more beautiful."

Giovanni Trapattoni: "I have seen the weather forecast and it looks like rain in the morning, so no problem if Spain want the pitch wet. But it really does not matter to us, because in Ireland, or in England, we are quite accustomed to the playing surface always being watered. In fact, if it doesn't rain on matchday, I will ask the groundsmen to water the pitch."

In order to spare the match surface, Spain train in Gniewino before hitting the Hotel Gdańsk Yachting for the night. Again, Pedro is used as a wing-back, not up front. While converted winger Juanfran has been an integral part of Atlético Madrid's Europa League triumph this season, he has not had Pedro's experience with Spain, he does not score as often and he is not as quick.

Booked against Italy, both Arbeloa and Alba are one yellow away from suspension. Del Bosque is preparing the Barça man, who is ambidextrous, to replace either one of the first choice full-backs if needed. There is a great emphasis placed on moves which start at the halfway line, involve a one-two pass and then a cross from wide to a central player. Ramos, Piqué, Alonso, Martínez, Torres, Fàbregas, Torres, Negredo and Llorente rotate as the player who receives the pass and spreads it to the wing, or the player who needs to get on the end of the cross. Alba, Arbeloa, Pedro, Navas and Silva are the wide men. One highlight is a spectacular mid-air, scissor-kick volley from Negredo past Reina. It is extraordinarily powerful, but will it have impressed Del Bosque sufficiently for the striker to start?

> **Meanwhile...**
> *Germany are on the verge of the quarter-finals after Mario Gómez scores two accomplished goals to leave Holland close to elimination. Four years after providing a personal gag-reel of misses, Gómez puts his marker down for the Golden Boot.*

— Day 10.
— June 14, 2012. Gdańsk, Poland
Spain v Ireland – UEFA European Championship Group C
Uno y dos y tres ... ganar y ganar y ganar!

Three minutes 49 seconds into this game, two things are crystal clear. It *does* make a difference to Spain when the pitch is fast and Del Bosque has done the right thing in ignoring Negredo and choosing Torres. In that time, Spain play at triple the speed of the Italy game. The ball fizzes across the surface, they take fewer touches and they score. Busquets shunts it forward, Xavi is running back towards him and Keith Andrews makes a bad decision in trying to intercept. Xavi shields with his bum, Kenny Dalglish-style, and volleys the pass off with a half-touch. On the wet surface, it flies to Iniesta and he needs a touch to control, one to push it past Glenn Whelan and a third to execute a sublime pass to David Silva, right between defenders Sean St Ledger and Stephen Ward. Richard Dunne slides in and blocks Silva's shot, but as he tries to pick himself up to clear, Torres roars past him, taking the ball away from the big defender, then past Ward before his shot explodes over Shay Given's head into the roof of the net.

The state and speed of the grass have played a massive part in ripping the Ireland game plan to shreds in less than four minutes.

Ireland play with intelligence and organisation against a significantly better team before Silva's goal ends the contest. Iniesta's shot is palmed out by Given and Silva controls. There are three men in front of him, plus the goalkeeper, jockeying to deny him shooting space. He dummies, alters his angle by an inch or two and gently side-foots a shot in off the right-hand post.

The third goal is a product of Spanish pressing. Ireland halt Iniesta for a second, but when the ball comes to Aiden McGeady, he is dozing. Silva is on him like a cobra, robs him and releases Torres, clean through for his second.

The fourth comes from a corner. In his report on Ireland, Paco Jiménez observed that they showed a strong trend of getting slack, physically and mentally tired towards the last 15 minutes of games – at least defensively. His report urged that Spain take throw-ins, free-kicks and corners quickly in the last 15 minutes. There are 83 minutes on the clock when Silva doesn't wait for Xavi, the designated corner taker, to get to the flag. Instead, he immediately glides the ball low and hard into the box, where substitute Fàbregas is on the run. The Catalan's first touch takes him past Paul Green and allows him to shoot firmly between Andrews and Given.

Roy Keane bemoans the fact that Ireland's supporters are praised for their singing – "let's not just turn up for the sing-song every now and then" – but the chorus of *The Fields of Athenry* that carries on over the final whistle impresses other participants. That night, Gerard Piqué, whose superstar girlfriend Shakira has also been stunned by the non-stop singing, phones his friend Luis Martín of the newspaper El País. He knows Lu is in touch with British football culture and he wants to know what the song was. Neither he nor his partner has ever heard anything like it, not so ferociously sustained, and certainly not in the face of a 4-0 defeat. Lu phones me for information, I pass on what I know and the Piqués can go look it all up on YouTube. Ireland are out, but they have been beaten by a very good performance and won the singing. Again.

Andrés Iniesta: "We were superior from start to finish, we imposed our game, our combination passing was quick and accurate and we go to the Croatia match in very exciting form. It helped us massively that the pitch was wet and that it rained because that made it quick. Now anyone who wasn't listening or taking us seriously can see that when we moaned the other day it wasn't because we were looking for an excuse after drawing with Italy. The state of the playing surface massively influences how well we play."

Giovanni Trapattoni: "Spain have developed such a technical capacity that it allows them not to use up so much energy during a match. Every player is involved and it is very rare for them to fail in a pass. Moreover, the majority of the players are from Spain's two biggest clubs and that is a big advantage for this team. When Italy were winning World Cups they could have six, seven or as many as nine from Juventus and those guys were just playing from memory. They knew each other inside out, just like these guys do."

Fernando Torres [UEFA man of the match]: "We wanted to score goals and make up for not having done so the other day. I'm happy to have played and this system worked, but that doesn't matter as far as the next game is concerned. The boss could and might play a completely different set-up, in which case it will just be someone else scoring the goals. There are 23 of us – it is the squad ethic which wins tournaments."

Spain 4 Republic of Ireland 0

Spain: Casillas, Arbeloa, Ramos, Piqué, Alba, Xavi, Busquets, Alonso (Martínez 65), Silva, Torres (Fàbregas 74), Iniesta (Cazorla 80)
Goals: Torres 4, 70, Silva 49, Fàbregas 83

Ireland: Given, O'Shea, St Ledger, Dunne, Ward, Duff (McClean 76), Andrews, Whelan (Green 80), McGeady, Cox (Walters 46), Keane

> ### Meanwhile...
> *Italy's Andrea Pirlo caresses a free-kick over the wall and into the top corner. It seems rude of Mario Mandžukić to squeeze a point out for Croatia, but his strike sees him join the tie for the Golden Boot.*

— Day 11.
— June 15, 2012. Gdańsk, Poland

A draw between Italy and Croatia means that if Spain win their remaining game, against Slaven Bilić's side, they will qualify as group winners. In fact, there are six different sets of results which will put Spain through, but one quirk of the group has conspiracy theorists chattering. If Spain and Croatia draw 2-2 then Italy are out.

The logic emanating from the Italian camp seems to be: 'Obviously! That's what *we* would do!'

Spain, meanwhile, are seeking as much relaxation as the paparazzi will allow. Shakira is, again, the main draw, but those players with young children in Poland do not want to be caught in the glare of celebrity. Many simply stay in their marina hotel until it is time to board the team bus back to Gniewino. Others in the squad head to the coast, a 25-minute drive north of their training complex.

One of the rare breed who will not be troubled by the photographers is the lesser-spotted Jordi Alba. This day off comes at a perfect juncture for him. His splendid season with Valencia, capped by a brilliant performance at winger/inside-forward against AZ Alkmaar in the quarter-final of the Europa League, seems to have brought his time at the Mestalla to an end. Alba was a La Masia (youth system) kid at Barcelona. Technically able and quick, he played in the Leo Messi positions – second striker, false No.9, a winger who could cut inside. His role model had always been the volatile Bulgarian striker from Barcelona's Dream Team of 1992, Hristo Stoichkov. However, even Barça's famed academy system is fallible. Alba was told the competition in his age group was too high and Barcelona released him.

The young Alba had industrial-strength self-confidence and a burning desire to play. If UE Cornella, a club based in Barcelona, near the location of Espanyol's new stadium, was where he was wanted, then that was where he would go. There, he showed up on the Valencia youth-system radar; at the Mestalla, injuries led to Alba's conversion from left winger to left-back and, under Unai Emery, a brave attack-minded coach, Alba established himself as a Spanish version of Dani Alves, Barcelona's raiding full-back.

During the summer of 2012, Barça want him back. It is a delicate situation, because Del Bosque has taken Alba aside after training and shared a startling prediction. Alba made his Valencia debut in late 2009, after going on loan to Gimnàstic, and did not start a game for Spain until five months before this tournament. Yet the national coach tells the 23-year-old that he can be the player of the tournament. Not Spain's player of the tournament, *the* player of the tournament.

Del Bosque's rationale is not only based on Alba's rich form at the end of the season, but the way opponents treat *La Roja*. Most teams try to press, harass, defend and counter attack against Spain. They mob Iniesta and Xavi, they try to stop the centre-backs from moving the ball upfield and they try to push the central striker as far from the goal as possible. Spain's forward players are no longer sprinters and opposing teams press higher and higher. Thus, Del Bosque tells Alba, 'your pace, your ability to beat a man one-on-one and your ability to score (honed as a Stoichkov-style striker at Barça) makes you our secret weapon'.

Del Bosque wants Alba to beat offside traps, running from deep and feeding off passes from the midfield. He wants opposition teams to fear Alba's extraordinary pace and to sit slightly deeper, thus relieving the smothering blanket of pressure in the middle of the pitch. However, if Barcelona's move to re-sign Alba drags on and distracts the player, it will be enormously frustrating for the national team coach and potentially ruinous for Alba, given that Pedro is excelling in a similar wing-back role in training.

A rest day like this is a chance for Alba's people to explain to him the latest situation with Barcelona, for agreements to be reached, for his future to be mapped out without damaging his here-and-now.

Today Barça confirm Tito Vilanova as their new coach – now they want to conclude a deal for Alba. How they do it will be as crucial as how much it costs. David Silva's move to Manchester City has worked out very well. He is better paid, he has improved as a world-class footballer and he is champion of England. However, the way the transfer played out two years ago almost certainly cost him game time at the World Cup. It is a lesson Alba cannot afford to ignore.

Meanwhile…

France are just beginning to soak up the atmosphere when their national anthem is interrupted by thunder and sheets of rain. It forces their match with Ukraine to be postponed by 58 minutes and concerns of the fixture being abandoned altogether grow with each one that passes. France adapt best to the delay and win 2-0; they top the group with England, 3-2 winners over Sweden after a winner from Danny Welbeck.

— **Day 12.**
— *June 16, 2012. Gdańsk, Poland*

Following their time off, a group of players are out on the training pitch a good 15 minutes early, having fun. To begin with there are tricks and keepy-uppy. Then free-kicks. The keepers are too smart to come out early, and of the players who take their turn in goal, Sergio Ramos's Superman dives are most impressive.

Gerard Piqué is chasing, or being chased. Inflicting physical punishment or trying to escape retribution. It is like watching a playground – a bit more transfer-market value, but the same nonsense, and the same basic love of the game.

The training, when it begins, is about chasing and catching, acting in groups, co-ordination, speed and decision-making. When the ball is used it flies between the players, forcing them to think and act at lightning speed.

Pedro is striking the ball brilliantly, regularly bulging the top corner of the net with shots and volleys. His eye is in and he looks brimful of energy.

Iniesta is looking more and more authoritative. In the mini-games where gaining an inch or two of space to unleash a pass is of prime importance, the Barça man is king.

Piqué looks fit, happy and relaxed: distinctly different from how he was during the pretty miserable season he's endured. Far beyond the questions about whether he would be able to get on with Ramos as a defensive partner was the feeling that he was losing some of his effervescent enjoyment of football. Whatever the condition of the relationship between him and Pep Guardiola, Piqué was played less in vital matches than at any time since returning from Manchester United.

During training, he and Ramos are always at the back together for one team, Albiol and Martínez for the other. Increasingly you can hear the dialogue between Ramos and Piqué, when they are dealing with situations, getting shorter, almost monosyllabic. For dining table conversation, this would be a bad sign. On the training pitch, it is a winning lottery ticket. They understand each other's movements, they trust each other and do not need to say very much any more: the bare minimum of info and they are on the case.

Better still, Busquets is gamboling around the field as if it were the first day of spring. He had a scan on a leg injury sustained during the Ireland game, but the news is good. To call him irreplaceable would be reckless, but Del Bosque and his team-mates view him as vital. The *doble pivote* debate should be over now. Spain have two pivots in the team, Busquets and Alonso, but the formation is now initially 4-3-3 and the Catalan is often the sole defensive midfielder, with Alonso encouraged to drive the play forward and, if possible, get into shooting positions.

Meanwhile...
Was it really eight days prior to this that the Czechs were teased and bullied by Russia? A goal by Petr Jiráček sends them to the quarter-finals at the expense of Poland. In fact, the Russians are going home too, after Greece beat them 1-0 to edge in front on the head-to-head.

— **Day 13.**
— *June 17, 2012. Gdańsk, Poland*
During Euro 2008, the third round of group fixtures was a bonus time for the squad players. With two wins in the bag, there were full games for Sergio Garcia, Rubén de la Red, Fernando Navarro and Pepe Reina. At the World Cup the situation was loaded with peril and there were no risks, and no minutes for players whose squad ranking was below 15.

The 90 minutes which De la Red or Navarro earned while beating Greece 2-1 at Euro 2008 puts them ahead of Javi Martínez (42 minutes) or Juan Mata (20 minutes) during their entire time at World Cup 2010, plus the first two games of Euro 2012. Mata just won the Champions League, Martínez just helped Athletic to the finals of the Europa League and the Copa del Rey (he is not far off a €40m move to Bayern). Yet they have their noses pressed against the window as far as this Spain team is concerned.

Here is another dilemma which has caused great squads to fall at the third hurdle of the tournament treble: disharmony, lack of game time, jealousy, boredom and rust. Del Bosque has started to repeat in interviews the phrase he used during one of our earlier meetings, when he talked about managing "players who don't even know where the bench is at their club". To strike the correct balance, he must untangle a Gordian Knot.

At Euro 2008, Xabi Alonso played 151 minutes out of a possible 540. If this is incredible in retrospect, it was due solely to Luis Aragonés' faith in Marcos Senna, and it stands as an indication of how difficult the squad husbandry in this golden Spanish era has become. Cesc Fàbregas, then captain of Arsenal, started two of six matches at Euro 2008 and played 305 of 540 minutes. At the World Cup, he made no starts and played only 126 minutes of a possible 630.

Currently, it is unclear where Fernando Llorente's game-time graph is going. His Clark Kent half hour against Portugal in the World Cup changed the course of Spain's tournament, but it only won him a medal, no more minutes at that tournament or this one. From a possible 750 tournament minutes between Poland/Ukraine and South Africa he is stuck on 32.

Del Bosque knows that while the Croatia game is both crucial and potentially very difficult, it is vital to plan who will get game time when the match is opening up and the opposition is tiring. Thus far, 15 players have been used: the basic XI with Fàbregas in the attack, plus Torres, Santi Cazorla, Jesús Navas and Javi Martínez. There has been no game time for Llorente, Álvaro Negredo, Pedro or Mata.

Can Del Bosque risk any radical change? For the last two days, Alba has worn a knee bandage in training, but his intensity of work suggests this is precautionary.

Álvaro Negredo: "The coach has three outright strikers here and each of us is pretty distinct from the next. Fernando [Torres] is very quick and mobile and that makes him very powerful in the last few metres in front of goal. Fernando Llorente is big and strong and when the rival won't let us dominate with our own football, he provides an out-ball we don't normally use, but which can be effective. As far as I'm concerned, I try to link well with my team-mates, be in the right place at the right time and it is these things I am trying to make the coach see."

Luka Modrić: "I fully expect Spain to dominate about 70% of possession and we will probably only have the ball at our feet for about 10 minutes in the whole match."

Fernando Torres: "Anyone who says we will try for a 2-2 draw in order to eliminate Italy is showing us a complete lack of respect."

Cesare Prandelli: "Spain will go out to win and we must never give in to the culture of the idle conspiracy theory." Bravo to that.

Meanwhile...
Holland suffer a third straight defeat in Group B – Cristiano Ronaldo scores twice to force Portugal into the last eight; Germany win by the same scoreline to leave Denmark outside the top two places. They are the only team in the tournament to move through the group stage with a perfect record.

— **Day 14.**
— *June 18, 2012. Gdańsk, Poland*
   Croatia v Spain – UEFA European Championship Group C
Uno y dos y tres … ganar y ganar y ganar!

Paco Jiménez is like a telescope for Del Bosque – he sees what is coming in the distance. Since the draw was made he has broken down every match Spain's Group C opponents have played. Already his work has inspired the last of the four goals Spain scored against Ireland.

His short presentation on Croatia stresses that Mario Mandžukić is on blazing form. Spain must not allow easy crosses or stupid free-kicks within 30 metres of goal. Luka Modrić, Jiménez adds, is tending to play deeper than he does for Tottenham Hotspur, in a similar area to that occupied by Sergio Busquets for Spain. The difference is Modrić will try to catch out his markers with runs to the edge of the opposition box. Jiménez concludes that Slaven Bilić's side is to be taken very seriously: some of the nous and technique of Italy, all the scrap and intensity of Ireland. So it proves.

Spain retain the XI which has beaten Ireland. 4-3-3: Casillas; Arbeloa, Piqué, Ramos, Alba; Xavi, Busquets, Alonso; Silva, Torres, Iniesta.

Croatia, slightly surprisingly, drop Nikica Jelavić and flood midfield, leaving Mandžukić up front on his own.

Croatia are intelligent and dogged in their organisation and their pressing. They are made to chase a great deal, but they do not mind. Spain do not create a plethora of goal chances and gradually Bilić's team shows more confidence in what they do with the ball. When one or two Spain moves break down in error, the tension ripples from *La Roja* fans, to the players and back again. The game situation changes when Antonio Cassano scores for Italy against Ireland in Poznan. Croatia must now win to progress; Casillas has some saves to make, from Ivan Rakitić when Modrić uses the outside of his right boot to curve an inswinging cross into the striker, and Ivan Perišić after a rampaging break down the left from Mandžukić.

As Croatia seek the win, however, Spain get more space in which to play and they dominate possession, using that advantage to put 10 of their 14 attempts at goal on target – seven more than their opponents. Crucially, one of Spain's efforts goes in.

Despite the fact that a breakaway goal will likely put them out, this Spain team is built to exploit space to score late goals as games stretch and legs tire. In this tournament they have scored in the 70th minute, the 83rd minute and now the 88th. Del Bosque banks on Croatia running out of steam. He is on the money with that and with his substitutions. Navas on the hour, Fàbregas 13 minutes later. By now some of Croatia's key players are at walking pace.

The Alonso-Fàbregas connection is working. The Madrid man is given space on the halfway line and Fàbregas drops into a huge pocket of space between Croatia's lines of midfield and defence. The first time it happens, Fàbregas feeds Iniesta and Stipe Pletikosa saves. Then exactly the same thing happens again. With all the time in the world, Alonso feeds Fàbregas, who is open. With his right boot he lofts the ball over the back line. Iniesta runs on to the pass, controls with the top of his chest. Navas is inside and onside, it is an open goal and he scores. Spain are group winners, Croatia are out and Bilić is off to coach Lokomotiv Moscow.

Navas explains to me later the reason he belts the ball high into the net, from six inches out. "It was such a relief of pressure that I instinctively hammered it."

There are no hugs, no celebrations, no punching the air and very few smiles.

For Spain, at this stage of the story, this is little more than taking care of business. The bar is set at winning the tournament.

Slaven Bilić: "We had our plan. We were playing the world and European champions – a team hungry for trophies – and we tried to neutralise them. We were waiting for them at the back in the first half; we weren't keen to attack them at that stage. Spain had a hard time against us. We could have won tonight, we went close. I was sure we would go through, but to play Spain is not easy, they are such a good tactical side."

Vicente del Bosque: "When you don't play your greatest game but manage to win, it gives confidence. Croatia closed up space well which caused us problems. It was a difficult win, but I think we had 17 shots on goal to their eight. We had more corners and more possession. They counter-attacked with menace, but I thought we were the better team. Our first touch tonight wasn't what it should have been, and that caused the game to be slower."

Spain are in the quarter-finals and, dependent on tomorrow night's matches, will face France or England.

Croatia 0 Spain 1

Croatia: Pletikosa, Vida (Jelavić 66), Ćorluka, Schildenfeld, Strinić, Srna, Rakitić, Vukojević (Eduardo 81), Modrić, Pranjić (Perišić 66), Mandžukić

Spain: Casillas, Arbeloa, Ramos, Piqué, Alba, Xavi (Negredo 89), Busquets, Alonso, Silva (Fàbregas 73), Torres (Navas 60), Iniesta
Goal: Navas 88

Meanwhile...
Even with Pirlo providing a metronomic presence in midfield, Italy seem hurried in their efforts to reach the quarter-finals. They are made to wait until the last minute of a victory over Ireland to be certain of progress, when Mario Balotelli hooks in a second goal to secure second place in Group B.

— Day 15.

— June 19, 2012. Gniewino, Poland

It is back to the Hotel Mistral and the training camp following the win over Croatia – no night off, no time at the luxurious Yachting Hotel, no more paparazzi. It is a pact between management and players. Spain have been surrounded by eager fans, tourists, news journalists and photographers every time they have wandered out of their city hotel. Del Bosque would like them isolated again, relaxing in peace and quiet – and he would like a tactical session mid-morning, the day after the game, to clear the air. He said after the game: "We got ourselves a bit tied up in knots." It's something he'd like to address.

Andrés Iniesta [UEFA man of the match]: "We're tired. That was a tough, complicated match, partly because of our situation. We were thinking all the time: 'Will this result do? Are we through? What happens if they score?' Moreover, Croatia were terrific. They contested the ball, they are quick passers and they had some chances to win. We went through very good patches, and some where we suffered a little. It is normal."

The relative hostility of questioning from the Spanish media at the Gdańsk Arena last night troubled Del Bosque so much that he retired to the briefing room in the Hotel Mistral at about 2am and watched the entire match once more. The *Mister* was getting angry.

Over the last few days the federation president, Ángel María Villar, has persuaded Del Bosque to renew his contract with Spain (plus those of all his staff with the exception of Jiménez, who wishes to retire) until after World Cup 2014. It is at times like these that Del Bosque raises his vigilance. He is being offered extra security and he wants to ensure no softness or rust has entered his project.

This is either his day off or one he could dedicate solely to preparing for the next game. Instead, he elects to face his critics. Repeatedly, he is asked inane or provocative questions – often the same question, worded slightly differently.

He uses two classic phrases. He talks about a "climate of pessimism". Then he says: "In Spain, as a football nation, perhaps we have gone from famine to feast too quickly. I have the feeling that people have lost the ability to appreciate how hard things are, to appreciate when things are going well." To my ear it sounds a clinically accurate dressing down of some parts of his national media.

Vicente del Bosque: "Last night I decided to review the whole game and now I have got quite a different idea than most of the judges who say we were so bad. I just don't think that. Okay, Croatia threatened us from time to time but, in general, we did things well. We didn't stretch the game enough and that meant there was always a threat of them creating a chance and converting it. I accept that people are not necessarily in favour of what I do. There is a lot of concern about 'did we suffer too much? Did Rakitić nearly score?' But the things we did well were important. The fact that Croatia had one good chance does not mean that they were on top – come on!

"All criticism has its place if it is constructive and not simply a product of the heat of the moment. I would ask some fans to stay calm. Everyone thinks he knows better than the coach, but I think we have done pretty well so far."

At this stage of the tournament Spain is the team with the most possession and the most time spent in possession in their opponents' half of the field. Spain have made the most passes, scored the most goals (6), had the most shots at goal (61, an average of 20 per game), conceded fewest goals (1) and conceded the fewest shots at goal (average of 6). Only Russia, who have been eliminated, won the ball back more times. His critics appear delusional.

Sweden roll over France and Ukraine succumb to Roy Hodgson's England. As a result, rather than facing England, *La Roja* will resurrect what has historically been an uneven and unsuccessful battle against *Les Bleus* for a place in the semi-final.

Six years after a streetwise mugging from France bundled Spain out of World Cup 2006, ushering in the revolution in playing style and attitude authored by Luis Aragonés, there is a chance for payback.

Meanwhile...
Sweden are knocked out but Zlatan Ibrahimovic does not take it lying down. Instead, the striker contorts his body in the air to direct a sumptuous volley past France goalkeeper Hugo Lloris, a wonderful goal which is supplemented by Sebastian Larsson in stoppage time.

Spain's training bases feature excellent pitches within a short walk of the hotel. This is the view from living quarters to 'the office' in 2012.
Photo: Offside/Marca

Iker Casillas' penalty saves are the product of countless duels with Pepe Reina, including this one at their pre-World Cup training base in Austria. 'Some evenings we're dragging them away as the lights are being switched off,' revealed José Manuel Ochotorena, Spain's goalkeeping coach.
Photo Offside/Marca

Sergio Ramos braves the mixed zone, where journalists crowd round players as they pass through post-match. Ramos has just executed a perfect 'Panenka' penalty against Portugal and Lu Martín, the great Spanish football writer, is setting about describing it over the player's right shoulder.
Photo: Graham Hunter

Manolo el del Bombo is a celebrity superfan of the Spanish national team and a character whom the author had to smuggle into the Loftus Versfeld Stadium after Manolo and his drum were refused entry to watch Spain face Chile at the 2010 World Cup.
Photo: Offside/Marca

Xabi Alonso marked his 100th cap with two goals against France to send Spain through to the semi-finals of Euro 2012.

Photo: AP

Before sending Spain into the final of Euro 2012 with the decisive fifth penalty, Cesc Fàbregas implored the ball, in Catalan: 'Don't fail me now. We have to make history again.' His celebration with Casillas came months after the two had been at the heart of a bitter and dangerous divide between players of Real Madrid and Barcelona. *Photos: Offside/Marca*

The starting XI about to create history by winning a third successive title, Kiev, July 1, 2012.
Back row: Casillas, Arbeloa, Alonso, Ramos, Busquets, Piqué; front row: Silva, Iniesta, Xavi, Fàbregas, Alba.

Photo: Ukrafoto / Demoti / PA

The celebrations following victory in the 2012 European Championships were low-key compared to the previous two tournaments; players were joined by their children both on the pitch and in the dressing room.

Photo: Offside/Marca

Gerard Piqué became used to being the centre of attention at Euro 2012, where his every move in the company of his girlfriend, Shakira, was tracked by paparazzi. After the 4-0 win over Italy in the final, he took centre stage by himself.

Picture: PA

Iker Casillas and Xavi signify the unity within a Spain squad which transcended a heightened Real Madrid-Barcelona rivalry to triumph in 2012. 'Iker helped to protect the ability of Barça and Madrid players to pull together so that we could win,' explained Vicente del Bosque.
Photo: Jake Badger/Landov/AP

Spain won the 2013 UEFA Under-21 Championship and have established a dominance at youth level that has never been seen before. From this group several players, including Isco, Koke, Dani Carvajal, Alberto Moreno and Thiago Alcántara, are now pushing for inclusion in the squad for the World Cup in Rio.
Photo: Offside/Marca

— Day 16.

— June 20, 2012. Gniewino, Poland

Away from the mini-tempest caused by Del Bosque wagging his finger at the Spanish media, Jesús Navas is doing something which, no more than three years ago, would have been impossible.

The Andaluz winger made his debut for the Sevilla first team aged only 16 and was recruited by the federation's *categorías inferiores*. However, he was afflicted with occasional yet fierce anxiety attacks if he was required to travel far from home turf. Spain coveted his talents and the Under-20 World Cup of 2005 should have been his stage, but he could not subjugate his nerves. Despite his wonderful skills, boundless energy, numerous goal assists and increasing maturity, the entire Luis Aragonés reign came and went without him.

In November 2009 I was in the hot, crowded mixed zone of Sevilla's Nervion stadium after a Navas goal gave them a 1-1 draw with Stuttgart in the Champions League. The rumour was that he'd advanced sufficiently to make himself fully available for national team selection. Other tactics had helped him address his phobia, but it is beyond dispute that the Champions League with its short, controlled experiences of match trips abroad helped to curb his anxiety attacks. Navas made it clear that he was up for the challenge, that he did not know how this would work out, but truly yearned to play for Spain.

Jesús Gómez, the press officer at Sevilla, told me a summary of how this had all come to pass.

Jesús Góméz: "The club did employ some sports psychology tactics to try to turn the situation around because they cared about Jesús making the most out of his footballing life, but the thing which eventually helped most of all was simply his absolute love of football. He's a straightforward guy who takes an enormous joy out of basic things like playing and training. Eventually, his will to turn this around plus the support from the guys of his own age in and around Sevilla meant that he was surer and surer of his ability to do what had previously been so difficult. Then his marriage, last year, really added the seal to his self-assurance and confidence."

In due course, Navas was the first substitute used in the World Cup final. He was first off the bench in Spain's opening match at Euro 2012 and created a golden chance for Torres. He was the first substitute used in the vital Group C decider against Croatia and scored.

Jesús may not walk on water, but he has come closer than anyone else in this squad. Navas is so fast that in Potchefstroom during the World Cup he would bet his team-mates that he could run across the loose canvas tarpaulin which protected the outdoor swimming pool at night, without falling in. The tarp was rudimentary, not stretched particularly taught. Only a very light, immensely quick person could even dream of doing it. Navas took cash off everyone who bet against him. He never got wet once. Aptly christened.

The time off which has been postponed post-match is reinstated. Instead of being holed up in the Gdańsk Hotel, closeted away from paparazzi, the players either go bowling in the private ten-pin alleys which are hidden away in the Hotel Mistral press centre, or go with their families to Sopot, the coastal resort where Ireland made their base.

— Day 17.
— June 21, 2012. Gniewino, Poland
This could be the last time Spain train here, and today there is a heavy emphasis on crossing: from the right, Navas and Juanfran, from the left Alba, Mata and Pedro. Torres, Alonso, Llorente, Martínez, Negredo, Busquets, Ramos and Piqué are the main recipients. Although he must be hurting at not getting on the pitch, Fernando Llorente scores two rocket-powered headers.

Paco Jiménez has seen all of France's group games, either in person or on tape, and it interests him that all three goals they've conceded have come from crosses into the box, resulting in one scoring header, one volley and one shot off the bar which is tucked away on the rebound. Philippe Mexès, the key central defender, is suspended, increasing this evident vulnerability to width.

As Spain enter the knockout phase, penalties also become an issue and today the few remaining witnesses at the end of the session – including Del Bosque and a couple of his staff – see the best in a long line of training ground shoot-outs between Iker Casillas and Pepe Reina. The goalkeepers take 10 penalties each against each other. Casillas is deadly off his left foot, as good as most regular penalty takers at the top clubs. Reina, however, is off the scale. He puts the ball to all four corners of the goal, he chips Casillas, he uses brutal power, he slides it like a bar of soap on an ice rink, he does a half-stop and rolls the ball one way as his team-mate goes the other. After 20 kicks, they are tied nine each. After another 10 in sudden death, Iker misses and Pepe wins – again. The victor drops to one knee and does the archer celebration which was the trademark of Kiko at Reina's beloved Atlético Madrid, ending the most extraordinary display of skill and intense competition.

The trip to Donetsk in Ukraine is looming. On average, it is costing the federation around €66,000 per day to accommodate, feed, move and protect the Spanish caravan of players, staff, directors, sponsors. By some distance, this makes it the cheapest tournament of the treble.

At this rate, Navas's goal against Croatia will pay for around eight days of expenses. It is a €500,000 goal. UEFA have allocated a €196m total prize pot for Euro 2012, up from €184m four years previously. Every team earns €8m just for qualifying, a further €1m per win and €500k per draw in the group stage. Winning the quarter-final is worth €2m, the semi-final €3m and victory in the final merits a cool €7.5m. Which means right now Spain are up €10.5m, are playing to make it €12.5m against France and in line for a total windfall of €23m if they win the final in Kiev.

This evening our little team stops for dinner in a pleasant but pretty basic pizza restaurant. Two tables away there is a group of Spaniards. I recognise Chus Llorente, brother of Fernando. Like us, they are checking out the Polish pizza standards while taking in the Portugal vs Czech Republic quarter-final on television.

I say a quick hello to Chus, representative for his brother and the man who nearly took Llorente to Tottenham Hotspur and then Liverpool in a couple of transfer markets separated by a few years. He is seated with his parents. I compliment his and Fernando's mother on what a decent pair of lads she has raised and share an anecdote about her more famous son, from the night of the World Cup final.

As I was walking down the tunnel at Soccer City, about to take up my position by Spain's dugout, I was suddenly swamped by a massive arm around my shoulder. On the other end of it, was Fernando Llorente. We had met once, briefly, and he was on his way to the bench for the biggest game in football, but he was relaxed and conversational: "How's it going? Are you looking forward to the game?" I was bowled over.

"I'm glad to hear all that," replies his mum. "I have always told both of them that football lasts for the blink of an eye but decent behaviour, family and friends are for life."

> *Meanwhile...*
> *Cristiano Ronaldo sticks his head on the end of a João Moutinho cross*
> *to break Czech resistance with 11 minutes left. It is the captain's second*
> *match-winning contribution and he also moves onto three goals for the*
> *tournament. Portugal await the winners of Spain's quarter-final.*

— Day 18.

— June 22, 2012. Donetsk, Ukraine

Immediately before writing this book I was discussing the quantum leap in Spanish football with Albert Ferrer, a member of Barça's Dream Team, a European Cup winner, a five-time Spanish champion, a European Cup Winners' Cup winner, a Copa del Rey winner, an FA Cup winner with Chelsea and an Olympic gold medallist with Spain.

The conversation turned to risk management and the strategies which Spain had used to turn the marginal moments when victory or elimination is determined in their favour.

Ferrer thought there were two key elements. Firstly, the possession philosophy: Ferrer insisted Spain keep the ball with the aim of scoring, creating space, tiring the opposition and winning – not as a purely defensive mechanism. But as well as handing Spain control of the game, this also gives them more ownership of the unpredictable elements which used to afflict them so badly at tournaments.

His analysis was fascinating. "Keep the ball, use it intelligently, use it productively and statistically there is a greater chance that bad things – errors of all shapes and sizes; bad luck, bad choices, anarchic actions by an official – will not happen to you."

Secondly, despite the rich success of his generation, Ferrer has no doubts that this era holds the greatest number of world-class players in Spain's history. His view is that this encompasses experience, toughness, intelligence and bravery. Spain always had talent, but not nearly this much of the psychological strength necessary to take great players to the final of international tournaments.

On day 18 of Spain's treble quest, Andrés Iniesta echoes Ferrer's analysis.

Andrés Iniesta: "At this stage of the tournament, against sides with such equal levels of quality, it is going to be about the side which reaches the opposition goalmouth twice and scores at least once."

This hints at the difference between what Spain used to be good at, and what they are good at now; the argument over efficiency and efficacy. Do something efficiently and it looks good, it feels good, it may bring admiration. Spain's play used to be technical, attacking, flowery, but not effective in tournaments.

If what you are doing efficiently is not the right thing to do, then you could continue forever without achieving your objective.

Fundamental to this historic era for Spain is the new drive to achieve the things which are vital, rather than that which comes naturally and which bring easy praise.

Increased efficacy and decreased errors look like being particularly important against France, a team which Spain have never beaten in a competitive match.

However, across in the opposition camp, fingers are being pointed after an apathetic display in the 2-0 defeat by Sweden.

Laurent Blanc: "When you win, things get brushed over but when you lose, the blood can boil. I admit that the temperatures got overheated in the dressing room after the Sweden game. There was a general feeling that not everyone gave everything they had. To win these types of game you have to play with everything you've got. It needed a few cold showers to cool things down. This isn't just something for the technical staff to analyse but for the players themselves to talk through."

The internal conflicts being discussed by the Spain players are by now historic. The *Clásico* war is *so* last season.

Sergio Ramos: "If anyone is still speaking of a crisis in the national team then they are making a mistake. What we have defended during the club year is one thing and defending the national team is another. There are no wounds and the objective of the national team is to win."

Sergio Busquets: "Everything has been forgotten, things were resolved and now we are all united to achieve the same objective. We defend the same colours and we've left everything in the past behind us."

Today is also the fourth anniversary of the Euro 2008 quarter-final shoot-out and Spain's captain, the hero of that episode, is in no doubt of its relevance to what has followed.

Iker Casillas: "Such memories! That liberated us, you feel a weight has been lifted off your shoulders. What we experienced was key to allow us to begin winning titles with the senior national team. If we had not made it past Italy, nothing which we achieved subsequently would have happened."

Meanwhile…
Greece have not so much got rid of the bus as given it a body-kit and a modern paint job. The alterations to their pragmatic tactics leave them less resolute – Germany score four times to reach the semi-finals, after all – yet Georgios Samaras levels the scores briefly, while his side also win a penalty in stoppage time to remain an irksome presence in Gdańsk.

—Day 19.
—June 23, 2012. Donbass Arena, Donetsk, Ukraine
France v Spain – UEFA European Championship quarter-final
Uno y dos y tres … ganar y ganar y ganar!

The good Laurent gives and the good Laurent taketh away.

Blanc says before the match: "Anyone who likes football must like the way Spain play. Spain have created something special in the last four years. It is a pleasure, a gift to watch them play."

Despite tossing those bouquets, he opts for thistles in his team, abandoning his attacking principles by playing two right-backs, Antony Réveillère and Mathieu Debuchy, one in front of the other, instead of using Samir Nasri or Jérémy Ménez in right midfield. Nasri and Ménez have both scored from the right side in this tournament, Hatem Ben Arfa has also played there, but Blanc opts for stultifying conservatism. All three of these dangerous French playmakers are on the bench. It is a negative tactic designed to suffocate the danger of Jordi Alba and Andrés Iniesta rather than try to pin them back by playing with a dangerous, rapid player like Nasri, the Manchester City winger.

France may have trouble in attack, too, as Karim Benzema, despite a terrific domestic season with Real Madrid, hasn't found the net yet.

Del Bosque promotes Cesc Fàbregas to the starting XI again. He's been flying in training and has two goals, while Fernando Torres' work against Croatia hasn't persuaded Del Bosque.

The night is sweltering. Spain are playing in a different country to their group matches, but it feels like a change of continent. Poland's Baltic coast was grey, chilly, drizzly and blustery. Donetsk is boiling. This will be an examination of their physical resources. Spain may have to go through the wall.

It takes Blanc one hour and three minutes to see the error of his ways. France are fortunate not to give away a penalty for a foul by Gael Clichy on Fàbregas early on, and then concede when Spain rip through the very area where Blanc has sought double protection.

Iniesta has been the player through the last two tournaments who has most frequently vaulted the defensive barricades of opponents. Xavi sets him off and he runs diagonally towards the right-back area, drawing Yohan Cabaye with him. Alba is by his side and Iniesta's pass splits Debuchy and Réveillère exquisitely. It is now a flat-out race between Debuchy and Alba. The Frenchman tries for a foul, fails and falls over.

Alba keeps his balance, takes a touch and, admirably, looks up to see Xabi Alonso thundering in at the back post. Alba's cross hangs there perfectly and the Real Madrid man nods the ball back across into the far panel of the net. It's a goal to mark his 100th cap and Paco Jiménez's predictive work has paid off again.

Spain end up with five on-target chances to France's one, but for 15 minutes after Blanc replaces Debuchy and Florent Malouda with Ménez and Nasri they are in this tie, owning the ball 55% to 45% – a rarity for teams playing Spain.

Instead of shoring up, Del Bosque sends on Pedro – who has been blistering in training – Torres and Cazorla. And so the thing which always happens… happens.

France are sluggish, there is space, Spain's substitutes are sharp, hungry and quick.

Xavi drags a marker out of defence, cedes the ball to Busquets and he feeds Cazorla, who turns and strikes an incisive pass to Pedro in the box. The winger's control is perfect, he produces a stepover trick to get away from Adil Rami and then Réveillère kicks Pedro down for a penalty. Alonso steps up, Hugo Lloris goes to his left, the ball goes to his right, Spain go through.

Les Bleus return home to accusing stares.

Le Parisien: France weren't up to this. Not once did they trouble Spain.

L'Equipe: *Les Bleus* did not inject either the quality nor the anarchy needed to upset the rhythm of a pitiless world champion.

Le Monde: France go home with their heads bowed.

France Football: An inglorious defeat.

Adil Rami: "We have played, and lost, to the best team in the world. There was nothing we could do. We defended well, they had three or four chances and scored from two of them. Top class."

Rami's analysis evokes Iniesta's pre-match call for efficacy.

Xabi Alonso [UEFA man of the match]: "There is not much more a guy can ask from a match. We worked our backsides off and the team did phenomenally well. Perhaps we didn't make our usual total of clear chances, but it felt like we were in total control of the game. To get two goals on my 100th appearance feels wonderful. Our critics? No, I don't feel stung by them because we, the players, know what it costs us to win these games. Some people mistakenly think it should just be a procession for us, but that is daft."

Alonso joins Spaniard centurions Casillas (135 caps), Zubizarreta (126), Xavi (113) and Raúl (102). There are a couple of hundred other players around world football who have made it. The win ratio of the members of this exclusive club now starts with Alonso (78%), Xavi (76%) and Casillas (73%). The first non-Spaniard on the list is Zinedine Zidane (69%). Spain's stats are extraordinary.

Iker Casillas [On Alonso reaching 100 caps]: "I believe it's important for Spanish football. A few years ago, it was unthinkable. There had only been one player who had surpassed 100 games, Zubizarreta. Then came Raúl. Later on, it was me and now there is a generation that has played a long time with the team, including Xavi, Puyol, Xabi Alonso, *El Niño* Torres, Sergio [Ramos]. All of them are at or around 100 caps, but Sergio has played so many games at a young age that it is up to him. If he takes care of himself and maintains his aspirations, he will possibly become the most capped player in Spanish history."

Vicente del Bosque: "We were playing with three forwards – Iniesta, Fàbregas and Silva – but we needed the help of the whole team. People talk about Xabi Alonso and Sergio Busquets, but I think that they are not that defensive – they know how to attack and they are exceptional players. In the last phase of the game France did not have the necessary strength, but they decided not to defend all the time and we needed to respond well as a team. We were tired at the end but that is normal."

Spain 2 France 0

Spain: Casillas, Arbeloa, Ramos, Piqué, Alba, Xavi, Busquets, Alonso, Silva (Pedro 65), Fàbregas (Torres 67), Iniesta (Cazorla 84)
Goals: Alonso 19, 90 pen

France: Lloris, Réveillère, Rami, Koscielny, Clichy, M'Vila (Giroud 79), Debuchy (Ménez 64), Cabaye, Malouda (Nasri 64), Ribéry, Benzema

— Day 20.
— June 24, 2012. Gniewino, Poland
Spain are exhausted. Not only was it extremely hot in Donetsk, the humidity factor was up around 80%. They sweated out litres of fluid – the long season past was in their legs and on their minds.

They do their media, they do the UEFA dope tests, they head from the Donbass Arena to the airport and they wait to board the two-and-a-half-hour flight to Gdańsk. It takes half an hour to disembark and get everyone onto the team bus. It is about an hour and 10 minutes to the Hotel Mistral in Gniewino at this time in the morning and the clock is just ticking on to 5am when they get there. By the time they utilise the fact this is a day off and get back into Gdańsk or Sopot, where their friends and families are living, it will be early afternoon and less than 48 hours before the next 2000km journey from Poland to Donetsk.

It may not compare with the expensive trials of endurance and hope supporters go through to follow their team, but repeated on heavy rotation, this routine takes a toll on the sharpness and motivation levels of every footballer at this level.

The semi-final is back at the Donbass Arena in Donetsk and the players know that it is too late to change the current arrangements. The gameplan for Portugal will be laid on the fields of the Mistral sports complex. However, these exhausted players have reached a consensus and they want to change what happens next.

Del Bosque and his staff, just like Aragonés before them, have planned this tournament intricately: the routines, the base, the pitch. Psychologically, Spain believe that to leave belongings at the team hotel and travel 'match-lite' for knockout games in a tournament gives the players a sense that they are not leaving the tournament each time they fly off from the training camp. For all these reasons, Del Bosque and his staff expect to return to Gniewino at around 5am on June 28 after another 2000km flight, if they defeat Portugal in the semi-final. They will rest, recuperate, train and then fly the 1200 km to Kiev, the venue for the final, on Saturday, June 30, in preparation for the match on Sunday night.

The players, particularly the senior members of the squad, have decided to lobby Del Bosque to abandon this strategy. Xavi, Casillas and company would prefer to stay the night in Donetsk after the semi-final, get a decent sleep, avoid two huge flights and remain in Ukraine until the final.

Based on the advantages of a planned and established training regime, the federation plan includes flights totalling 3200km [Donetsk-Gdańsk-Kiev] for a successful run to the final. The players' proposal includes flights totalling 730km [Donetsk-Kiev] – a net saving of several hours of sleep and avoiding an unnecessary 2500km on a plane.

This debate is not a major source of conflict, nor does it carry the weight of the cricket club meeting held in Potch after defeat by Switzerland. However, when the players petition the management for radical change to a previously successful strategy, there is obvious potential for discord and many managers in Del Bosque's position would say no on general principles. Some would view it as a direct authority challenge. Instead, the national coach listens to the request of his players and asks them to leave it with him. After thought and consultation, he agrees.

A fundamental factor in this decision is that Spain have just knocked out the team which was occupying the hotel and pitch attached to FC Shakhtar Donetsk's Kirsha training ground. The Spanish federation were not impressed with the availability of linked training and accommodation in Ukraine, compared to the five-star playing surface at Gniewino, a two-minute walk down the steps from the hotel. The elimination of France has changed that. Approximately 20 minutes from the Donbass Arena, Shakhtar's facility would not have been any use for Spain's group campaign, played out entirely in Gdańsk, Poland. Now that *La Roja's* players are so weary, it is perfect.

After such prosaic concerns earn a gain for Spain, the day ends with tragic news from Catalonia, where the 23-year-old Real Betis defender Miki Roqué has died. He had fought a malignant tumour in his pelvis since March the previous year, abandoning football in search of curative treatment. Carles Puyol, and Gerard Piqué in particular, who had befriended his fellow Catalan when the two of them were on the fringes at Liverpool and Manchester United respectively, had put time and personal resources into making sure Roqué got the best possible private treatment in Barcelona. Last June he had been given positive news after a six-hour operation to remove the tumour. Remission was at least a realistic goal.

A likeable, elegant defender who became Liverpool's youngest Champions League debutant when Rafa Benitez put him on aged 17 against Galatasaray, Roqué had been international class in the *categorías inferiores* and his loss is felt greatly by those who had come through the ranks with him.

Busquets is one. On the Spanish federation website this is what he writes:

"After hearing the tragic news that a team-mate has died I want to send all my support and my strength to the family and friends of Miki Roqué. We have lost a great person, a terrific sportsman, an example for everyone but, above all, a great friend with whom I shared many moments which I will never forget.

"What hits you first is a state of shock. Then you simply feel that life is completely unfair. Now, all that is left is the driving wish to do everything possible to win and dedicate this tournament to him. From now on we are playing for Miki."

Across social media, but also in phone calls and texts to friends and family, almost all of Spain's squad make it plain that they are deeply moved and affected by the death of this young man who was one of them.

Meanwhile...
Pirlo's chipped penalty in the shoot-out is a shining moment of the finals and England are made to seem uncomfortable in its glare, succumbing 4-2 after a goalless 120 minutes. It also places in the shadow the latest two fall guys for England in such circumstances: Ashley Cole and Ashley Young miss their spot-kicks.

— **Day 21.**
— June 25, 2012. Gniewino, Poland

If, following the death of Miki Roqué, there is something new riding on Spain winning this title, there is a *plus ça change* feel to the challenges ahead. Portugal were the World Cup last-16 opponents two years ago and after a gruelling quarter-final win over England, Italy, Spain's opening opponents in this tournament, remain possible finalists.

The world has been witnessing Panenka penalties since, well, Panenka in 1976, but Andrea Pirlo added an outstanding contribution in the shoot-out that decided Italy's quarter-final. It was executed with the cold eyes of a killer despite the high stakes.

Panenka. The man who robbed West Germany of this trophy treble in 1976.

Panenka. The man whose surname is a by-word for footballing audacity in Spain.

Panenka. The man whose technique can leave you humiliated and culpable if you attempt it and fail. Bear all that in mind if you will.

Spain versus Portugal is a very *Clásico* match-up. It is likely *La Roja* will field up to nine players from Real Madrid and Barcelona and it is sure that Portugal will use three. No Spaniard has forgotten that, in a friendly just after the World Cup, Portugal thrashed them 4-0. And it won't have escaped the notice of any Barça players in the Spain camp that José Mourinho is in Poland/Ukraine as a television match analyst with Al Jazeera.

Mourinho reckoned that Spain looked "sterile" with Fàbregas up front in place of a recognised striker in their opener. "It is not great to keep circulating between Xavi, Iniesta and Cesc without creating a great threat in Buffon's area. Without a striker they can be sterile."

Much of the focus, understandably, turns to Cristiano Ronaldo and whether Spain, who have conceded once so far, can blunt him after his blistering, Liga-winning season for Real Madrid. There is extra glare in the spotlight on Ronaldo given that he looked frustrated, disconnected and less potent against Spain in the World Cup.

Since Gerard Piqué returned from United in 2008, where he had a firm relationship with Ronaldo, circumstances have pitted the two men against one another 15 times. Once for Barcelona against Sir Alex Ferguson's side in the Rome Champions League final of 2009, again at the World Cup, plus 12 *Clásicos*. Piqué has won nine, drawn three and lost three.

Gerard Piqué: "This won't be a Cristiano-Piqué duel, so anyone who thinks that better get the idea out of their heads. Not any other one-on-one battle, not a Barça-Real Madrid game either. We are playing Spain vs Portugal and the better team will win. The team with the better collective spirit, not the one with the better individuals. It is true that it has almost always gone quite well when I have been marking Cristiano, both for Barça and for Spain, but I insist that people understand the value of the collective effort. It is always vital that there is a team-mate ready to help you out if there is a difficult moment and still more so that the players up front and in midfield do their duties in pressing the opposition."

— Day 22.
— June 26, 2012
Gniewino/Donetsk, Poland/Ukraine

One of the rare mistakes Spain have made during this tournament is not noticing that there were a few of their travelling support in Donetsk for the France match. Getting to the far south-east of Ukraine had proved beyond many due to high flight costs, a lack of available seats on the planes, a shortage of hotel accommodation and horrific road trip conditions. Tired, eager to get home and unaware of how many supporters there were in a stadium mostly filled by French and Ukrainians, only a few of Vicente del Bosque's men sought out the Spaniards in the crowd on Saturday.

As a consequence, in these last training days at Gniewino, those fans crammed in next to the fences at the entrance have been enjoying unusually high attention from the players. Every day here, some will sign autographs and pose for pictures. These last days, everyone has done so and proper time has been taken.

The senior players talk about erasing any thoughts of tiredness. The younger Jordi Alba throws in an aside: "I used to have to watch this on television – I'm enjoying a dream I don't want to wake up from!"

The role of the support staff now becomes still more important. It is not within their powers to win Spain the game, but mistakes in dealing with varying levels of mental and physical fatigue could end up costing Spain the title.

Javier Miñano: "Naturally it influences things that Portugal have 48 hours extra to rest, recuperate and prepare. We will just have to do our work very well to compensate. Against France we had an extra day ourselves, so we can't now use this as an excuse. What our boys' limits are we have yet to find out, but four or five seasons ago, talking about a group playing this well, this entertainingly after 72 games, or well over 6000 minutes in a season, was pretty unthinkable."

This time it is *adios* to Gniewino. Players sign everything which is not nailed down for the staff at the hotel, the spa, the bowling alley and the press centre. This place might not have the charm, the weather or the attractive surroundings of the Stubaital or Potch, but it has worked.

Donetsk is hot, sunny and the stadium is a wondrous place. Powerful-looking and elegant, lit to within a kilowatt of its life at night, this is a place of epic battles. The playing surface is not great, so Spain have opted to train on Shakhtar's pitch. Before that, Iniesta, Arbeloa and Negredo come to the Donbass to speak to the media. If Luis Aragonés had been there, he would have been proud of his former charges.

In the build-up to the 2008 semi-final against Russia, Aragonés told his players: "Don't be chatting to the referee or the linesmen and calling them ref or lino! Give them a high five, put an arm around their shoulder and make sure it's 'hi Joseph' or whatever. You'll see, the guy will go away thinking 'bloody hell, he knows my name!'"

Tomorrow's referee is Cüneyt Çakir from Turkey. He and his team of five assistants are trotting around the pitch, warming up and getting used to the stadium. Down at the mouth of the tunnel, following an interview with Negredo, I am having a brief chat with Arbeloa. Just then, Iniesta moves away from a small group he has been in and, all the while looking out the tunnel at the Turkish group, he asks me: "Which is the ref?"

I mistake him and answer: "You'll remember him, it's the guy who was in charge in the [Champions League semi-final] game against Chelsea at the Camp Nou in April."

"No, no, I know that. I mean which of them is he?" Iniesta replies, nodding at the pack of officials.

I point out Çakir and Iniesta joins our conversation as we lean on the wall around the mouth of the tunnel. By the time Çakir and his pals have completed their exercises, Iniesta makes sure that he is facing down the tunnel. As the officials approach there is a subtle nudging of elbows and exchange of knowing glances: *Look, that's the great Andrés Iniesta.* As they reach him, there is a general move to stop and politely exchange a handshake, but Iniesta picks out the referee, Çakir, for the first and warmest *'hola'.*

From afar, Puyol has been hectoring Piqué even more than he would had they been on the pitch together. For this tournament, his advice is restricted to texts about not losing concentration, about supporting Arbeloa and Alba should they go forward. It is also Puyol who breaks the news about Miki Roqué to Piqué.

Via the same medium of SMS, Negredo went back and forth with his Sevilla club mate, Ivan Rakitić, prior to the Croatia game, as did the Madrid contingent and Karim Benzema ahead of the quarter-final. However, Arbeloa reminds me: "I might play alongside Fabio Coentrão, Pepe and Cris [Ronaldo] at our club, but I will not speak to them until this game is done. There are no friends on the pitch until that point either."

I don't read much into the identity of the three players sent to face the media at the pre-match press conference. The following night, this will prove an error on my part. However, another thing which is of slightly more importance does catch my attention.

A half-hour bus ride takes us to Spain's training pitch. It is dark, mid evening and jungle hot. The pitch is fully enclosed by a wire cage and every 15 feet there is a fluorescent blue lantern into which flies and more particularly mosquitoes are attracted to their annihilation. The sound of zzzzzt... zzzzzt is like a Kraftwerk backing track to the players' work.

For once, our access is really poor. There are too many cameras and not enough space and I wander off. Down where the media are assembled, beside and behind Casillas, the major players are practising shooting, crosses and headers, free-kicks. Not everyone studies what is happening at the far end. Pepe Reina is keeping goal while an assortment of players including Santi Cazorla, Iniesta, Piqué and Arbeloa are taking penalties.

This is not one of their competitions and there is no shouting or joking. Nor is it drawing an audience. It is just five or six players, then a couple drop out and two others nip in for a few minutes. Ramos takes one, delaying his exit from the end of the session to do so. He strikes it hard and home. Middle right.

Previously, Xabi Alonso has told us: "I expect a very tight, balanced game against Portugal. Something along the lines of the England vs Italy game we watched the other night."

England vs Italy is scoreless, goes to extra-time and then penalties, which includes an Andrea Pirlo Panenka for the winners as they take the shoot-out by a score of 4-2. We look everywhere, but Donetsk does not make its bookmakers as obvious as one might like. Retrospectively that's a pity.

— Day 23.
— June 27 2012. Donbass Arena, Donetsk, Ukraine
Portugal v Spain – UEFA European Championship semi-final
Uno y dos y tres ... ganar y ganar y ganar!

Before a ball is kicked Spain, or at least Antonio Limones, has won the Game of Thrones. *La Roja* are tucked away exclusively, far from the madding crowd, in Shakhtar Donetsk's sumptuous training ground hotel. Those friends and family of the players who have taken an official package trip via the federation are, like us, in the Shakhtar Plaza hotel which is enormous, elegant and only 200 metres from the Donbass Arena, where the semi-final will be played. Portugal find that in their Hotel Victoria there are loads of journalists from all over the world, plus a large number of travelling Spanish fans. Nothing gets out of hand but Ronaldo, for example, is made aware that *La Roja's* fans are sharing his hotel whenever he makes himself visible.

Late afternoon I chat to a particularly close friend of a couple of *La Roja's* senior players and he tells us that the squad already know the line-up. Ten of the names are precisely as expected. One is not.

Paulo Bento: "Portugal is ready for Torres or Fàbregas starting, equally if it is Pedro or Silva. They are just minor variants on a basic playing scheme which we have well documented."

Well, one out of four ain't bad. There will be no Fàbregas, no Torres, no Pedro but there will be the surprise inclusion of Álvaro Negredo in attack. Spain line-up: Casillas; Arbeloa, Piqué, Ramos, Alba; Xavi, Busquets, Alonso; Silva, Negredo, Iniesta.

It is something of a surprise. Negredo was the starting striker in the last warm-up game (a 1-0 win over China in Seville) before heading for Poland. Subsequently, the debate over Fàbregas or Torres – to deploy a false No.9 or a conventional centre-forward – has somewhat overshadowed the fact that Negredo has had all of one minute this tournament – sixty seconds more than Fernando Llorente.

Each has been sharp in daily work, but Llorente has had a red-hot season. He was fundamental in Athletic's elimination of Manchester United and their march to the Europa League final. Two years ago it was his arrival off the bench against Portugal which changed the game, helped bring the winning goal and shaped Spain's World Cup destiny. Nevertheless, like Mata, who could barely walk when he came off the pitch having won the Champions League with Chelsea in Munich, the ravages of the season have cost Llorente.

Marcelo Bielsa, the Athletic coach, ran his players' legs off and their slump in the last four weeks across April and May is accounted for by physical and mental exhaustion. So, by a nose, it is Negredo.

Compared to the France game the temperature has dropped a little. Early in the week it rained, the atmosphere is suddenly a touch less humid and the grass has been watered a little bit more generously and cut just a shave shorter.

The first half provides further indication that this Spain team can be put on a low flame by athletic players with advantages in height and power, organisation, double marking and relentless pressing. However, as Sweden, Paraguay, Portugal, Holland, Croatia and France have discovered by employing these methods at the last two tournaments, this results in the defending team tiring in the last quarter and Spain scoring. Argentina and Portugal attacked Spain far more in their two friendly victories, but tournament football is more fearful. Teams put so much mental and physical effort into stopping Spain that they have too little left to impose their own creative or cutting-edge actions. For example, the semi-final of Euro 2012 will end without Casillas making a single save.

Spain have been open about how tired they are, and when Portugal throw a wet blanket of pressing defence on the European and world champions, excitement and flair rarely get through.

Negredo makes little impact and Bento's team look like they are bossing things until the game gets old. Fàbregas comes on. Navas come on. Portugal start to tire and from midway through the second half until the 120th minute, Spain are on the front foot and fierce. They go past tackles, Rui Patrício makes good saves – two of them are top quality. From a Navas shot, the keeper's work is tricky and he takes two bites at it, but he does not give up a rebound which would have resulted in a certain goal. From Iniesta, after a gorgeous set-up by Alba, the Portuguese keeper makes a diving point-blank stop that the Spain midfielder evidently can't believe. It is the best moment of the match.

Spain bring on two flying wingers in Navas and Pedro who, between them, have scored and created a goal each in the last two matches. They bring on Fàbregas, who has two goals in this tournament. Alba, nominally a full-back, spends more time in Portugal's penalty area than Nani or Ronaldo do in Spain's.

The final whistle goes at 12.12am. Even the clock can't be split. About 10 minutes earlier, Del Bosque turns to Toni Grande and asks him to draft a list of penalty takers. The two men already have a long-list prepared from the previous day, but Xavi, David Silva and Negredo (who have been subbed off) all featured.

This was the eventuality being prepared for on the Shakhtar training pitch last night. Del Bosque wanted those who habitually take very few penalties – players such as Cazorla, Mata, Iniesta, Piqué, Fàbregas, Ramos and Martínez – to hit at least one or two. He did not want Casillas in goals having penalty after penalty flying past him. Nor did he want to stage a full session in front of the world's media, whose headline would be written: Tired Spain Preparing For Penalties. Instead, Reina faced about 18 spot-kicks from six players who trotted over every now and again from other training drills. Now it is time for the real thing.

Spain's shoot-out victory over Portugal, which puts them in the final of Euro 2012, is further testimony to values other than talent.

Toni Grande suggests the order:

1) Alonso
2) Fàbregas
3) Piqué
4) Ramos
5) Iniesta

Del Bosque approves. Pedro and Alba are the other prime candidates, but for now there is no reason not to go with the Grande five. As they were at full-time, Spain's players are all up and about, sharing encouragement and some tactical thoughts.

Portugal, as with so many of Spain's rivals when they are through extra-time, have a few players who sit or lie down.

The coaches call their players into huddles. Toni Grande reads out his list and Fàbregas immediately objects. He wants the fifth penalty, for three reasons. He has had a premonition of scoring the winning goal. He scored the fifth penalty against Italy four years ago in the quarter-final. And he is not at all scared of the pressure and responsibility.

Grande is not particularly impressed. Time is short, some thought has been put in to his order, but while there is a brief chat between player and coach, Del Bosque is watching his player's body language like a hawk and listening intently. The boss judges that Fàbregas is not hiding from pressure, that it is a positive demand and agrees.

1) Alonso
2) Iniesta
3) Piqué
4) Ramos
5) Fàbregas

Paulo Bento also works as a benign dictator. He has his five candidates in mind: Moutinho, Pepe, Nani, Alves, Ronaldo. He is considering that order, but he is open to personal wishes from any players who have a specific preference. Unlike the Spanish bench there is minimal input from his assistants, João Aroso or Leonel Pontes, while the goalkeeper coach Ricardo Peres is working on some of the visualisation techniques upon which Rui Patrício, towel draped over his head, is completely focused. Ronaldo, like Fàbregas, is happy to take the responsibility of the fifth penalty, although his preference is to go first. Bento suggests he hits the final penalty and Ronaldo, who has a conversion rate for clubs and country of over 95%, agrees.

1) Moutinho
2) Pepe
3) Nani
4) Alves
5) Ronaldo

Meanwhile, Iker Casillas appears to have gone mad. Initially the players file up to pay homage to him, with the biggest hugs coming from Reina and Xavi. Then José Manuel Ochotorena appears and puts a *cordon sanitaire* around the keeper. This is Iker-time. Solitude. Which he uses to nip over to the bench, take off his gloves and unstrap his wrists. Then he drops his shorts, takes off the lycra cycle-shorts he has been wearing during the match and, now down to his smalls, he pulls up his football kit again. Ready now. Later, he will tell us he felt like the shorts were strangling him. Superheroes usually cape-up. *San Iker* strips off.

Back in the centre circle, Alonso has quite a lot to think about. He does not appreciate Pepe sneaking up to him to mutter in his ear that Rui Patrício is going to save everything. Ronaldo, another Real Madrid team-mate, runs over to Rui Patrício and cups his hand around the goalkeeper's ear, apparently passing on advice about Alonso's spot-kick technique. Alonso has taken 15 penalties for Liverpool, Real Madrid and Spain and scored 13, but his two failures have both been high-profile, in the Champions League final of 2005 and the World Cup quarter-final of 2010. Dida of Milan saved to Alonso's left; Justo Villar of Paraguay saved to Alonso's right. In the quarter-final only four days ago, Alonso took care of business from 11 metres against France, Hugo Lloris diving to Alonso's right, the ball going the other way.

The Basque has a distinctive technique. He lines up diagonally to the ball, not straight on. It looks as if he intends to strike his shot across the keeper and into the side panel of the goal to his right. Sometimes, as against France, he shapes to do that, but twists his right ankle round the ball and skews his shot left at something like a 70 degree angle from its apparent trajectory. Against France, he bet on red. This time on black. He shoots to his right but Rui Patrício has either read it or gets lucky. Alonso's penalty is well hit, it takes a really good save, but save he does.

Spain 0-0 Portugal

João Moutinho on the plate. This is a man used to pressure: Sporting Lisbon captain at the age of 19, a high-profile transfer to Porto not long in his past and renowned for striking the ball well. While not a prolific scorer he has nonetheless been a reasonably regular penalty taker. His most recent miss – playing for Bento and with Rui Patrício in the Sporting team – was against Steve McClaren's FC Twente in Champions League qualifying. Both Jiménez and Ochotorena have identified that Moutinho is so confident about his clean striking of the ball that he runs up with a series of dainty steps, looking at the keeper and assessing whether there is a 'tell' on offer. Then Moutinho usually shows a very strong preference for striking the shot to his left.

Casillas knows what is going to happen. Moutinho goes left and he makes the save.

Spain 0-0 Portugal

Casillas' mum is in the stadium again, as she was in Vienna. This time she doesn't faint, she just goes to the toilet to escape the tension.

Now it is Iniesta, not Fàbregas. He extends his arms wide in the style of David Beckham's free-kick technique, to feign that he is going to put the ball to his left. The goalkeeper goes *so* early that he is flat on the ground to that side of the goal while the ball is still three feet from crossing the line. Later Iniesta admits he saw the movement and, at the last second, changed his mind about shooting to his left.

Spain 1-0 Portugal

Now it is Pepe against his Real Madrid team-mate. The defender can sometimes seem raw and thuggish with no regard for propriety; sometimes an athletic and inspirational defender who, like Carlos Marchena, possesses a great deal more skill than most people realise.

In keeping with the theme of the tournament, Pepe starts his astonishingly long run-up in Poland and arrives in Donetsk to kick the ball, hard and low and in. It goes to the goalkeeper's right as Casillas has anticipated, but the Spain captain pretty much dives over Pepe's effort.

Spain 1-1 Portugal

Next, the man with the golden life. An IQ of 140, superstar girlfriend, athleticism, talent, youth, millionaire. Good right foot. Gerard Piqué puts the ball where Pepe did, but more firmly, so that Rui Patrício's full-length dive can't get him there in time to put a finger tip on it. In 277 professional matches, this is Piqué's first penalty. You'd never know.

Spain 2-1 Portugal

Bento has jotted down Nani as third taker, Bruno Alves as fourth. Just as Silvia Dorschnerova does for Spain, Portugal's match delegate passes the hand-written list to referee Cüneyt Çakir. This does not mean that they are dutybound to stick to that order. The five names must remain constant, but the order can change without notice. Alves, in the heat of the moment, forgets and sets off out of turn. He gets to within one stride of the penalty box, totally focused, when something happens for which he could not possibly have planned.

Nani runs from the halfway line to the penalty box to send Alves back so that he himself can take the third penalty for Portugal, as agreed. This Nani prioritises ahead of the risk of breaking Alves' concentration, or handing Spain the impression that Portugal haven't a clue what they are doing. Alves accepts the reprimand without hesitation and wanders back before Nani scores the best penalty of the night, incorporating a half-stop which sends Casillas off balance as the striker erupts a shot into the roof of the net.

Spain 2-2 Portugal

It is 84 days since Sergio Ramos and Casillas went through all of this in the semi-final of the Champions League, to much heartbreak, recrimination and then derision. Now here he is again, with a new haircut and a red shirt, not white – but still the same guy who sent a penalty rocketing up over Manuel Neuer's crossbar.

Nobody hammered Ronaldo and Kaká for missing Madrid's first two spot-kicks that April night, because Casillas saved from Toni Kroos and Philipp Lahm to send Ramos up with the shoot-out level again. The defender's effort was atrocious, taking off on the kind of upward trajectory you might get from a firework. Felix Baumgartner's world record parachute jump from space was only a few months old and there was a flood of YouTube videos showing the ball from Ramos's penalty hitting the Austrian on the head as he prepared to launch himself from his balloon, far above Earth. Over and above that, Ramos was pretty viciously castigated and mocked.

In the Donbass Arena Ramos' mum, Paqui, cannot watch because she knows what a hard time her younger son took in April for that miss. She is helping Pepe Reina's wife Yolanda by keeping their daughter, Grecia, on her knee. She leans down and buries her face in the little girl's shoulder until the ordeal is over.

Only his brother, René, and one of this Spain squad, knew that after such sustained abuse Ramos immediately took the decision that his next penalty, wherever, whenever and no matter the importance, would be converted in the style of Antonín Panenka.

Having sent the ball up into the galaxy last time, tonight the stars align. Portugal's goalkeeper is a diver, Ramos makes elegant, subtle contact and the ball arcs sweetly over Rui Patrício.

Spain 3-2 Portugal

Bruno Alves is the Portugal quarter-back. One of the facets of Paulo Bento's team is that this guy can ping accurate passes 40 and 50 metres across the pitch. However, as any golfer will tell you, you drive for show and putt for dough. What is he going to be like over 11 rather than 40 metres, particularly with Nani's intrusion still in the forefront of his mind?

Ronaldo has been pacing around his part of the centre circle like a caged tiger. Now he is quite still.

Alves sprints to the ball and strikes it sweetly, but his geometry is faulty by about 4 inches. The ball imprints its brand name on the face of the crossbar and cannons down away from the goal-line. Miss!

Spain 3-2 Portugal

Now it all seems to speed up. Jordi Alba goes to Cesc Fàbregas, whom he has known since he was eight, grasps the midfielder's head in both hands and says: "This is it, this is your moment!"

Fàbregas sets off. Racing through his mind is regret about telling his family not to waste money coming to the semi-final and to wait to meet him in Kiev. His parents were in Vienna when his penalty eliminated Italy and opened the portal to all this success and glory. He wishes they were here again. The duration of that thought has taken him to the edge of the box. The ball is sitting, waiting.

Fàbregas stops, bends down and starts talking to the ball as he picks it up.

"Don't fail me now," he says in Catalan. "Don't fail me, just go into the net like you did in Vienna. We have to make history again."

They do. Fàbregas takes about as long a run-up as Pepe's and cracks a right-footed shot in off the goalkeeper's right-hand post.

As he did against Buffon four years ago, he has changed his mind at the last moment and hit it to his own left instead of right. The Portuguese goalkeeper is so nearly there, but it is not enough. The ball has listened to Fàbregas and cannons off the inside of the post into the net. Spain are in the final.

Spain 4-2 Portugal

As in Vienna, Fàbregas is lost for a moment, but when he comes around, he provides an image to illustrate the whole *La Roja* spirit since Autumn 2006. Almost 10 months earlier, Fàbregas had been cut down by Marcelo during his long-awaited Camp Nou return. After the final whistle, Iker Casillas, talking about Fàbregas, said: "There will have been a tackle, one of them will have dived."

It has taken several months of internecine feuding followed by a conciliatory phone call, but here they are. Casillas, who has been standing on the touchline about 20 feet away from the Portugal goalmouth and Fàbregas, the winning penalty scorer again, beaming, arms open, eyes shining and about to embrace each other.

Never mind *Blancos* and *Blaugranas*. Never mind Mourinho. *Viva España!*

Portugal 0 Spain 0 (Spain win 4-2 on penalties)

Portugal: Rui Patrício, Joao Pereira, Alves, Pepe, Coentráo, Meireles (Varela 113), Veloso (Custódio 106), João Moutinho, Nani, Almeida (Oliveira 81), Ronaldo

Spain: Casillas, Arbeloa, Ramos, Piqué, Alba, Xavi (Pedro 87), Busquets, Alonso, Silva (Navas 60), Negredo (Fàbregas 54), Iniesta

—Day 24.
— June 28, 2012
   Donetsk/Kiev, Ukraine
It is well past 2am before the European Championship finalists leave the Donbass. The next 24 hours will include a short hop to Ukraine's capital city

on an 11am flight, installation at the new team hotel, no training and complete freedom to spend time with friends and family.

First, though, in the earliest hours of the new day and the immediate aftermath of the shoot-out, the players emerge.

Television cameras were focused tight on Del Bosque's face after Sergio Ramos executed his Panenka penalty over Rui Patrício. The coach didn't appear happy.

Sergio Ramos: "Del Bosque knows I'm a little bit *loco*. I had it all planned out because of the pain of the semi-final against Bayern. It wasn't so much missing, but the fact that people immediately questioned my will or my ability to face that responsibility and triumph. My pride was stung. I decided then to demonstrate in style that they were all wrong. Last night in training I deliberately chose not to practise that because I knew the media would pick up on it. When there is so much at stake the last thing a goalkeeper expects from a defender is to chip him. There is a risk, but if you execute it well there is a high chance of scoring, too. Just as I began my run up I could see that he was beginning to move and that sealed it for me. Now it is just an anecdote to tell my kids and my family, but what is important is that the whole world knows that Spain are going to do what nobody has ever managed – to win the big international tournaments back-to-back. Nobody understands what an effort this is costing us."

Jesús Navas: "He tells me everything. The night before the match I knew he was going to chip the keeper if there was a penalty."

Vicente del Bosque: "No way was I pissed off with him. Let him take more like that one! There is no doubt that watching him convert like that gave everyone's confidence a lift. I know he saw the keeper moving and chose to score like Pirlo did against England. It is in fashion now, you know?
"We took Xavi off because he was really, really tired and we needed pace and offensive power to try to win it. Controlling Cristiano was the work of Piqué and Arbeloa and Busquets when needed and they did great work, but everyone is right at their physical limit because of tiredness right now and I don't think he is an exception, however powerful and athletic he is."

Cesc Fàbregas: "In the morning I just had this intuition, like a premonition, that I was going to score the fifth penalty, the winning one. Look, you can't be sure that you won't miss, but it was a strong feeling and so I asked to change the order. Walking up to the ball I was thinking about my family, about four years ago. Then at the end someone handed me a mobile phone and it was my mum calling from Barcelona."

Vicente del Bosque: "Everyone we put on the first list immediately said they wanted to take one. We had put Cesc second, but he is one of the most confident when it comes to striking a penalty, so when he said he wanted to go fifth we decided to trust him, it was not something to have a big argument over."

Paulo Bento: "Cristiano did not demand to go fifth, we chose the order precisely the way we wanted, everyone agreed to it and I would not do it differently the next time. Everyone who is criticising now would be speaking very differently if it had been us with the fifth penalty to win it and Ronaldo had scored. I thought we were the better team in the first half but we lacked efficacy and then, ultimately, penalties are a lottery. We go home proud."

Andrés Iniesta [via Twitter]: "We are in the final!!! What joy!!! How great this team is …"

During this day there is a special toast between the father, mother and brother of Jordi Alba, who meet up with Spain's left-back to celebrate the fact that his €15m move to Barcelona is now official. The players' families are all holed up at the Kiev Holiday Inn, and after a day spent together they kiss goodnight and the squad returns to the Hotel Opera, Spain's base until they leave on Monday, to watch Germany vs Italy.

The German media, and to some extent the German squad, have begun to seem a little obsessed with *La Roja*. Jogi Löw wants the *Mannschaft* to play like Spain, his players think they are better than Spain and the German media report that this tournament has shown Del Bosque's team to be beatable.

Perhaps this focus on Spain is a factor in the semi-final, as Germany forget to defend and play like a unit for the first hour against Italy. The Mario Balotelli show, all pecs and power, knocks Germany out before they are even aware the match has got serious. Italy, the pre-tournament 14-1 shots, are in the final.

However, by the latter stages of this dramatic semi-final, Italy look very fatigued, Germany are knocking on the door for an equaliser and you can bet that Spain, with every player fit, happy and established in Kiev, go to bed very content with the world.

> **Meanwhile...**
> *Super Mario powers up – Balotelli joins Dzagoev, Mandžukić, Ronaldo and Gómez on three goals for the tournament. There is no contender from the world champions, but that could change in the final.*

— Day 25.
— *June 29, 2012*
 Kiev, Ukraine

Depending on your tastes, Kiev can be heaven or hell. If you like the staid and predictable, with no extremes, do not come here. If you like your life with a bagful of surprises, then this is the city for you.

Spain last played here in a qualifier for Euro 2004, but from the starting XI only Iker Casillas remains. For international qualifiers and for the players who come here on Champions League nights in spring or winter, it is a long trip to an incredibly cold destination. Both Barcelona and Del Bosque's Real Madrid were beaten here by Andriy Shevchenko's Dynamo in consecutive seasons in the late 1990s.

Now, in the summer, it is hot like home – not humid at all, just burning, dry heat.

The players have the first part of the day to themselves for rest and physio. Training is in the evening, closed-doors so that the last tactical work can be done in private before tomorrow's open session at the Olympic Stadium.

The theme linking Spain's draw here in 2003 and two humiliating defeats for the giants of Spanish football is Valeriy Vasylyovych Lobanovskyi. It was his Kiev team which humiliated Barcelona 4-0 in the group phase of the 1997/98 Champions League and then knocked out the holders, Madrid, at the quarter-final stage the following season. Shevchenko scored a hat-trick against Barça, and another three over the two legs of the quarter-final against Madrid, in his final season in Kiev.

Shortly after the 2-2 draw with Iñaki Sáez's Spain, less than a year after Lobanovskyi's death in May 2002, AC Milan won the Champions League final at Old Trafford and Shevchenko flew home to take the cup with the big ears to the shrine by his mentor's tomb. Dynamo's stadium – they choose to play home games there or at the larger, municipal Olympic Stadium – is now known as the Valeriy Lobanovskyi Dynamo Stadium. That is where Spain are training tonight, an hour and a quarter of tight, recuperative and then tactical work, to loosen limbs and sharpen minds.

Real Madrid have a stone in their shoe: the one major trophy they never won, and now cannot win because it was discontinued, is the European Cup Winners' Cup. Back in 1975 Del Bosque, playing the Sergio Busquets role for Madrid, reached the quarter-finals of that tournament but went out to Red Star Belgrade, while a pretty youthful Lobanovskyi coached Dynamo Kiev to the old Soviet Union's first major European trophy. Arriving at this picturesque stadium for today's press conference, Del Bosque, Fàbregas and Ramos find that the replica of that Cup Winners' Cup trophy, and the one Dynamo won in 1986, are on the floor, holding doors open.

When Fàbregas and the coach meet the press, focus turns for the first time to Italy and the final match of the treble quest.

Cesc Fàbregas: "Balotelli is a great footballer. That second goal he scored against Germany was a superstar finish. Against a team like Germany, in a semi-final, top corner – that is the work of a top-class centre-forward. He, Cassano and Pirlo need to be cut off by our work on Sunday night. Right now the record of winning three straight tournaments is not as important as simply winning this final. We have made history already, now we want to make more."

How much history will be written by the senior members of this remarkable group, though? Carles Puyol has watched this tournament on television in Spain, although he will travel to Ukraine for the final, and he will be 36 when the first ball is kicked in Brazil in the summer of 2014. Now it emerges that Xavi is considering closing the book on his international career after the final.

For the last three seasons he has had almost perpetual pain in his Achilles' tendons and his calf muscles, and it has badly affected his enjoyment of both life outside football – he is in almost constant remedial treatment when not playing or training – and also his athleticism, particularly when Spain or Barcelona are robbed of the ball and caught on a counter attack. So far he has coped, but this tournament has not felt quite as satisfying for him.

Xavi is used to being in control: of the ball, the tempo, the direction of attacks and of the result, by ensuring that the master-pass is made. Spain and Barcelona goals come with a 'Made By Xavi' stamp. That has not been happening so much at this tournament.

In South Africa, his position was slightly higher up the pitch, a little more often with his back to goal. The difference is not radical, but all these factors have cumulatively led him to a tipping point. Xavi is considering doing the right thing by Del Bosque and telling him that he intends to finish on a high this Sunday. When Pedro Proença's whistle goes it will finish the match, and Xavi's career in red. His mind turns to what to say. What the consequences will be. What it will be like to say goodbye.

Toni Grande: "We have had one or two differences of opinion about tactics over the years. For example, Xavi might have a preference to play alongside one player over another. He might want to play a bit further up or slightly deeper. Sometimes he persuades us and at others we manage to get him to see it our way."

Xavi: "After the semi-finals I told Del Bosque that I wanted to retire from the national team. He said to me: 'Are you going though some sort of depression? How can you contemplate missing the World Cup in Brazil?' He told me to take some time to think it over during the holidays, which I did. I took lots of advice – from my family, my mates, my girlfriend and in the end realised that I wouldn't be able to bear not being called up. The first friendly that I missed would most likely plunge me into a depression, for real. It was because of all the criticism rather that anything personal. I just thought, 'Enough is enough. We're playing well, we've made it to the final of the Euros and they're still saying I'm rubbish, I'm f***ing awful. People are sick of me, it's time to go, son'."

If Xavi is lost in reverie, so too is the Italian coach, even if for completely different reasons. Cesare Prandelli, a former team-mate of UEFA president Michel Platini at Juventus, is as elegant off the pitch as he wants his team to be on it. He is also a bit of a night-bird. He and his technical staff have agreed to mark each victory at this tournament with a pilgrimage to a religious site. After Italy defeat Ireland, Prandelli and Demetrio Albertini get clear of their stadium duties then walk, through the night, the 20km from their Wieliczka training ground to a monastery near Krakow. After eliminating England, they walk 11km to another monastery, nearer Wieliczka. After the titanic defeat of Germany, they march about 10km to the Sagrada Familia in Krakow, driving back to the team hotel and arriving at about 5am. Good for the spiritual side, perhaps less so for mental freshness.

— Day 26.
— June 30, 2012
Kiev, Ukraine

For the jumpy amongst the Spanish football community there are some causes for disquiet following Italy's semi-final win. Germany went into the game as the only side in the tournament to have won every game, and on a winning run of 15 matches in competitive fixtures – a world record. Italy had won once over 90 minutes at this tournament.

Once again, Italy triumph against the odds. Spain have still not beaten them without penalties in competition since 1920, so would the world champions take another shoot-out win if the game was tight?

Sergio Ramos: "Quite frankly, no. Over the past few days unforgettable memories from the last two tournaments are flooding through my mind and they motivate you even more to win this final. We all want to see the outpouring of joy across all the communities in Spain which victory in the last two tournaments brought. What is in play on Sunday night is putting the high benchmark of our work in an almost unreachable place for those who come after us. Whatever happens, we have already made history, but now we want our country to have the all-time record."

Iker Casillas: "I would much rather avoid a penalty shoot-out, every time. Winning them can come down to the tiniest of details, centimetres of a difference and there are so many things you can't control."

However, shoot-outs tend not to leave Spain injured any more. From 1984 until 1996, with Luis Arconada and Andoni Zubizarreta in goals, Spain went through three tournament penalty shoot-outs, winning one and losing two. In all that time, against 14 penalties, the keepers did not make a single save.

Since Casillas took over, there have been four shoot-outs: two in World Cup 2002, one in Euro 2008 and now this success against Portugal. Spain have won three and lost one. Of the 18 penalties he faced in those deciders, Casillas has saved five and two have hit the bar or gone over.

The Olympic Stadium is a vast ranch of land surrounding a bowl of an arena with a running track around the pitch. The players seem happy with the surface and once back down the tunnel there is a long warm-up zone covered in astroturf.

Italy train first and, as they begin to come back in, Spain are fidgeting, waiting to get out and get in contact with the ball again.

Balotelli, as usual, is dancing to a different tune. The *Azzurri* come down the stairs from the pitch, give some brief, stand-up interviews to the very few media accredited to be in this inner sanctum and head off to the dressing room. Not Mario. Stripped to the waist, just like he was after scoring that monster goal against Germany, he hangs around in his boots and shorts, waiting for David Silva to appear. The two Manchester City men lean against the wall, one about twice the size of the other, a Spaniard of Japanese extraction and an Italian of Ghanaian parentage, and they shoot the breeze about football.

Training is short and sharp and then the players head back for a night at the Opera Hotel. Del Bosque considers his starting XI. So far his decisions have been on the money, with the exception of the call to start Álvaro Negredo against France.

At the back it is automatic. The pairing of Ramos and Piqué has functioned brilliantly. Spain have not conceded a goal in knockout football since Zinedine Zidane scored France's third at World Cup 2006 – precisely 900 minutes ago.

Casillas; Arbeloa, Piqué, Ramos, Alba

In midfield there is still less doubt. Xavi tired in the humidity of Donetsk, Alonso took a sharp piece of Pepe's knee in his back during that semi-final, but the two warhorses will be fine and Busquets is allowing Del Bosque to live vicariously again – winning the ball, moving the ball, making the team tick.

Xavi, Busquets, Alonso

Up front, Cesc Fàbregas has earned his start. Against Italy in the group, precisely three weeks ago, he scored. Against Portugal in the semi-final, his arrival from the bench turned the game in Spain's favour. Given Negredo's poor performance when given a start against France and Llorente's absence from Del Bosque's mind, only Torres can challenge Fàbregas, but the Catalan has won that duel.

Silva, Fàbregas, Iniesta

Vicente del Bosque: "Many times it appears that experience of all this gives you a certain tranquility but as the years pass, they make you feel the responsibility of it all more strongly. We have little time for nerves because there is so much to do and to think about. You really have to centre your thoughts on the players, the formation and the tactics. Right now, of course, all we want is to get the final going. Between training camps in Spain and Austria and now the tournament we have been together 40 days. We are ready."

An interview with Sergio Ramos takes us to the Opera Hotel. About three-quarters of the squad are draped around various chairs, couches, benches and alcoves of this magnificent hotel's ornate reception area. Around them frolics an army of kids, from tiny toddlers to cute things of five and six years old. There are wives, girlfriends and, above all, there is an air that the football is just make believe. *This* is what matters to the guys we are watching.

While all this is going on, Xavi takes Del Bosque aside. He explains that this will be his farewell, that the physical and mental toll of fighting pain is becoming all consuming. He has a small thorn in his paw about the slight tactical variation between playing for Spain and for Barça, but this is far from the determining factor. He explains to Del Bosque that he believes sharing this information now is the grown-up way to handle the issue. If Spain lose, Del Bosque will understand that it is not a knee-jerk reaction. Should they win, it will be a perfect curtain call.

The Spain coach is strongly opposed to a firm decision. He urges Xavi to reconsider, to take time and to think about aiming to win the World Cup in Brazil. More practically, both Del Bosque and Toni Grande try to allay Xavi's worries about whether he truly is required to fulfill such a radically different role for Spain.

Six months after the tournament, I went to Las Rozas to talk to Del Bosque and asked him specifically about Xavi's position.

Vicente del Bosque: "I just don't agree with the idea that he is asked to play differently for Spain than for Barcelona. What players have to accept is that their role might be distinct between club and country, but we won't ask them to do things which aren't fully within their talents. Okay, at Barcelona, even back to the days of Pep Guardiola [playing] in the Dream Team, I know that they only play with one organising, controlling player in the centre of midfield [Guardiola then, Busquets now] while we use two. But I would remind everyone that, for example, Iniesta adapts to play a slightly distinct role on the left for Spain compared to his club. But when we talk about Xavi and Iniesta, these are universal players. They are world-class. Perhaps footballers don't always see things as their coaches do, but when I read about this change of position for Xavi with Spain, I think that people are really just making it an excuse if, one day, a performance isn't quite what they are used to. For example, for the day of the final against Italy in Kiev, I don't think we asked anything different of Xavi than usual and he – and we – were splendid in winning."

These are the themes Del Bosque emphasised to Xavi 24 hours before the final and the Catalan played dazzlingly. He had been excellent against Italy in the first match, vital in the demolition of Ireland, but was a little out of gas by the latter stages of the semi-final against Portugal.

This is the period, Toni Grande later reveals, when Xavi and the coaching staff talk about his preference for playing one organising midfielder and two attacking players, as is the style at Barcelona. Del Bosque appeases Xavi while sticking firmly to his tactical ethos.

Later in the day, I meet the federation president Ángel María Villar and it is agreed that I can take the only cameraman who will be allowed past security into the Spain dressing room in the Olympic Stadium, should they win the final.

— **Day 27.**
—*July 1, 2012*
  Olympic Stadium, Kiev, Ukraine.
  Spain v Italy – UEFA European Championship final
Uno y dos y tres … ganar y ganar y ganar!

"Nobody – *nobody* – remembers the losers."
Luis Aragonés, Vienna, June 28, 2008.

The Wise Man of Hortaleza was right about so many other things, I just hope he is wrong about that. Italy prove to be daring, threatening and admirable finalists. The way the night ends up does not reflect their contribution.

However, the way things unfold emphasises two important points. If you attempt to play football with this Spain side and they are in top shape, you will lose. And if a tactically acute set-up like the men behind *La Roja* are given two shots at unpicking a rival within three weeks, it is an advantage to them.

The tactical undressing of Italy began in the Opera Hotel on Saturday evening and continues with a second short session in the same meeting room at 6.45 on the evening of the final. Between Del Bosque, Toni Grande, Paco Jiménez and José Manuel Ochotorena there are some key points. One or two are obvious. Pirlo was given too much space in the first 70 minutes of the group match. That must change. This tournament, the little maestro has won three man-of-the-match awards. When he plays, Italy play. Next, Del Bosque tells his players something he cannot know for sure, but he intuits from all the footage he has watched and from the briefings Jiménez has given him.

"You are fitter, younger, quicker than Italy – they are even more tired than you." It is a message with its base partly in deduction, partly in psychology.

Del Bosque and his staff half-expect Italy to revert to the 3-5-2 which worked so well in the first group match, but which they have abandoned for a 4-1-3-2 formation since. Christian Maggio is available again after a suspension, but it is hard to second guess Italy's defence because injuries have led to Prandelli changing his back four in each of the three games since the defeat of Ireland. In fact, the list is ominous: Andrea Barzagli missing injured against Spain; Giorgio Chiellini missing injured against England; Daniele Di Rossi fighting against painful sciatica; Ignazio Abate left out against Germany because of muscle fatigue.

Finally, if Italy use a back four, Del Bosque will demand even more bravery from his full-backs, Arbeloa and Alba – they must push as high up the pitch as possible, squeezing Italy back and be ready to overlap or counter attack when the chance arises. He was not satisfied with his full-backs in the first game, pointing out that they allowed Italy to advance too far down either touchline.

It is a beautiful summer Sunday, with that dry heat which is familiar to the Spanish and they take their usual mid-morning *paseo* (stroll) in a Kiev park.

Carles Puyol and David Villa arrived in Kiev last night at the invitation of the Spanish federation. There had been a thought, inspired by one of the federation directors, that the two men should be with the squad for the whole tournament, funded by *La Roja*. The idea was to add experience and harmony to the group and to show solidarity to the two injured legends. It was not a practical initiative, but both players are grateful for the invitation to re-unite with their team-mates now that the chance to make history has arrived.

While Italy will not agree to watering the pitch at half-time, Prandelli has endorsed heavy watering before kick-off. He wants a pitch set up for quick passing, which leads Del Bosque to believe that Italy will try to do what they did against Germany: break devastatingly on the counter, score as early as possible and then attempt to see out the lead. It is an impression strengthened when he reads Prandelli's comments: "I really hope we can be positive and take the game to them. Spain's strength is not only possession, but also the way they win it back. We have got to pick our moments and work a numerical superiority in certain areas. We do not expect to be in charge from the first minute to the last, but we know we can play our own football when the opportunity arises."

Night time inside the Olympic Stadium. The estimated 12,000 Spanish fans who have braved the complicated and expensive journey to get here and are paying up to €5000 per night for a hotel room are streaming in.

Italy's dressing room is to the left as they come down the 27 steps from the pitch onto the astroturf vestibule where they will line up pre-match. Both dressing rooms are king-sized – in each are lockers, a physio space, showers, toilets, a huge Jacuzzi, a large drinks fridge full of isotonic liquids, tables full of fruit and television screens on the wall. You could move in.

Warm-up completed, pitch examined, Del Bosque gives his troops his final words before he goes off to send a text to the man who discovered him as a young, stick-thin footballer – Antonio 'Toñete' Martiño.

"We make sure that we start really, really strongly. It's really important that we mark our ground, that we lay down the law from the start. But we are footballers, nothing more than that. Not soldiers, this still is not a war. We will be brave like we were at Soccer City, nothing timid, nothing left in reserve. We work to win the ball, work to keep the ball, show humility and impose our game. You are still the examples for the kids back home – we will do this for them."

Tonight *Uno y dos y tres ... ganar y ganar y ganar!* stands for something more than victory on the evening. *Ganar y ganar y ganar!* Three wins. Three tournaments. History.

Spain, as expected, will be 4-3-3. Casillas; Arbeloa, Piqué, Ramos, Alba; Xavi, Busquets, Alonso; Silva, Fàbregas, Iniesta.

Italy tinker with the line-up again. Abate replaces Federico Balzaretti and Prandelli does not revert to the successful 3-5-2 of the Group C opener.

Italy are 4-1-3-2. Buffon; Abate, Barzagli, Bonucci, Chiellini; Pirlo; Marchisio, De Rossi, Montolivo; Cassano, Balotelli.

Spain are delighted that Italy have not opted for wing-backs, surprised that

Maggio is not reinstated. More confident now than ever.

As the teams line up, Sergio Ramos walks up and down giving a high five to each team-mate. Pirlo just stares at him.

Within the first 10 minutes there are four efforts at goal, the best of which is Xavi's neat one-two with Fàbregas which ends in Xavi shooting fractionally over Gianluigi Buffon's crossbar.

Italy are in the game, they look confident, but their tempo is not as high as Spain's and so their pressing is not quite getting there. Hence Spain make the breakthrough.

Jordi Alba starts a move of 10 passes which will end with the smallest man on the pitch, David Silva, heading home. The ball zings between Álvaro Arbeloa, Andrés Iniesta, Xavi and Silva, until Pirlo does not press Iniesta closely enough.

Silva has taken up the false No.9 position, Fàbregas has gone wide right and Iniesta gives the pass of the tournament inside Giorgio Chiellini. Fàbregas has never claimed to be fast, but he outpaces the Juventus defender, whose final will shortly be over due to the failing of a hamstring damaged earlier in the tournament. As Fàbregas reaches the byeline he lofts a little chip towards the penalty spot. Buffon is guarding his front post, Silva splits Andrea Barzagli and Leonardo Bonucci and the Manchester City magician directs a header into the empty net. The Fàbregas-Silva combination has now brought two goals in two games against Italy.

Italy come after the champions and Antonio Cassano has two efforts on target, the second of which really makes Casillas work. However, in the end Cassano's pressing of Casillas sparks the beginning of the end of the contest.

As Casillas is forced by Cassano to thump clear, his diagonal kick allows Fàbregas, now on Spain's left wing, to head a pass down to Alba. His first touch is on the thigh, his second touch a pass. Now Xavi has it and because Italy have been pressing up, neither Pirlo nor Daniele De Rossi are close enough to stop him advancing. As Alba starts his run there are eight Italians ahead of him, but he burns off four before Xavi releases his own contender for pass of the tournament, splitting Barzagli and Bonucci. Alba, told by Del Bosque that he would be Spain's secret weapon before Euro 2012 started, all but seals the historic treble with the finish of a born goalscorer.

Montolivo, and Di Natale – on at half-time for Cassano – threaten to score a goal that would change the momentum of the final, but then Thiago Motta, newly on as Italy's third substitute, pulls a muscle and is stretchered off leaving his team to fight the rampant world champions with only 10 men for the final 30 minutes.

Italy play intelligently but Spain do what killer sides do, what the great German, Brazilian and Italian sides would have done. They move the ball, wait for tiredness and errors and they exploit them ruthlessly.

With six minutes left, Arbeloa, playing high enough up the pitch to be second striker, presses De Rossi into an error in his return pass to Pirlo. Xavi intercepts and releases Fernando Torres to become the only man in history to score in two consecutive European Championship finals.

Sixty seconds after Mata has replaced Iniesta, Italy are dead on their feet and Ramos tries a long pass from the back. He finds Busquets, whose accurate pass releases Torres again. Torres knows his Chelsea team-mate is just inside him and he draws Buffon, slips the ball inside off the outstep of his boot and Mata makes it 4-0. Torres' goal placed him within the group of players on three for the tournament; now this assist breaks the tie and gives him the Golden Boot.

Not many notice that Casillas, as soon as the 90 minutes are up, taps his wrist and shouts to the additional assistant referee: "Ref! Come on! Show some respect for our rival!"

Spain make history. They are the first national team to win the treble. They have completed it with the biggest final-winning margin in the 52-year history of this competition. Spain have not lost a European Championship match since 2004, eight years ago. They have not conceded a goal in a knockout game since 2006, despite using a different back line in each of the three tournaments.

This has been a tournament during which this team has been accused of playing boring football. At Euro 2012 they scored the most goals (12, exactly the same number as at Euro 2008, when everyone swooned over their attacking brilliance); they shot on target more than everyone bar Italy. Spain hit the target 58 times in six games. Playing just one more game, Spain have 17 more shots on goal than a Germany side heralded for its attacking flair and 23 more than Portugal, the other beaten semi-finalist. Spain's average is just under 10 on-target efforts per game. England's average per game at Euro 2012 is 4.75.

A parallel criticism has Spain employing possession as a defensive tactic, yet Casillas makes 15 saves at this tournament. Only Joe Hart, Buffon and Shay Given make more. Spain make chances and they concede chances. They are just miles better than the rest when they have the ball at their feet.

In celebrations, the players don their various flags, scarves and dedicatory t-shirts. Ramos pays tribute to Antonio Puerta; Fàbregas commemorates Miki Roqué, Preciado, Dani Jarque and Puerta on his white t-shirt; Pepe Reina wears a

Real Betis Miki Roqué shirt back-to-front so that the name on the back is in the images seen around the world. These gestures do not win you trophies and these men are not saints, but it speaks about their priorities and their values.

Once Michel Platini gives the trophy to Casillas, the images of the on-pitch celebrations are of happy players with children everywhere. Well, it's the same in the dressing room.

It surprises me, once most of the players were inside, that there's such a low-key atmosphere, as if they'd had a good day at work, but not a great deal more than that.

It's a small indication of how matter-of-factly Spain take this triumph – 'it's no more than we were here to do' – that when UEFA nominate Iniesta as player of the tournament a well-placed friend gets to hear of it and texts the Barcelona midfielder, who has just arrived home, with the news. "Don't mess me about!" is the SMS reply he gets. Iniesta can't believe it's true. Not until he reads it on UEFA.com does he believe.

Retrospectively, the Spain squad also accept that there is a change in mentality, a change in what they perceive their role to be.

Santi Cazorla: "Ask any of the players and they'll all tell you that the best experience and the best celebration, indeed the best moment of their lives, was winning Euro 2008. The World Cup was great but not so explosive a celebration in the post-match. Then after Euro 2012, everyone who has kids, in Kiev you get them down onto the pitch. You have to be sure to pay tributes to the merit of winning this competition, and it's the third, and when you get to Madrid and see the entire nation partying again that changes your reaction a little. But it's true that the reaction to winning the last Euro was 'this is normal' and that there wasn't so much euphoria."

Fernando Torres: "The celebration of the last tournament was very different from the first one. I guess everything's special the first time. Vienna was a dream, we'd never done anything like it but we'd been searching for just that kind of achievement. The celebration was complete madness. None of us could believe it. The World Cup is the World Cup ... but it was won very far from Spain. Winning that final was impressive as an experience but it was different from the Euro. The strange situation of having this uncontrollable happiness and a plane to catch that we had to be hustled off into. It was like: 'Come on, come on – the plane's gonna be leaving.'

"This last Euro – well I'd say we expected to win it. In fact, winning was the only thing we could do. And while there was immense happiness at having made history it was a much more 'family' experience. Four years previously we had very few kids between us but by now almost all of us did. We were together for a month in a hotel, new friendships were made, wives and kids spent a lot of time together, and when we won we wanted everyone, the whole family, to be together immediately – enjoying it, savouring it and giving the kids this memory of what their dads had done. It was also different because we'd all changed from being hungry youngsters in Vienna to mature, hard-nosed professionals used to the demands of winning all the time; the journey from learning how to win to being accustomed to winning."

When our camera is pointed at them because King Juan Carlos's son, the Prince of Asturias, comes in to congratulate them, there is a brief rendition of *Campéones* sung in a huddle in the corner.

Casillas swigs out of a champagne bottle, one or two of the newer guys pose with the trophy; Vicente del Bosque leaves all this to his players and stands outside in the corridor chatting to his wife, Trini. His son, Álvaro, heads in to find his heroes and it is instantly apparent how much the players adore him.

Xavi is draped in the Catalan flag, Piqué in his goal net. Busquets is wearing the same Badia dels Vallès scarf he had on in the World Cup celebrations, celebrating the area of Barcelona from which he hails.

Torres brings his kids in, Valdés starts to play with them like a kindly uncle and Navas and Cazorla join in.

It is like a big company picnic. Ángel María Villar and the Prince of Asturias are beaming in a proprietorial way, Del Bosque is letting the workers relax, there are wives and kids everywhere and the pressure and drama of the office are left aside.

We are made welcome and beers are pressed in our hands, but we do our work and get out of their sanctum. I pass Villa and Puyol, who have given those who were stripped for action the respect of 10 minutes to celebrate their achievement before being joined for congratulations from two guys who wished they had been playing instead of watching. Puyol joins Casillas, Del Bosque and Xavi's future wife in a friendly counsel urging the midfielder, with one voice: "Don't retire." For the next couple of days of celebration he is urged to re-think, to see what a summer of rest will do for him, to dream of winning a second World Cup – this time in the dragon's layer. He does think again. He does change his mind. How he manages his body, how he is used by Del

Bosque — these are critical factors in Spain's quest for a fourth consecutive trophy. They are questions for another time.

Right now, the adrenalin is coursing through Spanish veins. They have confounded their critics with a flourish.

Cesare Prandelli: "Our only regret is that we were so tired. We were up against a great side, the world champions, and as soon as we went down to 10 men it was game over. We had a couple of chances at the start of the second half but did not take them and when Thiago Motta went off we had nothing left in the tank. When we did attack, we struggled to get back to cover. I think we have had a terrific European Championship and our only regret is that we did not have a few more days to rest before this game. We played against Spain in the group stage and I thought we were excellent then – because we were 100% fit. Against a team like Spain you need to be at your best going into tackles and tonight we simply were not. You have to pay credit to Spain. They have made history tonight and deservedly so. They may not play with a recognised striker, but they still cause a hell of a lot of problems."

Jordi Alba: "All my team-mates here had made history before, but this Euro has allowed me to do that with them again. It's gone so much better than I could have imagined. This time last year it was nothing but an idle dream to be a Spain player, now I am European champion. The people in the place I was born, Hospitalet, told me I was going to score in the final, so right now I am thinking of them, my family and friends who have always supported me."

Xavi: "I think we were superior to Italy throughout because we produced a very complete performance tonight – the best we have played this tournament. This time I was able to make some determining contributions whereas, in previous matches, my through-balls were not quite working. Today I hit two good ones for goals. The criticism we get is, I think, because we have set the bar so high. The demand is that we always win and we always win comfortably. That is not possible, but I prefer this kind of pressure compared to when the country did not believe in us."

In his words it is easy to detect a thorn in his paw being gently removed and the relief provided by the 'Made By Xavi' stamp of quality on two trophy-winning goals.

Gerard Piqué: "This is a feeling of enormous happiness. It is the trophy I was missing because I was not part of the 2008 squad. But best of all was how we played in the final. That was the real Spain."

Cesc Fàbregas: "What a game! Finals are not for playing, they are for winning, but if you can play well and enjoy it then that is the best of all."

Iker Casillas: "The basis of this triumph comes from a long time ago and requires lots of work that nobody sees in public. Moreover, this coach has known how to manage the transition between a couple of generations of players. When people look at the 4-0 scoreline they may think that it was easy, but I want people to think about and remember what it has cost us to get here and stay here. We are champions with dignity."

Trophy in hand, history written, families by their sides, Spain begin to party. And to dream about Rio.

Spain 4 Italy 0

Spain: Casillas, Arbeloa, Ramos, Piqué, Alba, Xavi (Pedro 87), Busquets, Alonso, Silva (Pedro 59), Fàbregas (Torres 75), Iniesta (Mata 87)
Goals: Silva 14, Alba 41, Torres 84, Mata 88

Italy: Buffon, Abate, Barzagli, Bonucci, Chiellini (Balzaretti 21), Pirlo, Marchisio, Montolivo (Motta 56), De Rossi, Balotelli, Cassano (Di Natale 46)

The Rough
Guide to Brazil

There will be some who look at the trophy-treble won by Spain and assume they didn't care that much about not lifting the Confederations Cup. In this era they competed at the tournament twice – in South Africa in 2009 and in Brazil in 2013 – and left without winners' medals.

That isn't quite the case and there is an image which tells the story of how much Spain invested in this competition. It was taken at the Estadio Casteláo in Fortaleza, during the 2013 semi-final.

Italy start that match by battering Spain. The world champions fight back to dominate extra-time but can't find a winner before it goes to penalties. The 11-metre shooting gallery is for the finest marksmen only. Twelve of them take aim and all 12 penalties leave Iker Casillas and Gigi Buffon without a hope. Then Leonardo Bonucci fires over the bar, Casillas vacates the goalmouth and Buffon is left to face Jesús Navas.

Casillas is a veteran of these shoot-outs; in the FIFA Under-20 tournament in 1999, he won a penalty competition against Ghana in the quarter-finals, on the way to his first world title. Since then he has seen everything, won everything. And yet he can't look.

In this moment he is right up against the advertising hoarding, about 20 metres to the left of Buffon, and while Navas prepares to take what will turn out to be the winning kick, Casillas has his back turned and his right glove up covering his eyes for double protection, despite the fact that he has turned away from the action. A quiet prayer is being muttered.

Anybody not yet convinced just needs to re-watch the footage of Sergio Ramos, Andrés Iniesta, Álvaro Arbeloa, Jordi Alba, Gerard Piqué and Javi Martínez roaring with joy and rushing to embrace their team-mate after he puts them in the final. They wanted that trophy.

However, after two tilts at the Confederations Cup, these players have nothing better than tired legs and a runners-up medal. What is it that makes this tournament Spain's Kryptonite?

Think of the 36-year-old boxer who hates the high-altitude training, road running at 6am, high-protein low-carb dieting, the isolation from his family and the endless sparring. But there's a belt to defend and a young buck of a challenger who might, perhaps, be a bout too far. The call of the ring subjugates all else.

A large percentage of this squad were not energised by the prospect of a long journey to Brazil, stifling heat and humidity, or of group games against Tahiti and Nigeria. Some of those whose limbs and brains were the most drained quietly briefed that South America was not their preferred destination for summer 2013. But when the bell rings and it is Italy or Brazil in the other corner, every last synapse tells them to come out fighting. Some of Vicente del Bosque's players felt apathy for this tournament as it began but cared deeply about the challenge as it neared its climax.

Similarly to 2009, one key player was missing. In South Africa it was Iniesta, in Brazil it was Xabi Alonso.

No good side relies wholly on one or two players, without whom they crumble. The Spain of this winning era has known how to adapt and deputise one player for another when injuries hit. But as this group ages and tires because of the relentless demands on it, the need for order on the pitch, and the fundamental requirement for there to be as few errors and as little extra running as possible, grow in importance. A few months before the Confederations Cup, draws against France and Finland in World Cup qualifiers showed that when Sergio Busquets and Alonso don't play together in midfield Spain tend to perform with less precision, order and impermeability.

At home to France in autumn 2012, Busquets deputised in central defence and, while Alonso didn't play badly, Spain kept the ball and the shape of their team less well.

For the shock home draw with Finland in spring 2013 Alonso wasn't fit to play and Busquets, used as the main midfield pivot, could not shore up all the space in the centre of the pitch, which was a principal factor in Teemu Pukki's equaliser.

In Brazil, Spain started like a runaway train against Uruguay. The football was devastatingly quick, accurate and entertaining – if a little short of end product.

By the time of the final, Del Bosque's key players were exhausted – feeling the impact of the climate and carrying the damage of a long, demanding season in legs and brains. They looked punch drunk.

That fact exacerbated the positional errors Spain made, it augmented the need to prevent Brazil powering upfield and camping in the Spain half. It heightened the need for the street-smartness, experience and anticipatory talents of the Busquets-Alonso tandem. With them in harness, Spain played seven knockout matches for a total of 690 minutes at World Cup 2010 and Euro 2012, without conceding a goal. Against Brazil they lost 3-0.

The best example is Brazil's second goal, less than two minutes before half-time. Busquets goes for, and misses, a challenge on Hulk. The lay-off leaves Oscar free to drive from near the halfway line to the edge of the Spain box and to set up Neymar for his goal.

Alonso's groin surgery, followed by his broken metatarsal as season 2013/4 began, constitutes the kind of hurdle which champions have always had to face and overcome. Restoring the Busquets-Alonso wall in midfield – or allowing Javi Martínez to demonstrate his importance in that role – is fundamental to Spain's chances in the 2014 World Cup.

The experience of the local climate which Spain gathered from the 2013 Confederations Cup presents a challenge Del Bosque and company can certainly be more aware of, but only sheer fluke can help them overcome it. Unless conditions in June 2013 prove to have been freakish, the combined heat and humidity of Recife, but especially Fortaleza, are factors which will hurt all European teams. If the draw asks Germany, Spain, England, France, Holland or Italy to repeatedly play in those venues then it will be an important handicap to them winning the tournament. The defending champions would view games further south, away from the tropical heat and humidity which decimated them in summer 2013, as an enormous bonus.

After the game against Nigeria in Fortaleza, one of two consecutive matches Spain played there, some players confided that by the time the pre-match warm-up was over it felt like they had already played a draining 90 minutes. The fact that both fixtures kicked off at 4pm local time, when temperatures are at their peak, in order to help advertisers and sponsors capture as much of the European market as possible, made things still worse.

"*Destrozado*" (destroyed) the Spain players darkly muttered when asked about their physical condition after two big games in that weather.

The geographical spread of games between Fortaleza, Recife and Rio meant thousands of kilometres of air travel, a factor likely to affect all teams in the World Cup. This experience served to underline the good fortune Spain had in Euro 2008, when they played two games in Innsbruck, one close by in Salzburg, then three games in Vienna; similarly, at the World Cup in 2010, when four of their seven games were in Jo'burg or Pretoria; and at Euro 2012 when all three group games were in Gdańsk.

Having watched all this unfold, and spoken to the men who devise Spain's off-field strategy, I am in no doubt that geography and logistics influence who wins and loses at a tournament.

Spain have made their training base a vital part of their armoury. It has become a competitive edge. They establish a base, with a terrific training pitch close by to avoid unnecessary travel, the geographical area chosen is secluded, even remote, so that the players and their families are given a good deal of time and space to relax in their down time.

However, at this Confederations Cup the Spanish felt ill at ease with the local organising committee and, from the outset, wanted to handle things differently.

Prior to the tournament the Spanish federation could not find a venue to replicate Neustift and Potchefstroom. Instead they were told where to stay and train, from a list of approved hotels and facilities.

In their Recife hotel several of Del Bosque's players were robbed of belongings and cash from their rooms. A sensationalist media story then falsely accused Spain of partying and allowing non-guests into their accommodation. No proof of this was ever offered and Del Bosque's players, many of whom had family, girlfriends, wives and children over with them, were infuriated.

Álvaro Arbeloa: "We are pretty pissed off. It's a very disagreeable experience even if the journalist is sued because while there could never be proof or CCTV images to back his story because nothing which he alleged actually happened, there is always a trace of suspicion left over once something is published. I hope that whoever wrote this rubbish gets a big fine just so that he knows what will happen the next time he considers inventing something."

Sergio Ramos: "The Spanish federation will pursue legal redress all the way and if not then the players will do so individually. Deliberately lying to besmirch our image is something we all view as a grave offence. But I know how to differentiate. Lots of people in Brazil treated us marvellously and we won't leave here with a bitter taste in our mouths because of one liar. We also know that a theft like that could have happened anywhere."

So, instead of setting up camp, Del Bosque's footballers were moved from hotel to hotel, from Recife to Fortaleza and Rio, to establishments which they found under-prepared to host a major international squad. Everywhere they went they were establishing new relationships with hotel staff, working out whether or not the lobby was safe from autograph hunters, whether or not the wifi worked, whether or not the food was as good as normal, discovering whether the room was comfortable, whether there was traffic noise or not. These small factors all contribute to how well a squad feels, trains, rests and plays. As did the fact that players found cockroaches which they joked about being the size of cats in their Recife hotel rooms – memories of Nigeria 1999 for some.

All around them the country was erupting into what Spain's players felt were understandable protests. As they spent time in the country, the Brazilian people the Spain players met talked about the need for jobs, schools, hospitals and bemoaned the spiralling cost of hosting the World Cup.

Most of us who love the sport find the idea of football's greatest tournament being hosted in *the* brand-name nation for the world's game hugely stimulating and evocative of great times past. Spain's players got there and discovered that vast sectors of the Brazilian people not only don't want the World Cup but feel exploited and bitter about it.

Perhaps by summer 2014 some social issues will have been sorted out – probably not.

But, again, Spain will be better prepared for the strange sensation of being in a soccer-mad nation where large parts of the population would happily ship this football jamboree off to anywhere else on the planet.

Much was made of the fact that the Brazilian public at the stadia booed and whistled Spain's every touch – this the squad found much more normal and stimulating.

Some observers claimed to be witnessing signs of the end of this incredible era for Spain and they might be right. While I see no sell-by date on the playing philosophy, and while there are budding talents pushing through such as Isco, Thiago Alcántara, Daniel Carvajal, Iñigo Martínez, Koke and Álvaro Morata, every playing group has a finite lifespan.

Brazil is going to present logistical difficulties which will probably put a magnifying glass to Spain's ageing process – the kind of travel, climatic and sociological difficulties which would not apply if the next World Cup were in England, Holland or France. *C'est la vie.*

In the playing sense, Spain are facing what Pep Guardiola's Barcelona team encountered sooner thanks to the fact that club teams play far more frequently than national sides: the other guy figuring you out.

> **Iker Casillas:** "Our rivals increasingly have us studied to the *nth* degree, they know how to find our defects and to complicate our gameplan. Things have changed, rivals know how to do us damage. The challenge is for us to improve again."

This group of players has always understood that if they are not at their best they are beatable.

They know that there will be an end, just as 2006 was the beginning – although it didn't look like it at the time. However, they also believe that their experience in Brazil in 2013 will help them get back in the ring to defend their world title in 2014.

> **Andrés Iniesta:** "At the World Cup we'll try to do our side of things better, drawing on the fact that we'll have more experience of what it's like to play competition football in that country and we'll find it easier to acclimatise."

Cesare Prandelli, the Italy coach, made an error not repeating his 3-5-2 formation of the first group game in Euro 2012 when it came to the final of that competition.

But he learned, and not only used the formation which – as Casillas says – was best at hurting Spain where they have problems, but inspired his players to a hard-working, aggressive and confident match in the semi-final of the Confederations Cup.

Inadvertently, Italy ensured that Spain, or at least the Spain team chosen by Del Bosque, weren't in shape to give the tournament the final it deserved.

The world champions worked their way back into the Italy semi-final, having been on the ropes, could easily have won it handsomely before the penalties and maintained focus and technique to win the shoot-out which strained Casillas' nerves. However, all this happened in 85-degree heat with 80 per cent humidity – it drained Spain to their core, which was why they were infuriated to find that FIFA's local organising committee either could not, or would not, accede to the Spanish federation's petition that they be allowed to fly to Rio that night, after the semi-final. Del Bosque's team managers wanted to squeeze a drop or two of extra juice out of the fatigued players, most of whom find it hard to sleep in the immediate aftermath of a big match, when adrenaline is still in their systems. Spain's plan was to do their media, head for the airport and get out of Fortaleza, fly the 2200km down to Rio (while many of the players would be awake anyway) install themselves in the team hotel, get a lie-in that morning, train the kinks out of tired minds and muscles that evening and then set their minds on preparing for the final.

The organising committee said no. No flights, no hotels and, by the way, Brazil had taken the specific hotel Spain wanted. It was galling enough, but exacerbated by the fact that the Spanish media corps did manage to fly out of Fortaleza that night after the semi-final. The world champion players were left behind.

Waiting for them in Rio were Phil Scolari's Brazil, a team now emanating power and momentum. Their trajectory during the tournament was that of an international squad beginning to play like a club side – a difficult but immensely valuable facet to achieve. The crowds were fanatical in their support, the players significantly raised their level and Neymar stood out for his skill, electric pace and confidence.

They were also very physical. In the final it was a Scolari tactic to break up Spain's play and to push physical contact to the edge of the rules – beyond if needed. Brazil committed 26 fouls against Spain, already a high total, and they didn't receive a single yellow card. Eight of the fouls were on Iniesta.

Holland were significantly more brutal during the final of World Cup 2010 and Spain still managed to win. Equally there will be some matches when Brazil's tactics will be punished, with both yellow and red, and others when referees are as tolerant as Bjorn Kuipers of Holland was that night.

Every single Spain player or staff member who spoke post-match acknowledged that Brazil had been superior in winning 3-0.

Vicente del Bosque: "From time to time it does no harm to taste defeat. Congratulations to Brazil, they deserved their win."

Gerard Piqué: "This loss will do us good if we take it as a firm message as far as the future is concerned. There are various aspects to improve. We have to give more if we want more back."

However, there were some positives for the world champions. After a sequence of errors allowed Brazil the lead, Pedro had an effort cleared off the line by David Luiz, one which could have sent the sides in at half-time tied at 1-1. Instead, Scolari's team went up the pitch and added a second, then showed an admirable winner's attitude by scoring the third quickly in the second half.

For Del Bosque to dwell on, however, will be the fact that with Spain down to 10 men after Piqué's red card, Sergio Ramos missed a penalty, Julio César needed to make two spectacular saves and a team which had looked physically shattered and completely out of the match, nearly clawed the most unlikely way back into it.

In his post-tournament assessments, I would expect the meticulous Del Bosque to re-examine his idea that 10 of the starting team which fought out that brutal 120-minute game of sauna-football against Italy on Thursday June 27, were in shape to do themselves justice against a Brazil side oozing power, youth and athleticism by that Sunday night. The only change was Juan Mata for David Silva, despite the presence on the bench of talents including Javi Martínez, Santi Cazorla and Roberto Soldado. Considering the condition and performance of some of the starters, the introduction of these reserves might have paid dividends. *Qué sé yo?* is one of Leo Messi's favourite expressions. What do I know?

Xavi, in particular, will probably need better husbandry come the World Cup. He played 90 minutes and 77 minutes in the group games, was excused the romp against Tahiti and then not only slogged out the full 120 against Italy, he scored the first penalty. Would a full-voltage 45 minutes in the second half of the final have been a better tactic? It is an issue which can only be resolved by Del Bosque and Xavi himself.

Some issues are beyond control. Spain's vital players are getting older and others have club problems to deal with. In the months before the World Cup, the Champions League will seem just as dominant, just as vital to win and most of Del Bosque's squad will be slogging it out to clinch the domestic titles in Spain, Germany or England.

The management of tiredness, mental fatigue, geographical logistics and the scouting of a training base will all assume still greater importance for the federation team of Antonio Limones and Javier Miñano, and those they work alongside.

If they get their jobs right, we can be certain they will find a group of players which still wants to, and still believes it can, win the World Cup at the Maracana Stadium on Sunday, July 13, 2014.

Into The Unknown

Spain are now in uncharted waters.

If no team has ever won three straight major international tournaments, then no manager, no squad has ever approached the hurdle of winning a fourth with all the inherent personnel management challenges for which there is no blueprint.

Win a continental trophy and a World Cup in succession, as Brazil, France and Germany have all managed, and either the natural wastage of injury and retirement or the natural temptation of hanging on too long to favoured, fundamental players have proved fatal flaws.

No blueprint, but echoes. Very distinct voices from the past.

There are themes facing Vicente del Bosque from now until the World Cup in Brazil which neatly match those that brought his undeserved downfall at Real Madrid all those years ago. Then, a process of renovation was needed. *Los Blancos'* hardcore of, say, 13 or 14 top players needed to expand by four or five. The team was winning trophies but began to look slightly jaded, in need of greater athleticism and stamina. Madrid's error was entrusting that process to their president, his acolytes and a series of weak coaches, rather than vesting faith in Del Bosque to renew and regenerate.

In fact, although Del Bosque was in charge of constant generational change as director of Real Madrid's youth academy, his trajectory of having had only two lengthy managerial posts means that this current challenge is one of his most complex ever. And, to an extent, it's fresh territory.

At Madrid he was gifted players from above. Florentino Pérez signed *Galácticos* and the time between mid-1999 and June 2003, when he was removed, wasn't long enough for Del Bosque to begin an overhaul of playing personnel. To his credit he has been gradually, calmly implementing just that with Spain since taking over in 2008.

At the time of writing, Nacho has just become the 35th new cap of Del Bosque's reign. From Manu del Moral and Bojan, who didn't make it, to Pedro, Sergio Busquets, Gerard Piqué, Jesús Navas and Jordi Alba who did. Five years in charge, an average of seven new players tested out per year. That's not what you'd call conservative.

He explains: "We have considerably increased our squad, but that doesn't mean we've stopped being confident in the group which has brought us such success. We simply can't take our attention off the production line of talent coming up because, these days, the process of developing youth footballers has accelerated. Nonetheless, this doesn't eliminate from our thinking any of the players who have made history."

But with a view to retaining the World Cup, the manager's more daunting task is choosing whether to finesse or to overhaul the starting XI in Brazil. Two quite different routes. First, he must make some tough decisions on his squad selection, as the ageing players who have made history find competition in those emerging from the most successful era in the history of international youth football.

Injury aside he'll have to perm between Álvaro Negredo, Juan Mata, Fernando Torres, David Villa, Roberto Soldado, Fernando Llorente, Álvaro Morata, Pedro, Cristian Tello and perhaps even Diego Costa up front.

Arguably, it's tougher still in midfield – even assuming that some will fall away due to form or injury. Think of Xabi Alonso, Xavi, Andrés Iniesta, Sergio Busquets, Cesc Fàbregas, Javi Martínez, Thiago Alcántara, Santi Cazorla, Jesús Navas, David Silva, Ander Herrera, Koke, Mario Suárez, Isco, Bruno, Beñat, Javi García and Asier Illarramendi. Eighteen credible names, who may have other challengers as the season progresses, but only nine will travel.

So far so good for Del Bosque, who will use tightly drawn criteria to delineate between one top player and another, a privilege for which most coaches would sell their soul.

The greater dilemma will definitely come in how to select the starting XI. Time and tide will mean the coach has significantly less margin for error than at any time during the last three major tournaments. He knows it.

Vicente del Bosque: "At the 2013 Confederations Cup I think we handled the tournament in the correct fashion but we reached that final very, very tired; physically depleted. We failed on the last day, Brazil were better. They were on top from the minute the anthems started playing. I've always thought that the way to handle defeat is to accept it, analyse it in the cold light of day and try to learn. Does that defeat indicate a tendency? I really think not. We'll be very attentive in the coming games – trying to feel sure that's the case. The trouble remains that many people obviously think that we must win really easily. But there are games which go against us, some of which are incredibly hard. It's not easy when you constantly have to beat a rival which doesn't really want to 'play'."

Some of the pillars of Del Bosque's success are now not going to be capable of seven 90-minute performances in wilting humidity after a 60-game season. The manager can't always reach for his favourites any more. This challenge, specifically, evokes another echo from the recent past.

In the lead-up to the 2006 World Cup Luis Aragonés was already convinced that the brand of football he had believed was essential to Spain's national characteristics no longer fitted the resources he had at his disposal. Further, he realised that *if* he could capitalise on the rich seam of technical talent and winning mentality which had been bred by Spain's *categorías inferiores* then something great could happen.

However, for once, *El Sabio* hesitated. He opted for too much conservatism, too much Raúl, Pernía, Antonio López, Pablo Ibañéz, Luis García and Joaquín ... not enough Iniesta, Carlos Marchena, Joan Capdevila, Xavi and Marcos Senna.

This World Cup is not identical. Spain neither need nor are likely to undergo a radical change of playing philosophy, coaching demands, squad atmosphere or on-pitch leadership such as followed Germany 2006. However, there might need to be a significant injection of youth to supplant proven experience. Different challenge, similar bravery and man-managerial skill required.

Brazil will present intense climate and travel difficulties – particularly if Spain's starting XI contains Xavi aged 34, Xabi Alonso aged 32, Carles Puyol aged 36 and David Villa aged 32.

When is the right time to discard? Which player will surprise and show no effects at all of the passing years? Which needs to be used more as an impact player than a starter? These are dilemmas for Del Bosque.

Eight years ago, when Aragonés intuited that he faced a titanic challenge in removing sacred cows, he shied from it and only found empowerment to drop Raúl, David Albelda, Santiago Cañizares, Joaquín, José Antonio Reyes and Luis García thanks to the humiliating defeat by France in the first knockout match, followed by qualifying losses to Northern Ireland and Sweden which left him staring into the abyss. He had no option but to follow his own beliefs.

The type of risk management facing Del Bosque doesn't include removing Xavi, Alonso, Villa or Puyol – but it strongly suggests that he leave one or two of them on the bench more often; to conserve their energy; to tap into the power, stamina, hunger and confidence of youth.

He'll be required to judge the deployment of hitherto stalwart players with the same success as has become his trademark in making second-half substitutions of players who go on to score or assist.

By autumn 2013 the Spain coach made his basic intention clear. Despite leaving out a variety of players – including Villa, Martínez, Cazorla, Torres and Mata – who might easily have played during matches against Ecuador, Finland or Chile, he believes that minor variations on an old tune will be sufficient to win the prize next summer.

In September 2013 he expressed his underlying ideal.

Vicente del Bosque: "If there have been guys with us from our outstanding under-21 squad who were European champions in the summer then it's because those guys are good enough to play for the full side. There is a new wave of very good players pushing through which we will introduce bit by bit. There are five or six who will fit in, without a great deal of fuss, and who can be extremely useful. But the truth is that the main block of those who won Euro 2012 have a great deal left in them. It's a stable national team in which relatively few of our players are over 30. This version of the national team still has a future and hopefully will still give us a lot of joy."

From an analytical point of view, I'd contend that two of those who require to be handed an immense amount of responsibility to help a brilliant but ageing squad punch its weight in difficult conditions are Isco and Javi Martínez. The latter is a great footballer, capable of scoring and preventing goals and a prodigious athlete –

what a combination. During extra-time against Italy in the 2013 Confederations Cup semi-final, Del Bosque used the Basque as an auxiliary centre-forward, a task that Martínez, though surprised, accepted with enthusiasm. Faced with the Bayern Munich midfielder, all of a sudden Italy's puzzled Giorgio Chiellini asked him at a corner: "Wait, didn't you used to be a defender?"

Maybe José Mourinho's Chelsea were asking the same thing when Martínez popped up to slot away an equaliser in the 2013 European Supercup before Bayern won on penalties.

Isco, well I think he is the pick of youth talent anywhere in the world right now. And I'm not alone.

Andrés Iniesta: "For us, the fact that there are young bucks with so much quality, for example Isco, is great news. When new guys like that come along it's down to us to ensure that we help them fit in as quickly as possible. As far as Isco is concerned he's shown in a tremendously short space of time that he has immense talent and quality. Hopefully he continues developing at this rate and, while he's clearly a part of Spain's future hopes, he's also a reality for this team right now."

Having exposed the stark truth that large swathes of the Spanish media have consistently misjudged Luis Aragonés and Vicente del Bosque and markedly underestimated the power of their playing squad, I'm not going to fall into that trap. Del Bosque, Toni Grande, Javier Miñano and company have proven beyond question that their experience, their talent, their man-management and their forward planning are exceptional. That they know far more than their jumpy media. Add the epoch-making technical ability and the sheer will to win within a squad which also has an unrivalled fraternal atmosphere, and the conclusion is that the changes should be incremental. If the choice is indeed between overhaul and finesse of the first team, it has to be the latter.

Minor calibrations at the right time could yield massive premiums, but the Brazil defeat showed that if Spain are unlucky with the climate, if certain key men are over-played, if team selection and rotation is not perfect, then *La Roja* is at its most vulnerable since 2006.

However, if Del Bosque gets some luck – a quality he, Casillas and Xavi have consistently noted has been on Spain's side over these three tournament victories – and if his squad-husbandry is first-rate, then *La Roja* are in a small group [Brazil, Argentina, Germany and perhaps Italy] from which the winner will emerge.

Having said all that, there are other skeletons in the closet. The Xavi-Casillas axis has been an enormously significant foundation stone for not only Spain's three trophy wins but the general state of health around their senior international camp for the last eight years. Individually they will rank as two of, if not *the* two great Spanish footballers of all time. Xavi will regularly argue that Iniesta is his better, as a player, and Spain's No.6 has become the key match-changer at the moment.

However, the personal leadership which Xavi and Casillas have been able to give, rewarded with the Principe de Asturias Prize in winter 2012, has been of towering importance. They set the example of standards in team spirit, how to welcome squad newcomers, levels of competitiveness, harmony between staunch Catalan and devoted *Madridista*, will-to-win. Every single thing, beyond pure talent, which a modern international playing group requires in order to win relentlessly, can be found in these two men.

Particularly, given how volatile and divided Spanish football can become, their almost fraternal relationship is remarkable, and is an influencer for other members of the squad.

Santi Cazorla: "Iker and Xavi are living proof that true friendship transcends sporting rivalry. You go out and play for your colours, for your team. You can even have a bit of aggro with your mate on the pitch but the minute that whistle blows, it's all forgotten. You leave it on the pitch and go off to a nice restaurant together. When things got tough, Xavi and Casillas showed how much they valued the friendship they'd built up over the years. They were prepared to make the effort after sharing so much and they sat down, talked it through and resolved their differences. In fact our three captains, Xavi, Casillas and Puyol have all had a huge impact on me. They lead by example in the national team and in their clubs and set the bar for the rest of us in terms of conduct and professionalism. They're guys who have something to share and you learn a huge amount just being around them."

All of which puts extra focus on the fact that Xavi's age and his chronic Achilles' problems, plus the uncertainty around Casillas' place in the Real Madrid first team, combine to leave the two key men of this era not assured of their position in the curtain call. In autumn 2013, Casillas was faced with the prospect of either playing only in the Champions League and Copa del Rey or leaving Real Madrid in search of full-time work in order to be sharp for the World Cup.

Del Bosque owes Casillas greatly: the penalty saves; the captaincy; the "eternal" moment of the one-on-one against Arjen Robben in the World Cup final; the phone calls to Xavi and Puyol after the *Clásico* madness of 2011.

When the Real Madrid keeper was picked to start the vital away game in Finland in September 2013, despite Casillas having been benched by Carlo Ancelotti, Victor Valdés, his deputy in the national squad, immediately gave an interview stating that he still thought Casillas was "the No.1".

Spain's manager is just incredibly fortunate in the depth of his riches. Valdés is top quality and always ready, as he proved in the 1-0 win in Paris in spring 2013. Pepe Reina, too – a high-level competitor who binds the squad together brilliantly during these tournaments. Behind them: David de Gea, who Del Bosque says will "mark an epoch" in terms of trophies and years of service to the senior squad once he takes over.

But Casillas is Casillas. Del Bosque's A-position will be that his captain is fit, happy, match-sharp and in pole position for the 2014 World Cup. If that is not the case then the manager again faces one of the major decisions of his career.

The same applies to Xavi. Perhaps the fact that Tata Martino at Barcelona has a stated aim of making sure that all his great players are rotated, so that the key men reach the April-May trophy-winning zone in fresher, sharper shape will help Xavi make more of an impact on the World Cup. On his game, he still dictates the rhythm and tempo of a Spain performance – and he still opens teams up.

However, where teams at first tried to stifle him and Iniesta with tight-marking and lots of bodies around them, the favoured tactic is increasingly targeted fouling and sufficient athleticism to repeatedly test whether the Catalan is willing to chase back when an opponent surges past him – with or without the ball. Xavi will be 34 when the World Cup is played out, and these are not unusual questions for opponents to ask of such an influential player as he reaches such an age.

I don't know where Vicente del Bosque ranks in the pantheon of managers and coaches. All I know, with some certainty, is that he doesn't care.

He's unique in having become world and European champion at club and international level.

However, if he were to add a second World Cup victory to his European Championship, plus two Champions League and two Spanish league titles, then would he have a rival?

Maybe the coming World Cup is the ultimate test of whether we should accord slightly greater importance to the player production system and the playing system itself, or to the golden generation which peaked between 2007 and 2012.

Proof of the former will be if Del Bosque can promote to his starting team players from the group of Martínez, Carvajal, Thiago Alcántara, Isco, Soldado and Negredo – and still win.

Proof of the latter would be the romantic one last hurrah where *La Roja* still, fundamentally, rely on Villa, Torres, Xavi, Puyol and Casillas for the biggest moments of a successful tournament.

I think from his comments we can infer that Spain's former director of football veers towards the idea that the systems are good, but the harvest has been great. Perhaps unrepeatable.

Fernando Hierro: "I'm one of those who believes that it will be extremely difficult to replace this extraordinary generation. There are good players, but when we are talking about being able to win the World Cup or conquer Europe we are talking about the absolute top level. I'm a major fan of this generation because of how they represent Spanish football on and off the pitch. I don't think I've ever seen such a talented group. If you look, player by player, the great majority are amongst the two or three best in their position in the world."

It's equally clear that the man who has now scored in five winning UEFA finals for club and country views the subject from a different perspective; one which hints at Spain having a better chance of victory in Brazil – because of the system.

Fernando Torres: "With attitude, but lacking talent, you can win things. With talent but no attitude ... not. But if you put the two things together then you've got a lot of options to win. The secret of Spain has been that across this time there have been impressive footballers in every single position. There hasn't really been a single weakness. And if there is one which is weaker than another then the strength of the rest of the team will compensate to erase that slight weakness. Both Luis and Vicente have been able to pick their teams from 23 top-class footballers, each of whom is important to his club. Yet they have known how to be substitutes for Spain when it had to be that way. I think this is the least known secret of our era. Because a team, or team spirit, begins to break up when you have too many players on the bench who are totally pissed off at being there. Obviously there is a lot of that, but knowing how to accept the manager's choice that you'll be a sub this time for the good of the team and the group – that's vital. Spain has kept on winning because it has produced a *team*. Once you are a team you can pick out Iniesta or Xavi or Iker for particular importance and praise, but I feel we are a little bit like Borussia Dortmund. There might be one or two stand out players, but nothing stands out more than the team spirit, the team play, the team work ethic. This is a team which, the day that Xavi and Alonso quit international football, Silva and Cesc will still be 25 or 26. This national team will be strong, winning, for a long time because in most positions there will be three top-level footballers who have understood how to stomach being on the bench for the good of the team and of the squad. It's the group which makes you champion. Notable players come out of a great team, it's not that a team is made great by having a couple of super footballers.

In 10 or 15 years what we've achieved will be valued more because right now there are still critics. 'This guy should play ... this guy shouldn't.' Let the skilled people work in peace, I say. They've made history, they aren't doing so badly. Previously they criticised because we weren't winning anything and now they criticise because we don't win every match 4-0. What will be bad will be the the day it all ends. That day will eventually come. But those of us who got lucky enough to live through all these times, I think we can be proud of ourselves."

So, ultimately, what's been achieved along the road means that whatever Spain do in Brazil this summer is a bonus – not the real heart of the matter.

They have changed football. The three trophies belong to the people you have met in these pages and I can't deny that being within the vicinity of their achievements has sometimes been joyful, other times tense – but always fun.

Where *La Roja* has done something eternal, something for the everyman who loves football, is to show what can be achieved by putting a premium on skill, vision, technique, planning, youth development and loving both having the ball and winning. Every nation – yours and mine – can aim at creating their version of it.

But this has also been a people story. These are some of the most remarkable men I've met and am ever likely to meet: hungry, dedicated winners. Fun, funny, ferocious.

At the end there's always Casillas. *San Iker*.

At the end of a penalty shoot-out; at the end of training, trying to out-psyche Pepe Reina [and failing]; at the end of a Robben breakaway; at the end of the match always willing to stop and speak when I ask him to; at the end of a tournament – lifting the trophy.

At the end of this book, too.

Iker Casillas: "In the past, Spaniards were used to celebrating victories in every sport but football. There were trophies galore for tennis, basketball, futbol sala, handball, waterpolo, hockey and all the rest. We weren't on the scene yet and Spanish football was nowhere. But there was a plan.

"Part of that plan was to take a bunch of kids and teach them how to win and keep on winning.

And it is that quality, combined with good fortune, greater maturity, a helping hand from fate and, at times, sheer blind luck that has got us where we are today. And we're completely committed to this project until the final whistle at the end of the final match and, let's face it, that may be sooner rather than later for some of us. Now we're in our thirties and heading towards the end.

"Has it been because our coaches, Luis and Vicente, both possess the code that unlocks all the latent talent? I don't know, but I see us like so many pieces of *Tetris*. We all fit together perfectly. But you can't stop time and everything goes in cycles. It'll be up to the coach to continue bringing in the younger guys to complement us old hands. What we do, what we have done, is make something very difficult appear completely normal."

Ganar y ganar y ganar

You Have Been Watching...

Iker Casillas
Euro 2008/ World Cup 2010/ Euro 2012
Starts: 18
As substitute: 0
Goals conceded: 6
Clean sheets: 13
Team of the Tournament: 2008/ 2010/ 2012

Pepe Reina
Euro 2008/ World Cup 2010/ Euro 2012
Starts: 1
As substitute: 0
Goals conceded: 1

Andrés Palop
Euro 2008
Starts: 0
As substitute: 0

Víctor Valdés
World Cup 2010/ Euro 2012
Starts: 0
As substitute: 0

Raúl Albiol
Euro 2008
Starts: 1
As substitute: 1

Fernando Navarro
Euro 2008
Starts: 1
As substitute: 0

Carlos Marchena
Euro 2008/ World Cup 2010
Starts: 5
As substitute: 3
Team of the Tournament: 2008

Carles Puyol
Euro 2008/ World Cup 2010
Starts: 12
As substitute: 0
Goals: 1
Team of the Tournament: 2008/ 2010

Joan Capdevila
Euro 2008/ World Cup 2010
Starts: 12
As substitute: 0
Assists: 1

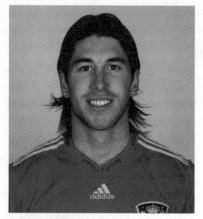

Sergio Ramos
Euro 2008/ World Cup 2010/ Euro 2012
Starts: 18
As substitute: 0
Team of the Tournament: 2010/ 2012

Álvaro Arbeloa
Euro 2008/ World Cup 2010/ Euro 2012
Starts: 7
As substitute: 1

Juanito
Euro 2008
Starts: 1
As substitute: 0

Gerard Piqué
World Cup 2010/ Euro 2012
Starts: 13
As substitute: 0

Jordi Alba
Euro 2012
Starts: 6
As substitute: 0
Goals: 1
Assists: 1
Team of the Tournament: 2012

Juanfran
Euro 2012
Starts: 0
As substitute: 0

Andrés Iniesta
Euro 2008/ World Cup 2010/ Euro 2012
Starts: 17
As substitute: 0
Goals: 2
Assists: 3
Team of the Tournament: 2010/ 2012

Xavi Hernández
Euro 2008/ World Cup 2010/ Euro 2012
Starts: 18
As substitute: 0
Goals: 1
Assists: 4
Team of the Tournament: 2008/ 2010/ 2012

Cesc Fàbregas
Euro 2008/ World Cup 2010/ Euro 2012
Starts: 5
As substitute: 11
Goals: 3
Assists: 5

Santi Cazorla
Euro 2008/ Euro 2012
Starts: 0
As substitute: 7

Xabi Alonso
Euro 2008/ World Cup 2010/ Euro 2012
Starts: 14
As substitute: 3
Goals: 2

Marcos Senna
Euro 2008
Starts: 5
As substitute: 0
Team of the Tournament: 2008

Sergio Busquets
World Cup 2010/ Euro 2012
Starts: 13
As substitute: 0

Javi Martínez
World Cup 2010/ Euro 2012
Starts: 0
As substitute: 2

David Silva
Euro 2008/ World Cup 2010/ Euro 2012
Starts: 12
As substitute: 1
Goals: 3
Assists: 4

Rúben de la Red
Euro 2008
Starts: 1
As substitute: 0
Goals: 1

David Villa
Euro 2008/ World Cup 2010
Starts: 11
As substitute: 0
Goals: 9
Assists: 1
Team of the Tournament: 2008/ 2010

Fernando Torres
Euro 2008/ World Cup 2010/ Euro 2012
Starts: 11
As substitute: 6
Goals: 5
Assists: 2

Sergio García
Euro 2008
Starts: 1
As substitute: 0
Assists: 1

Dani Güiza
Euro 2008
Starts: 1
As substitute: 3
Goals: 2
Assists: 1

Juan Mata
World Cup 2010/ Euro 2012
Starts: 0
As substitute: 2
Goals: 1

Jesús Navas
World Cup 2010/ Euro 2012
Starts: 1
As substitute: 5
Goals: 1
Assists: 1

Pedro
World Cup 2010/ Euro 2012
Starts: 2
As substitute: 6

Fernando Llorente
World Cup 2010
Starts: 0
As substitute: 1

Álvaro Negredo
Euro 2012
Starts: 1
As substitute: 1

Acknowledgements

I'd particularly like to express gratitude to those who were interviewed exclusively for this book: Vicente del Bosque – a man who's treated me with grace, humour and openness from day one; a noble man long before he gained his 'Marquis' title. President Ángel María Villar, Marcos Senna, Santi Cazorla, Fernando Torres, Gerard Piqué, Gines Mélendez, Paco Jiménez, José Manuel Ochotorena, Joan Capdevila, Dani Aranzubia, Carlos Marchena, Fernando Navarro, Sergio García, Victor Muñoz, Steve McManaman, Graeme Souness, Davie Provan, Gaizka Mendieta, Joan Gaspart, Javi Enríquez, Miguel Reina, Toñete, Albert Ferrer, Iñaki Sáez, Jesús Gómez and Thomas Hitzlsperger. Often, thanks to them, the search for anecdotes and quotes to explain certain themes became the discovery of inspiration and surprise.

Over the years the same goes for those I've interviewed, gossiped with, joked with and admired: Iker Casillas, Víctor Valdés, Andrés Palop, Pepe Reina, Álvaro Arbeloa, Carles Puyol, Xavi, Andrés Iniesta, Xabi Alonso, Pedro, David Villa, Fernando Llorente, Álvaro Negredo, Sergio Busquets, Roberto Soldado, Javi Martínez, Juan Mata, Jordi Alba, Raúl Albiol, Fernando Hierro, Cesc Fàbregas, Emilio Butragueño. David Silva, Luis Aragonés, Toni Grande, Javier Miñano, Raúl González, Kurt Jara and Manolo el del Bombo.

At the Spanish Football Federation I've found friendship and terrific professional help from Paloma Antoranz, who looks after *La Roja* with affection and intelligence, Atonio Bustamente, who has made me feel welcome and well looked after, María José Claramunt, Silvia Dorschnerova, Susana Barquero, José Manuel Ordás, Pablo Peña, Luis Arnáiz, Pedro Cortés, Juan Luis Larrea, Luis Uranga, Toni Guerra, Damián García and Joaquín Retamosa, Antolín Gonzalo Martín and Antonio Limones.

It needs to be said that for all the goals, saves, good training sessions and good fortune if the RFEF president, Ángel María Villar, didn't have the level of vision, patience, faith and ambition he does then this story wouldn't be written. Kudos to him.

When I called on them, top people like Hernán Sanz (Villarreal CF), Rafa Ramos (RCD Espanyol), Gareth Mills (Chelsea), Mark Gonella and Katie Baldwin (Arsenal), Arturo Canales, Ben Miller (legendary men both) and Chus Llorente, answered with enthusiasm. Thanks.

There are many people at UEFA.com, FIFA TV, HBS and IMG with whom I enjoy working at these tournaments, too many to mention them all. But, still, thanks to Nairn Salter, Keith and Andrin Cooper, Nick Moody, Rosemary Fagan, Thierry De Backer and David Ausseil, Rob Esteva, Alfredo Rodríguez, Andrew Haslam, Cathia Roth, David Farrelly, Dmitrijs Mamikins, John Atkin, Josh Hershman, Kadira Malkoc, Kevin Ashby, Martyn Hindley, Michael Harrold, Paul Nixon, Pavel Gognidze, Remy Wigmans, Sam Adams. Jim Agnew – from Vienna to Lisbon, what a journey. Simon and Patrick Hart. You know what I wish you. Hello to Juanita de Kock and family. Hola Evaristo y Miguel!
Thanks to Adidas, notably Carlos Rojo, Belén Fraguas and Luis Cano.

There is another terrific team *Roja*. Álvaro Macho, Delfín Ramírez, Paul Bryan, Santi 'I love to dance' Solsona and Roberto Hernández.

A work like this needs research and I'm indebted to those whose efforts allowed me to tell this story more fully. If, in error, I have failed to fully attribute a quote then it is without intention and I'd ask for understanding. If this story has, retrospectively and also reporting what I felt at the time, led me to be critical of some parts of the Spanish media then I must emphasise here that some of those who travel everywhere with *La Roja* are talented, honest, hard-working and great road-companions. They know who they are.

Aragonés versus Raúl
Aragonés was looking back on his decision to drop Raul in an interview with *Diario AS*.

Euro 2008
Fernando Torres was speaking before the first game of Euro 2008 to Manel Bruña of *El Mundo Deportivo*. Iker Casillas was talking about the unity in the squad on the television programme *Informe Robinson*. Prior to the Sweden game, Torres was speaking to Spanish television. Torres remembered his frustration at being substituted in his autobiography *El Niño: My Story*. Henrik Larsson was describing his admiration of Torres to Conchita Roura of *El Mundo Deportivo*. Sergio Ramos remembered his early waywardness under Luis Aragonés in Neustift in an interview with *El País* in 2009.

Arrigo Sacchi and Damiano Tomassi were talking with *El Mundo Deportivo*. Casillas was recalling his fear of Italy in *Mas Secretos de la Roja*, Dani Güiza and Cesc in *Informe Robinson* and *El Mundo Deportivo*. Luis Aragonés told the truth about the mood in the camp before the quarter-final to his friend Javier Matallanes in *Diario AS*. Carles Puyol was remembering the Russia team talk on *Informe Robinson* and bigging up the Sushi Crew to Lu Martín.

The Wise Man Of Hortaleza
Most of Luis Aragonés' historical quotes were researched from *El Mundo Deportivo* and *El País*.

Enrique Ibáñez was talking about Aragonés' decision to leave his post at Atlético to *El País* in July 1987. Aragonés discussed his phobic episodes in an interview with Jose Miguélez of *El País* in August 1991. Seven years later, he told the same journalist why he believed Spain should stand by their *Furia* heritage instead of adopting *tiki-taka*.

Everything You Always Wanted To Know About Winning Tournaments
Xavi was talking about his experiences on youth team duty with Spain to the newspaper *Marca* on the occasion of his 100th cap. Iker Casillas was remembering the Youth World Cup in Nigeria in his book *la Humildad del Campeón*.

The Man Behind The Moustache
Vicente del Bosque recalled his father with *El País*. The comments from his playing days about being easy for his critics to spot came from the same paper.

The Rough Guide To South Africa
Fernando Hierro was reviewing Spain's performance in South Africa in the summer of 2009 to José Sámano and Luis Martín of *El País*.

World Cup 2010
Andrés Iniesta was talking about his concerns over his physical and psychological well-being on *Informe Robinson,* as were Óscar Celadas and Emili Ricart. Fernando Torres was recounting his volcano-busting trans-European adventure on his own website. Vicente del Bosque was remembering the silence in the team bus before the Chile game on *Informe Robinson.* Villa, Xavi and Piqué, too. It's also where Torres contemplated taking retribution against Pedro. His feelings for South Africa were shared with *El Mundo Deportivo.*

Xavi and Villa spoke about the Portugal game on a Spanish federation film.

Johan Cruyff criticised Holland's final in *El Periodico,* Seedorf on the BBC. Iniesta's Van Bommel comments were to *Informe Robinson.* His Isaac Newton tribute came with Lu Martín of *El País.*

English Lessons
Xabi Alonso chatted to *El País*, Raúl wrote his open letter to Schalke 04 fans.

The Kids Are Alright
Cesc Fàbregas' recollection of youth football with Sergio Ramos was told to *Diario AS*.

Raúl was talking about his new life in Germany to Sid Lowe and Pete Jenson.

Euro 2012
Javier Miñano marvelled at the Spain players' commitment in *El País*, which is also where Cesc Fàbregas paid tribute to Luis Aragonés.

Toni Grande spoke about Xavi's chats with him and Del Bosque to *Diario de la Roja*. Xavi later stated that Grande had come to him and offered his apologies. Xavi made it clear he would never suggest one player over another to the Spain coach, only talk about matters which were "beneficial to the whole team".

Xavi spoke about choosing not to retire from international football to *El País*.

The Rough Guide To Brazil

Arbeloa and Ramos talked of their fury at false Brazilian reporting of the theft to *El País*.

Into The Unknown

Vicente del Bosque's Confederations Cup comments came on the RFEF website.

Fernando Hierro praised the current Spain generation of footballers on FIFA.com.

Iker Casillas spoke wonderfully, as ever, to Luis Martín. Who is exceptional.

Thank you

It's not digging coal and it's not putting rivets into a ship in the freezing cold but writing a book, at least trying to do so to the best of your ability, can test you until your mind is burnt and raw. More than ever in the beautiful lifetime we've spent together I needed my wonderful wife Louise. Smart, accurate, creative ... telepathic sometimes, her talents, even more than her infinite support, made this doable and better, *far* better, than it would otherwise have been. If she is moved by the story, I know it's worth telling.

Equally, one of my two fantastic daughters grew up in Spain and the other was born there. Watching players they know well excel is a good way to start life – thank you for your support Cara and Annie.

I hope my parents and brothers enjoy reading this, they've shrewdly left me to it as much as possible while I grumble and turn monosyllabic.

There is a Hollywood cast-list of those who've 'been there'. It begins with Graeme Runcie who helped me colonise Spain. Always, just about right. Sid Lowe, in the midst of writing an epic, and Pete Jenson hit me with bursts of advice and corrections just when I most needed them. Thank you. Rob Moore, Ivan Modia, Cordula Reinhardt, Aurelio Capaldi [Italian legend], Ian McGarry and the mighty Ronnie Reng were always there when I required help or advice. I'll do the same for you.

Carmelo Rubio, again, helped us with his generosity – a photographer who is always close to these great players. Dan Leydon, a fine talent, was as generous and sharp as ever.

Silvia González Poncelas is full of ability, energy and fun. She has done a fine job in helping me research this book, just as she did on Barça. I'd recommend her journalistic skills to anyone. Thank you. And to my friend Cheryl Jane Campbell.

While it's a happy privilege to work at them, these mammoth tournaments are becoming a real test of mental and physical stamina – especially if you want to keep pace with a winning team from beginning to end. As such I've drawn lucky hands each time. In 2008 Dani Huerta and Jürgen Pilger drove *La Roja* to victory, with help from the 'Wise Men Say' Ian Holyman.

In 2010 I had the life-changing experience of working with a true great, Adam 'Miami' Goldfinch and Glen 'defending the couch' Post, aka The Shadow. Go Square Go.

Two years later Miami was, justifiably, shipped in from the colonies, he's that good. And to be teamed up with Dani Huerta again, plus the golden-tonsilled Federico Ardiles was the jackpot. It led to gunplay, but all in the best possible taste.

When I'm at a tournament with Spain I know that there will be top quality reporting and writing from Santi Segurola, Manel Bruña and Miguel Angel Lara and my *Revista de la Liga* colleague Guillem Balague. But the daddy of them all must be the extraordinary Lu Martín, trusted and liked by the players, a terrific friend and what journalism should be about.

Finally, BackPage Press. To do what they do doesn't just take talent and vision, plus hard work, it takes *cojones*. The company was born in the middle of crushing economic times and the birth came because they believed things could, needed to, be done better. Their authors and their customers will agree they've achieved what they set out to. Neil White and Martin Greig, with the support of Carrie and Nic, are inspirational.

In other news, thank you all very much indeed for reading this and the Barça book, thank you for the positive reaction – and thank heavens for football.

Graham Hunter
Barcelona, October 2013

BACKPAGE PRESS

We welcome your feedback on this book and our other titles …
www.twitter.com/BackPagePress
www.facebook.com/BackPagePress
www.backpagepress.co.uk

We have a series of exclusive video diaries with Graham Hunter on our YouTube channel and release new content regularly.
Subscribe at www.youtube.com/backpage2010

DAN LEYDON

The illustrations in this book were specially commissioned and are the work of Irish illustrator Dan Leydon.
Shop: etsy.com/shop/footynews
Twitter: @danleydon